Hands-On Microservices with Kubernetes

Build, deploy, and manage scalable microservices on Kubernetes

Gigi Sayfan

BIRMINGHAM - MUMBAI

Hands-On Microservices with Kubernetes

Commissioning Editor: Pavan Ramchandani
Acquisition Editor: Rohit Rajkumar
Content Development Editor: Amitendra Pathak
Senior Editor: Rahul Dsouza
Technical Editor: Prachi Sawant
Copy Editor: Safis Editing
Project Coordinator: Jagdish Prabhu
Proofreader: Safis Editing
Indexer: Manju Arasan
Production Designer: Jayalaxmi Raja

First published: July 2019

Production reference: 1050719

Published by Packt Publishing Ltd.
Livery Place
35 Livery Street
Birmingham
B3 2PB, UK.

ISBN 978-1-78980-546-8

www.packtpub.com

Packt.com

Subscribe to our online digital library for full access to over 7,000 books and videos, as well as industry leading tools to help you plan your personal development and advance your career. For more information, please visit our website.

Why subscribe?

- Spend less time learning and more time coding with practical eBooks and Videos from over 4,000 industry professionals

- Improve your learning with Skill Plans built especially for you

- Get a free eBook or video every month

- Fully searchable for easy access to vital information

- Copy and paste, print, and bookmark content

Did you know that Packt offers eBook versions of every book published, with PDF and ePub files available? You can upgrade to the eBook version at www.packt.com and as a print book customer, you are entitled to a discount on the eBook copy. Get in touch with us at customercare@packtpub.com for more details.

At www.packt.com, you can also read a collection of free technical articles, sign up for a range of free newsletters, and receive exclusive discounts and offers on Packt books and eBooks.

Contributors

About the author

Gigi Sayfan is a principal software architect at Helix – a bioinformatics and genomics start-up – and author of *Mastering Kubernetes*, published by Packt. He has been developing software professionally for more than 20 years in domains as diverse as instant messaging, morphing, chip-fabrication process control, embedded multimedia applications for games consoles, and brain-inspired machine learning. He has written production code in many programming languages including Go, Python, C#, Java, Delphi, JavaScript, and even Cobol and PowerBuilder, for operating systems such as Windows, Linux, macOS, Lynx, and Sony PlayStation. His technical expertise covers databases, low-level networking, unorthodox user interfaces, and the general SDLC.

About the reviewers

Guang Ya Liu is a senior technical staff member for IBM Cloud Private and is currently focused on cloud computing, container technology, and distributed computing. He is also a member of the IBM Academy of Technology. He was an OpenStack Magnum Core member from 2015 to 2017, and now serves as an Istio maintainer, Kubernetes member, Kubernetes Federation V2 maintainer, Apache Mesos committer, and PMC member.

Shashidhar Soppin is a senior software architect with over 18 years' experience in IT. He has worked on virtualization, storage, the cloud and cloud architecture, OpenStack, machine learning, deep learning, and Docker container technologies. Primarily, his focus is on building new approaches and solutions for enterprise customers. He is an avid author of open source technologies (OSFY), a blogger (LinuxTechi), and a holder of patents. He graduated from BIET, Davangere, India. In his free time, he loves to travel and read books.

Packt is searching for authors like you

If you're interested in becoming an author for Packt, please visit `authors.packtpub.com` and apply today. We have worked with thousands of developers and tech professionals, just like you, to help them share their insight with the global tech community. You can make a general application, apply for a specific hot topic that we are recruiting an author for, or submit your own idea.

Table of Contents

Preface

Hands-On Microservices with Kubernetes is the book you have been waiting for. It will walk you though the parallel paths of developing microservices and deploying them on Kubernetes. The synergy between microservice-based architecture and Kubernetes is very powerful. This book covers all angles. It explains the concepts behind microservices and Kubernetes, discusses real-world concerns and trade-offs, takes you through the development of fully fledged microservice-based systems, shows you best practices, and provides ample recommendations.

This book covers an amazing amount of ground in great depth and with working code to illustrate. You will learn how to design a microservice-based architecture, build microservices, test the microservices you've built, and package them as Docker images. Then, you will learn how to deploy your system as a collection of Docker images to Kubernetes and manage it there.

Along the way, you will become familiar with most important trends to be aware of, such as automated **continuous integration / continuous delivery (CI/CD)**, gRPC-based microservices, serverless computing, and service meshes.

By the end of this book, you will have gained a lot of knowledge and hands-on experience with planning, developing, and operating large-scale cloud-native systems using microservice-based architecture deployed on Kubernetes.

Who this book is for

This book is targeted at software developers and DevOps engineers who want to be at the forefront of large-scale software engineering. It will help if you have experience with large-scale software systems that are deployed using containers on more than one machine and are developed by several teams.

What this book covers

Chapter 1, *Introduction to Kubernetes for Developers*, introduces you to Kubernetes. You will receive a whirlwind tour of Kubernetes and get an idea of how well it aligns with microservices.

Chapter 2, *Getting Started with Microservices*, discusses various aspects, patterns, and approaches to common problems in microservice-based systems and how they compare to other common architectures, such as monoliths and large services.

Chapter 3, *Delinkcious – the Sample Application*, explores why we should choose Go as the programming language of Delinkcious; then we will look at Go kit.

Chapter 4, *Setting Up the CI/CD Pipeline*, teaches you about the problem the CI/CD pipeline solves, covers the different options for CI/CD pipelines for Kubernetes, and finally looks at building a CI/CD pipeline for Delinkcious.

Chapter 5, *Configuring Microservices with Kubernetes*, moves you into the practical and real-world area of microservices configuration. Also, we will discuss Kubernetes-specific options and, in particular, ConfigMaps.

Chapter 6, *Securing Microservices on Kubernetes*, examines how to secure your microservices on Kubernetes in depth. We will also discuss the pillars that act as the foundation of microservice security on Kubernetes.

Chapter 7, *Talking to the World – APIs and Load Balancers*, sees us open Delinkcious to the world and let users interact with it from outside the cluster. Also, we will add a gRPC-based news service that users can hit up to get news about other users they follow. Finally, we will add a message queue that lets services communicate in a loosely coupled manner.

Chapter 8, *Working with Stateful Services*, delves into the Kubernetes storage model. We will also extend the Delinkcious news service to store its data in Redis, instead of in memory.

Chapter 9, *Running Serverless Tasks on Kubernetes*, dives into one of the hottest trends in cloud-native systems: serverless computing (also known as **Function as a Service**, or **FaaS**). Also, we'll cover other ways to do serverless computing in Kubernetes.

Chapter 10, *Testing Microservices*, covers the topic of testing and its various flavors: unit testing, integration testing, and all kinds of end-to-end testing. We also delve into how Delinkcious tests are structured.

Chapter 11, *Deploying Microservices*, deals with two related, yet separate, themes: production deployments and development deployments.

Chapter 12, *Monitoring, Logging, and Metrics*, focuses on the operational side of running a large-scale distributed system on Kubernetes, as well as on how to design the system and what to take into account to ensure a top-notch operational posture.

Chapter 13, *Service Mesh – Working with Istio*, reviews the hot topic of service meshes and, in particular, Istio. This is exciting because service meshes are a real game changer.

Chapter 14, *The Future of Microservices and Kubernetes*, covers the topics of Kubernetes and microservices, and will help us learn how to decide when it's the right time to adopt and invest in newer technologies.

To get the most out of this book

Any software requirements are either listed at the beginning of each chapter in the *Technical requirements* section, or, if the installation of a particular piece of software is part of the material of the chapter, then any instructions you need will be contained within the chapter itself. Most of the installations are software components that are installed into the Kubernetes cluster. This is an important part of the hands-on nature of the book.

Download the example code files

You can download the example code files for this book from your account at www.packt.com. If you purchased this book elsewhere, you can visit www.packt.com/support and register to have the files emailed directly to you.

You can download the code files by following these steps:

1. Log in or register at www.packt.com.
2. Select the **SUPPORT** tab.
3. Click on **Code Downloads & Errata**.
4. Enter the name of the book in the **Search** box and follow the onscreen instructions.

Once the file is downloaded, please make sure that you unzip or extract the folder using the latest version of:

- WinRAR/7-Zip for Windows
- Zipeg/iZip/UnRarX for Mac
- 7-Zip/PeaZip for Linux

The code bundle for the book is also hosted on GitHub at https://github.com/PacktPublishing/Hands-On-Microservices-with-Kubernetes. In case there's an update to the code, it will be updated on the existing GitHub repository.

We also have other code bundles from our rich catalog of books and videos available at https://github.com/PacktPublishing/. Check them out!

Download the color images

We also provide a PDF file that has color images of the screenshots/diagrams used in this book. You can download it here: `https://static.packt-cdn.com/downloads/9781789805468_ColorImages.pdf`.

Conventions used

There are a number of text conventions used throughout this book.

`CodeInText`: Indicates code words in text, database table names, folder names, filenames, file extensions, pathnames, dummy URLs, user input, and Twitter handles. Here is an example: "Note that I made sure it's executable via `chmod +x`."

A block of code is set as follows:

```
version: 2
jobs:
  build:
    docker:
    - image: circleci/golang:1.11
    - image: circleci/postgres:9.6-alpine
```

Any command-line input or output is written as follows:

```
$ tree -L 2
.
├── LICENSE
├── README.md
├── build.sh
```

Bold: Indicates a new term, an important word, or words that you see onscreen. For example, words in menus or dialog boxes appear in the text like this. Here is an example: "We can sync it by selecting **Sync** from the **ACTIONS** dropdown."

 Warnings or important notes appear like this.

 Tips and tricks appear like this.

Get in touch

Feedback from our readers is always welcome.

General feedback: If you have questions about any aspect of this book, mention the book title in the subject of your message and email us at `customercare@packtpub.com`.

Errata: Although we have taken every care to ensure the accuracy of our content, mistakes do happen. If you have found a mistake in this book, we would be grateful if you would report this to us. Please visit `www.packt.com/submit-errata`, selecting your book, clicking on the Errata Submission Form link, and entering the details.

Piracy: If you come across any illegal copies of our works in any form on the Internet, we would be grateful if you would provide us with the location address or website name. Please contact us at `copyright@packt.com` with a link to the material.

If you are interested in becoming an author: If there is a topic that you have expertise in and you are interested in either writing or contributing to a book, please visit `authors.packtpub.com`.

Reviews

Please leave a review. Once you have read and used this book, why not leave a review on the site that you purchased it from? Potential readers can then see and use your unbiased opinion to make purchase decisions, we at Packt can understand what you think about our products, and our authors can see your feedback on their book. Thank you!

For more information about Packt, please visit `packt.com`.

Introduction to Kubernetes for Developers
1

In this chapter, we will introduce you to Kubernetes. Kubernetes is a big platform and it's difficult to do justice to it in just one chapter. Luckily, we have a whole book to explore it. Don't worry if you feel a little overwhelmed. I'll mention many concepts and capabilities briefly. In later chapters, we will cover many of these in detail, as well as the connections and interactions between those Kubernetes concepts. To spice things up and get hands-on early, you will also create a local Kubernetes cluster (Minikube) on your machine. This chapter will cover the following topics:

- Kubernetes in a nutshell
- The Kubernetes architecture
- Kubernetes and microservices
- Creating a local cluster

Technical requirements

In this chapter, you will need the following tools:

- Docker
- Kubectl
- Minikube

Installing Docker

To install Docker, follow the instructions here: `https://docs.docker.com/install/` `#supported-platforms`. I will use Docker for macOS.

Installing kubectl

To install kubectl, follow the instructions here: `https://kubernetes.io/docs/tasks/` `tools/install-kubectl/`.

Kubectl is the Kubernetes CLI and we will use it extensively throughout the book.

Installing Minikube

To install Minikube, follow the instructions here: `https://kubernetes.io/docs/tasks/` `tools/install-minikube/`.

Note that you need to install a hypervisor too. For the macOS, I find VirtualBox the most reliable. You may prefer another hypervisor, such as HyperKit. There will be more detailed instructions later when you get to play with Minikube.

The code

- The code for the chapter is available here: `https://github.com/` `PacktPublishing/Hands-On-Microservices-with-Kubernetes/tree/master/` `Chapter01`
- There is another Git repository for the Delinkcious sample application that we will build together: `https://github.com/the-gigi/delinkcious`

Kubernetes in a nutshell

In this section, you'll get a sense of what Kubernetes is all about, its history, and how it became so popular.

Kubernetes – the container orchestration platform

The primary function of Kubernetes is deploying and managing a large number of container-based workloads on a fleet of machines (physical or virtual). This means that Kubernetes provides the means to deploy containers to the cluster. It makes sure to comply with various scheduling constraints and pack the containers efficiently into the cluster nodes. In addition, Kubernetes automatically watches your containers and restarts them if they fail. Kubernetes will also relocate workloads off problematic nodes to other nodes. Kubernetes is an extremely flexible platform. It relies on a provisioned infrastructure layer of compute, memory, storage, and networking, and, with these resources, it works its magic.

The history of Kubernetes

Kubernetes and the entire cloud-native scene is moving at breakneck speed, but let's take a moment to reflect on how we got here. It will be a very short journey because Kubernetes came out of Google in June 2014, just a few years ago. When Docker became popular, it changed how people package, distribute, and deploy software. But, it soon became apparent that Docker doesn't scale on its own for large distributed systems. A few orchestration solutions became available, such as Apache Mesos, and later, Docker's own swarm. But, they never measured up to Kubernetes. Kubernetes was conceptually based on Google's Borg system. It brought together the design and technical excellence of a decade of Google engineering, but it was a new open source project. At OSCON 2015, Kubernetes 1.0 was released and the floodgates opened. The growth of Kubernetes, its ecosystem, and the community behind it, was as impressive as its technical excellence.

Kubernetes means helmsman in Greek. You'll notice many nautical terms in the names of Kubernetes-related projects.

The state of Kubernetes

Kubernetes is now a household name. The DevOps world pretty much equates container orchestration with Kubernetes. All major cloud providers offer managed Kubernetes solutions. It is ubiquitous in enterprise and in startup companies. While Kubernetes is still young and innovation keeps happening, it is all happening in a very healthy way. The core is rock solid, battle tested, and used in production across lots and lots of companies. There are very big players collaborating and pushing Kubernetes forward, such as Google (obviously), Microsoft, Amazon, IBM, and VMware.

The **Cloud Native Computing Foundation** (**CNCF**) open source organization offers certification. Every 3 months, a new Kubernetes release comes out, which is the result of a collaboration between hundreds of volunteers and paid engineers. There is a large ecosystem surrounding the main project of both commercial and open source projects. You will see later how Kubernetes' flexible and extensible design encourages this ecosystem and helps in integrating Kubernetes into any cloud platform.

Understanding the Kubernetes architecture

Kubernetes is a marvel of software engineering. The architecture and design of Kubernetes are a big part in its success. Each cluster has a control plane and data plane. The control plane consists of several components, such as an API server, a metadata store for keeping the state of a cluster, and multiple controllers that are responsible for managing the nodes in the data plane and providing access to users. The control plane in production will be distributed across multiple machines for high availability and robustness. The data plane consists of multiple nodes, or workers. The control plane will deploy and run your pods (groups of containers) on these nodes, and then watch for changes and respond.

Here is a diagram that illustrates the overall architecture:

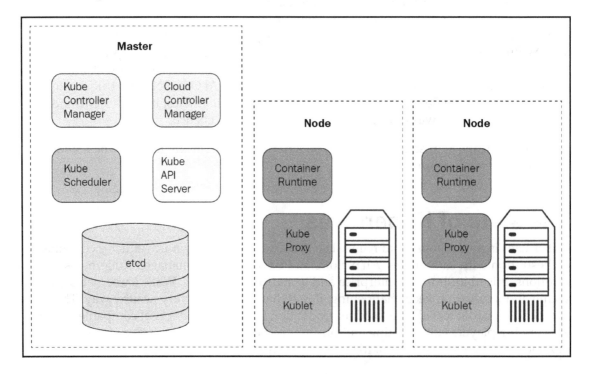

Let's review in detail the control plane and the data plane, as well as kubectl, which is the command-line tool you use to interact with the Kubernetes cluster.

The control plane

The control plane consists of several components:

- API server
- The etcd metadata store
- Scheduler
- Controller manager
- Cloud controller manager

Let's examine the role of each component.

The API server

The **kube-api-server** is a massive REST server that exposes the Kubernetes API to the world. You can have multiple instances of the API server in your control plane for high-availability. The API server keeps the cluster state in etcd.

The etcd store

The complete cluster is stored in etcd (`https://coreos.com/etcd/`), a consistent and reliable, distributed key-value store. The **etcd store** is an open source project (developed by CoreOS, originally).

It is common to have three or five instances of etcd for redundancy. If you lose the data in your etcd store, you lose your cluster.

The scheduler

The **kube-scheduler** is responsible for scheduling pods to worker nodes. It implements a sophisticated scheduling algorithm that takes a lot of information into account, such as resource availability on each node, various constraints specified by the user, types of available nodes, resource limits and quotas, and other factors, such as affinity, anti-affinity, tolerations, and taints.

The controller manager

The **kube-controller manager** is a single process that contains multiple controllers for simplicity. These controllers watch for events and changes to the cluster and respond accordingly:

- **Node controller**: Responsible for noticing and responding when nodes go down.
- **Replication controller**: This makes sure that there is the correct number of pods for each replica set or replication controller object.
- **Endpoints controller**: This assigns for each service an endpoints object that lists the service's pods.
- **Service account and token controllers**: These initialize new namespaces with default service accounts and corresponding API access tokens.

The data plane

The data plane is the collection of the nodes in the cluster that run your containerized workloads as pods. The data plane and control plane can share physical or virtual machines. This happens, of course, when you run a single node cluster, such as Minikube. But, typically, in a production-ready deployment, the data plane will have its own nodes. There are several components that Kubernetes installs on each node in order to communicate, watch, and schedule pods: kubelet, kube-proxy, and the container runtime (for example, the Docker daemon).

The kubelet

The **kubelet** is a Kubernetes agent. It's responsible for talking to the API server and for running and managing the pods on the node. Here are some of the responsibilities of the kubelet:

- Downloading pod secrets from the API server
- Mounting volumes
- Running the pod container via the **Container Runtime Interface** (**CRI**)
- Reporting the status of the node and each pod
- Probe container liveness

The kube proxy

The kube proxy is responsible for the networking aspects of the node. It operates as a local front for services and can forward TCP and UDP packets. It discovers the IP addresses of services via DNS or environment variables.

The container runtime

Kubernetes eventually runs containers, even if they are organized in pods. Kubernetes supports different container runtimes. Originally, only Docker was supported. Now, Kubernetes runs containers through an interface called **CRI**, which is based on **gRPC**.

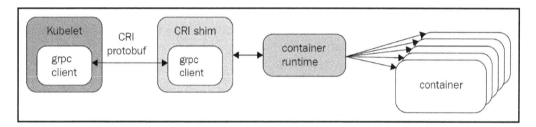

Each container runtime that implements CRI can be used on a node controlled by the **kubelet**, as shown in the preceding diagram.

Kubectl

Kubectl is a tool you should get very comfortable with. It is your **command-line interface** (**CLI**) to your Kubernetes cluster. We will use kubectl extensively throughout the book to manage and operate Kubernetes. Here is a short list of the capabilities kubectl puts literally at your fingertips:

- Cluster management
- Deployment
- Troubleshooting and debugging
- Resource management (Kubernetes objects)
- Configuration and metadata

Just type `kubectl` to get a complete list of all the commands and `kubectl <command> --help` for more detailed info on specific commands.

Kubernetes and microservices – a perfect match

Kubernetes is a fantastic platform with amazing capabilities and a wonderful ecosystem. How does it help you with your system? As you'll see, there is a very good alignment between Kubernetes and microservices. The building blocks of Kubernetes, such as namespaces, pods, deployments, and services, map directly to important microservices concepts and an agile **software development life cycle (SDLC)**. Let's dive in.

Packaging and deploying microservices

When you employ a microservice-based architecture, you'll have lots of microservices. Those microservices, in general, may be developed independently, and deployed independently. The packaging mechanism is simply containers. Every microservice you develop will have a Dockerfile. The resulting image represents the deployment unit for that microservice. In Kubernetes, your microservice image will run inside a pod (possibly alongside other containers). But an isolated pod, running on a node, is not very resilient. The kubelet on the node will restart the pod's container if it crashes, but if something happens to the node itself, the pod is gone. Kubernetes has abstractions and resources that build on the pod.

ReplicaSets are sets of pods with a certain number of replicas. When you create a ReplicaSet, Kubernetes will make sure that the correct number of pods you specify always run in the cluster. The deployment resource takes it a step further and provides an abstraction that exactly aligns with the way you consider and think about microservices. When you have a new version of a microservice ready, you will want to deploy it. Here is a Kubernetes deployment manifest:

```
apiVersion: apps/v1
kind: Deployment
metadata:
  name: nginx
  labels:
    app: nginx
spec:
  replicas: 3
  selector:
    matchLabels:
      app: nginx
  template:
    metadata:
      labels:
```

```
    app: nginx
spec:
  containers:
  - name: nginx
    image: nginx:1.15.4
    ports:
    - containerPort: 80
```

The file can be found at `https://github.com/the-gigi/hands-on-microservices-with-kubernetes-code/blob/master/ch1/nginx-deployment.yaml`.

This is a YAML file (`https://yaml.org/`) that has some fields that are common to all Kubernetes resources, and some fields that are specific to deployments. Let's break this down piece by piece. Almost everything you learn here will apply to other resources:

- The `apiVersion` field marks the Kubernetes resources version. A specific version of the Kubernetes API server (for example, V1.13.0) can work with different versions of different resources. Resource versions have two parts: an API group (in this case, `apps`) and a version number (`v1`). The version number may include **alpha** or **beta** designations:

  ```
  apiVersion: apps/v1
  ```

- The `kind` field specifies what resource or API object we are dealing with. You will meet many kinds of resources in this chapter and later:

  ```
  kind: Deployment
  ```

- The `metadata` section contains the name of the resource (`nginx`) and a set of labels, which are just key-value string pairs. The name is used to refer to this particular resource. The labels allow for operating on a set of resources that share the same label. Labels are very useful and flexible. In this case, there is just one label (`app: nginx`):

  ```
  metadata:
    name: nginx
    labels:
      app: nginx
  ```

- Next, we have a `spec` field. This is a ReplicaSet `spec`. You could create a ReplicaSet directly, but it would be static. The whole purpose of deployments is to manage its set of replicas. What's in a ReplicaSet spec? Obviously, it contains the number of `replicas` (3). It has a selector with a set of `matchLabels` (also `app: nginx`), and it has a pod template. The ReplicaSet will manage pods that have labels that match `matchLabels`:

```
spec:
  replicas: 3
  selector:
    matchLabels:
        app: nginx
  template:
      . . .
```

- Let's have a look at the pod template. The template has two parts: `metadata` and a `spec`. The `metadata` is where you specify the labels. The `spec` describes the `containers` in the pod. There may be one or more containers in a pod. In this case, there is just one container. The key field for a container is the image (often a Docker image), where you packaged your microservice. That's the code we want to run. There is also a name (`nginx`) and a set of ports:

```
metadata:
  labels:
      app: nginx
spec:
  containers:
  - name: nginx
    image: nginx:1.15.4
    ports:
    - containerPort: 80
```

There are more fields that are optional. If you want to dive in deeper, check out the API reference for the deployment resource at `https://kubernetes.io/docs/reference/generated/kubernetes-api/v1.13/#deployment-v1-apps`.

Exposing and discovering microservices

We deployed our microservice with a deployment. Now, we need to expose it, so that it can be used by other services in the cluster and possibly also make it visible outside the cluster. Kubernetes provides the `Service` resource for that purpose. Kubernetes services are backed up by pods, identified by labels:

```
apiVersion: v1
kind: Service
metadata:
  name: nginx
  labels:
    app: nginx
spec:
  ports:
  - port: 80
    protocol: TCP
  selector:
    app: nginx
```

Services discover each other inside the cluster, using DNS or environment variables. This is the default behavior. But, if you want to make a service accessible to the world, you will normally set an ingress object or a load balancer. We will explore this topic in detail later.

Securing microservices

Kubernetes was designed for running large-scale critical systems, where security is of paramount concern. Microservices are often more challenging to secure than monolithic systems because there is so much internal communication across many boundaries. Also, microservices encourage agile development, which leads to a constantly changing system. There is no steady state you can secure once and be done with it. You must constantly adapt the security of the system to the changes. Kubernetes comes pre-packed with several concepts and mechanisms for secure development, deployment, and operation of your microservices. You still need to employ best practices, such as principle of least privilege, security in depth, and minimizing blast radius. Here are some of the security features of Kubernetes.

Namespaces

Namespaces let you isolate different parts of your cluster from each other. You can create as many namespaces as you want and scope many resources and operations to their namespace, including limits, and quotas. Pods running in a namespace can only access directly their own namespace. To access other namespaces, they must go through public APIs.

Service accounts

Service accounts provide identity to your microservices. Each service account will have certain privileges and access rights associated with its account. Service accounts are pretty simple:

```
apiVersion: v1
kind: ServiceAccount
metadata:
  name: custom-service-account
```

You can associate service accounts with a pod (for example, in the pod `spec` of a deployment) and the microservices that run inside the pod will have that identity and all the privileges and restrictions associated with that account. If you don't assign a service account, then the pod will get the default service account of its namespace. Each service account is associated with a secret used to authenticate it.

Secrets

Kubernetes provides secret management capabilities to all microservices. The secrets can be encrypted at rest on etcd (since Kubernetes 1.7), and are always encrypted on the wire (over HTTPS). Secrets are managed per namespace. Secrets are mounted in pods as either files (secret volumes) or environment variables. There are multiple ways to create secrets. Secrets can contain two maps: `data` and `stringData`. The type of values in the data map can be arbitrary, but must be base64-encoded. Refer to the following, for example:

```
apiVersion: v1
kind: Secret
metadata:
  name: custom-secret
type: Opaque
data:
  username: YWRtaW4=
  password: MWYyZDFlMmU2N2Rm
```

Here is how a pod can load secrets as a volume:

```
apiVersion: v1
kind: Pod
metadata:
  name: db
spec:
  containers:
  - name: mypod
    image: postgres
    volumeMounts:
    - name: db_creds
      mountPath: "/etc/db_creds"
      readOnly: true
  volumes:
  - name: foo
    secret:
      secretName: custom-secret
```

The end result is that the DB credentials secrets that are managed outside the pod by Kubernetes show up as a regular file inside the pod accessible through the path `/etc/db_creds`.

Secure communication

Kubernetes utilizes client-side certificates to fully authenticate both sides of any external communication (for example, kubectl). All communication to the Kubernetes API from outside should be over HTTP. Internal cluster communication between the API server and the kubelet on the node is over HTTPS too (the kubelet endpoint). But, it doesn't use a client certificate by default (you can enable it).

Communication between the API server and nodes, pods, and services is, by default, over HTTP and is not authenticated. You can upgrade them to HTTPS, but note that the client certificate is checked, so don't run your worker nodes on public networks.

Network policies

In a distributed system, beyond securing each container, pod, and node, it is critical to also control communication over the network. Kubernetes supports network policies, which give you full flexibility to define and shape the traffic and access across the cluster.

Authenticating and authorizing microservices

Authentication and authorization are also related to security, by limiting access to trusted users and to limited aspects of Kubernetes. Organizations have a variety of ways to authenticate their users. Kubernetes supports many of the common authentication schemes, such as X.509 certificates, and HTTP basic authentication (not very secure), as well as an external authentication server via webhook that gives you ultimate control over the authentication process. The authentication process just matches the credentials of a request with an identity (either the original or an impersonated user). What that user is allowed to do is controlled by the authorization process. Enter RBAC.

Role-based access control

Role-based access control (**RBAC**) is not required! You can perform authorization using other mechanisms in Kubernetes. However, it is a best practice. RBAC is based on two concepts: role and binding. A role is a set of permissions on resources defined as rules. There are two types of roles: `Role`, which applies to a single namespace, and `ClusterRole`, which applies to all namespaces in a cluster.

Here is a role in the default namespace that allows the getting, watching, and listing of all pods. Each role has three components: API groups, resources, and verbs:

```
kind: Role
apiVersion: rbac.authorization.k8s.io/v1
metadata:
  namespace: default
  name: pod-reader
rules:
- apiGroups: [""] # "" indicates the core API group
  resources: ["pods"]
  verbs: ["get", "watch", "list"]
```

Cluster roles are very similar, except there is no namespace field because they apply to all namespaces.

A binding is associating a list of subjects (users, user groups, or service accounts) with a role. There are two types of binding, `RoleBinding` and `ClusterRoleBinding`, which correspond to `Role` and `ClusterRole`.

```
kind: RoleBinding
apiVersion: rbac.authorization.k8s.io/v1
metadata:
  name: pod-reader
  namespace: default
```

```
subjects:
- kind: User
  name: gigi # Name is case sensitive
  apiGroup: rbac.authorization.k8s.io
roleRef:
  kind: Role # must be Role or ClusterRole
  name: pod-reader # must match the name of the Role or ClusterRole you
bind to
  apiGroup: rbac.authorization.k8s.io
```

It's interesting that you can bind a `ClusterRole` to a subject in a single namespace. This is convenient for defining roles that should be used in multiple namespaces, once as a cluster role, and then binding them to specific subjects in specific namespaces.

The cluster role binding is similar, but must bind a cluster role and always applies to the whole cluster.

 Note that RBAC is used to grant access to Kubernetes resources. It can regulate access to your service endpoints, but you may still need fine-grained authorization in your microservices.

Upgrading microservices

Deploying and securing microservices is just the beginning. As you develop and evolve your system, you'll need to upgrade your microservices. There are many important considerations regarding how to go about it that we will discuss later (versioning, rolling updates, blue-green, and canary). Kubernetes provides direct support for many of these concepts out of the box and the ecosystem built on top of it to provide many flavors and opinionated solutions.

The goal is often zero downtime and safe rollback if a problem occurs. Kubernetes deployments provide the primitives, such as updating a deployment, pausing a roll-out, and rolling back a deployment. Specific workflows are built on these solid foundations. The mechanics of upgrading a service typically involve upgrading its image to a new version and sometimes changes to its support resources and access: volumes, roles, quotas, limits, and so on.

Scaling microservices

There are two aspects to scaling a microservice with Kubernetes. The first aspect is scaling the number of pods backing up a particular microservice. The second aspect is the total capacity of the cluster. You can easily scale a microservice explicitly by updating the number of replicas of a deployment, but that requires constant vigilance on your part. For services that have large variations in the volume of requests they handle over long periods (for example, business hours versus off hours or week days versus weekends), it might take a lot of effort. Kubernetes provides horizontal pod autoscaling, which is based on CPU, memory, or custom metrics, and can scale your service up and down automatically.

Here is how to scale our `nginx` deployment that is currently fixed at three replicas to go between 2 and 5, depending on the average CPU usage across all instances:

```
apiVersion: autoscaling/v1
kind: HorizontalPodAutoscaler
metadata:
    name: nginx
    namespace: default
spec:
    maxReplicas: 5
    minReplicas: 2
    targetCPUUtilizationPercentage: 90
    scaleTargetRef:
      apiVersion: v1
      kind: Deployment
      name: nginx
```

The outcome is that Kubernetes will watch CPU utilization of the pods that belong to the `nginx` deployment. When the average CPU over a certain period of time (5 minutes, by default) exceeds 90%, it will add more replicas until the maximum of 5, or until utilization drops below 90%. The HPA can scale down too, but will always maintain a minimum of two replicas, even if the CPU utilization is zero.

Monitoring microservices

Your microservices are deployed and running on Kubernetes. You can update the version of your microservices whenever it is needed. Kubernetes takes care of healing and scaling automatically. However, you still need to monitor your system and keep track of errors and performance. This is important for addressing problems, but also for informing you on potential improvements, optimizations, and cost cutting.

There are several categories of information that are relevant and that you should monitor:

- Third-party logs
- Application logs
- Application errors
- Kubernetes events
- Metrics

When considering a system composed of multiple microservices and multiple supporting components, the number of logs will be substantial. The solution is central logging, where all the logs go to a single place where you can slice and dice at your will. Errors can be logged, of course, but often it is useful to report errors with additional metadata, such as stack trace, and review them in their own dedicated environment (for example, sentry or rollbar). Metrics are useful for detecting performance and system health problems or trends over time.

Kubernetes provides several mechanisms and abstractions for monitoring your microservices. The ecosystem provides a number of useful projects too.

Logging

There are several ways to implement central logging with Kubernetes:

- Have a logging agent that runs on every node
- Inject a logging sidecar container to every application pod
- Have your application send its logs directly to a central logging service

There are pros and cons to each approach. But, the main thing is that Kubernetes supports all approaches and makes container and pod logs available for consumption.

 Refer to `https://kubernetes.io/docs/concepts/cluster-administration/logging/#cluster-level-logging-architectures` for an in-depth discussion.

Metrics

Kubernetes comes with cAdvisor (https://github.com/google/cadvisor), which is a tool for collecting container metrics integrated into the kubelet binary. Kubernetes used to provide a metrics server called **heapster** that required additional backends and a UI. But, these days, the best in class metrics server is the open source Prometheus project. If you run Kubernetes on Google's GKE, then Google Cloud Monitoring is a great option that doesn't require additional components to be installed in your cluster. Other cloud providers also have integration with their monitoring solutions (for example, CloudWatch on EKS).

Creating a local cluster

One of the strengths of Kubernetes as a deployment platform is that you can create a local cluster and, with relatively little effort, have a realistic environment that is very close to your production environment. The main benefit is that developers can test their microservices locally and collaborate with the rest of the services in the cluster. When your system is comprised of many microservices, the more significant tests are often integration tests and even configuration and infrastructure tests, as opposed to unit tests. Kubernetes makes that kind of testing much easier and requires much less brittle mocking.

In this section, you will install a local Kubernetes cluster and some additional projects, and then have some fun exploring it using the invaluable kubectl command-line tool.

Installing Minikube

Minikube is a single node Kubernetes cluster that you can install anywhere. I used macOS here, but, in the past, I used it successfully on Windows too. Before installing Minikube itself, you must install a hypervisor. I prefer HyperKit:

```
$ curl -LO
https://storage.googleapis.com/minikube/releases/latest/docker-machine-driv
er-hyperkit \
  && chmod +x docker-machine-driver-hyperkit \
  && sudo mv docker-machine-driver-hyperkit /usr/local/bin/ \
  && sudo chown root:wheel /usr/local/bin/docker-machine-driver-hyperkit \
  && sudo chmod u+s /usr/local/bin/docker-machine-driver-hyperkit
```

But, I've run into trouble with HyperKit from time to time. If you can't overcome the issues, I suggest using VirtualBox as the hypervisor instead. Run the following command to install VirtualBox via Homebrew:

```
$ brew cask install virtualbox
```

Now, you can install Minikube itself. Homebrew is the best way to go again:

```
brew cask install minikube
```

If you're not on macOS, follow the official instructions here: https://kubernetes.io/docs/tasks/tools/install-minikube/.

 You must turn off any VPN before starting Minikube with HyperKit. You can restart your VPN after Minikube has started.

Minikube supports multiple versions of Kubernetes. At the moment, the default version is 1.10.0, but 1.13.0 is already out and supported, so let's use that version:

```
$ minikube start --vm-driver=hyperkit --kubernetes-version=v1.13.0
```

If you're using VirtualBox as your hypervisor, you don't need to specify --vm-driver:

```
$ minikube start --kubernetes-version=v1.13.0
```

You should see the following:

```
$ minikube start --kubernetes-version=v1.13.0
Starting local Kubernetes v1.13.0 cluster...
Starting VM...
Downloading Minikube ISO
 178.88 MB / 178.88 MB [=========================================]
100.00% 0s
Getting VM IP address...
E0111 07:47:46.013804   18969 start.go:211] Error parsing version semver:
Version string empty
Moving files into cluster...
Downloading kubeadm v1.13.0
Downloading kubelet v1.13.0
Finished Downloading kubeadm v1.13.0
Finished Downloading kubelet v1.13.0
Setting up certs...
Connecting to cluster...
Setting up kubeconfig...
Stopping extra container runtimes...
```

```
Starting cluster components...
Verifying kubelet health ...
Verifying apiserver health ...Kubectl is now configured to use the cluster.
Loading cached images from config file.


Everything looks great. Please enjoy minikube!
```

 Minikube will automatically download the Minikube VM (178.88 MB) if it's the first time you are starting your Minikube cluster.

At this point, your Minikube cluster is ready to go.

Troubleshooting Minikube

If you run into some trouble (for example, if you forgot to turn off your VPN), try to delete your Minikube installation and restart it with verbose logging:

```
$ minikube delete
$ rm -rf ~/.minikube
$ minikube start --vm-driver=hyperkit --kubernetes-version=v1.13.0 --
logtostderr --v=3
```

If your Minikube installation just hangs (maybe waiting for SSH), you might have to reboot to unstick it. If that doesn't help, try the following:

```
sudo mv /var/db/dhcpd_leases /var/db/dhcpd_leases.old
sudo touch /var/db/dhcpd_leases
```

Then, reboot again.

Verifying your cluster

If everything is OK, you can check your Minikube version:

```
$ minikube version
minikube version: v0.31.0
```

Minikube has many other useful commands. Just type `minikube` to see the list of commands and flags.

Playing with your cluster

Minikube is running, so let's have some fun. Your kubectl is going to serve you well in this section. Let's start by examining our node:

```
$ kubectl get nodes
NAME        STATUS   ROLES    AGE      VERSION
minikube    Ready    master   4m       v1.13.0
```

Your cluster already has some pods and services running. It turns out that Kubernetes is dogfooding and many of its own services are plain services and pods. But, those pods and services run in namespaces. Here are all the namespaces:

```
$ kubectl get ns
NAME          STATUS   AGE
default       Active   18m
kube-public   Active   18m
kube-system   Active   18m
```

To see all the services in all the namespaces, you can use the `--all-namespaces` flag:

```
$ kubectl get svc --all-namespaces
NAMESPACE        NAME    TYPE    CLUSTER-IP   EXTERNAL-IP   PORT(S)   AGE
default     kubernetes    ClusterIP   10.96.0.1   <none>   443/TCP        19m
kube-system kube-dns    ClusterIP   10.96.0.10 <none>     53/UDP,53/TCP 19m
kube-system kubernetes-dashboard  ClusterIP 10.111.39.46 <none>
80/TCP           18m
```

The Kubernetes API server, itself, is running as a service in the default namespace and then we have `kube-dns` and the `kubernetes-dashboard` running in the `kube-system` namespace.

To explore the dashboard, you can run the dedicated Minikube command, `minikube dashboard`. You can also use `kubectl`, which is more universal and will work on any Kubernetes cluster:

```
$ kubectl port-forward deployment/kubernetes-dashboard 9090
```

Then, browse to `http://localhost:9090` and you will see the following dashboard:

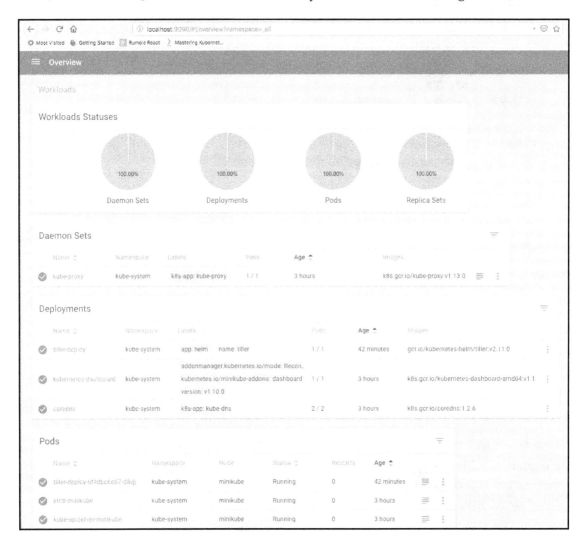

Installing Helm

Helm is the Kubernetes package manager. It doesn't come with Kubernetes, so you have to install it. Helm has two components: a server-side component called `tiller`, and a CLI called `helm`.

Let's install `helm` locally first, using Homebrew:

```
$ brew install kubernetes-helm
```

Then, properly initialize both the server and client type:

```
$ helm init
$HELM_HOME has been configured at /Users/gigi.sayfan/.helm.

Tiller (the Helm server-side component) has been installed into your
Kubernetes Cluster.

Please note: by default, Tiller is deployed with an insecure 'allow
unauthenticated users' policy.
To prevent this, run `helm init` with the --tiller-tls-verify flag.
For more information on securing your installation see:
https://docs.helm.sh/using_helm/#securing-your-helm-installation
Happy Helming!
```

With Helm in place, you can easily install all kinds of goodies in your Kubernetes cluster. There are currently 275 chars (the Helm term for a package) in the stable chart repository:

```
$ helm search | wc -l
275
```

For example, check out all the releases tagged with the db type:

```
$ helm search db
NAME                             CHART VERSION   APP VERSION
DESCRIPTION
stable/cockroachdb               2.0.6           2.1.1
CockroachDB is a scalable, survivable, strongly-consisten...
stable/hlf-couchdb               1.0.5           0.4.9         CouchDB
instance for Hyperledger Fabric (these charts are...
stable/influxdb                  1.0.0           1.7           Scalable
datastore for metrics, events, and real-time ana...
stable/kubedb                    0.1.3           0.8.0-beta.2  DEPRECATED
KubeDB by AppsCode - Making running production...
stable/mariadb                   5.2.3           10.1.37       Fast,
reliable, scalable, and easy to use open-source rel...
stable/mongodb                   4.9.1           4.0.3         NoSQL
document-oriented database that stores JSON-like do...
stable/mongodb-replicaset        3.8.0           3.6           NoSQL
document-oriented database that stores JSON-like do...
stable/percona-xtradb-cluster    0.6.0           5.7.19        free,
fully compatible, enhanced, open source drop-in rep...
stable/prometheus-couchdb-exporter 0.1.0         1.0           A Helm
chart to export the metrics from couchdb in Promet...
```

```
stable/rethinkdb              0.2.0          0.1.0        The open-
source database for the realtime web
jenkins-x/cb-app-slack        0.0.1                       A Slack
App for CloudBees Core
stable/kapacitor              1.1.0          1.5.1        InfluxDB's
native data processing engine. It can process ...
stable/lamp                   0.1.5          5.7          Modular
and transparent LAMP stack chart supporting PHP-F...
stable/postgresql             2.7.6          10.6.0       Chart for
PostgreSQL, an object-relational database manag...
stable/phpmyadmin             2.0.0          4.8.3        phpMyAdmin
is an mysql administration frontend
stable/unifi                  0.2.1          5.9.29       Ubiquiti
Network's Unifi Controller
```

We will use Helm a lot throughout the book.

Summary

In this chapter, you received a whirlwind tour of Kubernetes and got an idea of how well it aligns with microservices. The extensible architecture of Kubernetes empowers a large community of enterprise organizations, startup companies, and open source organizations to collaborate and create an ecosystem around Kubernetes that multiplies its benefits and ensures its staying power. The concepts and abstractions built into Kubernetes are very well suited for microservice-based systems. They support every phase of the SDLC, from development, through testing, and deployments, and all the way to monitoring and troubleshooting. The Minikube project lets every developer run a local Kubernetes cluster, which is great for experimenting with Kubernetes itself, as well as testing locally in an environment that is very similar to the production environment. The Helm project is a fantastic addition to Kubernetes and provides great value as the de facto package management solution. In the next chapter, we will dive into the world of microservices and learn why they are the best approach for developing complex and fast-moving distributed systems that run in the cloud.

Further reading

- If you want to learn more about Kubernetes, I recommend my book, *Mastering Kubernetes – Second Edition*, published by Packt: https://www.packtpub.com/application-development/mastering-kubernetes-second-edition

2
Getting Started with Microservices

In the previous chapter, you learned what Kubernetes is all about, and how it is well suited as a platform for developing, deploying, and managing microservices, and even played a little with your own local Kubernetes cluster. In this chapter, we are going to talk about microservices in general and why they are the best way to build complex systems. We will also discuss various aspects, patterns, and approaches that address common problems in microservice-based systems and how they compare to other common architectures, such as monolith and large services.

We will cover a lot of material in this chapter:

- Programming in the small – less is more
- Making your microservice autonomous
- Employing interfaces and contracts
- Exposing your service via APIs
- Using client libraries
- Managing dependencies
- Orchestrating microservices
- Taking advantage of ownership
- Understanding Conway's law
- Troubleshooting across multiple services
- Utilizing shared service libraries
- Choosing a source control strategy
- Creating a data strategy

Technical requirements

In this chapter, you'll see some code examples using Go. I recommend that you install Go and try to build and run the code examples yourself.

Installing Go with Homebrew on macOS

On macOS, I recommend using Homebrew:

```
$ brew install go
```

Next, make sure the go command is available:

```
$ ls -la `which go`
lrwxr-xr-x  1 gigi.sayfan  admin  26 Nov 17 09:03 /usr/local/bin/go ->
../Cellar/go/1.11.2/bin/go
```

To see all the options, just type go. Also, make sure that you define GOPATH in your .bashrc file and add $GOPATH/bin to your path.

Go comes with the Go CLI that provides many capabilities, but you may want to install additional tools. Check out https://awesome-go.com/.

Installing Go on other platforms

On other platforms, follow the official instructions here: https://golang.org/doc/install.

The code

You can find the code for this chapter here: https://github.com/PacktPublishing/Hands-On-Microservices-with-Kubernetes/tree/master/Chapter02.

Programming in the small – less is more

Think about the time you learned to program. You wrote little programs that accepted simple input, did a little processing, and produced some output. Life was good. You could hold the entire program in your head.

You understood every line of code. Debugging and troubleshooting was easy. For example, consider a program to convert temperatures between Celsius and Fahrenheit:

```go
package main

import (
        "fmt"
        "os"
        "strconv"
)

func celsius2fahrenheit(t float64) float64 {
        return 9.0/5.0*t + 32
}

func fahrenheit2celsius(t float64) float64 {
        return (t - 32) * 5.0 / 9.0
}

func usage() {
    fmt.Println("Usage: temperature_converter <mode> <temperature>")
    fmt.Println()
    fmt.Println("This program converts temperatures between Celsius and
Fahrenheit")
    fmt.Println("'mode' is either 'c2f' or 'f2c'")
    fmt.Println("'temperature' is a floating point number to be converted
according to mode")
    os.Exit(1)
}

func main() {
        if len(os.Args) != 3 {
                usage()
        }
        mode := os.Args[1]
        if mode != "f2c" && mode != "c2f" {
                usage()
        }

        t, err := strconv.ParseFloat(os.Args[2], 64)
        if err != nil {
                usage()
        }
        var converted float64
         if mode == "f2c" {
                converted = fahrenheit2celsius(t)
         } else {
                converted = celsius2fahrenheit(t)
```

```
        }
        fmt.Println(converted)
}
```

This program is pretty simple. It does a decent job of validating its input and displaying usage information if something goes wrong. The actual computation the program does is just two lines of code that convert the temperature, but it is 45 lines long. There aren't even any comments. Yet, those 45 lines are pretty readable and easy to test. There aren't any third-party dependencies (just the Go standard library). There is no IO (files, databases, network). There is no need for authentication or authorization. There is no need to rate limit calls. There is no logging, no metrics collection. There is no versioning, health checks, or configuration. There is no deployment to multiple environments and no monitoring in production.

Now, consider integrating this simple program into a big enterprise system. You'll have to take into account many of these aspects. Other parts of the system will start using the temperature conversion functionality. Suddenly, the simplest operations might have cascading impacts. Changes to other parts of the system might affect the temperature converter:

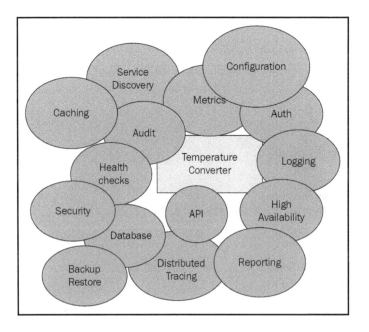

This jump in complexity is natural. Large enterprise systems have many requirements. The promise of microservices is that by following proper architectural guidelines and established patterns, the additional complexity can be neatly packaged and used across many small microservices that work together to accomplish the system goals. Ideally, service developers can be shielded from the encompassing system most of the time. However, it takes a lot of effort to provide the right degree of isolation and still also allow for testing and debugging in the context of the entire system.

Making your microservice autonomous

One of the best ways to fight complexity is to make your microservice autonomous. An autonomous service is a service that doesn't depend on other services in the system or third-party services. An autonomous service manages its own state and can be largely unaware of the rest of the system.

I like to think of autonomous microservices as similar to immutable functions. Autonomous services never change the state of other components in the system. The benefit of such services is that their complexity remains the same, regardless of how the rest of the system evolves and however they are being used by other services.

Employing interfaces and contracts

Interfaces are one of the best tools a software engineer can use. Once you expose something as an interface, you can freely change the implementation behind it. Interfaces are a construct that's being used within a single process. They are extremely useful for testing interactions with other components, which are plentiful in microservice-based systems. Here is one of the interfaces of our sample application:

```
type UserManager interface {
   Register(user User) error
   Login(username string, authToken string) (session string, err error)
   Logout(username string, session string) error
}
```

The `UserManager` interface defines a few methods, their inputs, and outputs. However, it doesn't specify the semantics. For example, what happens if the `Login()` method is called for an already logged-in user? Is it an error? Is the previous session terminated and a new session created? Is it returning the existing session without an error (idempotent approach)? These kinds of questions are answered by contracts. Contracts are difficult to specify fully and Go doesn't provide any support for contracts. But, contracts are important and they always exist, even if only implicitly.

 Some languages don't support interfaces as a first-class syntactic construct of the language. However, it is very easy to accomplish the same effect. Languages with dynamic typing, such as Python, Ruby, and JavaScript, allow you to pass any object that satisfies the set of attributes and methods used by the caller. Static languages, such as C and C++, get by with sets of function pointers (C) or structs with only pure virtual functions (C++).

Exposing your service via APIs

Microservices interact with each other and sometimes with the outside world over the network. A service exposes its capabilities through an API. I like to think of APIs as over-the-wire interfaces. Programming language interfaces use the syntax of the language they are written in (for example, Go's interface type). Modern network APIs also use some high-level representation. The foundation is UDP and TCP. However, microservices will typically expose their capabilities over web transports, such as HTTP (REST, GraphQL, SOAP), HTTP/2 (gRPC), or, in some cases, WebSockets. Some services may imitate other wire protocols, such as memcached, but this is useful in special situations. In 2019, there is really no reason to build your own custom protocol directly over TCP/UDP or use proprietary and language-specific protocols. Approaches such as Java RMI, .NET remoting, DCOM, and CORBA are better left in the past, unless you need to support some legacy code base.

There are two categories of microservices, which are as follows:

- Internal microservices are only accessible to other microservices running typically in the same network/cluster and those services can expose more specialized APIs because you're in control of both services and their clients (other services).
- External services are open to the world and often need to be consumed from web browsers or clients using multiple languages.

The benefit of using standard network APIs over standard language-agnostic transports is that it enables the polyglot promise of microservices. Each service may be implemented in its own programming language (for example, one service in Go and another in Python) and they may even migrate to a completely different language later (Rust, anyone?) without disruption, as all these services interact through the network API. We will examine later the polyglot approach and its trade-offs.

Using client libraries

Interfaces are very convenient to work with. You operate within your programming language environments, calling methods with native data types. Working with network APIs is different. You need to use a network library, depending on the transport. You need to serialize your payload and responses and deal with network errors, disconnects, and timeouts. The client library pattern encapsulates the remote service and all these decisions and presents you with a standard interface that, as a client of the service, you just call. The client library behind the scenes will take care of all the ceremony involved with invoking a network API. The law of leaky abstractions (`https://www.joelonsoftware.com/2002/11/11/the-law-of-leaky-abstractions/`) says that you can't really hide the network. However, you can hide it pretty effectively from the consumer service and configure it properly with policies regarding timeouts, retries, and caching.

 One of the greatest selling points of gRPC is that it generates a client library for you.

Managing dependencies

Modern systems have a lot of dependencies. Managing them effectively is a big part of the **software development life cycle** (**SDLC**). There are two kinds of dependencies:

- Libraries/packages (linked to the running service process)
- Remote services (accessible over the network)

Each of these dependencies can be internal or third party. You manage libraries or packages through your language's package management system. Go had no official package management system for a long time and several solutions, such as Glide and Dep, came along. These days (Go 1.12), Go modules are the official solution.

You manage remote services through the discovery of endpoints and tracking API versions. The difference between internal dependencies and third-party dependencies is the velocity of change. Internal dependencies will change much faster. With microservices, you'll have other microservices you depend on. Versioning and keeping track of the contracts behind the APIs become very important aspects of development.

Coordinating microservices

When comparing a monolith system with a microservice-based system, one thing is clear. There is more of everything. The individual microservices are simpler and it's much easier to reason, modify, and troubleshoot individual services. But, understanding the whole system, making changes across multiple services, and debugging problems are more challenging. Many more interactions also happen over the network between separate microservices, where, with a monolith, these interactions would occur within the same process. It means that to benefit from microservices, you need a disciplined approach, you need to apply best practices, and have good tools at your disposal.

The uniformity versus flexibility trade-off

Let's say you have a hundred microservices, but they are all very small and very similar. They all use the same data store (for example, the same type of relational database). They are all configured in the same way (for example, a configuration file). They all report errors and logs to a centralized log server. They are all implemented using the same programming language (for example, Go). Typically, the system will handle several use cases. Each use case will involve some subset of these hundred microservices. There will also be some generic microservices that are used in most use cases (for example, an authorization service). Then, it may not be that difficult to understand the system as a whole, given some good documentation. You can look at each use case separately and, when you extend the system and add more use cases, and maybe grow to a thousand microservices, the complexity remains bounded:

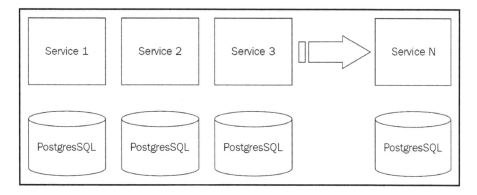

A good analogy is files and directories. Suppose you organize your music by genre, artist, and song. Initially, you had three genres, 20 artists, and 200 songs. Then, you expanded everything and now have 10 genres, 50 artists, and 3,000 songs. The organization is still the same old hierarchy of genre/artist/song. It's true that at some point when you scale, the sheer scale can present new problems. For example, with music, when you have so much music that it doesn't fit on your hard disk, you need a qualitatively different solution (for example, keep it in the cloud). The same is true for microservices, but the divide and conquer approach works well. If you reach internet-scale—Amazon, Google, Facebook—then, yes, you'll need much more elaborate solutions for every aspect.

But, with uniform microservices, you sacrifice a number of benefits. For example, teams and developers may be forced to use a programming language that is not best for the task, or they'll have to abide by strict operational standards of logging and error reporting, even for small non-critical internal services.

You need to understand the pros and cons of uniform versus diverse microservices. There is a spectrum ranging from totally uniform microservices to a jungle of anything goes, where each microservice is a unique snowflake. Your responsibility is to find the sweet spot along this spectrum for your system.

Taking advantage of ownership

Since microservices are small. A single developer can own a whole microservice and understand it completely. Other developers may also be familiar with it, but even if just a single developer is familiar with a service, it should be relatively simple and painless for a new developer to take over because the scope is so limited and ideally similar.

Sole ownership can be very powerful. The developer needs to communicate with the other developers and teams though the service API, but can iterate very fast on the implementation. You may still want other developers on the team to review the internal design and implementation, but even in the extreme case that the owner works completely on their own with no supervision, the potential damage is limited because the scope of each microservice is small and it interacts with the rest of the system through well-defined APIs.

The differences in productivity can be jaw-dropping.

Understanding Conway's law

Conway's law is defined as follows:

> *"Organizations which design systems ... are constrained to produce designs which are copies of the communication structures of these organizations."*

This means the structure of the system will reflect the structure of the team building it. A famous variation by Eric Raymond is this:

> *"If you have four groups building a compiler you'll get a 4-pass compiler."*

This is very insightful and I've personally witnessed it time and again in many different organizations. This is very relevant to microservice-based systems. With lots of small microservices, you don't need a dedicated team for each microservice. There will be some higher-level groups of microservices that work together to produce some aspect of the system. Now, the question is how to think about the high-level structure. There are three main options:

- Vertical
- Horizontal
- Matrix

Microservices can be very important in this regard. By being small autonomous components, they support all structures. But, what is even more important is when organizations need to transition from one approach to another. The usual trajectory is: horizontal | vertical | matrix.

The organization can perform those transitions with much less friction if the software follows a microservice-based architecture. It can even be a deciding factor. Even an organization that doesn't follow microservice-based architecture decides to stay with an inappropriate structure because the risk and effort of breaking the monolith is too high.

Vertical

The vertical approach takes a slice of functionality of the system that comprises multiple microservices and a team is fully responsible for that functionality, from design to implementation, through deployment and maintenance. Teams operate as silos and communication between them is typically limited and formal. This approach favors aspects of microservices, such as the following:

- Polyglot
- Flexibility
- Independently moving pieces
- End-to-end ownership
- Less formal contracts within the vertical slice
- Easy-to-scale to more vertical slices (just form another team)
- Difficult to apply changes across vertical slices, especially as the number of vertical slices scales

This approach is common in very large organizations due to its scalability advantages. It also requires a lot of creativity and effort to make improvements across the board. There will be duplication of effort between the silos. Aiming for complete reuse and coordination is futile. The trick with the vertical approach is to find the sweet spot, where common functionality is packaged in a way that can be used by multiple silos, but without requiring explicit coordination.

Horizontal

The horizontal approach looks at the system as a layered architecture. The team structure is organized along those layers. There may be a frontend group, backend group, and a DevOps group. Each group is responsible for all the aspects in their layer. Vertical functionality is implemented by a collaboration between different groups across all layers. This approach is more suitable for smaller organizations with a small numbers of products (sometimes just one).

The nice thing about the horizontal approach is that the organization can build expertise and share knowledge across entire horizontal layers. Typically, organizations start with a horizontal organization and, as they grow and then expand to more products, or possibly spread across multiple geographic locations, they divide into a more vertical structure. Within each silo, the structure is usually horizontal.

Matrix

The matrix organization is the most complicated. You have your vertical silos, but the organization recognizes that the amount of duplication and variation between the silos waste resources and also makes transferring people between vertical silos challenging if they diversify too much. With a matrix organization, in addition to the vertical silos, there are also cross-cutting groups that work with all vertical silos and try to bring some level of consistency, uniformity, and order. For example, the organization may dictate that all vertical silos must deploy their software to the cloud on AWS. In this case, there may be a cloud platform group that is managed outside the vertical silos and provides guidance, tooling, and other shared services for all the vertical silos. Security is another good example. Many organizations consider security an area that must be managed centrally and can't be left to the whims of each silo.

Troubleshooting across multiple services

Since most of the functions of the system will involve interactions between multiple microservices, it's important to be able to follow a request coming in across all those microservices and various data stores. One of the best ways to accomplish this is distributed tracing, where you tag each request and can follow it from beginning to end.

The subtleties of debugging distributed systems in general and microservice-based ones take a lot of expertise. Consider the following aspects along the path of a single request through the system:

- The microservices processing the request may use different programming languages.
- The microservices may expose APIs using different transports/protocols.
- Requests may be part of asynchronous workflows that involve waiting in queues and/or periodical processing.
- The persistent state of the request may be spread across many independent data stores controlled by different microservices.

When you need to debug a problem across the entire swath of microservices in the system, the autonomous nature of each microservice becomes a hindrance. You must build explicit support to be able to gain system-level visibility by aggregating internal information from multiple microservices.

Utilizing shared service libraries

If you choose the uniform microservices approach, it is very useful to have a shared library (or several libraries) that all services use and implement many cross-cutting concerns, such as the following:

- Configuration
- Secret management
- Service discovery
- API wrapping
- Logging
- Distributed tracing

This library may implement whole workflows, such as authentication and authorization, that interact with other microservices or third-party dependencies and do the heavy lifting for each microservice. This way, the microservice is only responsible for using these libraries properly and implements its own functionality.

This approach can work even if you choose the polyglot path and support multiple languages. You can implement this library for all the supported languages and the services themselves can be implemented in different languages.

However, there are costs associated with the maintenance and evolution of shared libraries and the rate of adopting them by all microservices. A real danger is that different microservices will use many versions of the shared libraries and cause subtle (or not so subtle) problems when services using different versions of the shared library try to communicate.

The service mesh approach that we will explore later in the book can provide some answers to this issue.

Choosing a source control strategy

This is a very interesting scenario. There are two main approaches: monorepo and multiple repos. Let's explore the pros and cons of each.

Monorepo

In the monorepo approach, your entire code base is in a single source control repository. It is very easy to perform operations over the entire code base. Whenever you make a change, it is reflected immediately in your entire code base. Versioning is pretty much off the table. That's great for keeping all your code in sync. But, if you do need to upgrade some parts of your systems incrementally, you'll need to come up with workarounds, such as creating a separate copy with your new changes. Also, the fact that your source code is always in sync doesn't mean that your deployed services are all using the latest version. If you always deploy all your services at once, you're pretty much building a monolith. Note that you may still have multiple repos if you contribute to third-party open source projects (even if you only use upstream versions after your changes were merged).

Another big issue with monorepo is that you might need a lot of custom tooling to manage your multi repo. Large companies, such as Google and Microsoft, use the multi-repo approach. They have special needs and the custom tooling aspect doesn't deter them. I'm on the fence if the multi-repo approach is appropriate for smaller organizations. However, I'll use a monorepo for the Delinkcious —the demo application—so, we will get to explore it together and form an opinion. A major downside is that many modern CI/CD tool chains use GitOps, which trigger changes in source control repos. When there is just one monorepo, you lose the one-to-one mapping between a source control repo and a microservice.

Multiple repos

The multiple repos approach is exactly the opposite. Each project, and often each library, has a separate source control repository. Projects consume each other just like third-party libraries. There are several advantages to this approach:

- Clear physical boundaries between projects and services.
- One-to-one mapping of source control repositories and services or projects.
- It is easy to map deployments of services to source control repositories.
- Uniform treatment of all dependencies—internal and third party.

However, there are significant costs to this approach, especially as the number of services and projects grows and the dependency graphs between them become more complicated:

- Applying changes often requires changes across multiple repositories.
- You often need to maintain multiple versions of a repository, as different services depend on different services.
- It is difficult to apply cross-cutting changes across all repositories.

Hybrid

The hybrid approach involves using a small number of repositories. Each repository contains multiple services and projects. Each repository is isolated from the other repositories, but within each repo, multiple services and projects can be developed in lockstep. This approach balances the pros and cons of monorepo and multiple repos. It may be useful when there are clear organizational boundaries and often geographical boundaries. For example, if a company has multiple product lines that are completely independent, it may be a good idea to break each product line into its own monorepo.

Creating a data strategy

One the most important responsibilities of a software system is to manage data. There are many types of data, and most of the data, should survive any failure of the system or you should be able to reconstruct it. Data often has complex relationships with other data. This is very explicit with relational databases, but exists in other types of data, too. Monoliths typically use large data stores that keep all the related data and, as a result, can perform queries and transactions over the entire set of data. Microservices are different. Each microservice is autonomous and responsible for its data. However, the system as a whole needs to query and operate over data that is now stored in many independent data stores and managed by many different services. Let's examine how to address this challenge using best practices.

One data store per microservice

The one data store per microservice is a crucial element of the microservice architecture. The moment two microservices can access directly the same data store, they are tightly coupled and are no longer independent. There are a few important nuances to understand. It may be OK for multiple microservices to use the same database instance, but they must not share the same logical database.

The database instance is a resource provisioning concern. In some cases, the team developing the microservice is responsible for provisioning its data stores too. In this case, the wise move may be to have physically separate DB instances for each microservice and not just logical ones. Note that when using cloud data stores, the microservice developer is not in control and unaware of the physical configuration of the data store.

We agree that two microservices shouldn't share the same data store. But, what about a single microservice managing two or more data stores? This is generally also frowned upon. If your design calls for two separate data stores, it's better to dedicate a microservice to each one:

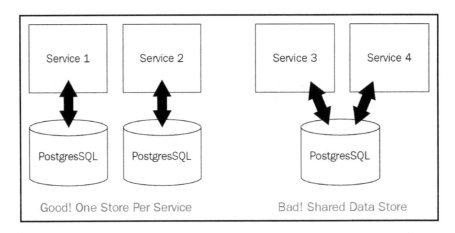

There is one common exception—you may want to manage an in-memory data store (cache) and a persistent data store by the same microservice. The workflow is that the service is writing to the persistent store and the cache and serving queries from the cache. The cache is either refreshed periodically, or based on change notification, or when there is a cache miss.

But, even in this case, it may be a better design to have a separate centralized cache, such as Redis managed by a separate microservice. Remember that each microservice may have multiple instances in a large system that serves many users.

Another reason to abstract away the physical configuration and provisioning of data stores from the microservices themselves is that those configurations may be different in different environments. Your production environment may have physically separate data stores for each microservice, but, in your development environment, it may be better to have just one physical database instance with lots of small logical databases.

Running distributed queries

We agree that each microservice should have its own data store. This means that the overall state of the system will be distributed across multiple data stores, accessible only from their own microservices. Most interesting queries will involve data available in multiple data stores. Each consumer could just access all these microservices and aggregate all the data to satisfy their query. However, that is sub-optimal for several reasons:

- Consumers are intimately aware of how data is managed by the system.
- Consumers need to get access to each and every service that stores data relevant to the query.
- Changing the architecture might require changes to a lot of consumers.

There are two common solutions to address this issue: CQRS and API composition. The cool thing about it is that the services that enable both solutions have the same API, so it is possible to switch from one solution to another, or even mix and match without impacting users. This means that some queries will be serviced by CQRS and others by API composition, all implemented by the same service. Overall, I recommend to start with API composition and transition to CQRS only if the proper conditions exist and benefits are compelling, due to its much higher complexity.

Employing Command Query Responsibility Segregation

With **Command Query Responsibility Segregation** (**CQRS**), the data from the various microservices is aggregated to a new read-only data store that is designed to answer specific queries. The meaning of the name is that you separate (segregate) the responsibility of updating data (commands) from the responsibility of reading data (queries). Different services are in charge of those activities. It is often implemented by watching for changes to all data stores and requires a change notification system in place. You could use polling too, but that's often undesirable. This solution shines when there are known queries that are used often.

Here is an illustration of CQRS in action. The CQRS service (responsible for queries) receives a change notification from the three microservices (responsible for updates) and aggregates them into its own data store.

When a query comes, the CQRS service responds by accessing its own aggregated view without hitting the microservices:

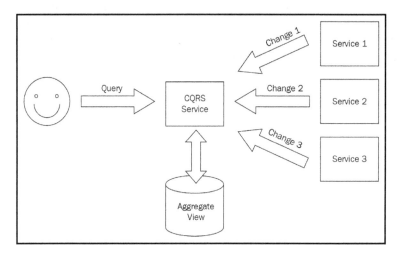

The pros are as follows:

- Queries don't interfere with updating the primary data store.
- The aggregator service exposes an API that is tailored to specific queries.
- It's easier to change the way data is managed behind the scenes without impacting consumers.
- Quick response time.

The cons are as follows:

- It adds complexity to the system.
- It duplicates the data.
- Partial views require explicit treatment.

Employing API composition

The API composition approach is much more lightweight. On the surface, it looks just like the CQRS solution. It exposes an API that can answer well-known queries across multiple microservices. The difference is that it doesn't keep its own data store. Whenever a request comes in, it will access the individual microservices that contain the data, compose the results, and return them. This solution shines when the system doesn't support event notification for data changes and when the load of running queries against the primary data store is acceptable.

Here is an illustration of API composition in action, where a query to an API composer service is translated under the covers to queries to three microservices:

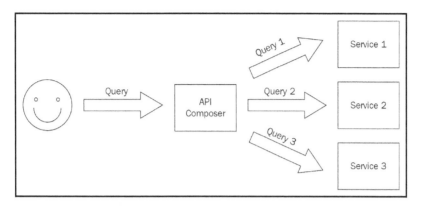

The pros are as follows:

- Lightweight solution.
- The aggregator service exposes an API that is tailored to specific queries.
- Results are always up to date.
- No architectural requirements, such as event notification.

The cons are as follows:

- The failure of any service will fail the query. This requires policy decisions around retries and timeouts.
- A high number of queries might impact primary data stores.

Using sagas to manage transactions across multiple services

The API composer and CQRS patterns provide adequate solutions for distributed queries when everything works well. However, maintaining distributed data integrity is a complex problem. If you store all your data in a single relational database and specify proper constraints in your schema, then you can rely on the database engine to take care of data integrity. The situation is very different with multiple microservices maintaining your data in isolated data stores (relational or non-relational). Data integrity is essential, but it must be maintained by your code. The saga pattern addresses this concern. Before diving into the saga pattern, let's understand data integrity in general.

Understanding ACID

A common measure of data integrity is that all transactions that modify data have the ACID properties:

- **Atomic**: All operations in the transaction succeed or they all fail.
- **Consistent**: The state of the data complies with all constraints before and after the transaction.
- **Isolated**: Concurrent transactions behave as if serialized.
- **Durable**: When a transaction completes successfully, the results are persisted.

The ACID properties are not specific to relational databases, but often used in that context, mostly because the relational schemas, with their formal constraints, provide a convenient measure of consistency. The isolation property often has serious performance implications and may be relaxed in some systems that prefer high-performance and eventual consistency.

The durability property is pretty obvious. There is no point going to all the trouble if your data can't be safely persisted. There are different levels of persistence:

- **Persistence to disk**: Can survive restart of the node, but no disk failure
- **Redundant memory on multiple nodes**: Can survive restart of a node and disk failure, but not temporary failure of all the nodes
- **Redundant disks**: Can survive the failure of a disk
- **Geo-distributed replicas**: Can survive a whole data center being down
- **Backups**: Cheaper to store a lot of information, but slower to restore and often lags behind real time

The atomicity requirement is also a no-brainer. Nobody likes partial changes, which can violate data integrity and break the system in unpredictable ways that are difficult to troubleshoot.

Understanding the CAP theorem

The CAP theorem states that a distributed system can't have all three properties at the same time:

- Consistency
- Availability
- Partition resiliency

In practice, you get to pick if you want a CP system or AP system. A **CP** system (**consistent and partition resilient**) is always consistent and will not serve queries or make changes if there is a network partitioning between components. It will function only when the system is fully connected. This obviously means that you don't have availability. On the other hand, an **AP** system (**available and partition resilient**) is always available and can operate in split-brain fashion. When the system splits, each part may continue to operate normally, but the system will be inconsistent because each part is unaware of transactions happening in the other part.

AP systems are often referred to as eventually consistent systems because, when connectivity is restored, some reconciliation process ensures the entire system syncs up again. An interesting variant is frozen systems, where, when a network partitioning occurs, they degrade gracefully and both parts continue to serve queries, but reject all modifications to the system. Note that there is no guarantee that, at the moment of partitioning, both parts are consistent because some transactions in one part may still not be replicated to the other part. Often, it is good enough because the divergence between the split part is small and will not increase over time because new changes are rejected.

Applying the saga pattern to microservices

Relational databases can provide ACID compliance for distributed systems through algorithms, such as two-phase commit and control over all the data. The two-phase commit algorithm works in two phases: prepare and commit. However, the services that participate in the distributed transaction must share the same database. That doesn't work for microservices that manage their own databases.

Enter the saga pattern. The basic idea of the saga pattern is that there is centralized management of the operations across all the microservices and that, for each operation, there is a compensating operation that will be executed if, for some reason, the entire transaction can't be completed. This achieves the atomicity property of ACID. But, the changes on each microservice are visible immediately and not only at the end of the entire distributed transaction. This violates the consistency and isolation properties. This is not a problem if you design your system as AP, also known as, **eventually consistent**. But, it requires your code to be aware of it and be able to work with data that may be partially inconsistent or stale. In many cases, this is an acceptable compromise.

How does a saga work? A saga is a set of operations and corresponding compensating operations on microservices. When an operation fails, its compensating operation and the compensating operations of all the previous operations are called in reverse order to roll back the entire state of the system.

Sagas are not trivial to implement because the compensating operations might fail too. In general, the transient state must be persistent and marked as such and a lot of metadata must be stored to enable reliable rollback. A good practice is to have an out-of-band process run frequently and clean up failed sagas that didn't manage to complete all their compensating operations in real time.

A good way to think about sagas is as workflows. Workflows are cool because they enable long processes that even involve humans and not just software.

Summary

In this chapter, we covered a lot of ground. We discussed the basic principle of microservices—less is more—and how breaking down your system to many small and self-contained microservices can help it scale. We also discussed the challenges that face developers utilizing the microservices architecture. We provided a slew of concepts, options, best practices, and pragmatic advice on architecting microservice-based systems. At this point, you should appreciate the flexibility that microservices offer, but also be a little apprehensive of the many ways you can choose to utilize them.

In the rest of the book, we will explore the terrain in detail and together build a microservice-based system using some of the best available frameworks and tools and deploy it on Kubernetes. In the next chapter, you'll meet Delinkcious—our sample application—that will serve as a hands-on laboratory. You will also get a glimpse into Go-kit, a microservice-based framework for constructing Go microservices.

Further reading

If you are interested in microservices, I recommend the following article as a starting point: https://www.martinfowler.com/

3
Delinkcious - the Sample Application

Delinkcious is a Delicious (`https://en.wikipedia.org/wiki/Delicious_ (website)`) wannabe. Delicious used to be an internet hit that managed links for users. It was acquired by Yahoo, was bounced around, and sold multiple times. It was eventually purchased by Pinboard, which runs a similar service and intends to shut down Delicious soon.

Delinkcious allows users store URLs in cool places on the web, tag them, and query them in various ways. Throughout this book, Delinkcious will serve as a live lab to demonstrate many microservices and Kubernetes concepts, as well as features in the context of a real-world application. The focus will be on the backend, so there will be no snazzy frontend web application or mobile app. I'll leave those as the dreaded exercise for you.

In this chapter, we will understand why I chose Go as the programming language of Delinkcious, and then look at **Go kit** – an excellent Go microservice toolkit that I'll use to build Delinkcious. Then, we will dissect the different aspects of Delinkcious itself using the social graph service as a running example.

We will be covering the following topics:

- The Delinkcious microservices
- The Delinkcious data storage
- The Delinkcious API
- The Delinkcious client libraries

Technical requirements

If you have followed along with this book so far, you will have already installed Go. I recommend installing a good Go IDE to follow the code in this chapter since there will be a lot to go through. Let's go through a couple of good options.

Visual Studio Code

Visual Studio Code, also known as **VS Code** (`https://code.visualstudio.com/docs/languages/go`), is an open source IDE from Microsoft. It isn't Go-specific but has deep integration with Go via a dedicated and sophisticated Go extension. It is considered the best free Go IDE.

GoLand

JetBrains' GoLand (`https://www.jetbrains.com/go/`) is my personal favorite. It follows the great tradition of IntelliJ IDEA, PyCharm, and other great IDEs. This is a paid version with a 30-day free trial. There is no Community Edition, unfortunately. If you can afford it, I highly recommend it. If you can't or don't want to pay for an IDE (totally reasonable), check out the other options.

LiteIDE

LiteIDE or LiteIDE X (`https://github.com/visualfc/liteide`) is a very interesting open source project. It is one of the earliest Go IDEs and it predates both GoLand and the Go extension for VS Code. I used it in the early days and was surprised by its quality. I eventually dropped it due to difficulties with interactive debugging via the **GNU Project Debugger** (**GDB**). It is actively developed, has a lot of contributors, and supports all the latest and greatest Go features, including Go 1.1 and the Go modules. You can now debug using Delve, which is the best of class Go debugger.

Other options

If you're a die-hard command-line person and don't like IDEs at all, you have options available. Most programming and text editors have some form of Go support. The Go wiki (`https://github.com/golang/go/wiki/IDEsAndTextEditorPlugins`) has a big list of IDEs and text editor plugins, so go and check that out.

The code

In this chapter, there are no code files since you'll just be getting to know the Delinkcious application:

- It is hosted in its own GitHub repository, which can be found at: `https://github.com/the-gigi/delinkcious`.
- Check out the **v0.1 Tags | Releases**: `https://github.com/the-gigi/delinkcious/releases/tag/v0.1`.
- Clone it and use your favorite IDE or text editor to follow up.
- Remember that the general code examples for this book are in another GitHub repository: `https://github.com/PacktPublishing/Hands-On-Microservices-with-Kubernetes/`.

Choosing Go for Delinkcious

I wrote and shipped production backend code in many fine languages such as C/C++, Python, C#, and, of course, Go. I also used a few not-so-fine languages, but let's leave those out of the discussion. I decided to use Go as the programming language for Delinkcious because it is a superb language for microservices:

- Go compiles to a single binary with no external dependencies (awesome for simple Dockerfiles).
- Go is very readable and easy to learn.
- Go has excellent support for network programming and concurrency.
- Go is the implementation language of many cloud-native data stores, queues, and frameworks (including Docker and Kubernetes).

You may argue that microservices are supposed to be language agnostic and that I shouldn't focus on one language. This is true, but my goal is to be very hands-on in this book and dive deep into all the fine details of building microservices on Kubernetes. To do that, I had to make specific choices and stick to them. Trying to get the same level of depth in multiple languages would have been futile. That being said, the microservice boundaries are very clear (one of the advantages of microservices) and you can see how implementing a microservice in another language will present a few issues to the rest of the system.

Getting to know Go kit

You can write your microservices from scratch (in Go or any other language) and they will interact with each other just fine through their APIs. However, in a real-world system, there will be a large number of shared and/or cross-cutting concerns that you want to be consistent:

- Configuration
- Secret management
- Central logging
- Metrics
- Authentication
- Authorization
- Security
- Distributed tracing
- Service discovery

In practice, microservices in most large production systems will need to comply with certain policies for those concerns.

Enter Go kit (`https://gokit.io/`). Go kit takes a very modular approach to the microservices space. It provides a high degree of separation of concerns, a recommended approach for structuring your microservice, and a lot of flexibility. As the website says, *Few opinions, lightly held.*

Structuring microservices with Go kit

Go kit is all about best practices. Your business logic is implemented as pure Go libraries that only deal with interfaces and Go structs. All the complex aspects involved in APIs, serialization, routing, and networking will be relegated to clearly separate layers that are taking advantage of Go kit concepts and infrastructures such as transports, endpoints, and services. This makes for a great development experience, where you can evolve and test your application code in the simplest environment possible. Here is the interface for one of Delinkcious' services – the social graph. Note that it is in plain Go. There is no notion of API, microservice, or even Go kit imports:

```
type SocialGraphManager interface {
    Follow(followed string, follower string) error
    Unfollow(followed string, follower string) error

    GetFollowing(username string) (map[string]bool, error)
    GetFollowers(username string) (map[string]bool, error)
}
```

The implementation of this interface resides in a Go package that is still completely agnostic of Go kit or even the fact it is being used in a microservice:

```
package social_graph_manager

import (
    "errors"
    om "github.com/the-gigi/delinkcious/pkg/object_model"
)

type SocialGraphManager struct {
    store om.SocialGraphManager
}

func (m *SocialGraphManager) Follow(followed string, follower string) (err
error) {
    ...
}

func (m *SocialGraphManager) Unfollow(followed string, follower string)
(err error) {
    ...
}

func (m *SocialGraphManager) GetFollowing(username string)
(map[string]bool, error) {
    ...
}
```

```
func (m *SocialGraphManager) GetFollowers(username string)
(map[string]bool, error) {
    ...
}
```

A good way to think of a Go kit service is as an onion with different layers. At the core is your business logic and layered on top are various concerns such as routing, rate limiting, logging, and metrics, which are eventually exposed to other services or the world over transports:

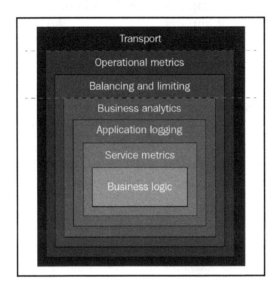

Go kit primarily supports RPC-style communication by using a request-response model.

Understanding transports

One of the biggest concerns about microservices is that they interact with each other and clients over a network; that is, at least an order of magnitude more complicated than calling methods inside the same process. Go kit provides explicit support for the networking aspect of microservices through the transport concept.

A Go kit transport encapsulates all the complexity and integrates with other Go kit constructs such as requests, responses, and endpoints. Go kit officially supports the following transports out of the box:

- HTTP
- gRPC
- Thrift
- net/rpc

However, there are several more transports in its GitHub repository, including AMQP and NATS transports for message queuing and pub/sub. One cool thing about Go kit transports is that you can expose the same service through multiple transports without changing your code.

Understanding endpoints

A Go kit microservice is really just a set of endpoints. Each endpoint corresponds to one method in your service interface. An endpoint is always associated with at least one transport and a handler that you implement to service the request. The Go kit endpoints support the RPC style of communication and have request and response structs.

Here is the factory function for the `Follow()` method endpoint:

```
func makeFollowEndpoint(svc om.SocialGraphManager) endpoint.Endpoint {
    return func(_ context.Context, request interface{}) (interface{}, error)
{
        req := request.(followRequest)
        err := svc.Follow(req.Followed, req.Follower)
        res := followResponse{}
        if err != nil {
            res.Err = err.Error()
        }
        return res, nil
    }
}
```

I will explain what's going on here soon. For now, just note that it accepts an `svc` argument of the `om.SocialGraphManager` type, which is an interface, and it invokes its `Follow()` method.

Understanding services

This is where your code plugs into the system. When the endpoint is called, it invokes the corresponding method in your service implementation to do all the work. All the hard work of encoding and decoding requests and responses is done by the endpoint wrapper. You can focus on your application logic using the best abstractions that make sense.

Here is the implementation of the `SocialGraphManager` function's `Follow()` method:

```
func (m *SocialGraphManager) Follow(followed string, follower string) (err
error) {
    if followed == "" || follower == "" {
        err = errors.New("followed and follower can't be empty")
        return
    }

    return m.store.Follow(followed, follower)
}
```

Understanding middleware

Go kit is composable, as demonstrated in the preceding onion diagram. In addition to the mandatory transports, endpoints, and services, Go kit uses the decorator pattern to optionally wrap services and endpoints with cross-cutting concerns, such as the following:

- Resiliency (for example, retries with exponential backoff)
- Authentication and authorization
- Logging
- Metrics collection
- Distributed tracing
- Service discovery
- Rate limiting

This approach of a solid core with a small number of abstractions, such as transports, endpoints, and services, that can be extended using a uniform mechanism of middleware is easy to comprehend and work with. Go kit strikes the right balance between providing enough built-in functionality for middleware and leaving the floor open to your needs. For example, when running on Kubernetes, service discovery is taken care of for you. It's great that you don't have to work around Go kit in this case. Features and capabilities that you don't absolutely need are optional.

Understanding clients

In Chapter 2, *Getting Started with Microservices*, we discussed the client library principle of microservices. A microservice that talks to another microservice ideally utilizes a client library that's exposed through an interface. Go kit provides excellent support and guidelines for writing such client libraries. The using microservice simply receives an interface. It is actually totally agnostic to the fact it is talking to another service. For (almost) all intents and purposes, the remote service could be running in the same process. This is excellent for testing or for refactoring services and breaking a slightly too large service into two separate services.

Go kit has client endpoints that are similar to service endpoints but work in the opposite direction. Service endpoints decode requests, delegate work to the service, and encode responses. Client endpoints encode requests, invoke the remote service over the network, and decode the response.

Here is what the `Follow()` method of the client looks like:

```go
func (s EndpointSet) Follow(followed string, follower string) (err error) {
    resp, err := s.FollowEndpoint(context.Background(),
FollowRequest{Followed: followed, Follower: follower})
    if err != nil {
        return err
    }
    response := resp.(SimpleResponse)

    if response.Err != "" {
        err = errors.New(response.Err)
    }
    return
}
```

Generating the boilerplate

The clean separation of concerns and neat architectural layering of Go kit has a price. The price is a lot of boring, mind-numbing, and error-prone boilerplate code for translating requests and responses between different structs and method signatures. It is useful to see and understand how Go kit can support strongly-typed interfaces in a generic way, but for large-scale projects, the preferred solution is to generate all the boilerplate from the Go interfaces and data types. There are several projects for this task, including one under development by Go kit itself called **kitgen** (`https://github.com/go-kit/kit/tree/master/cmd/kitgen`).

It is considered experimental at the moment. I'm a big fan of code generation and highly recommend it. However, in the following sections, we will look at a lot of manual boilerplate code to make it clear what's going on and avoid any magic.

Introducing the Delinkcious directory structure

The Delinkcious system at this stage of initial development consists of three services:

- Link service
- User service
- Social graph service

The high-level directory structure includes the following sub directories:

- cmd
- pkg
- svc

The `root` directory also includes some common files such as `README.md` and the important `go.mod` and `go.sum` files to support the Go modules. I use the monorepo approach here, so the entire Delinkcious system will live in this directory structure and is considered a single Go module, albeit with many packages:

```
$ tree -L 1
.
├── LICENSE
├── README.md
├── go.mod
├── go.sum
├── cmd
├── pkg
└── svc
```

The cmd subdirectory

The `cmd` subdirectory contains various tools and commands to support development and operations, as well as end-to-end tests that involve multiple actors, services, or external dependencies; for example, testing a microservice via its client library.

At the moment, it only contains a single end-to-end test for the social graph service:

```
$ tree cmd
cmd
└── social_graph_service_e2e
    └── social_graph_service_e2e.go
```

The pkg subdirectory

The pkg subdirectory is where all the packages live. It includes the implementation of the microservices, the client libraries, the abstract object model, other support packages, and unit tests. The bulk of the code is in the form of Go packages that are simple to develop and test before they are bundled into actual microservices:

```
$ tree pkg
pkg
├── link_manager
│   ├── abstract_link_store.go
│   ├── db_link_store.go
│   ├── db_link_store_test.go
│   ├── in_memory_link_store.go
│   ├── link_manager.go
│   └── link_manager_suite_test.go
├── link_manager_client
│   └── client.go
├── object_model
│   ├── README.md
│   ├── interfaces.go
│   └── types.go
├── social_graph_client
│   ├── client.go
│   └── endpoints.go
├── social_graph_manager
│   ├── db_scoial_graph_store.go
│   ├── db_social_graph_manager_test.go
│   ├── in_memory_social_graph_manager_test.go
│   ├── in_memory_social_graph_store.go
│   ├── social_graph_manager.go
│   └── social_graph_manager_suite_test.go
└── user_manager
    ├── db_user_manager_test.go
    ├── db_user_store.go
    ├── in_memory_user_manager.go
    ├── in_memory_user_manager_test.go
    ├── in_memory_user_store.go
    └── user_manager_suite_test.go
```

The svc subdirectory

The `svc` subdirectory is where the Delinkcious microservices live. Each microservice is a separate binary with its own main package. `delinkcious_service` is a public umbrella service that follows the API gateway (`https://microservices.io/patterns/apigateway.html`) pattern:

```
$ tree svc
svc
├────── delinkcious_service
│       └────── README.md
├────── link_service
│       ├────── link_service.go
│       └────── transport.go
├────── social_graph_service
│       ├────── social_graph_service.go
│       └────── transport.go
└────── user_service
        ├────── transport.go
        └────── user_service.go
```

Introducing the Delinkcious microservices

Let's examine the Delinkcious services in detail and peel the onion. We'll actually work our way from the inside out, starting with the service layer and going through the endpoints all the way to the transports.

There are three different services:

- Link service
- User service
- Social graph service

Together, they collaborate to provide the functionality of Delinkcious, which is to manage links for users and keep track of their social graph (followed/follower relationships).

The object model

The object model is the collection of all the interfaces and related data types that are implemented by the services. I chose to put all of them in a single package: github.com/the-gigi/delinkcious/pkg/object_model. It contains two files: interfaces.go and types.go.

The interfaces.go file contains the interfaces for the three Delinkcious services:

```
package object_model

type LinkManager interface {
    GetLinks(request GetLinksRequest) (GetLinksResult, error)
    AddLink(request AddLinkRequest) error
    UpdateLink(request UpdateLinkRequest) error
    DeleteLink(username string, url string) error
}

type UserManager interface {
    Register(user User) error
    Login(username string, authToken string) (session string, err error)
    Logout(username string, session string) error
}

type SocialGraphManager interface {
    Follow(followed string, follower string) error
    Unfollow(followed string, follower string) error

    GetFollowing(username string) (map[string]bool, error)
    GetFollowers(username string) (map[string]bool, error)
}

type LinkManagerEvents interface {
    OnLinkAdded(username string, link *Link)
    OnLinkUpdated(username string, link *Link)
    OnLinkDeleted(username string, url string)
}
```

The types.go file contains the structs that are used in the signatures of the various interface methods:

```
package object_model

import "time"

type Link struct {
    Url         string
```

```
    Title        string
    Description  string
    Tags         map[string]bool
    CreatedAt    time.Time
    UpdatedAt    time.Time
}

type GetLinksRequest struct {
    UrlRegex         string
    TitleRegex       string
    DescriptionRegex string
    Username         string
    Tag              string
    StartToken       string
}

type GetLinksResult struct {
    Links          []Link
    NextPageToken  string
}

type AddLinkRequest struct {
    Url          string
    Title        string
    Description  string
    Username     string
    Tags         map[string]bool
}

type UpdateLinkRequest struct {
    Url          string
    Title        string
    Description  string
    Username     string
    AddTags      map[string]bool
    RemoveTags   map[string]bool
}

type User struct {
    Email string
    Name  string
}
```

The object_model package is just using basic Go types, standard library types
(time.Time), and user-defined types for the Delinkcious domain. It is all pure Go. At this
level, there is no dependency or awareness of networking, APIs, microservices, or Go kit.

The service implementation

The next layer is implementing the service interfaces as simple Go packages. At this point, each service has its own package:

- github.com/the-gigi/delinkcious/pkg/link_manager
- github.com/the-gigi/delinkcious/pkg/user_manager
- github.com/the-gigi/delinkcious/pkg/social_graph_manager

Note that these are Go package names and not URLs.

Let's examine the social_graph_manager package. It imports the object_model package as om because it needs to implement the om.SocialGraphManager interface. It defines a struct called SocialGraphManager that has a field called store of the om.SocialGraphManager type. So, the interface of the store field is identical to the interface of the manager in this case:

```
package social_graph_manager

import (
    "errors"
    om "github.com/the-gigi/delinkcious/pkg/object_model"
)

type SocialGraphManager struct {
    store om.SocialGraphManager
}
```

This may be a little confusing. The idea is that the store field implements the same interface so that the top-level manager can implement some validation logic and delegate the heavy lifting to the store. You will see this in action soon.

In addition, the fact that the store field is an interface allows us to use different stores that implement the same interface. This is very useful. The NewSocialGraphManager() function accepts a store field that must not be nil, and then returns a new instance of SocialGraphManager with the provided store:

```
func NewSocialGraphManager(store om.SocialGraphManager)
(om.SocialGraphManager, error) {
    if store == nil {
        return nil, errors.New("store can't be nil")
    }
    return &SocialGraphManager{store: store}, nil
}
```

The `SocialGraphManager` struct itself is pretty simple. It performs some validity checks and then delegates the work to its `store`:

```
func (m *SocialGraphManager) Follow(followed string, follower string) (err
error) {
   if followed == "" || follower == "" {
      err = errors.New("followed and follower can't be empty")
      return
   }

   return m.store.Follow(followed, follower)
}

func (m *SocialGraphManager) Unfollow(followed string, follower string)
(err error) {
   if followed == "" || follower == "" {
      err = errors.New("followed and follower can't be empty")
      return
   }

   return m.store.Unfollow(followed, follower)
}

func (m *SocialGraphManager) GetFollowing(username string)
(map[string]bool, error) {
   return m.store.GetFollowing(username)
}

func (m *SocialGraphManager) GetFollowers(username string)
(map[string]bool, error) {
   return m.store.GetFollowers(username)
}
```

The social graph manager is a pretty simple library. Let's continue peeling the onion and look at the service itself, which lives under the `svc` subdirectory: `https://github.com/the-gigi/delinkcious/tree/master/svc/social_graph_service`.

Let's start with the `social_graph_service.go` file. We'll go over the main parts that are similar for most services. The file lives in the `service` package, which is a convention I use. It imports several important packages:

```
package service

import (
   httptransport "github.com/go-kit/kit/transport/http"
   "github.com/gorilla/mux"
   sgm "github.com/the-gigi/delinkcious/pkg/social_graph_manager"
```

```
    "log"
    "net/http"
)
```

The Go kit `http` transport package is necessary for services that use the HTTP transport. The `gorilla/mux` package provides top-notch routing capabilities. `social_graph_manager` is the implementation of the service that does all the heavy lifting. The `log` package is for logging, and the `net/http` package is for serving HTTP since it's an HTTP service.

There is just one function called `Run()`. It starts by creating a data store for the social graph manager and then creates the social graph manager itself, passing it the `store` field. So, the functionality of `social_graph_manager` is implemented in the package, but the `service` is responsible for making the policy decisions and passing a configured data store. If anything goes wrong at this point, the service just exits with a `log.Fatal()` call because there is no way to recover at this early stage:

```
func Run() {
    store, err := sgm.NewDbSocialGraphStore("localhost", 5432, "postgres",
"postgres")
    if err != nil {
        log.Fatal(err)
    }
    svc, err := sgm.NewSocialGraphManager(store)
    if err != nil {
        log.Fatal(err)
    }
```

The next part is constructing the handler for each endpoint. This is done by calling the `NewServer()` function of the HTTP transport for each endpoint. The parameters are the `Endpoint` factory function, which we will review soon, a request decoder function, and the `response` encoder function. For HTTP services, it is common for requests and responses to be encoded as JSON:

```
followHandler := httptransport.NewServer(
    makeFollowEndpoint(svc),
    decodeFollowRequest,
    encodeResponse,
)

unfollowHandler := httptransport.NewServer(
    makeUnfollowEndpoint(svc),
    decodeUnfollowRequest,
    encodeResponse,
)
```

```
getFollowingHandler := httptransport.NewServer(
    makeGetFollowingEndpoint(svc),
    decodeGetFollowingRequest,
    encodeResponse,
)

getFollowersHandler := httptransport.NewServer(
    makeGetFollowersEndpoint(svc),
    decodeGetFollowersRequest,
    encodeResponse,
)
```

At this point, we have `SocialGraphManager` properly initialized and the handlers for all the endpoints. It's time to expose them to the world via the `gorilla` router. Each endpoint is associated with a route and a method. In this case, the `follow` and `unfollow` operations use the POST method and the `following` and `followers` operations use the GET method:

```
r := mux.NewRouter()
r.Methods("POST").Path("/follow").Handler(followHandler)
r.Methods("POST").Path("/unfollow").Handler(unfollowHandler)
r.Methods("GET").Path("/following/{username}").Handler(getFollowingHandler)
r.Methods("GET").Path("/followers/{username}").Handler(getFollowersHandler)
```

The last part is just passing the configured router to the `ListenAndServe()` method of the standard HTTP package. This service is hardcoded to listen on port 9090. Later on in this book, we will see how to configure things in a flexible and more industrial-strength way:

```
log.Println("Listening on port 9090...")
log.Fatal(http.ListenAndServe(":9090", r))
```

Implementing the support functions

As you may recall, the social graph implementation in the `pkg/social_graph_manager` package is completely transport agnostic. It implements the `SocialGraphManager` interface in terms of Go and couldn't care less whether the payload is JSON or protobuf and coming over the wire through HTTP, gRPC, Thrift, or any other method. The service is responsible for translation, encoding, and decoding. These support functions are implemented in the `transport.go` file.

For each endpoint, there are three functions, which are the input to the HTTP transport's `NewServer()` function of Go kit:

- The `Endpoint` factory function
- The `request` decoder
- The `response` encoder

Let's start with the `Endpoint` factory function, which is the most interesting. Let's use the `GetFollowing()` operation as an example. The `makeGetFollowingEndpoint()` function takes a `SocialGraphManager` interface as input (as you saw earlier, in practice, it will be the implementation in `pkg/social_graph_manager`). It returns a generic `endpoint.Endpoint` function, which a function that takes a `Context` and a generic `request` and returns a generic `response` and `error`:

```
type Endpoint func(ctx context.Context, request interface{}) (response
interface{}, err error)
```

The job of the `makeGetFollowingEndpoint()` method is to return a function that complies with this signature. It returns such a function that, in its implementation, takes the generic request (the empty interface) and type before asserting it to a concrete request, that is, `getByUsernameRequest`:

```
req := request.(getByUsernameRequest)
```

This is a key concept. We cross the boundary from a generic object, which could be from anything to a strongly typed struct. This ensures that, even though the Go kit endpoints operate in terms of empty interfaces, the implementation of our microservice is type checked. If the request doesn't contain the right fields, it panics. I could also check whether it's possible to do the type assert and return an error instead of panicking, which might be more appropriate in some contexts:

```
req, ok := request.(getByUsernameRequest)
if !ok {
    ...
}
```

Let's take a look at the request itself. It is simply a struct with a single string field called `Username`. It has the JSON struct tag, which is optional in this case because the JSON package can automatically work with field names that differ from the actual JSON just by case like (`Username` versus `username`):

```
type getByUsernameRequest struct {
    Username string `json:"username"`
}
```

Note that the request type is `getByUsernameRequest` and not `getFollowingRequest`, as you may expect in order to be consistent with the operation it is supporting. The reason for this is that I actually use the same request for multiple endpoints. The `GetFollowers()` operation also requires a `username`, and `getByUsernameRequest` serves both `GetFollowing()` and `GetFollowers()`.

At this point, we have the username from the request and we can invoke the `GetFollowing()` method of the underlying implementation:

```
followingMap, err := svc.GetFollowing(req.Username)
```

The result is a map of the users that the requested user is following and the standard error. However, this is an HTTP endpoint, so the next step is to package this information into the `getFollowingResponse` struct:

```
type getFollowingResponse struct {
    Following map[string]bool `json:"following"`
    Err       string          `json:"err"`
}
```

The following map can be translated into a JSON map of `string->bool`. However, there is no direct equivalent to the Go error interface. The solution is to encode the error as a string (via `err.Error()`), where an empty string represents no error:

```
res := getFollowingResponse{Following: followingMap}
if err != nil {
    res.Err = err.Error()
}
```

Here is the entire function:

```
func makeGetFollowingEndpoint(svc om.SocialGraphManager) endpoint.Endpoint
{
    return func(_ context.Context, request interface{}) (interface{}, error)
    {
        req := request.(getByUsernameRequest)
        followingMap, err := svc.GetFollowing(req.Username)
        res := getFollowingResponse{Following: followingMap}
        if err != nil {
            res.Err = err.Error()
        }
        return res, nil
    }
}
```

Now, let's take a look at the `decodeGetFollowingRequest()` function. It accepts the standard `http.Request` object. It needs to extract the username from the request and return a `getByUsernameRequest` struct that the endpoint can use later. At the HTTP request level, the username will be a part of the request path. The function will parse the path, extract the username, prepare the request, and return it or an error if anything goes wrong (for example, no username is provided):

```
func decodeGetFollowingRequest(_ context.Context, r *http.Request)
(interface{}, error) {
   parts := strings.Split(r.URL.Path, "/")
   username := parts[len(parts)-1]
   if username == "" || username == "following" {
      return nil, errors.New("user name must not be empty")
   }
   request := getByUsernameRequest{Username: username}
   return request, nil
```

The last support function is the `encodeResonse()` function. In theory, each endpoint can have its own custom `response` encoding function. However, in this case, I am using a single generic function that knows how to encode all the responses into JSON:

```
func encodeResponse(_ context.Context, w http.ResponseWriter, response
interface{}) error {
   return json.NewEncoder(w).Encode(response)
}
```

This requires all the response structs to be JSON serializable, which was taken care of by translating the Go error interface into a string by the endpoint implementation.

Invoking the API via a client library

The social graph manager is now accessible through an HTTP REST API. Here is a quick local demo. First, I will launch the Postgres DB (I have a Docker image called `postgres`), which is used as the data store, and then I will run the service itself in the `service` directory, that is, `delinkcious/svc/social_graph_service`:

```
$ docker restart postgres
$ go run main.go

2018/12/31 10:41:23 Listening on port 9090...
```

Let's add a couple of follower/following relationships by invoking the /follow endpoint. I will use the excellent HTTPie (https://httpie.org/), which is a better curl in my honest opinion. However, you can use curl if you prefer:

```
$ http POST http://localhost:9090/follow followed=liat follower=gigi
HTTP/1.1 200 OK
Content-Length: 11
Content-Type: text/plain; charset=utf-8
Date: Mon, 31 Dec 2018 09:19:01 GMT

{
    "err": ""
}

$ http POST http://localhost:9090/follow followed=guy follower=gigi
HTTP/1.1 200 OK
Content-Length: 11
Content-Type: text/plain; charset=utf-8
Date: Mon, 31 Dec 2018 09:19:01 GMT

{
    "err": ""
}
```

These two calls made the gigi user follow the liat and guy users. Let's use the /following endpoint to verify this:

```
$ http GET http://localhost:9090/following/gigi
HTTP/1.1 200 OK
Content-Length: 37
Content-Type: text/plain; charset=utf-8
Date: Mon, 31 Dec 2018 09:37:21 GMT

{
    "err": "",
    "following": {
        "guy": true
        "liat": true
    }
}
```

The JSON response has an empty error, and the following map contains the guy and liat users, as expected.

While a REST API is cool, we can do better. Instead of forcing the caller to understand the URL schema of our service and decode and encode JSON payloads, why not provide a client library that does all of that? This is especially true for internal microservices that all talk to each other using a small number of languages, and in many cases, just one language. The service and client can share the same interface and, maybe even some common types. In addition, Go kit provides support for client-side endpoints that are pretty similar to service-side endpoints. This translates directly into a very streamlined end-to-end developer experience, where you just stay in the programming language space. All the endpoints, transports, encoding, and decoding can remain hidden as an implementation detail for the most part.

The social graph service provides a client library that lives in the pkg/social_graph_client package. The client.go file is similar to the social_graph_service.go file and is responsible for creating a set of endpoints in the NewClient() function and returning the SocialGraphManager interface. The NewClient() function takes the base URL as an argument and then constructs a set of client endpoints using Go kit's NewClient() function of the HTTP transport. Each endpoint requires a URL, a method (GET or POST, in this case), a request encoder, and a response decoder. It's like a mirror image of the service. Then, it assigns the client endpoints to the EndpointSet struct, which can expose them through the SocialGraphManager interface:

```
func NewClient(baseURL string) (om.SocialGraphManager, error) {
    // Quickly sanitize the instance string.
    if !strings.HasPrefix(baseURL, "http") {
        baseURL = "http://" + baseURL
    }
    u, err := url.Parse(baseURL)
    if err != nil {
        return nil, err
    }

    followEndpoint := httptransport.NewClient(
        "POST",
        copyURL(u, "/follow"),
        encodeHTTPGenericRequest,
        decodeSimpleResponse).Endpoint()

    unfollowEndpoint := httptransport.NewClient(
        "POST",
        copyURL(u, "/unfollow"),
        encodeHTTPGenericRequest,
        decodeSimpleResponse).Endpoint()
```

```
        getFollowingEndpoint := httptransport.NewClient(
            "GET",
            copyURL(u, "/following"),
            encodeGetByUsernameRequest,
            decodeGetFollowingResponse).Endpoint()

        getFollowersEndpoint := httptransport.NewClient(
            "GET",
            copyURL(u, "/followers"),
            encodeGetByUsernameRequest,
            decodeGetFollowersResponse).Endpoint()

        // Returning the EndpointSet as an interface relies on the
        // EndpointSet implementing the Service methods. That's just a simple
bit
        // of glue code.
        return EndpointSet{
            FollowEndpoint:        followEndpoint,
            UnfollowEndpoint:      unfollowEndpoint,
            GetFollowingEndpoint:  getFollowingEndpoint,
            GetFollowersEndpoint:  getFollowersEndpoint,
        }, nil
    }
```

The `EndpointSet` struct is defined in the `endpoints.go` file. It contains the endpoints themselves, which are functions, and it implements the `SocialGraphManager` method, where it delegates the work to the endpoint's functions:

```
    type EndpointSet struct {
        FollowEndpoint        endpoint.Endpoint
        UnfollowEndpoint      endpoint.Endpoint
        GetFollowingEndpoint  endpoint.Endpoint
        GetFollowersEndpoint  endpoint.Endpoint
    }
```

Let's examine the `EndpointSet` struct's `GetFollowing()` method. It accepts the username as a string, and then it calls the endpoint with a `getByUserNameRequest` that's populated with the input username. If calling the endpoint function returned an error, it just bails out. Otherwise, it does type assertion to convert the generic response into a `getFollowingResponse` struct. If its error string wasn't empty, it creates a Go error from it. Eventually, it returns the following users from the response as a map:

```
    func (s EndpointSet) GetFollowing(username string) (following
    map[string]bool, err error) {
        resp, err := s.GetFollowingEndpoint(context.Background(),
    getByUserNameRequest{Username: username})
        if err != nil {
```

```
        return
    }

    response := resp.(getFollowingResponse)
    if response.Err != "" {
        err = errors.New(response.Err)
    }
    following = response.Following
    return
}
```

Storing data

We've seen how Go kit and our own code take an HTTP request with a JSON payload, translate it into a Go struct, invoke the service implementation, and encode the response as a JSON to return to the caller. Now, let's take a deeper look at the persistent storage of the data. The social graph manager is responsible for maintaining the followed/follower relationships between users. There are many options for storing such data, including relational databases, key-value stores, and, of course, graph databases, which may be the most natural. I chose to use a relational database at this stage because it is familiar, reliable, and can support the following necessary operations well:

- Follow
- Unfollow
- Get followers
- Get following

However, if we later discover that we prefer a different data store or extend the relational DB with some caching mechanism, it will be very easy to do so because the data store of the social graph manager is hidden behind an interface. It is actually using the very same interface, that is, `SocialGraphManager`. As you may remember, the social graph manager package accepts a store argument of the `SocialGraphManager` type in its factory function:

```
func NewSocialGraphManager(store om.SocialGraphManager)
(om.SocialGraphManager, error) {
    if store == nil {
        return nil, errors.New("store can't be nil")
    }
    return &SocialGraphManager{store: store}, nil
}
```

Since the social graph manager interacts with its data store through this interface, changing implementations can be done without any code changes to the social graph manager itself. I will take advantage of this for unit testing, where I use an in-memory data store that is easy to set up, can be quickly populated with test data, and allows me to run tests locally.

 Let's look at the in-memory social graph data store, which can be found at `https://github.com/the-gigi/delinkcious/blob/master/pkg/social_graph_manager/in_memory_social_graph_store.go`.

It has very few dependencies – just the `SocialGraphManager` interface and the standard errors package. It defines a `SocialUser` struct, which contains a username and the names of the users it is following, as well as the names of the users that they are followed by:

```
package social_graph_manager

import (
    "errors"
    om "github.com/the-gigi/delinkcious/pkg/object_model"
)

type Followers map[string]bool
type Following map[string]bool

type SocialUser struct {
    Username   string
    Followers Followers
    Following Following
}

func NewSocialUser(username string) (user *SocialUser, err error) {
    if username == "" {
        err = errors.New("user name can't be empty")
        return
    }

    user = &SocialUser{Username: username, Followers: Followers{},
Following: Following{}}
    return
}
```

The data store itself is a struct called `InMemorySocialGraphStore` that contains a map between usernames and the corresponding `SocialUser` struct:

```
type SocialGraph map[string]*SocialUser

type InMemorySocialGraphStore struct {
    socialGraph SocialGraph
}

func NewInMemorySocialGraphStore() om.SocialGraphManager {
    return &InMemorySocialGraphStore{
        socialGraph: SocialGraph{},
    }
}
```

This is all pretty pedestrian. The `InMemorySocialGraphStore` struct implements the `SocialGraphManager` interface methods. For example, here is the `Follow()` method:

```
func (m *InMemorySocialGraphStore) Follow(followed string, follower string)
(err error) {
    followedUser := m.socialGraph[followed]
    if followedUser == nil {
        followedUser, _ = NewSocialUser(followed)
        m.socialGraph[followed] = followedUser
    }

    if followedUser.Followers[follower] {
        return errors.New("already following")
    }

    followedUser.Followers[follower] = true

    followerUser := m.socialGraph[follower]
    if followerUser == nil {
        followerUser, _ = NewSocialUser(follower)
        m.socialGraph[follower] = followerUser
    }

    followerUser.Following[followed] = true

    return
```

At this point, there is no need to focus on how it works too much. The main point I want to get across is that by using interfaces as abstractions, you can get a lot of flexibility and clean separation of concerns that helps a lot when you want to develop specific parts of the system or a service during testing. If you want to make significant changes, such as changing your underlying data stores or using multiple data stores interchangeably, then having an interface in place is a life saver.

Summary

In this chapter, you got a close look at the Go kit toolkit, the overall Delinkcious system and its microservices, and got to drill down into the social graph component of Delinkcious. The main theme of this chapter is that Go kit provides clean abstractions, such as services, endpoints and transports, and generic functionality for breaking microservices into layers. Then, you add your code for a consistent system of loosely-coupled yet cohesive microservices. You also followed the path of a request from the client, all the way to the service and back through all the layers. At this point, you should have a general grasp of how Go kit helps shape the Delinkcious architecture and how it would benefit any other system. You may be a little overwhelmed by all of this information, but remember that the complexity it neatly packaged and that you can ignore it most of the time, focus on your application, and just reap the benefits.

In the next chapter, we'll address a very critical part of any modern microservices-based system – the CI/CD pipeline. We'll create a Kubernetes cluster, configure CircleCI, deploy the Argo CD continuous delivery solution, and see how to deploy Delinkcious on Kubernetes.

Further reading

Let's refer to the following references:

- To learn more about Go kit, check out `https://gokit.io/`.
- To better understand the SOLID design principles that Delinkcious utilizes, check out `https://en.wikipedia.org/wiki/SOLID`.

Setting Up the CI/CD Pipeline

4

In a microservice-based system, there are many moving parts. Kubernetes is a rich platform that provides a lot of building blocks for your system. Managing and deploying all of these components reliably and predictably requires a high level of organization and automation. Enter the CI/CD pipeline.

In this chapter, we will understand the problem the CI/CD pipeline solves, cover the different options for CI/CD pipelines for Kubernetes, and finally build a CI/CD pipeline for Delinkcious.

In this chapter, we will discuss the following topics:

- Understanding a CI/CD pipeline
- Options for Kubernetes CI/CD pipelines
- GitOps
- Automated CI/CD
- Building your images with CircleCI
- Setting up continuous delivery for Delinkcious

Technical requirements

In this chapter, you will work with CircleCI and Argo CD. I will show you how to install Argo CD in the Kubernetes cluster later. To set up CircleCI, for free, follow *Getting started* instructions on their website at `https://circleci.com/docs/2.0/getting-started/`.

The code

The Delinkcious release for this chapter can be found at `https://github.com/the-gigi/` `delinkcious/releases/tag/v0.2`.

We will be working on the main Delinkcious code base, so there are no code snippets or examples.

Understanding a CI/CD pipeline

The development life cycle of software systems goes from code, through testing, generating artifacts, even more testing, and eventually, deployment to production. The basic idea is that whenever a developer commits changes to their source control system (for example, GitHub), these changes are detected by the **continuous integration** (**CI**) system, which immediately runs the tests.

This is often followed by a review by peers and merging the code changes (or a pull request) from a feature branch or development branch into the master. In the context of Kubernetes, the CI system is also responsible for building the Docker images for the services and pushing them to the image registry. At this point, we have Docker images that contain new code. This is where the CD system comes in.

When a new image becomes available, the **continuous delivery** (**CD**) system will deploy it to the target environment(s). CD is the process of ensuring that the overall system is in a desired state, which is done though provisioning and deployments. Sometimes, deployment can occur as a result of configuration change if the system doesn't support dynamic configuration. We will discuss configuration in great detail in `Chapter 5`, *Configuring Microservices with Kubernetes*.

So, a CI/CD pipeline is a set of tools that detect code changes and can take them all the way to production according to the processes and policies of the organization. It is typically the responsibility of DevOps engineers to build and maintain this pipeline, and it is used heavily by developers.

Every organization and company (or even different groups within the same company) will have a specific process. In one of my first jobs, my first task was to replace a Perl-based build system (that's what CI/CD pipelines were called back then) with lots of recursive makefiles that nobody understood any more. That build system had to run code generation steps on Windows using some modeling software, compile and run C++ unit tests on two flavors of Unix (including an embedded flavor) using two different toolchains, and trigger open CVS. I chose Python and had to create everything from scratch.

It was fun, but very specific to this company. It's common to think of CI/CD pipelines as a workflow of steps driven by events.

The following diagram demonstrates a simple CI/CD pipeline:

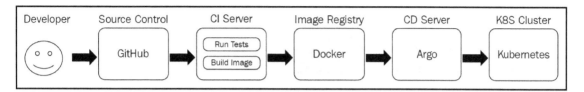

The stages in this pipeline function as follows:

1. The developer commits their changes to GitHub (source control)
2. The CI server runs the tests, builds a Docker image, and pushes the image to DockerHub (image registry)
3. The Argo CD server detects that there is a new image available and deploys to the Kubernetes cluster

Now that we have understood the CI/CD pipeline, let's examine a specific CI/CD pipeline choice.

Options for the Delinkcious CI/CD pipeline

Choosing a CI/CD pipeline for your system is a major decision. When I faced this decision for Delinkcious, I looked into several alternatives. There isn't an obvious choice here. Kubernetes is moving fast and the tooling and processes struggle to catch up. I evaluated a few choices and settled on CircleCI for continuous integration and Argo CD for continuous delivery. I initially considered a one-stop shop for the entire CI/CD pipeline and, after reviewing some options, I decided that I preferred to consider them as two separate entities and chose a different solution for CI and CD. Let's briefly review some of these options (there are many, many more):

- Jenkins X
- Spinnaker
- Travis CI and CircleCI
- Tekton
- Argo CD
- Rolling your own

Jenkins X

Jenkins X was my first choice and favorite. I read some articles and watched some presentations that made me want to like it. It provides all the features you want, including some advanced capabilities:

- Automated CI/CD
- Environment promotion via GitOps
- Pull request preview environments
- Automatic feedback on your commit and pull requests

Under the cover, it utilizes Jenkins, which is a mature, albeit complex, product. The premise of Jenkins X is that it will mask the complexity of Jenkins and provide a Kubernetes-specific streamlined workflow.

I was disappointed by a couple of issues when I tried to actually use Jenkins X:

- It doesn't work out of the box and troubleshooting is complicated.
- It is very opinionated.
- It doesn't support the monorepo approach well (or at all).

I tried to make it work for a while, but after reading about other people's experiences and seeing the lack of response in the Jenkins X slack community channels, I was turned off Jenkins X. I still like the idea, but it really has to be super stable before I try it again.

Spinnaker

Spinnaker is an open source CI/CD solution from Netflix. It has many benefits, including the following:

- It has been adopted by many companies.
- It has a lot of integration with other products.
- It supports a lot of best practices.

The downsides of Spinnaker are as follows:

- It is a large and complicated system.
- It has a steep learning curve.
- It is not Kubernetes-specific.

In the end, I decided to skip on Spinnaker – not because of any fault of Spinnaker itself, but because I don't have experience with it. I didn't want to learn such a large product from scratch while developing Delinkcious itself and writing this book. You may very well find that Spinnaker is the right CI/CD solution for you.

Travis CI and CircleCI

I prefer to separate the CI solution from the CD solution. Conceptually, the role of the CI process is to generate a container image and push it to a registry. It doesn't need to be aware of Kubernetes at all. The CD solution, on the other hand, must be Kubernetes-aware, and it ideally runs inside the cluster.

For CI, I considered Travis CI and CircleCI. Both provide free CI services for open source projects. I settled on CircleCI because it is more feature-complete and has a nicer UI, which is important. I'm sure Travis CI would work well too. I use Travis CI in some of my other open source projects. It's important to note that the CI part of the pipeline is completely Kubernetes-agnostic. The end result is a Docker image in an image registry. This Docker image can be used for other purposes and not necessarily deployed in a Kubernetes cluster.

Tekton

Tekton is a very interesting project. It is Kubernetes-native and has great abstractions of steps, tasks, runs, and pipelines. It is relatively young, but seems very promising. It was also selected as one of the inaugural projects of the CD Foundation: `https://cd.foundation/projects/`.

It will be interesting to see how it evolves.

The advantages of Tekton are as follows:

- Modern design and clean conceptual model
- Supported by the CD foundation
- Built on top of prow (the CI/CD solution of Kubernetes itself)
- Kubernetes-native solution

The disadvantages of Tekton are as follows:

- It's still fairly new and unstable.
- It doesn't have all the features and capabilities of other solutions.

Argo CD

The CD solution, as opposed to the CI solution, is very specific to Kubernetes. I picked Argo CD for several reasons:

- Kubernetes-aware
- Implemented on top of a general-purpose workflow engine (Argo)
- Great UI
- Runs on your Kubernetes cluster
- Implemented in Go (not that important, but I like it)

Argo CD has a number of disadvantages, too:

- It isn't a member of the CD foundation or the CNCF (less recognition in the community).
- Intuit, the primary company behind it, is not a major cloud-native powerhouse.

Argo CD is a young project that comes from Intuit, who acquired the original developers of the Argo project – Applatix. I really like its architecture and, when I tried it, everything worked like a charm.

Rolling your own

I briefly considered creating my own simple CI/CD pipeline. The operations are not complicated. For the purpose of this book, I didn't need a very reliable solution, and it would have been easy to explain exactly what happens at each step. However, with the reader in mind, I decided that it was best to use existing tools that can be utilized directly and also save me time developing a poor CI/CD solution.

At this point, you should have a good idea of the different options for CI/CD solutions on Kubernetes. We reviewed most of the popular solutions and chose CircleCI and Argo CD as the best fit for the Delinkcious CI/CD solution. Next, we'll discuss the hot new trend of GitOps.

GitOps

GitOps is a new buzzword, although the concept is not very new. It is another variant of *Infrastructure as Code*. The basic idea is that your code, configuration, and the resources it requires should all be described and stored in a source control repository where they are version controlled. Whenever you push a change to the repository, your CI/CD solution will respond and take the correct action. Even rollbacks can be initiated just by reverting to a previous version in your repository. The repository doesn't have to be Git, of course, but GitOps sounds way better than Source Control Ops, and most people use Git anyway, so here we are.

Both CircleCI and Argo CD fully support and advocate the GitOps model. When your `git push` code changes, CircleCI will trigger on it and start building the correct images. When you `git push` changes to the Kubernetes manifests, Argo CD will trigger and deploy those changes to your Kubernetes cluster.

Now that we're clear on what GitOps is, we can start implementing the continuous integration part of the pipeline for Delinkcious. We will use CircleCI to build Docker images from source code.

Building your images with CircleCI

Let's dive in and look at the Delinkcious CI pipeline. We will go over each step in the continuous integration process, which includes the following:

- Reviewing the source tree
- Configuring the CI pipeline
- Understanding the build script
- Dockerizing a Go service with a multi-stage Dockerfile
- Exploring the CircleCI user interface

Reviewing the source tree

Continuous integration is about building and testing stuff. The first step is to understand what needs to be built and tested in Delinkcious. Let's have another look at the Delinkcious source tree:

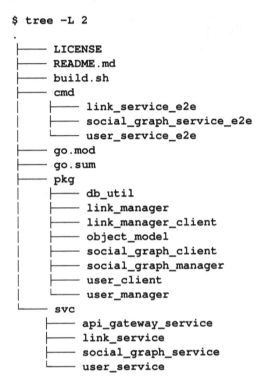

```
$ tree -L 2
.
├── LICENSE
├── README.md
├── build.sh
├── cmd
│   ├── link_service_e2e
│   ├── social_graph_service_e2e
│   └── user_service_e2e
├── go.mod
├── go.sum
├── pkg
│   ├── db_util
│   ├── link_manager
│   ├── link_manager_client
│   ├── object_model
│   ├── social_graph_client
│   ├── social_graph_manager
│   ├── user_client
│   └── user_manager
└── svc
    ├── api_gateway_service
    ├── link_service
    ├── social_graph_service
    └── user_service
```

The `pkg` directory contains packages that are used by services and commands. We should run the unit tests of these packages. The `svc` directory contains our microservices. We should build those services, package each one in a properly versioned Docker image, and push those images to DockerHub (the image registry). The `cmd` directory currently contains end-to-end tests. Those are designed to run locally and don't need to be built by the CI pipeline (this can be changed if you want to add end-to-end tests to our testing processes).

Configuring the CI pipeline

CircleCI is configured by a single YAML file with a standard name and location, that is, `<root directory>/.circleci/config.yaml`:

```
version: 2
jobs:
  build:
    docker:
    - image: circleci/golang:1.11
    - image: circleci/postgres:9.6-alpine
      environment: # environment variables for primary container
        POSTGRES_USER: postgres
    working_directory: /go/src/github.com/the-gigi/delinkcious
    steps:
    - checkout
    - run:
        name: Get all dependencies
        command: |
          go get -v ./...
          go get -u github.com/onsi/ginkgo/ginkgo
          go get -u github.com/onsi/gomega/...
    - run:
        name: Test everything
        command: ginkgo -r -race -failFast -progress
    - setup_remote_docker:
        docker_layer_caching: true
    - run:
        name: build and push Docker images
        shell: /bin/bash
        command: |
          chmod +x ./build.sh
          ./build.sh
```

Let's break it apart and understand what's going on. The first part specifies the build job, and below that are the necessary Docker images (`golang` and `postgres`) and their environment. Then, we have the working directory, where the `build` commands should be executed:

```
version: 2
jobs:
 build:
 docker:
 - image: circleci/golang:1.11
 - image: circleci/postgres:9.6-alpine
     environment: # environment variables for primary container
       POSTGRES_USER: postgres
     working_directory: /go/src/github.com/the-gigi/delinkcious
```

The next part is the build steps. The first step is just checkout. In the CircleCI UI, I associated the project with the Delinkcious GitHub repository so that it knows where to checkout from. If the repository is not public, then you'll need to provide an access token, too. The second step is a `run` command that gets all the Go dependencies of Delinkcious:

```
steps:
- checkout
- run:
    name: Get all dependencies
    command: |
      go get -v ./...
      go get -u github.com/onsi/ginkgo/ginkgo
      go get -u github.com/onsi/gomega/...
```

I had to explicitly `go get` the `ginkgo` framework and the `gomega` library because they are imported using Golang dot notation, which makes them invisible to `go get ./...`.

Once we have all the dependencies, we can run the tests. I am using the `ginkgo` test framework in this case:

```
- run:
    name: Test everything
    command: ginkgo -r -race -failFast -progress
```

The next section is where it builds and pushes the Docker images. Since it requires access to the Docker daemon, it needs special setup via the `setup_remote_docker` step. The `docker_layer_caching` option is used to make everything more efficient and faster by reusing previous layers. The actual build out and push is handled by the `build.sh` script, which we will look at in the next section. Note that I made sure it's executable via `chmod +x`:

```
- setup_remote_docker:
    docker_layer_caching: true
- run:
    name: build and push Docker images
    shell: /bin/bash
    command: |
      chmod +x ./build.sh
      ./build.sh
```

I'm just scratching the surface here. There is much more to CircleCI, with orbs for reusable configuration, workflows, triggers, and artifacts.

Understanding the build.sh script

The `build.sh` script is available at `https://github.com/the-gigi/delinkcious/blob/master/build.sh`.

Let's examine it bit by bit. There are several best practices we will follow here. First, it's a good idea to add a shebang with the path of the binary that will execute your script – that is, if you know where it is located. If you try to write a cross-platform script that works on many different platforms, you may need to rely on the path or other techniques. `set -eo pipefail` will fail out immediately (even in the middle of a pipe) if anything goes wrong.

This is highly recommended for production environments:

```
#!/bin/bash

set -eo pipefail
```

The next few lines just set some variables for directories and the tags for the Docker images. There are two tags: STABLE_TAB and TAG. The STABLE_TAG tag has a major and minor version and doesn't change in every build. The TAG includes the CIRCLE_BUILD_NUM provided by CircleCI and is incremented in every build. This means that the TAG is always unique. This is considered a best practice for tagging and versioning images:

```
IMAGE_PREFIX='g1g1'
STABLE_TAG='0.2'

TAG="${STABLE_TAG}.${CIRCLE_BUILD_NUM}"
ROOT_DIR="$(pwd)"
SVC_DIR="${ROOT_DIR}/svc"
```

Next, we go to the svc directory, which is the parent directory of all our services, and log in to DockerHub using the environment variables we set in the CircleCI project.

```
cd $SVC_DIR
docker login -u $DOCKERHUB_USERNAME -p $DOCKERHUB_PASSWORD
```

Now, we get to the main event. The script iterates over all the subdirectories of the svc directory looking for Dockerfile. If it finds a Dockerfile, it builds an image, tags it using a combination of service name and both TAG and STABLE_TAG, and finally pushes the tagged images to the registry:

```
cd "${SVC_DIR}/$svc"
    if [[ ! -f Dockerfile ]]; then
        continue
    fi
    UNTAGGED_IMAGE=$(echo "${IMAGE_PREFIX}/delinkcious-${svc}" | sed -e
's/_/-/g' -e 's/-service//g')
    STABLE_IMAGE="${UNTAGGED_IMAGE}:${STABLE_TAG}"
    IMAGE="${UNTAGGED_IMAGE}:${TAG}"
    docker build -t "$IMAGE" .
    docker tag "${IMAGE}" "${STABLE_IMAGE}"
    docker push "${IMAGE}"
    docker push "${STABLE_IMAGE}"
done
cd $ROOT_DIR
```

Dockerizing a Go service with a multi-stage Dockerfile

The Docker images you build in a microservice system are very important. You will build many of them, and each one many, many times. These images will also be shipped back and forth over the wire, and they present a target for attackers. With this in mind, it makes sense to build images that have the following properties:

- Lightweight
- Present minimal attack surface

This can be done by using a proper base image. For example, Alpine is very popular due to its small footprint. However, nothing beats the scratch base image. With Go-based microservices, you can literally create an image that just contains your service binary. Let's continue peeling the onion and look into the Dockerfile of one of the services. Spoiler alert: they are all virtually identical, and just differ in terms of their service names.

 You can find the `Dockerfile` of `link_service` at https://github.com/ the-gigi/delinkcious/blob/master/svc/link_service/Dockerfile.

We are using the multi-stage `Dockerfile` here. We will build the image using the standard Golang image. The arcane magic in the last line is what it takes to build a truly static and self-contained Golang binary that doesn't require a dynamic runtime library:

```
FROM golang:1.11 AS builder
ADD ./main.go main.go
ADD ./service service
# Fetch dependencies
RUN go get -d -v

# Build image as a truly static Go binary
RUN CGO_ENABLED=0 GOOS=linux go build -o /link_service -a -tags netgo -
ldflags '-s -w' .
```

We then copy the final binary into a scratch base image and create the smallest and most secure image possible. We exposed the `7070` port, which is the port the service listens on:

```
FROM scratch
MAINTAINER Gigi Sayfan <the.gigi@gmail.com>
COPY --from=builder /link_service /app/link_service
EXPOSE 7070
ENTRYPOINT ["/app/link_service"]
```

Exploring the CircleCI UI

CircleCI has a very friendly UI. Here, you can set various project settings, explore your builds, and drill down into specific builds. Remember that we used a monorepo approach and that, in the `build.sh` file, we took care of building multiple services. From CircleCI's point of view, Delinkcious is a single cohesive project. Here is the project's view of Delinkcious, which displays the recent builds:

Let's drill down into a successful build. All is well and green:

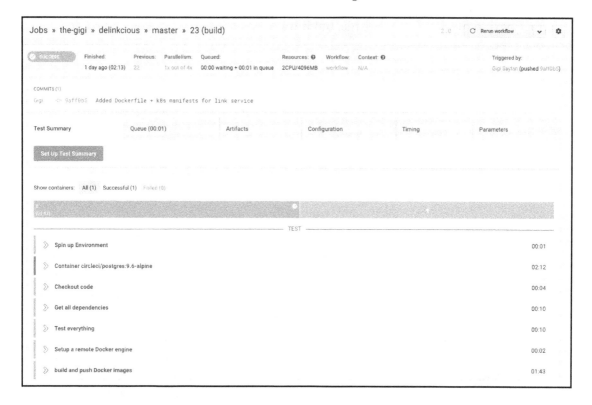

You can even expand any step and check the console output. Here's the output of the test stage:

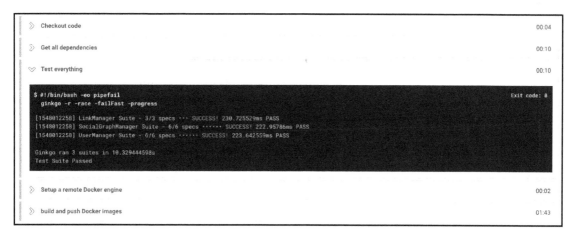

This is cool, but it's even more useful when things go wrong and you need to figure out why. For example, at one point, I tried to hide the `build.sh` script inside the `.circleci` directory next to the `config.yaml` file, but it wasn't added to the Docker context and produced the following error:

Considering future improvements

The Dockerfiles are pretty much duplicates, and there are some assumptions that can be parameterized. In the Kubernetes ecosystem, there are some interesting projects that help to address these concerns. Some of the solutions are for local development and can automatically generate the necessary Dockerfiles, while others are more targeted toward consistent and uniform production setups. We will look into some of these in later chapters. In this chapter, I want to keep it simple and avoid overwhelming you with too many options and layers of indirection.

Another opportunity for improvement is to test and build only services that have changed (or their dependencies have changed). As it stands, the `build.sh` script always builds all the images and tags them all with the same tags.

So far, we've built a complete CI pipeline using CircleCI and Docker. The next phase is to set up Argo CD as a continuous delivery pipeline.

Setting up continuous delivery for Delinkcious

With continuous integration in CircleCI under our belt, we can turn our attention to continuous delivery. First, we'll see what it takes to deploy a Delinkcious microservice to a Kubernetes cluster, then we'll look into Argo CD itself, and finally, we'll set up complete continuous delivery for Delinkcious via Argo CD.

Deploying a Delinkcious microservice

Each Delinkcious microservice has a set of Kubernetes resources defined in YAML manifests in its `k8s` subdirectory. Here is the link service `k8s` directory:

```
]$ tree k8s
k8s
├──── db.yaml
└──── link_manager.yaml
```

The `link_manager.yaml` file contains two resources: the Kubernetes deployment and the Kubernetes service. The Kubernetes deployment is as follows:

```
apiVersion: apps/v1
kind: Deployment
metadata:
  name: link-manager
  labels:
    svc: link
    app: manager
spec:
  replicas: 1
  selector:
    matchLabels:
      svc: link
      app: manager
  template:
```

```
metadata:
  labels:
    svc: link
    app: manager
spec:
  containers:
  - name: link-manager
    image: g1g1/delinkcious-link:0.2
    ports:
    - containerPort: 8080
```

The Kubernetes service is as follows:

```
apiVersion: v1
kind: Service
metadata:
  name: link-manager
spec:
  ports:
  - port:  8080
  selector:
    svc: link
    app: manager
```

The `db.yaml` file describes the database the link service uses to persist its state. Both can be deployed via `kubectl` in a single command by passing the `k8s` directory to `kubectl apply`:

```
$ kubectl apply -f k8s
deployment.apps "link-db" created
service "link-db" created
deployment.apps "link-manager" created
service "link-manager" created
```

 The main difference between kubectl create and `kubectl apply` is that `create` will return an error if a resource already exists.

Deploying from the command line with `kubectl` is nice, but our goal is to automate the process. Let's understand this.

Understanding Argo CD

Argo CD is an open source continuous delivery solution for Kubernetes. It was created by Intuit and adopted by many other companies, including Google, NVIDIA, Datadog, and Adobe. It has an impressive set of features, which are as follows:

- Automated deployment of apps to specific target environments
- CLI and web visualization of applications and differences between the desired and live states
- Hooks for supporting advanced deployment patterns (blue/green and canary)
- Support for multiple config management tools (plain YAML, ksonnet, kustomize, Helm, and so on)
- Continuous monitoring of all deployed applications
- Manual or automated sync of applications to the desired state
- Rollback to any application state that's committed in the Git repository
- Health assessment for all the components of the application
- SSO integration
- GitOps webhook integration (GitHub, GitLab, and BitBucket)
- Service account/access key management for integration with CI pipelines
- Audit trails for application events and API calls

Argo CD is built on Argo

Argo CD is a specialized CD pipeline, but it is built on the solid Argo workflow engine. I like this layered approach a lot, where you have a robust general-purpose foundation for the problem of orchestrating a workflow composed of steps and then build on top of it with CD-specific features and capabilities.

Argo CD utilizes GitOps

Argo CD adheres to the GitOps approach. The basic principle is that the state of your system is stored in Git. Argo CD manages your live state versus the desired state by examining Git diffs and using Git primitives to roll back and reconcile the live state.

Getting started with Argo CD

Argo CD follows best practices and expects to be installed in a dedicated namespace on your Kubernetes cluster:

```
$ kubectl create namespace argocd
$ kubectl apply -n argocd -f
https://raw.githubusercontent.com/argoproj/argo-cd/stable/manifests/install
.yaml
```

Let's see what was created. Argo CD installed four types of objects: pods, services, deployments, and replica sets. Here are the pods:

```
$ kubectl get all -n argocd
NAME                                                 READY  STATUS   RESTARTS  AGE
pod/argocd-application-controller-7c5cf86b76-2cp4z   1/1    Running  1         1m
pod/argocd-repo-server-74f4b4845-hxzw7                      1/1    Running  0         1m
pod/argocd-server-9fc58bc5d-cjc95                           1/1    Running  0         1m
pod/dex-server-8fdd8bb69-7dlcj                              1/1    Running  0         1m
```

Here are the services:

```
NAME                                     TYPE       CLUSTER-IP
EXTERNAL-IP   PORT(S)
service/argocd-application-controller ClusterIP    10.106.22.145    <none>
8083/TCP
service/argocd-metrics                   ClusterIP  10.104.1.83      <none>
8082/TCP
service/argocd-repo-server               ClusterIP  10.99.83.118     <none>
8081/TCP
service/argocd-server                    ClusterIP  10.103.35.4      <none>
80/TCP,443/TCP
service/dex-server                       ClusterIP  10.110.209.247   <none>
5556/TCP,5557/TCP
```

Here are the deployments:

```
NAME                                              DESIRED   CURRENT   UP-TO-
DATE      AVAILABLE    AGE
deployment.apps/argocd-application-controller     1         1         1
1              1m
deployment.apps/argocd-repo-server                1         1         1
1              1m
deployment.apps/argocd-server                     1         1         1
1              1m
deployment.apps/dex-server                        1         1         1
1              1m
```

Finally, here are the replica sets:

```
NAME                                                        DESIRED
CURRENT    READY       AGE
replicaset.apps/argocd-application-controller-7c5cf86b76    1              1
1              1m
replicaset.apps/argocd-repo-server-74f4b4845                1              1
1              1m
replicaset.apps/argocd-server-9fc58bc5d                     1              1
1              1m
replicaset.apps/dex-server-8fdd8bb69                        1              1
1              1m
```

However, Argo CD also installs two **custom resource definitions (CRDs)**:

```
$ kubectl get crd
NAME                       AGE
applications.argoproj.io   7d
appprojects.argoproj.io    7d
```

CRDs allow various projects to extend the Kubernetes API and add their own domain objects, as well as controllers to monitor them and other Kubernetes resources. Argo CD adds the concepts of an application and project to the world of Kubernetes. Soon, you will see how they integrate for the purposes of continuous delivery with built-in Kubernetes resources such as deployments, services, and pods. Let's get started:

1. Install the Argo CD CLI:

   ```
   $ brew install argoproj/tap/argocd
   ```

2. Port-forward to access the Argo CD server:

   ```
   $ kubectl port-forward -n argocd svc/argocd-server 8080:443
   ```

3. The initial password for the admin user is the name of the Argo CD server:

```
$ kubectl get pods -n argocd -l app.kubernetes.io/name=argocd-
server -o name | cut -d'/' -f 2
```

4. Log in to the server:

```
$ argocd login :8080
```

5. If it complains about an insecure login, just confirm by pressing *y*:

```
WARNING: server certificate had error: tls: either ServerName or
InsecureSkipVerify must be specified in the tls.Config. Proceed
insecurely (y/n)?
```

6. Alternatively, to skip the warning, type in the following:

```
argocd login --insecure :8080
```

Then, you can change the password.

7. If you store your password in an environment variable (for example, ARGOCD_PASSWORD), then you can have a one-liner so that you can log in with no further questions being asked:

```
argocd login --insecure --username admin --password
$ARGOCD_PASSWORD :8080
```

Configuring Argo CD

Remember to port-forward the argocd-server:

```
$ kubectl port-forward -n argocd svc/argocd-server 8080:443
```

Then, you can just browse to https://localhost:8080 and provide the admin user's password to log in:

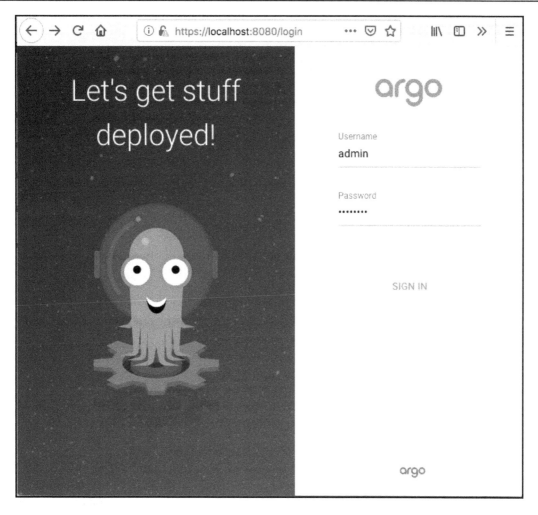

Configuring Argo CD is a pleasure. Its UI is very pleasant and easy to work with. It supports the Delinkcious monorepo out of the box, and there are no assumptions that each Git repository contains one application or project.

It will ask you for a Git repository to watch for changes, a Kubernetes cluster (defaults to the cluster it is installed on), and then it will try to detect the manifests in the repository. Argo CD supports multiple manifest formats and templates, such as Helm, ksonnet, and kustomize. We will introduce some of these fine tools later in this book. To keep things simple, we have configured each application with the directory that contains its raw k8s YAML manifests, which Argo CD also supports.

When all is said and done, the Argo CD is ready to go!

Using sync policies

By default, Argo CD detects when an application's manifests are out of sync, but doesn't sync automatically. This is a good default. In some cases, more tests need to run in dedicated environments before pushing changes to production. In other cases, a human must be in the loop. However, in many other cases, it's OK to automatically deploy changes to the cluster immediately and without human intervention. The fact that Argo CD follows GitOps also makes it very easy to sync back to any previous version (including the last one).

For Delinkcious, I chose auto sync because it is a demo project and the consequences of deploying a bad version are negligible. This can be done in the UI or from the CLI:

```
argocd app set <APPNAME> --sync-policy automated
```

The auto sync policy doesn't guarantee that the application will always be in sync. There are limitations that govern the auto sync process, which are as follows:

- Applications in error state will not attempt automated sync.
- Argo CD will attempt only a single auto sync for a specific commit SHA and parameters.
- If auto sync failed for whatever reason, it will not attempt it again.
- You can't roll back an application with auto sync.

In all of these cases, you either have to make a change to the manifests to trigger another auto sync or sync manually. To roll back (or, in general, sync to a previous version), you must turn auto sync off.

Argo CD offers another policy for pruning resources on deployment. When an existing resource no longer exists in Git, Argo CD will not delete it by default. This is a safety mechanism that's used to avoid destroying critical resources if someone makes a mistake while editing Kubernetes manifests. However, if you know what you're doing (for example, for stateless applications), you can turn on automatic pruning:

```
argocd app set <APPNAME> --auto-prune
```

Exploring Argo CD

Now that we have logged in and configured Argo CD, let's explore it a little bit. I really like the UI, but you can do everything from the command line or through a REST API, too, if you want to access it programmatically.

I already configured Argo CD with the three Delinkcious microservices. Each service is considered an application in Argo CD speak. Let's take a look at the **Applications** view:

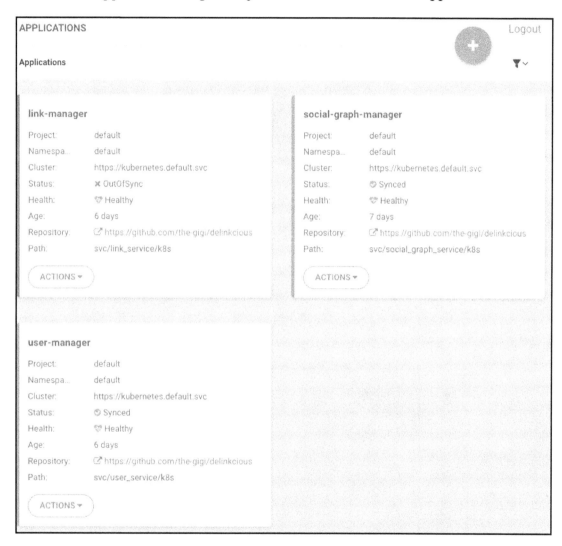

There are a few interesting things here. Let's talk about each one:

- The project is an Argo CD concept for grouping applications.
- The namespace is the Kubernetes namespace where the application should be installed.

- The cluster is the Kubernetes cluster, that
  is, `https://kubernetes.default.svc` and this is the cluster where Argo CD
  is installed.
- The status tells you if the current application is in sync with its YAML manifests
  in the Git repository.
- The health tells you if the application is OK.
- The repository is the application's Git repository.
- The path is the relative path within the repository where the `k8s` YAML
  manifests live (Argo CD monitors this directory for changes).

Here is what you get from the `argocd` CLI:

```
$ argocd app list
NAME                         CLUSTER                         NAMESPACE   PROJECT
STATUS       HEALTH   SYNCPOLICY   CONDITIONS
link-manager                 https://kubernetes.default.svc  default     default
OutOfSync    Healthy  Auto-Prune   <none>
social-graph-manager  https://kubernetes.default.svc  default     default
Synced       Healthy  Auto-Prune   <none>
user-manager                 https://kubernetes.default.svc  default     default
Synced       Healthy  Auto-Prune   <none>
```

As you can see (both in the UI and in the CLI), `link-manager` is out of sync. We can sync it
by selecting **Sync** from the **ACTIONS** dropdown:

Alternatively, you can do this from the CLI:

```
$ argocd app sync link-manager
```

One of the coolest things about the UI is how it presents all the k8s resources associated with an application. By clicking on the social-graph-manager application, we get the following view:

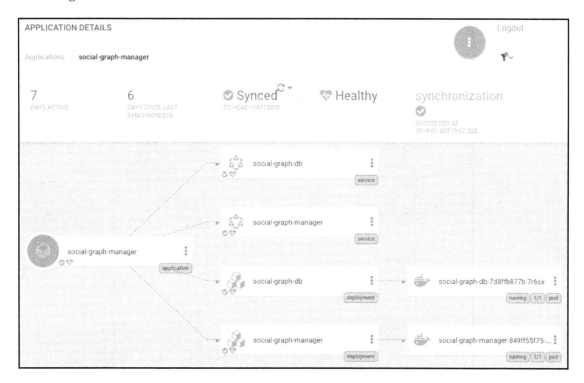

We can see the application itself, the services, the deployments, and the pods, including how many pods are running. This is actually a filtered view and, if we want to, we can add the replica sets associated with each deployment and the endpoints of each service to the display. However, these aren't interesting most of the time, so Argo CD doesn't display them by default.

We can click on a service and view a **SUMMARY** of its information, including the **MANIFEST**:

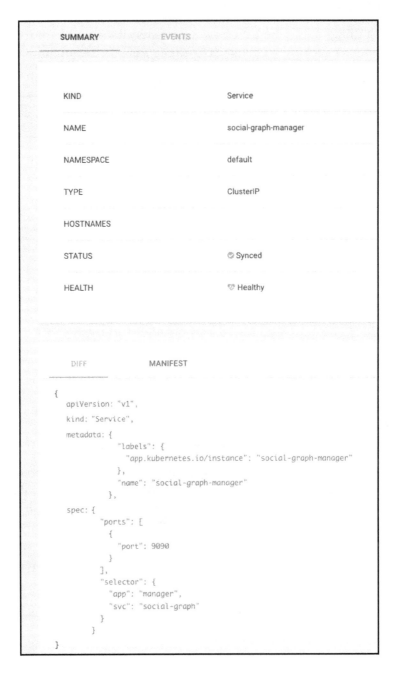

For pods, we can even check the logs, as shown in the following screenshot, all from the comfort of the Argo CD UI:

Argo CD can already take you a long way. However, it has a lot more to offer, and we will dive into these offerings later on in this book.

Summary

In this chapter, we discussed the importance of a CI/CD pipeline for a microservices-based distributed system. We reviewed some CI/CD options for Kubernetes and settled on a combination of CircleCI for the CI part (code change | Docker image) and Argo CD for the CD part (k8s manifest change | deployed application).

We also covered the best practices for building Docker images using multi-stage builds, the k8s YAML manifests for Postgres DB, and the deployment and service k8s resources. Then, we installed Argo CD in the cluster, configured it to build all our microservices, and explored the UI and the CLI. At this point, you should have a clear understanding of the concept of CI/CD and how important it is, the pros and cons of various solutions, and how to choose the best option for your system.

However, there is much more to come. In later chapters, we will improve our CI/CD pipeline with additional tests, security checks, and advanced multi-environment deployment options.

In the next chapter, we will turn out attention to configuring our services. Configuration is a huge part of developing complex systems that need to be developed, tested, and deployed by large teams. We will explore various conventional configuration options, such as command-line arguments, environment variables, and configuration files, as well as more dynamic configuration options and the special configuration features of Kubernetes.

Further reading

You can refer to the following sources for more information regarding what was covered in this chapter:

- Here are some good resources to expand your knowledge of the CI/CD options on Kubernetes. First and foremost, here are the two projects I use for the Delinkcious CI/CD solution:
    - **CircleCI**: https://circleci.com/docs/
    - **Argo**: https://argoproj.github.io/docs/argo-cd/docs/
- Then, there's this free mini ebook about CI/CD with Kubernetes:
    - https://thenewstack.io/ebooks/kubernetes/ci-cd-with-kubernetes/
- Finally, here are a couple of the other options I discarded for Delinkcious, but may be a good option for you:
    - **Jenkins X**: https://jenkins-x.io/
    - **Spinnaker**: https://www.spinnaker.io/

Configuring Microservices with Kubernetes

5

In this chapter, we're moving into the practical and real-world area of microservices configuration. Configuration is a big part of building complex distributed systems. In general, configuration concerns any aspect of the system that the code should be aware of, but that isn't encoded in the code itself. Here are the topics we will discuss in this chapter:

- What is configuration all about?
- Managing configuration the old-fashioned way
- Managing configuration dynamically
- Configuring microservices with Kubernetes

By the end of this chapter, you will have a solid understanding of the value of configuration. You will also have learned the many ways to configure software both statically and dynamically, as well as the special configuration options that Kubernetes provides (one of its best features). You will have also gained the insights and knowledge to benefit from the flexibility and control Kubernetes provides you as a developer and operator.

Technical requirements

In this chapter, we will look at a lot of Kubernetes manifests and will extend the capabilities of Delinkcious. There will be no need to install anything new.

The code

As usual, the code is split between two Git repositories:

- You can find the code samples at `https://github.com/PacktPublishing/Hands-On-Microservices-with-Kubernetes/tree/master/Chapter05`
- You can find the updated Delinkcious application at `https://github.com/the-gigi/delinkcious/releases/tag/v0.3`

What is configuration all about?

Configuration is a very overloaded term. Let's define it clearly for our purpose here: configuration mostly refers to operational data that's needed for computation. The configuration may be different between environments. Here are some typical configuration items:

- Service discovery
- Support testing
- Environment-specific metadata
- Secrets
- Third-party configuration
- Feature flags
- Timeouts
- Rate limits
- Various defaults

In general, the code that processes the input data utilizes configuration data to control operational aspects of the computation, but not algorithmic aspects. There are special cases where, via configuration, you can switch between different algorithms at runtime, but that's crossing into gray areas. Let's keep it simple for our purposes.

When considering configuration, it's important to think about who is supposed to create and update the configuration data. It may or may not be the developer of the code—for example, rate limits may be determined by a DevOps team member, but feature flags will be set by the developer. Also, in different environments, different people may modify the same value. You'll typically have the most restrictions in production.

Configuration and secrets

Secrets are credentials that are used to access databases and other services (internal and/or external). Technically, they are configuration data, but in practice, because of their sensitivity, they often need to be encrypted at rest and controlled more carefully. It is common to have secrets stored and managed separately from regular configurations.

In this chapter, we will consider only nonsensitive configuration. In the next chapter, we will discuss secrets in detail. Kubernetes also separates configuration from secrets at the API level.

Managing configuration the old-fashioned way

When I say the old-fashioned way, I mean pre-Kubernetes static configuration. But as you'll see, the old-fashioned way is sometimes the best way, and is often well supported by Kubernetes too. Let's go over the various ways to configure a program, consider their pros and cons, and when they are appropriate. The configuration mechanisms we will cover here are as follows:

- No configuration (convention over configuration)
- Command-line arguments
- Environment variables
- Configuration files

While Delinkcious is implemented mostly in Go, we will use different programming languages to demonstrate the configuration options just for fun and variety.

Convention over configuration

Sometimes, you don't really need configuration; the program can just make some decisions, document them, and that's that. For example, the name of the directory of the output file could be configurable, but the program can just decide that it's going to *output* and that's that. The upside of this approach is that it is very predictable: you don't have to think about configuration, and just by reading the code of the program, you know exactly what it does and where everything is supposed to be. The operators have very little work to do. The downside is that if more flexibility is needed, you have no recourse (for example, maybe there isn't enough space on the volume the program is running on).

Note that convention over configuration doesn't mean that there is no configuration at all. It means that you can reduce the amount of configuration when using convention.

Here is a little Rust program that prints the Fibonacci sequence up to 100 to the screen. By convention, it makes the decision that it will not go over 100. You can't configure it to print more or fewer numbers without changing the code:

```
fn main() {
    let mut a: u8 = 0;
    let mut b: u8 = 1;
    println!("{}", a);
    while b <= 100 {
        println!("{}", b);
        b = a + b;
        a = b - a;
    }
}

Output:

0
1
1
2
3
5
8
13
21
34
55
89
```

Command-line flags

Command-line flags or arguments are a staple of programming. When you run your program, you provide arguments that the program uses to configure itself. There are pros and cons of using them:

- **Pros:**
  - Very flexible
  - Familiar and available in every programming language
  - There are established best practices for short and long options
  - Works well with interactive usage documentation

- **Cons**:
  - Arguments are always strings
  - Need to quote arguments that contain spaces
  - Difficult to deal with multiline arguments
  - Restrictions on the number of command-line arguments
  - Restrictions on the size of each argument

 Command-line arguments are often used for input in addition to configuration. The boundaries between input and configuration can be a little murky sometimes. In most cases, it doesn't really matter, but it can make it confusing to users that just want to pass their input to a program through a command-line argument and are presented with a large and confusing array of configuration options.

Here is a little Ruby program that writes the Fibonacci sequence up to a number that's provided as a command-line argument:

```
if __FILE__ == $0
  limit = Integer(ARGV[0])
  a = 0
  b = 1
  puts a
  while b < limit
    puts b
    b = a + b
    a = b - a
  end
end
```

Environment variables

Environment variables are another favorite. They are useful when your program runs in an environment that may be set up by another program (or a shell script). Environment variables are typically inherited from the parent environment. They are also used for running interactive programs when the user always wants to provide the same option (or set of options) to the program. Instead of typing a long command line with the same options again and again, it is much more convenient to set an environment variable once (maybe even in your profile) and just run the program with no arguments. A good example is the AWS CLI, which allows you to specify many configuration options as environment variables (for example, `AWS_DEFAULT_REGION` or `AWS_PROFILE`).

Here is a little Python program that writes the Fibonacci sequence up to a number that is provided as an environment variable. Note that the FIB_LIMIT environment variable is read as a string and the program has to convert it into an integer:

```
import os

limit = int(os.environ['FIB_LIMIT'])
a = 0
b = 1
print(a)
while b < limit:
    print(b)
    b = a + b
    a = b - a
```

Configuration files

Configuration files are particularly useful when you have a lot of configuration data, especially when that data has a hierarchical structure. In most cases, it would be too overwhelming to configure an application with tens or even hundreds of options via command-line arguments or environment variables. Configuration files have another advantage, which is that you can chain multiple configuration files. Often, applications have a search path where they look for configuration files, such as /etc/conf, and then the home directory and then the current directory. This provides a lot of flexibility since you have common configuration while you're also able to override some parts per user or per run.

Configuration files are great! You should think about what format is best for your use case. There are many options. Configuration file formats follow trends, and every few years a new star shines. Let's review some of the older formats, as well as some of the newer ones.

INI format

INI files were once all the rage on Windows. INI stands for **initialization**. Mucking around with windows.ini and system.ini to get something working was very common in the eighties. The format itself was very simple and included sections with sets of key–value pairs and comments. Here is a simple INI file:

```
[section]
a=1
b=2
```

```
; here is a comment
[another_section]
c=3
d=4
e=5
```

The Windows API has functions for reading and writing INI files, so a lot of Windows applications used them as their configuration files.

XML format

XML (https://www.w3.org/XML/) is a W3C standard that was very popular in the nineties. It stands for **eXtensible Markup Language**, and it was used for *everything*: data, documents, APIs (SOAP), and, of course, configuration files. It is very verbose, and its main claim to fame is that it is self-describing and contains its own metadata. XML had schemas and many standards built on top of it. At some point, people thought that it would replace HTML (remember XHTML?). That's all in the past now. Here is a sample XML configuration file:

```
<?xml version="1.0" encoding="UTF-8"?>
    <startminimized value="False">
  <width value="1024">
  <height value = "768">
  <dummy />
  <plugin>
    <name value="Show Warning Message Box">
    <dllfile value="foo.dll">
    <method value = "warning">
  </plugin>
  <plugin>
    <name value="Show Error Message Box">
    <dllfile value="foo.dll">
    <method value = "error">
  </plugin>
  <plugin>
    <name value="Get Random Number">
    <dllfile value="bar.dll">
        <method value = "random">
  </plugin>
</xml>
```

JSON format

JSON (`https://json.org/`) stands for **JavaScript Object Notation**. It became popular with the growth of dynamic web applications and REST APIs. Its conciseness compared to XML was a breath of fresh air, and it quickly took over the industry. Its claim to fame is that it translates one-to-one to JavaScript objects. Here is a simple JSON file:

```
{
  "firstName": "John",
  "lastName": "Smith",
  "age": 25,
  "address": {
    "streetAddress": "21 2nd Street",
    "city": "New York",
    "state": "NY",
    "postalCode": "10021"
  },
  "phoneNumber": [
    {
      "type": "home",
      "number": "212 555-1234"
    },
    {
      "type": "fax",
      "number": "646 555-4567"
    }
  ],
  "gender": {
    "type": "male"
  }
}
```

I personally never liked JSON as a configuration file format; it doesn't support comments, it is unnecessarily strict about extra commas at the end of arrays, and serializing dates and times to JSON is always a struggle. It is also pretty verbose, with all the quotes, parentheses, and the need to escape many characters (although it is not as bad as XML).

YAML format

You've seen a lot of YAML (`https://yaml.org/`) already in this book, since the Kubernetes manifests are often written as YAML. YAML is a superset of JSON, but it also provides a much more concise syntax that is extremely human readable, as well as many more features, such as references, the autodetection of types, and support for aligned multiline values.

Here is a sample YAML file with more fancy features than you typically see in a normal Kubernetes manifest:

```
# sequencer protocols for Laser eye surgery
---
- step: &id001                          # defines anchor label &id001
    instrument:      Lasik 3000
    pulseEnergy:     5.4
    pulseDuration:   12
    repetition:      1000
    spotSize:        1mm

- step: &id002
    instrument:      Lasik 3000
    pulseEnergy:     5.0
    pulseDuration:   10
    repetition:      500
    spotSize:        2mm
- step: *id001                          # refers to the first step (with anchor
&id001)
- step: *id002                          # refers to the second step
- step:
    <<: *id001
    spotSize: 2mm                       # redefines just this key, refers rest
from &id001
- step: *id002
```

YAML is not as popular as JSON, but it slowly gathered momentum. Big projects such as Kubernetes and AWS CloudFormation use YAML (alongside JSON, because it's a superset) as their configuration format. CloudFormation added YAML support later; Kubernetes started with YAML.

It is currently my favorite configuration file format; however, YAML has its gotchas and critics, especially when you're using some of its more advanced features.

TOML format

Enter TOML (`https://github.com/toml-lang/toml`)—**Tom's Obvious Minimal Language**. TOML is like an INI file on steroids. It is the least known of all the formats, but it has started to gain momentum since it is used by Cargo, Rust's package manager. TOML is between JSON and YAML on the expressiveness spectrum. It supports autodetected data types and comments, but it's not as powerful as YAML. That said, it is the easiest for humans to read and write. It supports nesting mostly via dot notation as opposed to indentation.

Here is an example of a TOML file; see how readable it is:

```
# This is how to comment in TOML.

title = "A TOML Example"

[owner]
name = "Gigi Sayfan"
dob = 1968-09-28T07:32:00-08:00 # First class dates

# Simple section with various data types
[kubernetes]
api_server = "192.168.1.1"
ports = [ 80, 443 ]
connection_max = 5000
enabled = true

# Nested section
[servers]

  # Indentation (tabs and/or spaces) is optional
  [servers.alpha]
  ip = "10.0.0.1"
  dc = "dc-1"

  [servers.beta]
  ip = "10.0.0.2"
  dc = "dc-2"

[clients]
data = [ ["gamma", "delta"], [1, 2] ]

# Line breaks are OK when inside arrays
hosts = [
  "alpha",
  "omega"
]
```

Proprietary formats

Some applications just come up with their own formats. Here is a sample configuration file for an Nginx web server:

```
user        www www;  ## Default: nobody
worker_processes  5;  ## Default: 1
error_log  logs/error.log;
pid        logs/nginx.pid;
```

```
worker_rlimit_nofile 8192;

events {
  worker_connections  4096;  ## Default: 1024
}

http {
  include     conf/mime.types;
  include     /etc/nginx/proxy.conf;
  include     /etc/nginx/fastcgi.conf;
  index       index.html index.htm index.php;

  default_type application/octet-stream;
  log_format    main '$remote_addr - $remote_user [$time_local]  $status '
    '"$request" $body_bytes_sent "$http_referer" '
    '"$http_user_agent" "$http_x_forwarded_for"';
  access_log    logs/access.log  main;
  sendfile      on;
  tcp_nopush    on;
  server_names_hash_bucket_size 128; # this seems to be required for some
vhosts

  server { # php/fastcgi
    listen       80;
    server_name  domain1.com www.domain1.com;
    access_log   logs/domain1.access.log  main;
    root         html;

    location ~ \.php$ {
      fastcgi_pass   127.0.0.1:1025;
    }
  }
}
```

I don't recommend inventing yet another poorly conceived configuration format for your application. Between JSON, YAML, and TOML you should find the sweet spot between expressiveness, human readability, and familiarity. Also, there are libraries in all languages to parse and compose those familiar formats.

 Don't invent your own configuration format!

Hybrid configuration and defaults

So far, we have reviewed the primary configuration mechanisms:

- Convention over configuration
- Command-line arguments
- Environment variables
- Configuration files

These mechanisms are not mutually exclusive. Many applications will support some and even all of them. Very often, there will be a configuration resolution mechanism where a configuration file has a standard name and location, but you will still be able to specify a different configuration file via an environment variable and override even that for a specific run using a command-line argument. You don't have to look very far. Kubectl is a program that looks for its configuration file in $HOME/.kube by default; you can specify a different file via the KUBECONFIG environment variable. You can specify a special config file for a particular command by passing the --config command-line flag.

Speaking of which, kubectl uses YAML as its configuration format as well. Here is my Minikube configuration file:

```
$ cat ~/.kube/config
apiVersion: v1
clusters:
- cluster:
    certificate-authority: /Users/gigi.sayfan/.minikube/ca.crt
    server: https://192.168.99.121:8443
  name: minikube
contexts:
- context:
    cluster: minikube
    user: minikube
  name: minikube
current-context: minikube
kind: Config
preferences: {}
users:
- name: minikube
  user:
    client-certificate: /Users/gigi.sayfan/.minikube/client.crt
    client-key: /Users/gigi.sayfan/.minikube/client.key
```

Kubectl supports multiple clusters/contexts in the same config file. You can switch between them via `kubectl use-context`; however, many people who work regularly with multiple clusters don't like to keep them all in the same config file, and prefer to have a separate file for each cluster and then switch between them using the `KUBECONFIG` environment variable or by passing `--config` on the command-line.

Twelve factor app configuration

Heroku was one of the pioneers of cloud platform as a service. In 2011, they published the 12 factor methodology for building web applications. It's a pretty solid approach, and was very innovative at the time. It also happened to be the best way to build applications that could be deployed easily on Heroku itself.

 For our purposes, the most interesting part of their website is the config section, which can be found at `https://12factor.net/config`.

In short, they recommend that web services and applications always store the configuration in environment variables. This is a safe but somewhat limited guideline. It means that the service has to be restarted whenever a configuration changes, and suffers from the general limitations of environment variables.

Later, we will see how Kubernetes supports configuration as environment variables and configuration as configuration files, as well as a few special twists. But first, let's discuss dynamic configuration.

Managing configuration dynamically

So far, the configuration options we have discussed have been static. You have to restart and, in some cases (such as with embedded configuration files), redeploy your service to change its configuration. The nice thing about restarting your service when the configuration changes is that you don't have to worry about the impact of the new configuration changes on the in-memory state and the processing of in-flight requests because you're starting from scratch; however, the downside is that you lose all your in-flight requests (unless you are using a graceful shutdown) and any warmed-up caches or one-time initialization work, which could be substantial. You can mitigate this somewhat, though, by using rolling updates and blue-green deployments.

Understanding dynamic configuration

Dynamic configuration means that the service keeps running with the same code and the same in-memory state, but it can detect that the configuration has changed, and will dynamically adjust its behavior according to the new configuration. From the operator's perspective, when the configuration needs to change, they can just update the central configuration store and don't need to force a restart/redeployment of a service whose code didn't change.

It's important to understand that this is not a binary choice; some configuration may be static, and when it changes, you must restart the service, but some other configuration items may be dynamic.

Since dynamic configuration can change the behavior of the system in a way that is not captured by source control, it's a common practice to keep a history and audit of who changed what and when. Let's look at when you should use dynamic configuration and when you shouldn't!

When is dynamic configuration useful?

Dynamic configuration is useful in the following cases:

- If you just have a single instance of your service, then restarting means a mini-outage
- If you have feature flags that you want to switch back and forth quickly
- If you have services where initialization or dropping in-flight requests is expansive
- If your service doesn't support advanced deployment strategies, such as rolling updates, or blue-green or canary deployments
- When redeploying a new configuration file may pull in unrelated code changes from source control that are not ready for deployment yet

When should you avoid dynamic configuration?

However, dynamic configuration is not a panacea for all situations. If you want to play it totally safe, then restarting your service when configuration changes makes things easier to comprehend and analyze. That being said, microservices are often simple enough that you can grasp all the implications of configuration changes.

In the following situations, it may be better to avoid dynamic configuration:

- Regulated services where configuration change must go through a vetting and approval process
- Critical services where the low risk of static configuration trumps any benefit of dynamic configuration
- A dynamic configuration mechanism doesn't exist and the benefits don't justify the development of such a mechanism
- Existing system with a large number of services where the benefits of migration to a dynamic configuration doesn't justify the cost
- Advanced deployment strategies provide the benefits of dynamic configuration with static configuration and restarts/redeployments
- The added complexity of keeping track of and auditing configuration changes is too high

Remote configuration store

One of the options for dynamic configuration is a remote configuration store. All service instances can periodically query the configuration store, check whether the configuration has changed, and read the new configuration when it does. Possible options include the following:

- Relational databases (Postgres, MySQL)
- Key–value stores (Etcd, Redis)
- Shared filesystems (NFS, EFS)

In general, if all/most of your services already work with a particular type of store, it is often simpler to put your dynamic configuration there. An anti-pattern is to store the configuration in the same store as the service-persistent store. The problem here is that the configuration will be spread across multiple data stores, and some configuration changes are central. It will be difficult to manage, keep track of, and audit configuration changes across all services.

Remote configuration service

A more advanced approach is to create a dedicated configuration service. The purpose of this service is to provide a one-stop shop for all configuration needs. Each service will only have access to its configuration, and it's easy to implement control mechanisms for each and every configuration change. The downside of a configuration service is that you need to build it and maintain it. It can become a **single point of failure** (**SPOF**) too, if you're not careful.

So far, we have covered the many options for system configurations in great detail. Now, it's time to study what Kubernetes brings to the table.

Configuring microservices with Kubernetes

With Kubernetes or any container orchestrator, you have an interesting mix of configuration options. Kubernetes runs your containers for you. There is no way to set different environment options and command-line arguments for a specific run because Kubernetes decides when and where to run your container. What you can do is embed configuration files in your Docker image or change the command it is running; however, that means baking a new image for each configuration change and deploying it to your cluster. It's not the end of the world, but it's a heavyweight operation. You can also use the dynamic configuration options I mentioned earlier:

- Remote configuration store
- Remote configuration service

However, Kubernetes has some very neat tricks when it comes to dynamic configuration. The most innovative dynamic configuration mechanism is ConfigMaps. You can also get much fancier with custom resources. Let's dive in.

Working with Kubernetes ConfigMaps

ConfigMaps are Kubernetes resources that are managed by Kubernetes per namespace, and can be referenced by any pod or container. Here is the ConfigMap for the `link-manager` service:

```
apiVersion: v1
kind: ConfigMap
metadata:
  name: link-service-config
  namespace: default
data:
  MAX_LINKS_PER_USER: "10"
  PORT: "8080"
```

The `link-manager` deployment resource imports it into the pod by using the `envFrom` key:

```
apiVersion: apps/v1
kind: Deployment
metadata:
  name: link-manager
  labels:
    svc: link
    app: manager
spec:
  replicas: 1
  selector:
    matchLabels:
      svc: link
      app: manager
  template:
    metadata:
      labels:
        svc: link
        app: manager
    spec:
      containers:
      - name: link-manager
        image: g1g1/delinkcious-link:0.2
        ports:
        - containerPort: 8080
        envFrom:
        - configMapRef:
            name: link-manager-config
```

The effect of this is that the key–value pairs in the ConfigMap's `data` section are projected as environment variables when the `link-manager` service runs:

```
MAX_LINKS_PER_PAGE=10
PORT=9090
```

Let's see how Argo CD visualizes that the `link-manager` service has a ConfigMap. Note the top box named `link-service-config`:

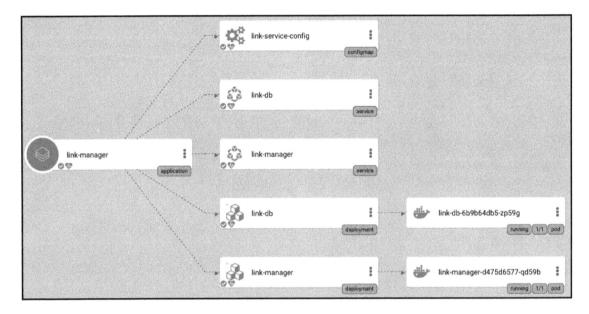

You can even drill down and inspect the ConfigMap itself from the Argo CD UI by clicking on the **ConfigMap** box. Very slick:

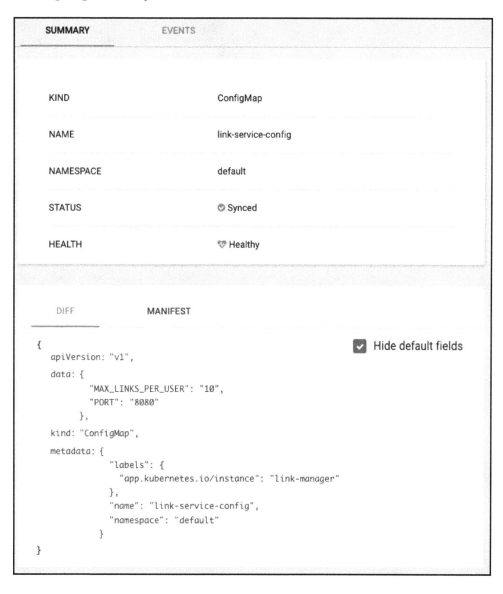

Note that since the ConfigMap is consumed as environment variables, this is static configuration. If you want to change any of it, you'll need to restart the service. In Kubernetes, this can be done in a couple of ways:

- Killing the pods (the replica set of the deployment will create new pods)
- Deleting and recreating the deployment (this has the same effect, but you don't need to kill pods explicitly)
- Applying some other change and redeploying

Let's see how the code uses it. This code can be found at `svc/link_manager/service/link_manager_service.go`:

```
port := os.Getenv("PORT")
if port == "" {
    port = "8080"
}

maxLinksPerUserStr := os.Getenv("MAX_LINKS_PER_USER")
if maxLinksPerUserStr == "" {
    maxLinksPerUserStr = "10"
}
```

The `os.Getenv()` standard library function gets `PORT` and `MAX_LINKS_PER_USER` from the environment. This is great because it allows us to test the service outside of the Kubernetes cluster and still configure it properly. For example, the link service end-to-end test—which is designed for local testing outside of Kubernetes—sets the environment variables before launching the social graph manager and the `link-manager` services:

```
func runLinkService(ctx context.Context) {
    // Set environment
    err := os.Setenv("PORT", "8080")
    check(err)

    err = os.Setenv("MAX_LINKS_PER_USER", "10")
    check(err)

    runService(ctx, ".", "link_service")
}

func runSocialGraphService(ctx context.Context) {
    err := os.Setenv("PORT", "9090")
    check(err)

    runService(ctx, "../social_graph_service", "social_graph_service")
}
```

Now that we've looked at how Delinkcious uses ConfigMaps, let's move on to the nuts and bolts of working with ConfigMaps.

Creating and managing ConfigMaps

Kubernetes gives you multiple ways to create ConfigMaps:

- From command-line values
- From one or more files
- From a whole directory
- By directly creating a ConfigMap YAML manifest

In the end, all ConfigMaps are a set of key–value pairs. What the keys and values are depends on the method of creating the ConfigMap. When playing with ConfigMaps, I find it useful to use the `--dry-run` flag so that I can see what ConfigMap will be created before committing to actually creating it. Let's look at some examples. Here is how to create a ConfigMap from command-line arguments:

```
$ kubectl create configmap test --dry-run --from-literal=a=1 --from-
literal=b=2 -o yaml
apiVersion: v1
data:
  a: "1"
  b: "2"
kind: ConfigMap
metadata:
  creationTimestamp: null
  name: test
```

This method should be used mostly for playing around with ConfigMaps. You have to specify each config item individually with a cumbersome `--from-literal` argument.

Creating a ConfigMap from a file is a much more viable method. It works well with the GitOps concept, where you can keep a history of the source configuration files that are used to create your ConfigMaps. We can create a very simple YAML file called `comics.yaml`:

```
superhero: Doctor Strange
villain: Thanos
```

Next, let's create a ConfigMap from this file using the following command (well, just a dry run):

```
$ kubectl create configmap file-config --dry-run --from-file comics.yaml -o yaml

apiVersion: v1
data:
  comics.yaml: |+
    superhero: Doctor Strange
    villain: Thanos

kind: ConfigMap
metadata:
  creationTimestamp: null
  name: file-config
```

What's interesting here is that the entire contents of the file are mapped to a single key: `comics.yaml`. The value is the entire contents of the file. The `|+` in YAML means that the following multiline block is one value. If we add additional `--from-file` arguments, then each file will have its own key in the ConfigMap. Similarly, if the argument to `--from-file` is a directory, then each file in the directory becomes a key in the ConfigMap.

Finally, let's look at a manually constructed ConfigMap. It's not that difficult to do this: just add a bunch of key–value pairs under the `data` section:

```
apiVersion: v1
kind: ConfigMap
metadata:
  name: env-config
  namespace: default
data:
  SUPERHERO: Superman
  VILLAIN: Lex Luthor
```

Here, we created dedicated `SUPERHERO` and `VILLAIN` keys.

Let's see how pods can consume these ConfigMaps. The pod gets its environment from the `env-config` ConfigMap. It executes a command that watches the values of the `SUPERHERO` and `VILLAIN` environment variables and every two seconds echos the current values:

```
apiVersion: v1
kind: Pod
metadata:
  name: some-pod
```

```
spec:
  containers:
  - name: some-container
    image: busybox
    command: [ "/bin/sh", "-c", "watch 'echo \"superhero: $SUPERHERO
villain: $VILLAIN\"'" ]
    envFrom:
    - configMapRef:
        name: env-config
  restartPolicy: Never
```

The ConfigMap must be created before the pod is started!

```
$ kubectl create -f env-config.yaml
configmap "env-config" created

$ kubectl create -f some-pod.yaml
pod "some-pod" created
```

The `kubectl` command is super useful for checking the output:

```
$ kubectl logs -f some-pod

Every 2s: echo "superhero: $SUPERHERO villain: $VILLAIN"        2019-02-08
20:50:39

superhero: Superman villain: Lex Luthor
```

As expected, the values match the ConfigMap. But what happens if we change the ConfigMap? The `kubectl edit configmap` command lets you update an existing ConfigMap in your editor:

```
$ kubectl edit configmap env-config

# Please edit the object below. Lines beginning with a '#' will be ignored,
# and an empty file will abort the edit. If an error occurs while saving
this file will be
# reopened with the relevant failures.
#
apiVersion: v1
data:
  SUPERHERO: Batman
  VILLAIN: Joker
kind: ConfigMap
metadata:
  creationTimestamp: 2019-02-08T20:49:37Z
  name: env-config
  namespace: default
```

```
  resourceVersion: "874765"
  selfLink: /api/v1/namespaces/default/configmaps/env-config
  uid: 0c83dee5-2be3-11e9-9999-0800275914a6

configmap "env-config" edited
```

We've changed the superhero and villain to Batman and Joker. Let's verify the changes:

```
$ kubectl get configmap env-config -o yaml

apiVersion: v1
data:
  SUPERHERO: Batman
  VILLAIN: Joker
kind: ConfigMap
metadata:
  creationTimestamp: 2019-02-08T20:49:37Z
  name: env-config
  namespace: default
  resourceVersion: "875323"
  selfLink: /api/v1/namespaces/default/configmaps/env-config
  uid: 0c83dee5-2be3-11e9-9999-0800275914a6
```

The new values are there. Let's check our pod logs. Nothing should change because the pod consumes the ConfigMap as environment variables that can't be changed from the outside while the pod is running:

```
$ kubectl logs -f some-pod

Every 2s: echo "superhero: $SUPERHERO villain: $VILLAIN"     2019-02-08
20:59:22

superhero: Superman villain: Lex Luthor
```

However, if we delete and recreate the pod, the picture is different:

```
$ kubectl delete -f some-pod.yaml
pod "some-pod" deleted

$ kubectl create -f some-pod.yaml
pod "some-pod" created

$ kubectl logs -f some-pod

Every 2s: echo "superhero: $SUPERHERO villain: $VILLAIN" 2019-02-08
21:45:47

superhero: Batman villain: Joker
```

I saved the best for last. Let's look at some dynamic configuration in action. The pod named some-other-pod is consuming the ConfigMap called file-config as a file. First, it creates a volume called config-volume that gets populated from the file-config ConfigMap. Then, this volume is mounted into /etc/config. The command that's running is simply watching the /etc/config/comics file:

```
apiVersion: v1
kind: Pod
metadata:
  name: some-other-pod
spec:
  containers:
  - name: some-container
    image: busybox
    command: [ "/bin/sh", "-c", "watch \"cat /etc/config/comics\"" ]
    volumeMounts:
    - name: config-volume
      mountPath: /etc/config
  volumes:
  - name: config-volume
    configMap:
      name: file-config
  restartPolicy: Never
```

Here is the file-config ConfigMap:

```
apiVersion: v1
kind: ConfigMap
metadata:
  name: file-config
  namespace: default
data:
  comics: |+
    superhero: Doctor Strange
    villain: Thanos
```

It has a key called comics (the filename), and the value is a multiline YAML string with superhero and villain entries (Doctor Strange and Thanos). When all is said and done, the contents of the comics key under the ConfigMap data section will be mounted inside the container as the /etc/config/comics file.

Let's verify this:

```
$ kubectl create -f file-config.yaml
configmap "file-config" created

$ kubectl create -f some-other-pod.yaml
```

```
pod "some-other-pod" created

$ kubectl logs -f some-other-pod

Every 2s: cat /etc/config/comics        2019-02-08 22:15:08

superhero: Doctor Strange
villain: Thanos
```

This is looking good so far. Now for the main attraction. Let's change the contents of the ConfigMap to the superhero Wonder Woman and villain Medusa. We'll use the `kubectl apply` command this time instead of deleting and recreating the ConfigMap. The ConfigMap is updated properly, but we also get a warning for our efforts (it's OK to ignore this):

```
$ kubectl apply -f file-config.yaml
Warning: kubectl apply should be used on resource created by either kubectl
create --save-config or kubectl apply
configmap "file-config" configured

$ kubectl get configmap file-config -o yaml
apiVersion: v1
data:
  comics: |+
    superhero: Super Woman
    villain: Medusa

kind: ConfigMap
metadata:
  annotations:
    kubectl.kubernetes.io/last-applied-configuration: |
      {"apiVersion":"v1","data":{"comics":"superhero: Super Woman\nvillain:
Medusa\n\n"},"kind":"ConfigMap","metadata":{"annotations":{},"name":"file-
config","namespace":"default"}}
  creationTimestamp: 2019-02-08T22:14:01Z
  name: file-config
  namespace: default
  resourceVersion: "881662"
  selfLink: /api/v1/namespaces/default/configmaps/file-config
  uid: d6e892f4-2bee-11e9-9999-0800275914a6
```

Note the preceding annotation. It's interesting that it stores the last applied change, which is available in the data and not the previous values for historical context.

```
$ kubectl logs -f some-other-pod

Every 2s: cat /etc/config/comics      2019-02-08 23:02:58

superhero: Super Woman
villain: Medusa
```

Yes, this has been a great success! The pod now prints the updated configuration information with no need to restart.

In this section, we have demonstrated how dynamic configuration works using ConfigMaps mounted as files. Let's look at what we should do when the configuration needs of large-scale systems are developed by multiple teams over long periods of time.

Applying advanced configuration

For large-scale systems with lots of services and lots of configuration, you may want to have services that consume multiple ConfigMaps. This is separate from the fact that a single ConfigMap may contain multiple files, directories, and literal values, in any combination. For example, each service may have its own specific configuration, but it might also use some shared libraries that need to be configured as well. In this scenario, you can have one ConfigMap for the shared library and a separate ConfigMap for each service. In this case, the services will consume both their ConfigMap and the shared library's ConfigMap.

Another common scenario is to have different configuration for different environments (development, staging, and production). Since in Kubernetes each environment typically has its own namespace, you need to be creative here. ConfigMaps are scoped to their namespace. This means that even if your configuration across environments is identical, you still need to create a copy in each namespace. There are various solutions that you can use to manage this proliferation of configuration files and Kubernetes manifests in general. I will not get into the details of these, and will just mention some of the more popular options here in no particular order:

- **Helm**: https://helm.sh/
- **Kustomize**: https://kustomize.io/
- **Jsonnet**: https://jsonnet.org/articles/kubernetes.html
- **Ksonnet**: https://github.com/ksonnet/ksonnet (not maintained anymore)

You can also build some tooling yourself to do this. In the next section, we'll look at another alternative, which is very cool but more complicated—custom resources.

Kubernetes custom resources

Kubernetes is a very extensible platform. You can add your own resources to the Kubernetes API and enjoy all the benefits of the API machinery, including kubectl support to manage them. Yes, it's that good. The first thing you need to do is define a custom resource, also known as a CRD. The definition will specify endpoints on the Kubernetes API, the version, scope, kind, and the names that are used to interact with resources of this new type.

Here is a superheroes CRD:

```
apiVersion: apiextensions.k8s.io/v1beta1
kind: CustomResourceDefinition
metadata:
  # name must match the spec fields below, and be in the form:
<plural>.<group>
  name: superheros.example.org
spec:
  # group name to use for REST API: /apis/<group>/<version>
  group: example.org
  # list of versions supported by this CustomResourceDefinition
  versions:
  - name: v1
    # Each version can be enabled/disabled by Served flag.
    served: true
    # One and only one version must be marked as the storage version.
    storage: true
  # either Namespaced or Cluster
  scope: Cluster
  names:
    # plural name to be used in the URL: /apis/<group>/<version>/<plural>
    plural: superheros
    # singular name to be used as an alias on the CLI and for display
    singular: superhero
    # kind is normally the CamelCased singular type. Your resource
manifests use this.
    kind: SuperHero
    # shortNames allow shorter string to match your resource on the CLI
    shortNames:
    - hr
```

Custom resources are available from all namespaces. The scope is relevant when constructing the URL from which it will be available and when deleting all objects from a namespace (a namespace scope CRD will be deleted with its namespace).

Let's create some superhero resources. The antman superhero has the same API version and kind that is defined in the superheroes CRD. It has a name in metadata, and spec is totally open. You can define whatever fields you want there. In this case, the fields are superpower and size:

```
apiVersion: "example.org/v1"
kind: SuperHero
metadata:
  name: antman
spec:
  superpower: "can shrink"
  size: "tiny"
```

Let's check out the Hulk. It's very similar, but also has a color field in its spec:

```
apiVersion: "example.org/v1"
kind: SuperHero
metadata:
  name: hulk
spec:
  superpower: "super strong"
  size: "big"
  color: "green"
```

Let's create the whole gang, starting with the CRD itself:

```
$ kubectl create -f superheros-crd.yaml
customresourcedefinition.apiextensions.k8s.io "superheros.example.org"
created

$ kubectl create -f antman.yaml
superhero.example.org "antman" created

$ kubectl create -f hulk.yaml
superhero.example.org "hulk" created
```

Now let's examine them with kubectl. We can use the short name, hr, here:

```
$ kubectl get hr
NAME            AGE
antman          5m
hulk            5m
```

We can also check the details of the superheroes:

```
$ kubectl get superhero hulk -o yaml
apiVersion: example.org/v1
kind: SuperHero
metadata:
  creationTimestamp: 2019-02-09T09:58:32Z
  generation: 1
  name: hulk
  namespace: default
  resourceVersion: "932374"
  selfLink: /apis/example.org/v1/namespaces/default/superheros/hulk
  uid: 4256d27b-2c51-11e9-9999-0800275914a6
spec:
  color: green
  size: big
  superpower: super strong
```

This is cool, but what can you do with custom resources? Well, a lot. If you think about it, you get a free CRUD API with CLI support and reliable persistent storage. Just invent your object model and create, get, list, update, and delete as many custom resources as you want. But it goes much further: you can have your own controller that watches over your custom resources and takes action when needed. This is actually how Argo CD works, as you can see from the following command:

```
$ kubectl get crd -n argocd
NAME                           AGE
applications.argoproj.io       20d
appprojects.argoproj.io        20d
```

How does that help with configuration? Since custom resources are available across the cluster, you can use them for shared configuration across namespaces. CRDs can serve as centralized remote configuration services, as we discussed earlier in the *Dynamic configuration* section, but you don't need to implement anything yourself. Another option is to create a controller that watches over these CRDs and then copies them to proper ConfigMaps for each namespace automatically. You are only limited by your imagination with Kubernetes. The bottom line is that for large complicated systems where managing configuration is a large endeavor, Kubernetes gives you tools to scale your configuration. Let's turn our attention to one aspect of configuration that often causes a lot of difficulties on other systems—service discovery.

Service discovery

Kubernetes has built-in support for service discovery, without any additional work having to be done on your part. Each service has an endpoints resource that Kubernetes keeps up to date with the addresses of all the backing pods for that service. Here are the endpoints for a single node Minikube cluster. Note how each pod has its own IP address, even though there is only one physical node. This demonstrates the vaunted flat networking model of Kubernetes. Only the Kubernetes API server has a public IP address:

```
$ kubectl get endpoints
NAME                   ENDPOINTS               AGE
kubernetes             192.168.99.122:8443     27d
link-db                172.17.0.13:5432        16d
link-manager           172.17.0.10:8080        16d
social-graph-db        172.17.0.8:5432         26d
social-graph-manager   172.17.0.7:9090         19d
user-db                172.17.0.12:5432        18d
user-manager           172.17.0.9:7070         18d
```

Normally, you don't deal directly with the endpoints resource. Each service is automatically exposed to other services in the cluster via both DNS and environment variables.

If you deal with the discovery of external services running outside the Kubernetes cluster, then you're on your own. A good approach could be to add them to a ConfigMap and update it when those external services need to change. If you need to manage secret credentials to access those external services (which is very likely), it's best to put those in Kubernetes secrets, which we will cover in the next chapter.

Summary

In this chapter, we discussed everything related to configuration, not including secret management. First, we considered classic configuration, and then we looked at dynamic configuration, focusing on remote configure stores and remote configuration services.

Next, we discussed Kubernetes-specific options and in particular ConfigMaps. We went over all the ways a ConfigMap can be created and managed. We also saw how a pod can consume a ConfigMap as either environment variables (static configuration) or as configuration files in mounted volumes that get updated automatically when the corresponding ConfigMap is modified by an operator. Finally, we looked at even more powerful options, such as custom resources, and discussed the special yet very important case of service discovery. At this point, you should have a clear picture of configuration in general, and the available options to configure microservices either traditionally or in Kubernetes-specific ways.

In the next chapter, we will look at the crucial topic of security. Microservice-based systems that are deployed in Kubernetes clusters often provide essential services and manage critical data. Securing both the data and the system itself is, in many cases, a top priority. Kubernetes provides multiple mechanisms across different layers to assist in building secure systems when following best practices.

Further reading

Here are some resources for you to use so that you can understand the fine details of the concepts and mechanisms we discussed in this chapter:

- **12 Factor Apps**: https://12factor.net/
- **Program Configuration in Python**: http://www.drdobbs.com/open-source/program-configuration-in-python/240169310
- **Building a dynamic configuration service**: https://www.compose.com/articles/building-a-dynamic-configuration-service-with-etcd-and-python/
- **Extending Kubernetes (video)**: https://www.youtube.com/watch?v=qVZnU8rXAEU

6
Securing Microservices on Kubernetes

In this chapter, we will examine how to secure your microservices on Kubernetes in depth. This is a broad topic and we will focus on the aspects that are most relevant to developers who are building and deploying microservices in a Kubernetes cluster. You must be very rigorous with security because your adversaries will actively try to find cracks, infiltrate your system, access sensitive information, run botnets, steal your data, corrupt your data, destroy your data, and make your system unavailable. Security should be designed into the system and not sprinkled on top as an afterthought. We will address this by covering general security principles and best practices before delving into the security mechanisms that Kubernetes puts at your disposal.

In this chapter, we will cover the following topics:

- Applying sound security principles
- Differentiating between user accounts and service accounts
- Managing secrets with Kubernetes
- Managing permissions with RBAC
- Controlling access with authentication, authorization, and admission
- Hardening Kubernetes by using security best practices

Technical requirements

In this chapter, we will look at a lot of Kubernetes manifests, and make Delinkcious more secure. There is no need to install anything new.

The code

The code is split between two Git repositories:

- You can find the code samples here: `https://github.com/PacktPublishing/Hands-On-Microservices-with-Kubernetes/tree/master/Chapter06`
- You can find the updated Delinkcious application here: `https://github.com/the-gigi/delinkcious/releases/tag/v0.4`

Applying sound security principles

There are many universal principles. Let's review the most important principles and understand how they assist in preventing attacks and making attacks more difficult, thus minimizing the damage caused by any attack and assisting in recovering from these attacks:

- **Defense in depth**: Defense in depth means multiple and redundant layers of security. The purpose is to make it difficult for an attacker to compromise your system. Multi-factor authentication is a great example. You have a username and password, but you must also type in a one-time code that's sent to your phone. If an attacker discovers your credentials, but doesn't have access to your phone, they won't be able to log in to the system and wreak havoc. There are multiple benefits to defense in depth, such as the following:
  - Make your system more secure
  - Make the cost of breaking your security too high for an attacker to even try
  - Better protection from non-malicious mistakes
- **Principle of least privilege**: The principle of least privilege is similar to the famous *need to know basis* from the spy world. You can't divulge what you don't know. You can't compromise what you have no access to. Any agent can be compromised. Limiting privileges just to the necessary ones will minimize damage if a breach occurs and will help in the auditing, mitigation, and analysis of incidents.

- **Minimize the attack surface**: This principle is very clear. The smaller your attack surface is, the easier it is to protect it. Please keep the following things in mind:
  - Don't expose APIs that you don't need
  - Don't keep data that you don't use
  - Don't provide different ways to perform the same task

The most secure code is code that's not written. It's also the most efficient and bug-free code. Consider the business value of each new feature you want to add very carefully. When migrating to some new technology or system, make sure not to leave legacy items behind. In addition to preventing many attack vectors, when a breach does occur the smaller attack surface will help a lot in terms of focusing the investigation and finding the root cause.

- **Minimize the blast radius**: Take it as a given that your system will be compromised or may have already been compromised. However, there are different levels of threat. Minimizing the blast radius means that compromised components can't easily reach out to other components and spread throughout our system. It also means that the resources that are available to those compromised components don't exceed the needs of the legitimate workload that is supposed to run there.
- **Trust no one**: Here is a partial list of entities you shouldn't trust:
  - Your users
  - Your partners
  - Vendors
  - Your cloud provider
  - Open source developers
  - Your developers
  - Your admins
  - Yourself
  - Your security

When we say *don't trust*, we don't mean that necessarily in a malicious way. Everyone is fallible and honest mistakes can be just as detrimental as targeted attacks. The great thing about the *Trust no one* principle is that you don't have to make a judgement call. The same approach of minimal trust will help you prevent and mitigate mistakes and attacks.

- **Be conservative**: The Lindy effect says that for some non-perishable things, the longer they exist, the longer you can expect them to exist. For example, if a restaurant exists for 20 years, you can expect it to exist for many more years, whereas a brand new restaurant that has just opened is much more likely to shut down within a short period of time. This is very true for software and technology. The latest JavaScript framework may have the lifetime expectancy of a fruit fly, but something like jQuery will be around for a while. From a security standpoint, there are other benefits from using more mature and battle-hardened software whose security has undergone a baptism of fire. It's often better to learn from other people's experiences. Take the following things into account:
  - Don't upgrade to the latest and greatest (unless explicitly fixing a security vulnerability).
  - Prefer stability over ability.
  - Prefer simplicity over power.

This goes hand in hand with the *trust no one* principle. Don't trust new shiny stuff and don't trust newer versions of your current dependencies. Of course, microservices and Kubernetes are relatively new technologies and the ecosystem is evolving fast. In this case, I assume that you've made a decision that the overall benefits of these innovations and their current status are mature enough to build on.

- **Be vigilant**: Security is not a one-shot thing. You have to actively keep working on it. The following are globally some ongoing activities you should perform and processes you should follow:
  - Patch your systems regularly.
  - Rotate your secrets.
  - Use short-lived keys, tokens, and certificates.
  - Follow up on CVEs.
  - Audit everything.
  - Test the security of your systems.

- **Be ready**: When the inevitable breach happens, be ready and ensure you do or have done the following:
  - Set up an incident management protocol.
  - Follow your protocol.
  - Plug the holes.
  - Restore system security.
  - Perform post-mortem for security incidents.
  - Evaluate and learn.

- Update your process, tools, and security to improve your security posture.

- **Do not write your own crypto**: A lot of people are excited about crypto and/or are disappointed when a strong crypto impacts performance. Contain your excitement and/or disappointment. Let the experts do crypto. It's much harder than it seems and the stakes are too high.

Now that we're clear about the general principles of good security, let's look at what Kubernetes offers in terms of security.

Differentiating between user accounts and service accounts

Accounts are a central concept in Kubernetes. Every request to the Kubernetes API server must originate from a particular account that the API server will authenticate, authorize, and admit before going through with it. There are two types of account:

- User accounts
- Service accounts

Let's examine both account types and understand the differences and when it's appropriate to use each one.

User accounts

User accounts are for humans (cluster administrators or developers) who typically operate Kubernetes from the outside via kubectl or programmatically. End users shouldn't have Kubernetes user accounts, only application-level user accounts. This is unrelated to Kubernetes. Remember, Kubernetes manages your containers for you – it has no idea what's going on inside and what your application is actually doing.

Your user credentials are stored in the `~/.kube/config` file. If you are working with multiple clusters, then you may have multiple clusters, users, and contexts in your `~/.kube/config` file. Some people prefer to have a separate config file for each cluster and switch between them using the `KUBECONFIG` environment variable. This is up to you. The following is my config file for a local Minikube cluster:

```
apiVersion: v1
clusters:
```

```
  - cluster:
      certificate-authority: /Users/gigi.sayfan/.minikube/ca.crt
      server: https://192.168.99.123:8443
    name: minikube
contexts:
- context:
      cluster: minikube
      user: minikube
    name: minikube
current-context: minikube
kind: Config
preferences: {}
users:
- name: minikube
    user:
      client-certificate: /Users/gigi.sayfan/.minikube/client.crt
      client-key: /Users/gigi.sayfan/.minikube/client.key
```

As you can see in the preceding code block, this is a YAML file that follows the conventions of typical Kubernetes resources, although it's not an object you can create in your cluster. Note that everything is plural: clusters, contexts, users. In this case, there is just one cluster and one user. However, you can create multiple contexts that are a combination of clusters and users so that you have multiple users with different privileges in the same cluster, or even multiple clusters in the same Minikube configuration file. `current-context` determines the target of each operation of `kubectl` (which cluster to access with what user credentials). User accounts have cluster-scope, which means that we can access resources in any namespace.

Service accounts

Service accounts are a different story. Each pod has a service account associated with it, and all the workloads running in this pod use that service account as their identity. Service accounts are scoped to a namespace. When you create a pod (directly or via a deployment), you may specify a service account. If you create a pod without specifying a service account, then the namespace's default service account is used. Each service account has a secret associated with it for talking to the API server.

The following block shows the default service account in the default namespace:

```
$ kubectl get sa default -o yaml
apiVersion: v1
kind: ServiceAccount
metadata:
  creationTimestamp: 2019-01-11T15:49:27Z
```

```
  name: default
  namespace: default
  resourceVersion: "325"
  selfLink: /api/v1/namespaces/default/serviceaccounts/default
  uid: 79e17169-15b8-11e9-8591-0800275914a6
secrets:
- name: default-token-td5tz
```

The service account can have more than one secret. We will talk about secrets very soon. The service account allows the code running in the pod to talk to the API server.

You can fetch a token and CA certificate from:
/var/run/secrets/kubernetes.io/serviceaccount and then construct a REST HTTP request by passing these credentials via an authorization header. For example, the following code block shows a request to list pods in the default namespace:

```
# TOKEN=$(cat /var/run/secrets/kubernetes.io/serviceaccount/token)
# CA_CERT=$(cat /var/run/secrets/kubernetes.io/serviceaccount/ca.crt)
# URL="https://${KUBERNETES_SERVICE_HOST}:${KUBERNETES_SERVICE_PORT}"

# curl --cacert "$CERT" -H "Authorization: Bearer $TOKEN"
"$URL/api/v1/namespaces/default/pods"
{
  "kind": "Status",
  "apiVersion": "v1",
  "metadata": {

  },
  "status": "Failure",
  "message": "pods is forbidden: User
\"system:serviceaccount:default:default\" cannot list resource \"pods\" in
API group \"\" in the namespace \"default\"",
  "reason": "Forbidden",
  "details": {
    "kind": "pods"
  },
  "code": 403
}
```

The result is 403 forbidden. The default service account is not allowed to list the pods, and actually it's not allowed to do anything. In the Authorization section, we will see how to grant privileges to service accounts.

If you don't feel comfortable with manually constructing curl requests, you can also do it programmatically via the client library. I created a Python-based Docker image that includes the official Python client (https://github.com/kubernetes-client/python) library for Kubernetes and a few other goodies, such as vim, IPython, and HTTPie.

Here is the Dockerfile that builds the image:

```
FROM python:3

RUN apt-get update -y
RUN apt-get install -y vim
RUN pip install kubernetes \
                 httpie        \
                 ipython


CMD bash
```

I uploaded it to DockerHub as `g1g1/py-kube:0.2`. Now, we can run it as a pod in the cluster and have a nice troubleshooting or interactive exploration session:

$ kubectl run trouble -it --image=g1g1/py-kube:0.2 bash

Executing the preceding command will drop you into a command-line prompt where you can do whatever you want with Python, IPython, HTTPie, and of course the Kubernetes Python client package that's available. Here is how we can list the pods in the default namespace from Python:

```
# ipython
Python 3.7.2 (default, Feb  6 2019, 12:04:03)
Type 'copyright', 'credits' or 'license' for more information
IPython 7.2.0 -- An enhanced Interactive Python. Type '?' for help.

In [1]: from kubernetes import client, config
In [2]: config.load_incluster_config()
In [3]: api = client.CoreV1Api()
In [4]: api.list_namespaced_pod(namespace='default')
```

The result will be similar – a Python exception – because the default account is forbidden to list pods. Note that, if your pod doesn't need to access the API server (very common), you can make it explicit by setting `automountServiceAccountToken: false`.

This can be done at the service account level or in the pod spec. This way, even if something or someone outside your control adds permissions to the service account at a later date, since there is no token mounted, the pod will fail to authenticate to the API server and will not get unintended access. Delinkcious services currently have no need to access the API server, so by following the principle of least privilege, we can add this to their spec in the deployment.

Here is how you can create a service account for the LinkManager (without access to the API server) and add it to the deployment:

```
apiVersion: v1
kind: ServiceAccount
metadata:
  name: link-manager
  automountServiceAccountToken: false
---
apiVersion: apps/v1
kind: Deployment
metadata:
  name: link-manager
  labels:
    svc: link
    app: manager
spec:
  replicas: 1
  selector:
    matchLabels:
      svc: link
      app: manager
  serviceAccountName: link-manager
...
```

Before granting our service account super powers using RBAC, let's review how Kubernetes manages secrets. Kubernetes stores secrets in etcd by default. It is possible to integrate etcd with third-party solutions, but in this section we will focus on vanilla Kubernetes. Secrets should be encrypted at rest and in transit, and etcd has supported this since version 3.

Now that we understand how accounts work in Kubernetes, let's see how to manage secrets.

Managing secrets with Kubernetes

Before granting our service account super powers using RBAC, let's review how Kubernetes manages secrets. Kubernetes stores secrets in etcd (`https://coreos.com/etcd/`) by default. There are different types of secret Kubernetes can manage. Let's look at the various secret types and then create our own secrets and pass them to containers. Finally, we'll build a secure pod together.

Understanding the three types of Kubernetes secret

There are three distinct types of secret:

- Service account API token (credentials for talking to the API server)
- Registry secret (credentials for pulling images from private registries)
- Opaque secret (your secrets that Kubernetes knows nothing about)

The service account API token is built-in for each service account (unless you specified `automountServiceAccountToken: false`). Here is the secret for the service account API token for the `link-manager`:

```
$ kubectl get secret link-manager-token-zgzff | grep link-manager-token
link-manager-token-zgzff    kubernetes.io/service-account-token   3    20h
```

The `pull secrets` image is a little more complicated. Different private registries behave differently and require different secrets. Also, some private registries require that you refresh your tokens often. Let's look at an example with DockerHub. DockerHub lets you have a single private repository by default. I converted `py-kube` into a private repository, as shown in the following screenshot:

I deleted the local Docker image. To pull it, I need to create a registry secret:

```
$ kubectl create secret docker-registry private-dockerhub \
  --docker-server=docker.io \
  --docker-username=g1g1 \
  --docker-password=$DOCKER_PASSWORD \
  --docker-email=$DOCKER_EMAIL
secret "private-dockerhub" created
```

```
$ kubectl get secret private-dockerhub
NAME                     TYPE                              DATA     AGE
private-dockerhub        kubernetes.io/dockerconfigjson    1        16s
```

The last type of secret is `Opaque` and is the most interesting type of secret. You store your sensitive information in opaque secrets that Kubernetes doesn't touch. It just provides you with a robust and secure store for your secrets and an API for creating, reading, and updating those secrets. You can create opaque secrets in many ways, such as the following:

- From literal values
- From a file or directory
- From an `env` file (key-value pairs in separate lines)
- Create a YAML manifest with `kind`

This is very similar to ConfigMaps. Now, let's create some secrets.

Creating your own secrets

One of the simplest and most useful ways to create secrets is via a simple `env` file that contains key-value pairs:

```
a=1
b=2
```

We can create a secret by using the `-o yaml` flag (YAML output format) to see what was created:

```
$ kubectl create secret generic generic-secrets --from-env-file=generic-
secrets.txt -o yaml

apiVersion: v1
data:
  a: MQ==
  b: Mg==
kind: Secret
metadata:
  creationTimestamp: 2019-02-16T21:37:38Z
  name: generic-secrets
  namespace: default
  resourceVersion: "1207295"
  selfLink: /api/v1/namespaces/default/secrets/generic-secrets
  uid: 14e1db5c-3233-11e9-8e69-0800275914a6
type: Opaque
```

The type is `Opaque` and the returned values are base64-encoded. To fetch the values and decode them, you can use the following command:

```
$ echo -n $(kubectl get secret generic-secrets -o jsonpath="{.data.a}") |
base64 -D
1
```

The `jsonpath` output format lets you drill-down into specific parts of the object. You can also use `jq` (`https://stedolan.github.io/jq/`) if you prefer.

 Note that secrets are not stored or transmitted; they are just encrypted or encoded in base-64, which anyone can decode. When you create a secret using your user account (or get secrets), you get back the base-64 encoded representation of the decrypted secret. However, it is encrypted at rest on disk and also encrypted in transit since you communicate with the Kubernetes API server over HTTPS.

Now that we have understood how to create secrets, we will make them available to workloads that are running in containers.

Passing secrets to containers

There are many ways to pass secrets to containers, such as the following:

- You can bake secrets into the container image.
- You can pass them into environment variables.
- You can mount them as files.

The most secure way is to mount your secrets as files. When you bake your secret into the image, anyone with access to the image can retrieve your secrets. When you pass your secrets as environment variables, they can be viewed via `docker inspect`, `kubectl describe pod`, and by child processes if you don't clean up the environment. In addition, it is common to log your entire environment when reporting an error, which takes discipline from all your developers to sanitize and redact secrets. Mounted files don't suffer from these weaknesses, but note that anyone who can `kubectl exec` into your container can examine any mounted files, including secrets, if you don't manage permissions carefully.

Let's create a secret from a YAML manifest. When choosing this method, it's your responsibility to base64-encode the values:

```
$ echo -n top-secret | base64
dG9wLXNlY3JldA==

$ echo -n bottom-secret | base64
Ym90dG9tLXNlY3JldA==

apiVersion: v1
kind: Secret
type: Opaque
metadata:
  name: generic-secrets2
  namespace: default
data:
  c: dG9wLXNlY3JldA==
  d: Ym90dG9tLXNlY3JldA==
```

Let's create the new secrets and verify that they were created successfully by getting them using kubectl get secret:

```
$ kubectl create -f generic-secrets2.yaml
secret "generic-secrets2" created

$ echo -n $(kubectl get secret generic-secrets2 -o jsonpath="{.data.c}") |
base64 -d
top-secret

$ echo -n $(kubectl get secret generic-secrets2 -o jsonpath="{.data.d}") |
base64 -d
bottom-secret
```

Now that we know how to create opaque/generic secrets and pass them to containers, let's connect all the dots and build a secure pod.

Building a secure pod

The pod has a custom service that doesn't need to talk to the API server (so there's no need to auto-mount a service account token); instead, the pod offers imagePullSecret to pull our private repository and also has some generic secrets mounted as a file.

Let's get started and learn how to build a secure pod:

1. The first step is the custom service account. Here is the YAML manifest:

```
apiVersion: v1
kind: ServiceAccount
metadata:
  name: service-account
automountServiceAccountToken: false
```

Let's create it:

```
$ kubectl create -f service-account.yaml
serviceaccount "service-account" created
```

2. Now, we'll attach it to our pod and also set the imagePullSecret we created earlier. There's a lot going on here. I attached a custom service account, created a secret volume that references the generic-secrets2 secret, then a volume mount that mounts it into /etc/generic-secrets2; finally, I set imagePullSecrets to the private-dockerhub secret:

```
apiVersion: v1
kind: Pod
metadata:
  name: trouble
spec:
  serviceAccountName: service-account
  containers:
  - name: trouble
    image: g1g1/py-kube:0.2
    command: ["/bin/bash", "-c", "while true ; do sleep 10 ; done"]
    volumeMounts:
    - name: generic-secrets2
      mountPath: "/etc/generic-secrets2"
      readOnly: true
  imagePullSecrets:
  - name: private-dockerhub
  volumes:
  - name: generic-secrets2
    secret:
      secretName: generic-secrets2
```

3. Next, we can create our pod and start playing around:

```
$ kubectl create -f pod-with-secrets.yaml
pod "trouble" created
```

Kubernetes was able to pull the image from the private repository. We expect no API server token (there shouldn't be `/var/run/secrets/kubernetes.io/serviceaccount/`), and our secrets should be mounted as files in `/etc/generic-secrets2`. Let's verify this by starting an interactive shell using `kubectl exec -it` and check that the service account file doesn't exist, but that the generic secrets `c` and `d` do:

```
$ kubectl exec -it trouble bash

# ls /var/run/secrets/kubernetes.io/serviceaccount/
ls: cannot access '/var/run/secrets/kubernetes.io/serviceaccount/':
No such file or directory

# cat /etc/generic-secrets2/c
top-secret

# cat /etc/generic-secrets2/d
bottom-secret
```

Yay, it works!

Here, we focused a lot on managing custom secrets and built a secure pod that can't access the Kubernetes API server, but often you need to carefully manage the access of different entities have to the Kubernetes API server. Kubernetes has a well-defined **role-based access control model** (also known as **RBAC**). Let's see it in action.

Managing permissions with RBAC

RBAC is a mechanism that's used to manage access to Kubernetes resources. With effect from Kubernetes 1.8, RBAC is considered stable. Start the API server with `--authorization-mode=RBAC` to enable it. RBAC works as follows when a request to the API server comes in:

1. First, it authenticates the request via the user credentials or service account credentials of the caller (returns 401 unauthorized if it fails).
2. Next, it checks the RBAC policies to verify whether the requester is authorized to perform the operation on the target resource (returns 403 forbidden if it fails).
3. Finally, it runs through an admission controller that may reject or modify the request for various reasons.

The RBAC model consists of identities (user and service accounts), resources (Kubernetes objects), verbs (standard actions such as `get`, `list`, and `create`), roles, and role bindings. Delinkcious services don't need to access the API server, so they don't need access. However, Argo CD, the continuous delivery solution, definitely needs access as it deploys our services and all related objects.

Let's look at the following snippet from a role and understand it in detail. You can find the source here: `https://github.com/argoproj/argo-cd/blob/master/manifests/install.yaml#L116`:

```yaml
apiVersion: rbac.authorization.k8s.io/v1
kind: Role
metadata:
  labels:
    app.kubernetes.io/component: server
    app.kubernetes.io/name: argo-cd
  name: argocd-server
rules:
- apiGroups:
  - ""
  resources:
  - secrets
  - configmaps
  verbs:
  - create
  - get
  - list
  ...
- apiGroups:
  - argoproj.io
  resources:
  - applications
  - appprojects
  verbs:
  - create
  - get
  - list
  ...
- apiGroups:
  - ""
  resources:
  - events
  verbs:
  - create
  - list
```

A role has rules. Each rule assigns a list of allowed verbs to each API group and resources within that API group. For example, for the empty API group (indicates the core API group) and the `configmaps` and `secrets` resources, the Argo CD server can apply all of these verbs:

```
- apiGroups:
  - ""
  resources:
  - secrets
  - configmaps
  verbs:
  - create
  - get
  - list
  - watch
  - update
  - patch
  - delete
```

The `argoproj.io` API group and the `applications` and `appprojects` resources (both are CRDs defined by Argo CD) have another list of verbs. Finally, for the `events` resource of the core group, it can only use the `create` or `list` verb:

```
- apiGroups:
  - ""
  resources:
  - events
  verbs:
  - create
- list
```

An RBAC role applies only to the namespace it was created in. This means that the fact that Argo CD can do anything with `configmaps` and `secrets` is not too scary if it's created in a dedicated namespace. As you may recall, I installed Argo CD on the cluster in a namespace called `argocd`.

However, similar to a role, RBAC also has a `ClusterRole` where the permissions that are listed are allowed across the cluster. Argo CD has cluster roles too. For example, `argocd-application-controller` has the following cluster role:

```
apiVersion: rbac.authorization.k8s.io/v1
kind: ClusterRole
metadata:
  labels:
    app.kubernetes.io/component: application-controller
    app.kubernetes.io/name: argo-cd
```

```
      name: argocd-application-controller
  rules:
  - apiGroups:
      - '*'
      resources:
      - '*'
      verbs:
      - '*'
  - nonResourceURLs:
      - '*'
      verbs:
  - '*'
```

This pretty much gives access to anything on the cluster. It is equivalent to not having RBAC at all. I'm not sure why the Argo CD application controller needs such global access. My guess is that it's just easier to get access to anything than explicitly list everything if it's a big list. However, this is not the best practice from a security standpoint.

Roles and cluster roles are just a list of permissions. To make it all work, you need to bind a role to a set of accounts. That's where role bindings and cluster role bindings come into play. Role bindings only work in their namespace. You can role-bind both a role and a cluster role (in which case the cluster role will be active in the target namespace only). Here is an example:

```
  apiVersion: rbac.authorization.k8s.io/v1
  kind: RoleBinding
  metadata:
    labels:
      app.kubernetes.io/component: application-controller
      app.kubernetes.io/name: argo-cd
    name: argocd-application-controller
  roleRef:
    apiGroup: rbac.authorization.k8s.io
    kind: Role
    name: argocd-application-controller
  subjects:
  - kind: ServiceAccount
  name: argocd-application-controller
```

A cluster role binding applies across the cluster and can bind a cluster role only (because a role is restricted to its namespace).

Now that we understand how to control access to Kubernetes resources using RBAC, let's move on to controlling access to our own microservices.

Controlling access with authentication, authorization, and admission

Kubernetes has an interesting access control model that goes above and beyond standard access control. For your microservices, it provides the troika of authentication, authorization, and admission. You're probably familiar with authentication (who is calling?) and authorization (what is the caller allowed to do?). Admission is not as common. It can be used for a more dynamic situation where a request may be rejected, even if the caller is properly authenticated and authorized.

Authenticating microservices

Service accounts and RBAC are a good solution to manage identity and access for Kubernetes objects. However, in a microservice architecture, there will be a lot of communication between microservices. This communication happens inside the cluster and may be considered less prone to attacks. But the defense in depth principle guides us to encrypt, authenticate, and manage this communication as well. There are several approaches here. The most robust approach requires your own **private key infrastructure** (**PKI**) and **certificate authority** (**CA**) that can deal with issuing, revoking, and updating certificates as service instances come and go. This is pretty complicated (if you use a cloud provider, they may provide it for you). A somewhat simpler approach is to utilize Kubernetes secrets and create shared secrets between each of the two services that can talk to each other. Then, when a request comes in, we can check whether the calling service passed the correct secret, which authenticates it.

Let's create a mutual secret for `link-manager` and `graph-manager` (remember that it must be base64-encoded):

```
$ echo -n "social-graph-manager: 123" | base64
c29jaWFsLWdyYXBoLW1hbmFnZXI6IDEyMw==
```

Then, we will create a secret for `link-manager`, as follows:

```
apiVersion: v1
kind: Secret
type: Opaque
metadata:
  name: mutual-auth
  namespace: default
data:
  mutual-auth.yaml: c29jaWFsLWdyYXBoLW1hbmFnZXI6IDEyMw==
```

Never commit secrets to source control. I have done it here for educational purposes only.

To see the value of the secret using `kubectl` and the `jsonpath` format, you need to escape the dot in `mutual-auth.yaml`:

```
$ kubectl get secret link-mutual-auth -o "jsonpath={.data['mutual-
auth\.yaml']}" | base64 -D
social-graph-manager: 123
```

We'll repeat the process for `social-graph-manager`:

```
$ echo -n "link-manager: 123" | base64
bGluay1tYW5hZ2VyOiAxMjM=
```

Then, we will create a secret for `social-graph-manager`, as follows:

```
apiVersion: v1
kind: Secret
type: Opaque
metadata:
  name: mutual-auth
  namespace: default
data:
  mutual-auth.yaml: bGluay1tYW5hZ2VyOiAxMjM=
```

At this point, `link-manager` and `social-graph-manager` have a shared secret that we can mount to the respective pods. Here is the pod spec in the `link-manager` deployment that mounts the secret from a volume into `/etc/delinkcious`. The secret will show up as the `mutual-auth.yaml` file:

```
spec:
  containers:
  - name: link-manager
    image: g1g1/delinkcious-link:0.3
    imagePullPolicy: Always
    ports:
    - containerPort: 8080
    envFrom:
    - configMapRef:
        name: link-manager-config
    volumeMounts:
    - name: mutual-auth
      mountPath: /etc/delinkcious
      readOnly: true
```

```
volumes:
- name: mutual-auth
  secret:
    secretName: link-mutual-auth
```

We can apply the same convention to all services. The result is that each pod will have a file called /etc/delinkcious/mutual-auth.yaml with the tokens of all the services it needs to talk to. Based on this convention, we created a little package called auth_util that reads the file, populates a couple of maps, and exposes a couple of functions for mapping and matching callers and tokens. The auth_util package expects the file itself to be a YAML file with key-value pairs in the format of <caller>: <token>.

Here are the declarations and maps:

```
package auth_util

import (
    _ "github.com/lib/pq"
    "gopkg.in/yaml.v2"
    "io/ioutil"
    "os"
)

const callersFilename = "/etc/delinkcious/mutual-auth.yaml"

var callersByName = map[string]string{}
var callersByToken = map[string][]string{}
```

The init() function reads the file (unless the env variable, DELINKCIOUS_MUTUAL_AUTH, is set to false), unmarshals it into the callersByName map, and then iterates over it and populates the reverse callersByToken map, where the tokens are the keys and the callers are the values (with possible duplicates):

```
func init() {
    if os.Getenv("DELINKCIOUS_MUTUAL_AUTH") == "false" {
        return
    }

    data, err := ioutil.ReadFile(callersFilename)
    if err != nil {
        panic(err)
    }
    err = yaml.Unmarshal(data, callersByName)
    if err != nil {
        panic(err)
    }
```

```
    for caller, token := range callersByName {
        callersByToken[token] = append(callersByToken[token], caller)
    }
}
```

Finally, the `GetToken()` and `HasCaller()` functions provide the external interface to the package that's used by services and clients that communicate with each other:

```
func GetToken(caller string) string {
    return callersByName[caller]
}

func HasCaller(caller string, token string) bool {
    for _, c := range callersByToken[token] {
        if c == caller {
            return true
        }
    }

    return false
}
```

Let's see how the link service calls the `GetFollowers()` method of the social graph service. The `GetFollowers()` method extracts the authentication token from the environment and compares it to the token that's provided in the headers (this is only known to the link service) to verify that the caller is really the link service. As usual, the core logic doesn't change. The entire authentication scheme is isolated to the transport and client layers. Since the social graph service uses the HTTP transport, the client stores the token in a header called `Delinkcious-Caller-Service`. It gets the token from the `auth_util` package via the `GetToken()` function without knowing anything about where the secret is coming from (in our case, the Kubernetes secret is mounted as a file):

```
// encodeHTTPGenericRequest is a transport/http.EncodeRequestFunc that
// JSON-encodes any request to the request body. Primarily useful in a
client.
func encodeHTTPGenericRequest(_ context.Context, r *http.Request, request
interface{}) error {
    var buf bytes.Buffer
    if err := json.NewEncoder(&buf).Encode(request); err != nil {
        return err
    }
    r.Body = ioutil.NopCloser(&buf)

    if os.Getenv("DELINKCIOUS_MUTUAL_AUTH") != "false" {
        token := auth_util.GetToken(SERVICE_NAME)
        r.Header["Delinkcious-Caller-Token"] = []string{token}
    }
```

```
        return nil
    }
```

On the service side, the social graph service transport layer ensures that `Delinkcious-Caller-Token` exists and that it contains the token of a valid caller:

```
func decodeGetFollowersRequest(_ context.Context, r *http.Request)
(interface{}, error) {
    if os.Getenv("DELINKCIOUS_MUTUAL_AUTH") != "false" {
        token := r.Header["Delinkcious-Caller-Token"]
        if len(token) == 0 || token[0] == "" {
            return nil, errors.New("Missing caller token")
        }

        if !auth_util.HasCaller("link-manager", token[0]) {
            return nil, errors.New("Unauthorized caller")
        }
    }
    parts := strings.Split(r.URL.Path, "/")
    username := parts[len(parts)-1]
    if username == "" || username == "followers" {
        return nil, errors.New("user name must not be empty")
    }
    request := getByUsernameRequest{Username: username}
    return request, nil
}
```

The beauty of this mechanism is that we keep all the gnarly plumbing stuff of parsing files and extracting headers from HTTP requests in the transport layer and keep the core logic pristine.

In `Chapter 13`, *Service Mesh – Working with Istio*, we will look at another solution for authenticating microservices using a service mesh. Now, let's move on to authorizing microservices.

Authorizing microservices

Authorizing microservices can be very simple or very complicated. In the simplest case, if a calling microservice is authenticated, then it is authorized to perform any operation. However, sometimes, this is not enough and you need very sophisticated and fine-grained authorization, depending on other request parameters. For example, in a company I used to work at, I developed an authorization scheme for a sensor network with both spatial and temporal dimensions. Users could query the data, but they might be limited to certain cities, buildings, floors, or rooms.

If they requested data from a location they were not authorized to query, their request was rejected. They were also limited by time range and couldn't query outside their designated time range.

For Delinkcious, you can imagine that users may be limited to viewing their own links and the links of users they follow (if approved).

Admitting microservices

Authentication and authorization are very well-known and familiar mechanisms for access control (although not easy to implement robustly). Admission is yet another step that follows authorization. Even if a request is authenticated and authorized, it may not be possible to satisfy the request at the moment. This could be due to a rate limit or some other intermittent issue on the server side. Kubernetes implements additional capabilities, such as mutating requests as part of admission. For your own microservices, it may not be needed.

So far, we have discussed accounts, secrets, and access control. However, there's still a lot of work to be done in order to get closer to a secure and hardened cluster.

Hardening your Kubernetes cluster using security best practices

In this section, we will cover various best practices and we'll see how close Delinkcious gets to getting it right.

Securing your images

One of the top priorities is making sure that the images that you deploy to the cluster are secure. There are several good guidelines to follow here.

Always pull images

In the container spec, there is an optional key called `ImagePullPolicy`. The default is `IfNotPresent`. There are a few problems with this default, as follows:

- If you use tags such as *latest* (you shouldn't), then you will not pick up updated images.

- You may have conflicts with other tenants on the same node.
- Other tenants on the same node can run your images.

Kubernetes has an admission controller called `AlwaysPullImages` that sets the `ImagePullPolicy` of every pod to `AlwaysPullImages`. This prevents all the issues at the expense of pulling images, even if they are present and you had the right to use them. You turn on this admission controller by adding it to the list of enabled admission controllers that are passed to `kube-apiserver` via the `--enable-admission-controllers` flag.

Scan for vulnerabilities

Vulnerabilities in your code or dependencies allow attackers to get access to your system. The national vulnerability database (`https://nvd.nist.gov/`) is a good place to learn about new vulnerabilities and processes for managing them, such as the **Security Content Automation Protocol** (**SCAP**).

Open-source solutions such as Claire (`https://github.com/coreos/clair`) and Anchore (`https://anchore.com/kubernetes/`) are available, as well as commercial solutions. Many image registries provide scanning services too.

Update your dependencies

Keep your dependencies up-to-date, especially if they fix known vulnerabilities. This is where you need to find the right balance between being vigilant and being conservative.

Pinning the versions of your base images

Pinning versions of base images is critical for ensuring repeatable builds. If your base image version is not specified, you will pick up the latest version, which may or may not be what you want.

Using minimal base images

The principle of minimizing the attack surface exhorts you to use as many minimal base images as possible; the smaller and more restricted, the better. In addition to these security benefits, you also enjoy faster pulling and pushing (although layers should make it relevant only when upgrading your base image). Alpine is a very popular base image. Delinkcious services take this approach to the extreme and use the `SCRATCH` image as a base image.

Pretty much the entire service is just the Go executable, and that's it. It's small, fast, and secure, but you pay for it when you need to troubleshoot issues and there are no tools to help you.

If we follow all of these guidelines, our images will be secure, but we should still apply the basic principles of least privilege and zero trust, and minimize the blast radius at the network level. If a container, pod, or node somehow gets compromised, they shouldn't be allowed to reach another part of the network except what's needed by the workloads running on these components. This is where namespaces and network policies come into the picture.

Dividing and conquering your network

In addition to authentication as part of defense in depth, you can ensure that services talk to each other only if they're supposed to by utilizing namespaces and network policies. Namespaces are a very intuitive yet powerful concept. However, on their own, they don't prevent pods in the same cluster from communicating with each other. In Kubernetes, all the pods in a cluster share the same flat networking address space. This is one of the great simplifications of the Kubernetes networking module. Your pods can be on the same nodes or a different node – it doesn't matter.

Each pod will have its own IP address (even if multiple pods run on the same physical node or VM with a single IP address). This is where network policies come into the picture. A network policy is basically a set of rules that specify both intra-cluster communication between pods (east-west traffic), as well as communication between services in the cluster and the outside world (north-south traffic). If no network policy is specified, all incoming traffic (ingress) is allowed by default on all the ports of every pod. From a security perspective, this is unacceptable.

Let's start by blocking all ingress and later open up selectively as needed:

```
apiVersion: networking.k8s.io/v1
kind: NetworkPolicy
metadata:
  name: deny-all
spec:
  podSelector: {}
  policyTypes:
  - Ingress
```

Note that network policies work at the pod level. You specify pods with labels, which is one of the primary reasons why you should properly group your pods using meaningful labels.

Before applying this policy, it's good to know that it works from the troubleshooting pod, as shown in the following code block:

```
# http GET http://$SOCIAL_GRAPH_MANAGER_SERVICE_HOST:9090/following/gigi

HTTP/1.1 200 OK
Content-Length: 37
Content-Type: text/plain; charset=utf-8
Date: Mon, 18 Feb 2019 18:00:52 GMT

{
    "err": "",
    "following": {
        "liat": true
    }
}
```

However, after applying the `deny-all` policy, we get a timeout error, as follows:

```
# http GET http://$SOCIAL_GRAPH_MANAGER_SERVICE_HOST:9090/following/gigi

http: error: Request timed out (30s).
```

Now that all the pods are isolated, let's allow `social-graph-manager` to talk to its database. Here is a network policy that allows only `social-graph-manager` to access `social-graph-db` on port `5432`:

```
apiVersion: networking.k8s.io/v1
kind: NetworkPolicy
metadata:
  name: allow-social-graph-db
  namespace: default
spec:
  podSelector:
    matchLabels:
      svc: social-graph
      app: db
  ingress:
  - from:
    - podSelector:
        matchLabels:
          svc: social-graph
          app: manger
    ports:
    - protocol: TCP
      port: 5432
```

And the following additional policy allows ingress to `social-graph-manager` on port `9090` from the `link-manager`, as shown in the following code:

```
apiVersion: networking.k8s.io/v1
kind: NetworkPolicy
metadata:
  name: allow-link-to-social-graph
  namespace: default
spec:
  podSelector:
    matchLabels:
        svc: social-graph
        app: manager
  ingress:
  - from:
    - podSelector:
        matchLabels:
            svc: link
            app: manger
    ports:
    - protocol: TCP
      port: 9090
```

In addition to the security benefits, the network policies serve as live documentation to the flow of information across the system. You can tell exactly which services talk to which other services, as well as external services.

We have gotten our network under control. Now, it's time to turn our attention to our image registry. After all, this is where we get our images, which we give a lot of permissions to.

Safeguarding your image registry

It is highly recommended to use private image registries. If you have proprietary code, then you must not publish your containers with public access because reverse-engineering your images will grant attackers access. However, there are other reasons for this too. You get better control over (and auditing of) pulling and pushing images from the registry.

There are two options here:

- Use a private registry managed by a third party like AWS, Google, Microsoft, or Quay.
- Use your own private registry.

The first option makes sense if you deploy your system on a cloud platform that has good integration with its own image registry or if you don't manage your own registry in the sprint of cloud-native computing and you prefer to let a third party such as Quay do it for you.

The second option (running your own container registry) may be best if you need extra control over all the images, including base images and dependencies.

Granting access to Kubernetes resources as needed

The principle of least privilege directs you to grant access to Kubernetes resources only to services that actually need it (for example, Argo CD). RBAC is a great option here since everything is locked down by default and you can explicitly add privileges. However, beware of falling into the trap of giving wildcard access to everything just to get over difficulties with RBAC configuration. For example, let's take a look at a cluster role with the following rule:

```
rules:
- apiGroups:
  - '*'
  resources:
  - '*'
  verbs:
  - '*'
- nonResourceURLs:
  - '*'
  verbs:
  - '*'
```

This is worse than disabling RBAC because it gives you a false sense of security. Another option for a more dynamic situation is dynamic authentication, authorization, and admission control via webhooks and external servers. Those give you the ultimate flexibility.

Using quotas to minimize the blast radius

Limits and quotas are a Kubernetes mechanism where you can control various limited resources such as CPU and memory which are allocated to clusters, pods, and containers. They are very useful for multiple reasons:

- Performance.
- Capacity planning.
- Cost management.
- They help Kubernetes schedule pods based on resource utilization.

When your workloads operate within a budget, everything becomes more predictable and easier to reason about, although you have to do the leg work of figuring out how many resources are actually needed and adjust this as time goes by. This is not as bad as it sounds since, with horizontal pod autoscaling, you can let Kubernetes dynamically adjust the number of pods for a service, even if each pod has a very strict quota.

From a security perspective, if an attacker gains access to a workload running on your cluster, it limits the amount of physical resources it can use. One of the most common attacks these days is just saturating targets with crypto currency mining. Similar types of attacks are fork bombs, which just consume all the available resources by having a rogue process replicate itself uncontrollably. Network policies limit the blast radius of compromised workloads by limiting access to other pods on the network. Resource quotas minimize the blast radius from utilizing the resources on the hosting node of the compromised pod.

There are several types of quota, such as the following:

- Compute quota (CPU and memory)
- Storage quota (disks and external storage)
- Objects (Kubernetes object)
- Extended resources (non-Kubernetes resources like GPUs)

Resource quotas are quite nuanced. There are several concepts you need to understand, such as units and scopes, as well as the difference between requests and limits. I'll explain the basics and demonstrate them by adding resource quotas for the Delinkcious user service. A resource quota is allocated for container, so you add it to the container spec as follows:

```
apiVersion: apps/v1
kind: Deployment
metadata:
  name: user-manager
```

```
    labels:
      svc: user
      app: manager
spec:
  replicas: 1
  selector:
    matchLabels:
      svc: user
      app: manager
  template:
    metadata:
      labels:
        svc: user
        app: manager
    spec:
      containers:
      - name: user-manager
        image: g1g1/delinkcious-user:0.3
        imagePullPolicy: Always
        ports:
        - containerPort: 7070
        resources:
          requests:
            memory: 64Mi
            cpu: 250m
          limits:
            memory: 64Mi
            cpu: 250m
```

There are two sections under resources:

- **Requests**: Requests are what the container requests in order to start. If Kubernetes can't satisfy a request for a particular resource, it will not start the pod. Your workload can be sure that it will have that much CPU and memory allocated to it throughout its life, and you can take it to the bank.

  In the preceding block, I specified a request of `64Mi` of memory and `250m` units of CPU (see the following section for an explanation of these units).

- **Limits**: Limits are the ceiling for resources a workload may have access to. A container that exceeds its memory limits might be killed and the entire pod may be evicted from the node. Kubernetes will restart the container if killed and reschedule the pod if evicted, like it does with any type of failure. If a container exceeds its CPU limits, it will not be killed and may even get away with it for a while but, since the CPU is much easier to control, it will probably just not get all the CPU it requests and will sleep a lot to remain within its limits.

It is often the best approach to specify requests as limits, like I did for the user manager. The workload knows that it already has all the resources it will ever need and doesn't have to worry about trying to get closer to the limit in the presence of other hungry neighbors on the same node who may all compete for the same resource pool.

While resources are specified per container, when pods have multiple containers, it's important to consider the total resource requests of the entire pod (the sum of all the container requests). The reason for this is that pods are always scheduled as one unit. If you have a pod that has 10 containers, with each one asking for 2 Gib of memory, then it means that your pod requires a node with 20 Gib of free memory.

Units for requests and limits

You can use the following suffixes for memory requests and limits: E, P, T, G, M, and K. You can also use the power of two suffixes (which are always a little larger), that is, Ei, Pi, Ti, Gi, Mi, and Ki. You can also just use integers, including the exponent notation for bytes.

The following are approximately the same: 257,988,979, 258e6, 258M, and 246Mi. CPU units are relative to the hosting environment, as follows:

- 1 AWS vCPU
- 1 GCP Core
- 1 Azure vCore
- 1 IBM vCPU
- 1 hyperthread on a bare-metal Intel processor with hyperthreading

You can request CPU in fractions of resolutions of 0.001. A more convenient method is to use milliCPU and just integers with the m suffix; for example, 100 m is 0.1 CPU.

Implementing security contexts

Sometimes, pods and containers need escalated privileges or access to the node. This will be very rare for your application workloads. However, when necessary, Kubernetes has the concept of a security context that encapsulates and allows you to configure multiple Linux security concepts and mechanisms. This is critical from a security perspective because you open up a tunnel out of the container world into the host machine.

Here is a list of some mechanisms that are covered by security contexts:

- Allowing (or forbidding) privilege escalation
- Access control via user IDs and group IDs (`runAsUser`, `runAsGroup`)
- Capabilities as opposed to unrestricted root access
- Using AppArmor and seccomp profiles
- SELinux configuration

There are many details and interactions that are beyond the scope of this book. I'll just share an example of `SecurityContext`:

```
apiVersion: v1
kind: Pod
metadata:
  name: secure-pod
spec:
  containers:
  - name: some-container
    image: g1g1/py-kube:0.2
    command: ["/bin/bash", "-c", "while true ; do sleep 10 ; done"]
    securityContext:
      runAsUser: 2000
      allowPrivilegeEscalation: false
      capabilities:
        add: ["NET_ADMIN", "SYS_TIME"]
      seLinuxOptions:
        level: "s0:c123,c456"
```

The security policy does different things, such as setting the user ID inside the container to `2000` and not allowing privilege escalation (getting root), as follows:

```
$ kubectl exec -it secure-pod bash

I have no name!@secure-pod:/$ whoami
whoami: cannot find name for user ID 2000

I have no name!@secure-pod:/$ sudo su
bash: sudo: command not found
```

Security contexts are a very good way to centralize the security aspects of a pod or container, but in a large cluster where you potentially install third-party packages such as helm charts, it's difficult to ensure that every pod and container gets the right security context. That's where pod security policies come into the picture.

Hardening your pods with security policies

A pod security policy allows you set a global policy that applies to all newly created pods. It is enforced as part of the admission stage of access control. The pod security policy can create a security context for pods with no security context or reject pod creation and updating if they have a security context that doesn't match the policy. Here is a security policy that will prevent pods from getting a privileged status that allows access to host devices:

```
apiVersion: policy/v1beta1
kind: PodSecurityPolicy
metadata:
  name: disallow-privileged-access
spec:
  privileged: false
  allowPrivilegeEscalation: false
  # required fields.
  seLinux:
    rule: RunAsAny
  supplementalGroups:
    rule: RunAsAny
  runAsUser:
    rule: RunAsAny
  fsGroup:
    rule: RunAsAny
  volumes:
  - '*'
```

Here are some good policies to enforce (if you don't need the capabilities):

- Read-only root filesystem
- Control mounting host volumes
- Prevent privileged access and escalation

Last but not least, let's make sure that the tools we will use to work with our Kubernetes cluster are secure as well.

Hardening your toolchain

Delinkcious is pretty well-contained. The main tool it uses is Argo CD. Argo CD, which can potentially cause a lot of damage, is running inside the cluster and pulls from GitHub. However, it has a lot of permissions. Before I decided to use Argo CD as the continuous delivery solution for Delinkcious, I reviewed it seriously from a security perspective. The Argo CD developers did a great job of thinking how to make Argo CD secure. They made sensible choices, implemented them, and documented how to run Argo CD securely. Here are the security features that Argo CD provides:

- Authentication of the admin user via JWT tokens
- Authorization via RBAC
- Secure communication over HTTPS
- Secret and credential management
- Audits
- Cluster RBAC

Let's take a look at them briefly.

Authentication of admin user via JWT tokens

Argo CD has a built-in admin user. All other users must use **Single-Sign on** (**SSO**). Authentication to the Argo CD server always uses **JSON Web Token** (**JWT**). Admin user credentials are converted into JWT too.

It also supports automation via the `/api/v1/projects/{project}/roles/{role}/token` endpoint, which generates automation tokens that are issued and signed by Argo CD itself. These tokens are limited in scope and expire pretty fast.

Authorization via RBAC

Argo CD authorizes requests by mapping the user's JWT group claims to RBAC roles. This is a very nice combination of industry-standard authentication with the Kubernetes authorization model via RBAC.

Secure communication over HTTPS

All communication to/from Argo CD, as well as between its own components, is done over HTTPS/TLS.

Secret and credentials management

Argo CD needs to manage a lot of sensitive information, such as the following:

- Kubernetes secrets
- Git credentials
- OAuth2 client credentials
- Credentials to external clusters (when not installed in the cluster)

Argo CD makes sure to keep all of these secrets to itself. It never leaks them by returning them in responses or logging them. All API responses and logs are scrubbed and redacted.

Audits

You can audit most of the activity just by looking at git commit logs, which triggers everything in Argo CD. However, Argo CD also sends various events to capture in-cluster activity for additional visibility. This combination is powerful.

Cluster RBAC

By default, Argo CD uses a cluster-wide admin role. This isn't necessary.
The recommendation is to restrict its write privileges only to the namespaces it needs to manage.

Summary

In this chapter, we took a serious look at a serious topic: security. Microservice-based architectures and Kubernetes make the most sense to large-scale enterprise-distributed systems that support mission-critical objectives and often manage sensitive information. On top of the challenges of developing and evolving such complex systems, we must be aware that such systems present very enticing targets to attackers.

We must use a rigorous process and best practices to protect the system, the users, and the data. From here, we covered security principles and best practices, and we also saw how they support each other and how Kubernetes dedicates a lot of effort to allowing them to develop and operate our system securely.

We also discussed the pillars that act as the foundation of microservice security on Kubernetes: the triple A of authentication/authorization/admission, secure communication inside and outside the cluster, strong secret management (encrypted at rest and in transit), and layered security policies.

At this point, you should have a clear understanding of the security mechanisms that are at your disposal and enough information to decide how to integrate them into your system. Security is never complete, but utilizing best practices will allow you to find the right balance between security and the other requirements of your system at each point in time.

In the next chapter, we will finally open Delinkcious to the World! We will look at public APIs, load balancers, and the important considerations for performance and security that we need to be aware of.

Further reading

There are many good resources for Kubernetes security. I've collected some very good external resources that will aid you in your journey:

- **Kubernetes security**: https://kubernetes-security.info/
- **Microsoft SDL practices**: https://www.microsoft.com/en-us/securityengineering/sdl/practices

The following Kubernetes documentation pages expand on a lot of the topics we have covered in this chapter:

- **Network Policies**: https://kubernetes.io/docs/concepts/services-networking/network-policies/
- **Resource Quotas**: https://kubernetes.io/docs/concepts/policy/resource-quotas/
- **Configure a Security Context for a Pod or Container**: https://kubernetes.io/docs/tasks/configure-pod-container/security-context/

Talking to the World - APIs and
Load Balancers

7

In this chapter, we're finally going to open Delinkcious to the world and let users interact with it from outside the cluster. This is important because Delinkcious users can't access the internal services running inside the cluster. We're going to significantly expand the capabilities of Delinkcious by adding a Python-based API gateway service and expose it to the world (including social login). We'll add a gRPC-based news service that users can hit to get news about other users they follow. Finally, we will add a message queue that lets services communicate in a loosely coupled manner.

In this chapter, we will cover the following topics:

- Getting familiar with Kubernetes services
- East-west versus north-south communication
- Understanding ingress and load balancing
- Providing and consuming a public REST API
- Providing and consuming an internal gRPC API
- Sending and receiving events via a message queue
- Preparing for service meshes

Technical requirements

In this chapter, we will add a Python service to Delinkcious. There is no need to install anything new. We will build a Docker image for the Python service later.

The code

You can find the updated Delinkcious application here: `https://github.com/the-gigi/delinkcious/releases/tag/v0.5`

Getting familiar with Kubernetes services

Pods (one or more containers bundled together) are the units of work in Kubernetes. Deployments make sure that there are enough pods running. However, individual pods are ephemeral. Kubernetes services are where the action is and how you can expose your pods as a coherent service to other services in the cluster or even externally to the world. A Kubernetes service provides a stable identity and typically maps 1:1 to an application service (which may be a microservice or a traditional fat service). Let's look at all the services:

```
$ kubectl get svc
NAME                   TYPE           CLUSTER-IP       EXTERNAL-IP   PORT(S)       AGE
api-gateway            LoadBalancer   10.103.167.102   <pending>     80:31965/TCP
6m2s
kubernetes             ClusterIP      10.96.0.1        <none>        443/TCP
25m
link-db                ClusterIP      10.107.131.61    <none>        5432/TCP
8m53s
link-manager           ClusterIP      10.109.32.254    <none>        8080/TCP
8m53s
news-manager           ClusterIP      10.99.206.183    <none>        6060/TCP
7m45s
news-manager-redis     ClusterIP      None             <none>        6379/TCP
7m45s
social-graph-db        ClusterIP      10.106.164.24    <none>        5432/TCP
8m38s
social-graph-manager   ClusterIP      10.100.107.79    <none>        9090/TCP
8m37s
user-db                ClusterIP      None             <none>        5432/TCP
8m10s
user-manager           ClusterIP      10.108.45.93     <none>        7070/TCP
8m10s
```

You've seen how the Delinkcious microservices are deployed using Kubernetes services and how they can discover and call each other through the environment variables Kubernetes provides. Kubernetes also provides DNS-based discovery.

Each service can be accessed inside the cluster via the DNS name:

```
<service name>.<namespace>.svc.cluster.local
```

I prefer to use environment variables because it allows me to run the services outside of Kubernetes for testing.

Here is how to find the IP address of the `social-graph-manager` service using both environment variables and DNS:

```
$ dig +short social-graph-manager.default.svc.cluster.local
10.107.162.99

$ env | grep SOCIAL_GRAPH_MANAGER_SERVICE_HOST
SOCIAL_GRAPH_MANAGER_SERVICE_HOST=10.107.162.99
```

Kubernetes associates a service with its backing pods by specifying a label selector. For example, as shown in the following code, `news-service` is backed by pods that have the `svc: link` and `app: manager` labels:

```
spec:
  replicas: 1
  selector:
    matchLabels:
      svc: link
      app: manager
```

Then, Kubernetes manages the IP addresses of all the pods that match the label selector using an `endpoints` resource, as follows:

```
$ kubectl get endpoints
NAME                   ENDPOINTS
AGE
api-gateway            172.17.0.15:5000
1d
kubernetes             192.168.99.137:8443
51d
link-db                172.17.0.19:5432
40d
.
.
.
social-graph-db        172.17.0.16:5432
50d
social-graph-manager   172.17.0.18:9090
43d
```

The `endpoints` resource always keeps an up-to-date list of the IP addresses and ports of all the backing pods of a service. When pods are added, removed, or recreated with another IP address and port, the `endpoints` resource is updated. Now, let's see what types of services are available in Kubernetes.

Service types in Kubernetes

Kubernetes services always have a type. It's important to understand when to use each type of service. Let's go over the various service types and the differences between them:

- **ClusterIP (default)**: The ClusterIP type means that the service is only accessible inside the cluster. This is the default, and it's perfect for microservices to communicate with each other. For testing purposes, you can expose such services using `kube-proxy` or `port-forwarding`. It is also a good way to view the Kubernetes dashboard or other UIs of internal services, such as Argo CD in Delinkcious.

  If you don't specify a type of ClusterIP, set the `ClusterIP` to `None`.

- **NodePort**: A service that's of the NodePort type is exposed to the world through a dedicated port on all the nodes. You can access the service through `<Node IP>:<NodePort>`. The NodePort will be selected from a range you can control via `--service-node-port-range` to the Kubernetes API server if you run it yourself (by default, this is 30000-32767).

  You can also explicitly specify NodePort in your service definition. If you have a lot of services exposed via node ports that you specify, you'll have to manage those ports carefully to avoid conflicts. When a request comes into any node though the dedicated NodePort, the kubelet will take care of forwarding it to a node that has one of the backing pods on it (you can find it via endpoints).

- **LoadBalancer**: This type of service is most common when your Kubernetes cluster runs on a cloud platform that provides load balancer support. Although there are Kubernetes-aware load balancers for on-premise clusters too, the external load balancer will be in charge of accepting external requests and routing them through the service to the backing pods. There are often cloud provider-specific intricacies such as special annotations or having to create dual services to handle internal and external requests. We will use the LoadBalancer type to expose Delinkcious to the world of minikube, which provides a load balancer emulation.

- **ExternalName**: These services just resolve requests to the service to an externally provided DNS name. This is useful if your services need to talk to external services not running in the cluster, but you still want to be able to find them as if they were Kubernetes services. This may be useful if you plan to migrate those external services to the cluster at some point.

Now that we understand what services are all about, let's discuss the differences between cross-service communication inside the cluster and exposing services outside the cluster.

East-west versus north-south communication

East-west communication is when services/pods/containers communicate with each other inside the cluster. As you may recall, Kubernetes exposes all the services inside the cluster via both DNS and environment variables. This solves the service discovery problem inside the cluster. It is up to you to impose further restrictions via network policies or other mechanisms. For example, in `Chapter 5`, *Configuring Microservices with Kubernetes*, we established mutual authentication between the link service and the social graph service.

North-south communication is about exposing services to the world. In theory, you could expose just your services via NodePort, but this approach is beset by numerous problems, including the following:

- You have to deal with secure/encrypted transport yourself
- You can't control which pods will actually service requests
- You have to either let Kubernetes choose random ports for your services or manage port conflicts carefully
- Only one service can be exposed via each port (for example, the coveted port `80` can't be reused)

The production approved methods for exposing your services are used via an ingress controller and/or a load balancer.

Understanding ingress and load balancing

The ingress concept in Kubernetes is about controlling access to your services and potentially providing additional features, such as the following:

- SSL termination
- Authentication
- Routing to multiple services

There is an ingress resource that defines routing rules for other relevant information, and there is also an ingress controller that reads all the ingress resources defined in the cluster (across all namespaces). The ingress resource receives all the requests and routes to the target services that distribute them to the backing pods. The ingress controller serves as a cluster-wide software load balancer and router. Often, there will be a hardware load balancer that sits in front of the cluster and sends all traffic to the ingress controller.

Let's go ahead and put all of these concepts together and expose Delinkcious to the world by adding a public API gateway.

Providing and consuming a public REST API

In this section, we will build a whole new service in Python (API gateway) to demonstrate that Kubernetes is really language-agnostic. Then, we will add user authentication via OAuth2 and expose the API gateway service externally.

Building a Python-based API gateway service

The API gateway service is designed to receive all requests from outside the cluster and route them to the proper services. Here is the directory's structure:

```
$ tree
.
├── Dockerfile
├── README.md
├── api_gateway_service
│   ├── __init__.py
│   ├── api.py
│   ├── config.py
│   ├── news_client.py
│   ├── news_client_test.py
│   ├── news_pb2.py
```

```
    |        ├──── news_pb2_grpc.py
    |        └──── resources.py
    ├──── k8s
    |        ├──── api_gateway.yaml
    |        ├──── configmap.yaml
    |        └──── secrets.yaml
    ├──── requirements.txt
    ├──── run.py
    └──── tests
             └──── api_gateway_service_test.py
```

This is a little different from the Go services. The code is under the `api_gateway_service` directory, which is also a Python package. The Kubernetes resources are under the `k8s` subdirectory, and there is a `tests` subdirectory too. In the top directory, the `run.py` file is the entry point, as defined in the `Dockerfile`. The `main()` function in `run.py` invokes the `app.run()` method of the app that's imported from the `api.py` module:

```python
import os
from api_gateway_service.api import app

def main():
    port = int(os.environ.get('PORT', 5000))
    login_url = 'http://localhost:{}/login'.format(port)
    print('If you run locally, browse to', login_url)
    host = '0.0.0.0'
    app.run(host=host, port=port)

if __name__ == "__main__":
    main()
```

The `api.py` module is responsible for creating the app, hooking up the routing, and implementing social login.

Implementing social login

The `api-gateway` service utilizes several Python packages to assist in implementing social login via GitHub. Later, we will cover the user flow, but first, we will take a look at the code that implements it. The `login()` method is reaching out to GitHub and requesting authorization to the current user, who must be logged in to GitHub and give authorization to Delinkcious.

The `logout()` method just removed the access token from the current session. The `authorized()` method is getting called by GitHub as a redirect after a successful login attempt and provides an access token that is displayed for the user in their browser. This access token must be passed as a header to all future requests to the API gateway:

```
@app.route('/login')
def login():
    callback = url_for('authorized', _external=True)
    result = app.github.authorize(callback)
    return result


@app.route('/login/authorized')
def authorized():
    resp = app.github.authorized_response()
    if resp is None:
        # return 'Access denied: reason=%s error=%s' % (
        #     request.args['error'],
        #     request.args['error_description']
        # )
        abort(401, message='Access denied!')
    token = resp['access_token']
    # Must be in a list or tuple because github auth code extracts the
first
    user = app.github.get('user', token=(token,))
    user.data['access_token'] = token
    return jsonify(user.data)

@app.route('/logout')
def logout():
    session.pop('github_token', None)
    return 'OK'
```

When a user is passing a valid access token, Delinkcious can retrieve their name and email from GitHub. If the access token is missing or invalid, the request will be rejected with a 401 access denied error. This happens in the `_get_user()` function in `resources.py`:

```
def _get_user():
    """Get the user object or create it based on the token in the session

    If there is no access token abort with 401 message
    """
    if 'Access-Token' not in request.headers:
        abort(401, message='Access Denied!')

    token = request.headers['Access-Token']
    user_data = github.get('user', token=dict(access_token=token)).data
```

```
    if 'email' not in user_data:
        abort(401, message='Access Denied!')

    email = user_data['email']
    name = user_data['name']

    return name, email
```

The GitHub object is created and initialized in the `create_app()` function of the `api.py` module. First, it imports a few third-party libraries, that is, `Flask`, `OAuth`, and `Api` class:

```
import os

from flask import Flask, url_for, session, jsonify
from flask_oauthlib.client import OAuth
from flask_restful import Api, abort
from . import resources
from .resources import Link
```

Then, it initializes the `Flask` app with a GitHub `Oauth` provider:

```
def create_app():
    app = Flask(__name__)
    app.config.from_object('api_gateway_service.config')
    oauth = OAuth(app)
    github = oauth.remote_app(
        'github',
        consumer_key=os.environ['GITHUB_CLIENT_ID'],
        consumer_secret=os.environ['GITHUB_CLIENT_SECRET'],
        request_token_params={'scope': 'user:email'},
        base_url='https://api.github.com/',
        request_token_url=None,
        access_token_method='POST',
        access_token_url='https://github.com/login/oauth/access_token',
        authorize_url='https://github.com/login/oauth/authorize')
    github._tokengetter = lambda: session.get('github_token')
    resources.github = app.github = github
```

Finally, it sets the routing map and stores the initialized `app` object:

```
api = Api(app)
    resource_map = (
        (Link, '/v1.0/links'),
    )

    for resource, route in resource_map:
        api.add_resource(resource, route)
```

```
        return app


app = create_app()
```

Routing traffic to internal microservices

The main job of the API gateway service is to implement the API gateway pattern we discussed in Chapter 2, *Getting Started with Microservices*. For example, here is how it routes the get links requests to the proper method of the link microservice.

The Link class is derived from the Resource base class. It gets the host and port from the environment and constructs the base URL.

The get() method is called when a GET request for the links endpoint comes in. It extracts the username from the GitHub token in the _get_user() function and parses the query part of the request URL for the other parameter. Then, it makes its own request to the link manager service:

```
class Link(Resource):
    host = os.environ.get('LINK_MANAGER_SERVICE_HOST', 'localhost')
    port = os.environ.get('LINK_MANAGER_SERVICE_PORT', '8080')
    base_url = 'http://{}:{}/links'.format(host, port)

    def get(self):
        """Get all links

        If user doesn't exist create it (with no goals)
        """
        username, email = _get_user()
        parser = RequestParser()
        parser.add_argument('url_regex', type=str, required=False)
        parser.add_argument('title_regex', type=str, required=False)
        parser.add_argument('description_regex', type=str, required=False)
        parser.add_argument('tag', type=str, required=False)
        parser.add_argument('start_token', type=str, required=False)
        args = parser.parse_args()
        args.update(username=username)
        r = requests.get(self.base_url, params=args)

        if not r.ok:
            abort(r.status_code, message=r.content)

        return r.json()
```

Utilizing base Docker images to reduce build time

When we built Go microservices for Delinkcious, we used the scratch image as the base and just copied the Go binary. The images are super lightweight, at less than 10 MB. However, the API gateway is almost 500 MB, even when using `python:alpine`, which is much lighter than the standard Debian-based Python image:

```
$ docker images | grep g1g1.*0.3
g1g1/delinkcious-user            0.3      07bcc08b1d73    38 hours ago
6.09MB
g1g1/delinkcious-social-graph    0.3      0be0e9e55689    38 hours ago
6.37MB
g1g1/delinkcious-news            0.3      0ccd600f2190    38 hours ago
8.94MB
g1g1/delinkcious-link            0.3      9fcd7aaf9a98    38 hours ago
6.95MB
g1g1/delinkcious-api-gateway     0.3      d5778d95219d    38 hours ago
493MB
```

In addition, the API gateway needs to build some bindings to native libraries. Installing the C/C++ toolchain and then building the native libraries takes a long time (more than 15 minutes). Docker shines here with reusable layers and base images. We can put all the heavyweight stuff into a separate base image at `svc/shared/docker/python_flask_grpc/Dockerfile`:

```
FROM python:alpine
RUN apk add build-base
COPY requirements.txt /tmp
WORKDIR /tmp
RUN pip install -r requirements.txt
```

The `requirements.txt` file contains the dependencies for `Flask` applications that execute social login and need to consume a gRPC service (more on this later):

```
requests-oauthlib==1.1.0
Flask-OAuthlib==0.9.5
Flask-RESTful==0.3.7
grpcio==1.18.0
grpcio-tools==1.18.0
```

With all of this in place, we can build the base image, and then the API gateway Dockerfile can be based on it. The following is the super-simple build script at `svc/shared/docker/python_flask_grpc/build.sh` that builds the base image and pushes it to DockerHub:

```
IMAGE=g1g1/delinkcious-python-flask-grpc:0.1
docker build . -t $IMAGE
docker push $IMAGE
```

Let's take a look at the Dockerfile for the API gateway service at `svc/api_gateway_service/Dockerfile`. It is based on our base image. Then, it copies the `api_gate_service` directory, exposes the `5000` port, and executes the `run.py` script:

```
FROM g1g1/delinkcious-python-flask-grpc:0.1
MAINTAINER Gigi Sayfan "the.gigi@gmail.com"
COPY . /api_gateway_service
WORKDIR /api_gateway_service
EXPOSE 5000
ENTRYPOINT python run.py
```

The benefit is that as long as the heavy base image doesn't change, then making changes to the actual API service gateway code will result in lightning fast Docker image builds. We're talking a few seconds compared to 15 minutes. At this point, we have a nice and quick build-test-debug-deploy for the API gateway service. Now is a good time to add ingress to the cluster.

Adding ingress

On Minikube, you must enable the ingress add-on:

```
$ minikube addons enable ingress
  ingress was successfully enabled
```

On other Kubernetes clusters, you may want to install your own favorite ingress controller (such as Contour, Traefik, or Ambassador).

The following code is for the ingress manifest for the API gateway service. By using this pattern, our entire cluster will have a single ingress that funnels every request to our API gateway service, which will route it to the proper internal service:

```
apiVersion: extensions/v1beta1
kind: Ingress
metadata:
  name: api-gateway
  annotations:
```

```
      nginx.ingress.kubernetes.io/rewrite-target: /
spec:
  rules:
  - host: delinkcio.us
    http:
      paths:
      - path: /*
        backend:
          serviceName: api-gateway
          servicePort: 80
```

The single ingress service is simple and effective. On most cloud platforms, you pay per ingress resource, since a load balancer is created for each ingress resource. You can scale the number of API gateway instances easily since it is totally stateless.

 Minikube does a lot of magic under the covers with networking, simulating load balancers, and tunneling traffic. I don't recommend using Minikube to test ingress to the cluster. Instead, we will use a service of the LoadBalancer type and access it through the Minikube cluster IP.

Verifying that the API gateway is available outside the cluster

Delinkcious uses GitHub as a social login provider. You must have a GitHub account to follow along.

The user flow is as follows:

1. Find the Delinkcious URL (on Minikube, this will change frequently).
2. Log in and get an access token.
3. Hit the Delinkcious API gateway from outside the cluster.

Let's dive in and go over this in detail.

Finding the Delinkcious URL

In a production cluster, you'll have a well-known DNS name configured and a load balancer hooked up to that name. With Minikube, we can get the API gateway service URL using the following command:

```
$ minikube service api-gateway --url
http://192.168.99.138:31658
```

It's convenient to store it in an environment variable for interactive use with commands, as follows:

```
$ export DELINKCIOUS_URL=$(minikube service api-gateway --url)
```

Getting an access token

Here are the steps for getting an access token:

1. Now that we have the API gateway URL, we can browse to the login endpoint, that is, `http://192.168.99.138:31658/login`. If you're signed into your GitHub account, you'll see the following dialog box:

2. Next, if this is the first time your logging in to Delinkcious, GitHub will ask you to authorize Delinkcious to get access to your email and name:

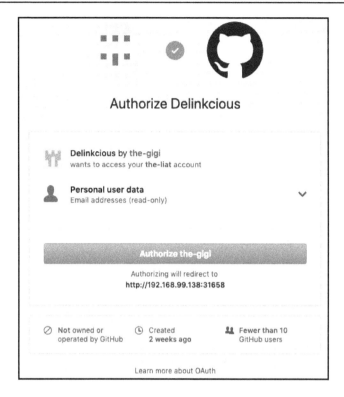

3. If you approve of this, then you'll be redirected to a page that will show you a lot of information about your GitHub profile, but, most importantly, provide you with an access token, as shown in the following screenshot:

Let's store the access token in an environment variable, too:

```
$ export DELINKCIOUS_TOKEN=def7de18d9c05ce139e37140871a9d16fd37ea9d
```

Now that we have all the information we need to access Delinkcious from the outside, let's take it for a test drive.

Hitting the Delinkcious API gateway from outside the cluster

We'll use HTTPie to hit the API gateway endpoint at `${DELINKCIOUS_URL}/v1.0/links`. To authenticate, we must provide the access token as a header, that is, `"Access-Token: ${DELINKCIOUS_TOKEN}"`.

Starting with a clean slate, let's verify that there are no links whatsoever:

```
$ http "${DELINKCIOUS_URL}/v1.0/links" "Access-Token: ${DELINKCIOUS_TOKEN}"
HTTP/1.0 200 OK
Content-Length: 27
Content-Type: application/json
Date: Mon, 04 Mar 2019 00:52:18 GMT
Server: Werkzeug/0.14.1 Python/3.7.2

{
    "err": "",
    "links": null
}
```

Alright – so far, so good. Let's add a couple of links by sending a POST request to the `/v1.0/links` endpoint. Here is the first link:

```
$ http POST "${DELINKCIOUS_URL}/v1.0/links" "Access-Token:
${DELINKCIOUS_TOKEN}" url=http://gg.com title=example
HTTP/1.0 200 OK
Content-Length: 12
Content-Type: application/json
Date: Mon, 04 Mar 2019 00:52:49 GMT
Server: Werkzeug/0.14.1 Python/3.7.2

{
    "err": ""
}
```

And here is the second link:

```
$ http POST "${DELINKCIOUS_URL}/v1.0/links" "Access-Token:
${DELINKCIOUS_TOKEN}" url=http://gg2.com title=example
HTTP/1.0 200 OK
Content-Length: 12
Content-Type: application/json
Date: Mon, 04 Mar 2019 00:52:49 GMT
Server: Werkzeug/0.14.1 Python/3.7.2

{
```

```
    "err": ""
}
```

No errors. That's great. By getting the links again, we can see the new links we just added:

```
$ http "${DELINKCIOUS_URL}/v1.0/links" "Access-Token: ${DELINKCIOUS_TOKEN}"
HTTP/1.0 200 OK
Content-Length: 330
Content-Type: application/json
Date: Mon, 04 Mar 2019 00:52:52 GMT
Server: Werkzeug/0.14.1 Python/3.7.2

{
    "err": "",
    "links": [
        {
            "CreatedAt": "2019-03-04T00:52:35Z",
            "Description": "",
            "Tags": null,
            "Title": "example",
            "UpdatedAt": "2019-03-04T00:52:35Z",
            "Url": "http://gg.com"
        },
        {
            "CreatedAt": "2019-03-04T00:52:48Z",
            "Description": "",
            "Tags": null,
            "Title": "example",
            "UpdatedAt": "2019-03-04T00:52:48Z",
            "Url": "http://gg2.com"
        }
    ]
}
```

We have successfully established an end-to-end flow, including user authentication, thus hitting a Python API gateway service that talks to a Go microservice via its internal HTTP REST API and stores information in a relational DB. Now, let's up the ante and add yet another service.

This time, it will be a Go microservice that uses a gRPC transport.

Providing and consuming an internal gRPC API

The service we will implement in this section is called the news service. Its job is to keep track of link events, such as link added or link updated, and return new events to users.

Defining the NewsManager interface

This interface exposes a single GetNews() method. Users may invoke it and receive a list of link events from users they follow. Here is the Go interface and related structs. It doesn't get much simpler: a single method with a request struct with username and token fields, as well as a result struct. The resulting struct contains a list of Event structs with the following information: EventType, Username, Url, and Timestamp:

```go
type NewsManager interface {
        GetNews(request GetNewsRequest) (GetNewsResult, error)
}

type GetNewsRequest struct {
        Username   string
        StartToken string
}

type Event struct {
        EventType EventTypeEnum
        Username  string
        Url       string
        Timestamp time.Time
}

type GetNewsResult struct {
        Events    []*Event
        NextToken string
}
```

Implementing the news manager package

The implementation of the core logic service is in pkg/news_manager. Let's take a look at the new_manager.go file. The NewsManager struct has an InMemoryNewsStore called eventStore that implements the GetNews() method for the NewsManager interface. It delegates the work of actually fetching the news to the store.

However, it is aware of pagination and takes care of converting the token from a string into an integer to match the store preferences:

```
package news_manager

import (
        "errors"
        "github.com/the-gigi/delinkcious/pkg/link_manager_events"
        om "github.com/the-gigi/delinkcious/pkg/object_model"
        "strconv"
        "time"
)

type NewsManager struct {
        eventStore *InMemoryNewsStore
}

func (m *NewsManager) GetNews(req om.GetNewsRequest) (resp
om.GetNewsResult, err error) {
        if req.Username == "" {
                err = errors.New("user name can't be empty")
                return
        }

        startIndex := 0
        if req.StartToken != "" {
                startIndex, err := strconv.Atoi(req.StartToken)
                if err != nil || startIndex < 0 {
                        err = errors.New("invalid start token: " +
req.StartToken)
                        return resp, err
                }
        }

        events, nextIndex, err := m.eventStore.GetNews(req.Username,
startIndex)
        if err != nil {
                return
        }

        resp.Events = events
        if nextIndex != -1 {
                resp.NextToken = strconv.Itoa(nextIndex)
        }

        return
}
```

The store is very basic and just keeps a map between usernames and all their events, as follows:

```
package news_manager

import (
        "errors"
        om "github.com/the-gigi/delinkcious/pkg/object_model"
)

const maxPageSize = 10

// User events are a map of username:userEvents
type userEvents map[string][]*om.Event

// InMemoryNewsStore manages a UserEvents data structure
type InMemoryNewsStore struct {
        userEvents userEvents
}

func NewInMemoryNewsStore() *InMemoryNewsStore {
        return &InMemoryNewsStore{userEvents{}}
}
```

The store implements its own GetNews() method (a different signature from the interface method). It just returns the requested slice for the target user based on the start index and the maximum page size:

```
func (m *InMemoryNewsStore) GetNews(username string, startIndex int)
(events []*om.Event, nextIndex int, err error) {
        userEvents := m.userEvents[username]
        if startIndex > len(userEvents) {
                err = errors.New("Index out of bounds")
                return
        }

        pageSize := len(userEvents) - startIndex
        if pageSize > maxPageSize {
                pageSize = maxPageSize
                nextIndex = startIndex + maxPageSize
        } else {
                nextIndex = -1
        }

        events = userEvents[startIndex : startIndex+pageSize]
        return
}
```

It also has a method for adding new events:

```
func (m *InMemoryNewsStore) AddEvent(username string, event *om.Event) (err
error) {
        if username == "" {
                err = errors.New("user name can't be empty")
                return
        }

        if event == nil {
                err = errors.New("event can't be nil")
                return
        }

        if m.userEvents[username] == nil {
                m.userEvents[username] = []*om.Event{}
        }

        m.userEvents[username] = append(m.userEvents[username], event)
        return
}
```

Now that we've implemented the core logic of storing and providing news to users, let's look at how to expose this functionality as a gRPC service.

Exposing NewsManager as a gRPC service

Before diving into the gRPC implementation of the news service, let's see what all the fuss is about. The gRPC is a collection of a wire protocol, payload format, conceptual framework, and code generation facilities for interconnecting services and applications. It originated in Google (hence the g in gRPC) and is a highly performant and mature RPC framework. It has many things going for it, such as the following:

- Cross-platform
- Wide spread adoption by industry
- Idiomatic client libraries for all relevant programming languages
- Extremely efficient wire protocols
- Google protocol buffers for strongly typed contracts
- HTTP/2 support enables bi-directional streaming
- Highly extensible (customize your own authentication, authorization, load balancing, and health checking)
- Excellent documentation

The bottom line is that for internal microservices, it is superior in almost every way to HTTP-based REST APIs.

For Delinkcious, it's a great fit because Go-kit, which we selected as our microservice framework, has great support for gRPC.

Defining the gRPC service contract

gRPC requires that you define a contract for your service in a special DSL inspired by protocol buffers. It is pretty intuitive and lets gRPC generate a lot of boilerplate code for you. I chose to locate the contract and the generated code in a separate top-level directory called **pb** (common short name for **protocol buffers**) because different parts of the generated code will be used by services and consumers. In these cases, it is often best to put the shared code in a separate location and not arbitrarily throw it into the service or the client.

Here is the pb/new-service/pb/news.proto file:

```
syntax = "proto3";
package pb;

import "google/protobuf/timestamp.proto";

service News {
    rpc GetNews(GetNewsRequest) returns (GetNewsResponse) {}
}

message GetNewsRequest {
    string username = 1;
    string startToken = 2;
}

enum EventType {
    LINK_ADDED = 0;
    LINK_UPDATED = 1;
    LINK_DELETED = 2;
}

message Event  {
        EventType eventType = 1;
        string username = 2;
        string url = 3;
        google.protobuf.Timestamp timestamp = 4;
}
```

```
message GetNewsResponse {
        repeated Event events = 1;
        string nextToken = 2;
    string err = 3;
}
```

We don't need to go over the syntax and meaning of each and every line. The short version is that requests and responses are always messages. Service-level errors need to be embedded in the response message. Other errors, such as network or invalid payloads, will be reported separately. One interesting tidbit is that, in addition to primitive data types and embedded messages, you can use other high-level types, such as the `google.protobuf.Timestamp` data type. This elevates the abstraction level significantly and brings the benefits of strong typing for things such as dates and timestamps that you always have to serialize and deserialize yourself when working with JSON over HTTP/REST.

The service definition is cool, but we need some actual code to connect the dots. Let's see how gRPC can help with this task.

Generating service stubs and client libraries with gRPC

The gRPC model is used to generate both service stubs and client libraries using a tool called `protoc`. We need to generate both Go code for the news service itself and Python code for the API gateway that consumes it.

You can generate `news.pb.go` by running the following command:

```
protoc --go_out=plugins=grpc:. news.proto
```

You can generate `news_pb2.py` and `news_pb2_grpc.py` by running the following command:

```
python -m grpc_tools.protoc -I. --python_out=. --grpc_python_out=. news.proto
```

At this point, both the Go client code and Python client code can be used to call the news service from Go code or from Python code.

Using Go-kit to build the NewsManager service

Here is the implementation of the service itself in `news_service.go`. It looks very similar to an HTTP service. Let's dissect the important sections. First, it imports some libraries, including the generated gRPC code in `pb/news-service-pb`, `pkg/news_manager`, and a general gRPC library called `google.golang.org/grpc`. At the beginning of the `Run()` function, it gets the `service` port to listen from the environment:

```
package service

import (
        "fmt"
        "github.com/the-gigi/delinkcious/pb/news_service/pb"
        nm "github.com/the-gigi/delinkcious/pkg/news_manager"
        "google.golang.org/grpc"
        "log"
        "net"
        "os"
)

func Run() {
        port := os.Getenv("PORT")
        if port == "" {
                port = "6060"
        }
```

Now, we need to create a standard TCP listener on the target port:

```
listener, err := net.Listen("tcp", ":"+port)
        if err != nil {
                log.Fatal(err)
        }
```

Furthermore, we have to connect to a NATS message queue service. We'll discuss this in detail in the next section:

```
natsHostname := os.Getenv("NATS_CLUSTER_SERVICE_HOST")
        natsPort := os.Getenv("NATS_CLUSTER_SERVICE_PORT")
```

Here comes the main initialization code. It instantiates a new news manager, creates a new gRPC server, creates a news manager object, and registers the news manager with the gRPC server. The `pb.RegisterNewsManager()` method was generated by gRPC from the `news.proto` file:

```
svc, err := nm.NewNewsManager(natsHostname, natsPort)
        if err != nil {
                log.Fatal(err)
```

```
        }

        gRPCServer := grpc.NewServer()
        newsServer := newNewsServer(svc)
        pb.RegisterNewsServer(gRPCServer, newsServer)
```

Finally, the gRPC server starts listening on the TCP listener:

```
fmt.Printf("News service is listening on port %s...\n", port)
        err = gRPCServer.Serve(listener)
        fmt.Println("Serve() failed", err)
}
```

Implementing the gRPC transport

The last piece of the puzzle is implementing the gRPC transport in the `transport.go` file.
It is similar, conceptually, to the HTTP transport, but there are a few details that are
different. Let's break it down so it's clear how all the pieces fit together.

First, all the relevant packages are imported, including the gRPC transport from go-kit.
Note that in `news_service.go`, there is no mention of go-kit anywhere. You can definitely
implement a gRPC service directly in Go with the general gRPC libraries. However, here,
go-kit will help make this much easier via its service and endpoints concepts:

```
package service

import (
        "context"
        "github.com/go-kit/kit/endpoint"
        grpctransport "github.com/go-kit/kit/transport/grpc"
        "github.com/golang/protobuf/ptypes/timestamp"
        "github.com/the-gigi/delinkcious/pb/news_service/pb"
        om "github.com/the-gigi/delinkcious/pkg/object_model"
)
```

The `newEvent()` function is a helper that adopts `om.Event` from our abstract object model
to the gRPC-generated event object. The most important part is translating the event type
and the timestamp:

```
func newEvent(e *om.Event) (event *pb.Event) {
        event = &pb.Event{
                EventType: (pb.EventType)(e.EventType),
                Username:  e.Username,
                Url:       e.Url,
        }
```

```
        seconds := e.Timestamp.Unix()
        nanos := (int32(e.Timestamp.UnixNano() - 1e9*seconds))
        event.Timestamp = &timestamp.Timestamp{Seconds: seconds, Nanos:
nanos}
        return
}
```

Decoding the request and encoding the response is pretty trivial – there's no need to serialize or deserialize any JSON code:

```
func decodeGetNewsRequest(_ context.Context, r interface{}) (interface{},
error) {
        request := r.(*pb.GetNewsRequest)
        return om.GetNewsRequest{
                Username:   request.Username,
                StartToken: request.StartToken,
        }, nil
}

func encodeGetNewsResponse(_ context.Context, r interface{}) (interface{},
error) {
        return r, nil
}
```

Creating the endpoint is similar to the HTTP transport you've seen with other services. It invokes the actual service implementation and then translates the response and handles errors, if there are any:

```
func makeGetNewsEndpoint(svc om.NewsManager) endpoint.Endpoint {
        return func(_ context.Context, request interface{}) (interface{},
error) {
                req := request.(om.GetNewsRequest)
                r, err := svc.GetNews(req)
                res := &pb.GetNewsResponse{
                        Events:    []*pb.Event{},
                        NextToken: r.NextToken,
                }
                if err != nil {
                        res.Err = err.Error()
                }
                for _, e := range r.Events {
                        event := newEvent(e)
                        res.Events = append(res.Events, event)
                }
                return res, nil
        }
}
```

The handler implements the gRPC news interface from the code generated:

```
type handler struct {
        getNews grpctransport.Handler
}


func (s *handler) GetNews(ctx context.Context, r *pb.GetNewsRequest)
(*pb.GetNewsResponse, error) {
        _, resp, err := s.getNews.ServeGRPC(ctx, r)
        if err != nil {
                return nil, err
        }

        return resp.(*pb.GetNewsResponse), nil
}
```

The `newNewsServer()` function ties everything together. It returns a gRPC handler wrapped in a Go-kit handler that hooks up the endpoint, the request decoder, and the response encoder:

```
func newNewsServer(svc om.NewsManager) pb.NewsServer {
        return &handler{
                getNews: grpctransport.NewServer(
                        makeGetNewsEndpoint(svc),
                        decodeGetNewsRequest,
                        encodeGetNewsResponse,
                ),
        }
}
```

This may seem very confusing, with all the layers and nested functions, but the bottom line is that you have to write very little glue code (and can generate it, which is ideal) and end up with a very clean, safe (strongly typed), and efficient gRPC service.

Now that we have a gRPC news service that can serve the news, let's see how we can feed it the news.

Sending and receiving events via a message queue

The news service needs to store link events for each user. The link service knows when links are added, updated, or deleted by different users. One approach to solve this problem is to add another API to the news service and have the link service invoke this API and notify the news service for each relevant event. However, this approach creates a tight coupling between the link service and the news service. The link service doesn't really care about the news service since it doesn't need anything from it. Instead, let's go for a loosely-coupled solution. The link service will just send events to a general-purpose message queue service. Then, independently, the news service will subscribe to receive messages from that messages queue. There are several benefits to this approach, as follows:

- No need for more complicated service code
- Fits perfectly with the interaction model of event notification
- Easy to add additional listeners to the same events without changing the code

The terms that I used here, that is, *message*, *event*, and *notification*, are interchangeable. The idea is that a source has some information to share with the world in a fire-and-forget way.

It doesn't need to know who is interested in the information (this could be nobody or multiple listeners) and whether it was processed successfully. Delinkcious uses the NATS messaging system for loosely coupled communication between services.

What is NATS?

NATS (https://nats.io/) is an open source message queue service. It is a **Cloud Native Computing Foundation** (**CNCF**) project that's implemented in Go and is considered one of the top contenders when you need a message queue in Kubernetes. NATS supports multiple models of message passing, such as the following:

- Publish-subscribe
- Request-reply
- Queueing

NATS is very versatile and can be used for many use cases. It can also run in a highly available cluster. For Delinkcious, we will use the publish-subscribe model. The following diagram illustrates the pub-sub message passing model. A publisher publishes a message and all the subscribers receive the same message:

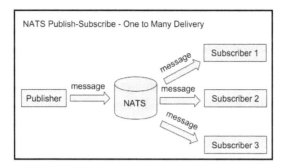

Let's deploy NATS in our cluster.

Deploying NATS in the cluster

First, let's install the NATS operator (`https://github.com/nats-io/nats-operator`). The NATS operator helps you to manage NATS clusters in Kubernetes. Here are the commands to install it:

```
$ kubectl apply -f
https://github.com/nats-io/nats-operator/releases/download/v0.4.5/00-prereq
s.yaml
$ kubectl apply -f
https://github.com/nats-io/nats-operator/releases/download/v0.4.5/10-deploy
ment.yaml
```

The NATS operator provides a NatsCluster **Custom Resource Definition** (**CRD**) that we will use to deploy NATS in our Kubernetes cluster. Don't get confused by this NATS cluster within the Kubernetes cluster relationship. This is really nice since we can deploy the NATS cluster just like built-in Kubernetes resources. Here is the YAML manifest that's available in `svc/shared/k8s/nats_cluster.yaml`:

```
apiVersion: nats.io/v1alpha2
kind: NatsCluster
metadata:
  name: nats-cluster
spec:
  size: 1
  version: "1.3.0"
```

Let's deploy it using `kubectl` and verify that it was deployed properly:

```
$ kubectl apply -f nats_cluster.yaml
natscluster.nats.io "nats-cluster" configured
```

```
$ kubectl get svc -l app=nats
NAME                 TYPE        CLUSTER-IP     EXTERNAL-IP    PORT(S)    AGE
nats-cluster         ClusterIP   10.102.48.27   <none>         4222/TCP   5d
nats-cluster-mgmt    ClusterIP   None           <none>
6222/TCP,8222/TCP,7777/TCP    5d
```

This looks good. The `nats-cluster` service listening on port `4222` is the NATS server. The other service is a management service. Let's send some events to the NATS server.

Sending link events with NATS

As you may recall, we defined a `LinkManagerEvents` interface in our object model:

```
type LinkManagerEvents interface {
        OnLinkAdded(username string, link *Link)
        OnLinkUpdated(username string, link *Link)
        OnLinkDeleted(username string, url string)
}
```

The `LinkManager` package receives this event link in its `NewLinkManager()` method:

```
func NewLinkManager(linkStore LinkStore,
        socialGraphManager om.SocialGraphManager,
        eventSink om.LinkManagerEvents,
        maxLinksPerUser int64) (om.LinkManager, error) {
        if linkStore == nil {
                return nil, errors.New("link store")
        }

        if eventSink != nil && socialGraphManager == nil {
                msg := "social graph manager can't be nil if event sink is
not nil"
                return nil, errors.New(msg)
        }

        return &LinkManager{
                linkStore:          linkStore,
                socialGraphManager: socialGraphManager,
                eventSink:          eventSink,
                maxLinksPerUser:    maxLinksPerUser,
        }, nil
}
```

Later, when a link is added, updated, or deleted, `LinkManager` will call the corresponding `OnLinkXXX()` method. For example, when `AddLink()` is called, the `OnLinkAdded()` method is called on the sink for each follower:

```
if m.eventSink != nil {
                followers, err :=
m.socialGraphManager.GetFollowers(request.Username)
                if err != nil {
                        return err
                }

                for follower := range followers {
                        m.eventSink.OnLinkAdded(follower, link)
                }
        }
```

This is great, but how are these events going to get to the NATS server? That's where the link service comes into the picture. When instantiating the `LinkManager` object, it will pass a dedicated event sender object as the sink that implements `LinkManagerEvents`. Whenever it receives an event such as `OnLinkAdded()` or `OnLinkUpdated()`, it publishes the event to the NATS server on the `link-events` subject. It ignores the `OnLinkDeleted()` event for now. This object lives in `pkg/link_manager_events` package/`sender.go`:

```
package link_manager_events

import (
        "github.com/nats-io/go-nats"
        "log"

        om "github.com/the-gigi/delinkcious/pkg/object_model"
)

type eventSender struct {
        hostname string
        nats     *nats.EncodedConn
}
```

Here is the implementation of the `OnLinkAdded()`, `OnLinkUpdated()`, and `OnLinkDeleted()` methods:

```
func (s *eventSender) OnLinkAdded(username string, link *om.Link) {
        err := s.nats.Publish(subject, Event{om.LinkAdded, username, link})
        if err != nil {
                log.Fatal(err)
        }
```

```
}

func (s *eventSender) OnLinkUpdated(username string, link *om.Link) {
        err := s.nats.Publish(subject, Event{om.LinkUpdated, username,
link})
        if err != nil {
                log.Fatal(err)
        }
}

func (s *eventSender) OnLinkDeleted(username string, url string) {
        // Ignore link delete events
}
```

The NewEventSender() factory function accepts the URL of the NATS service it will send
the events to and returns a LinkManagerEvents interface that can serve as a sink for
LinkManager:

```
func NewEventSender(url string) (om.LinkManagerEvents, error) {
        ec, err := connect(url)
        if err != nil {
                return nil, err
        }
        return &eventSender{hostname: url, nats: ec}, nil
}
```

Now, all the link service has to do is figure out the URL for the NATS server. Since the
NATS server runs as a Kubernetes service, its hostname and port are available through
environment variables, just like the Delinkcious microservices. The following is the relevant
code from the Run() function of the link service:

```
natsHostname := os.Getenv("NATS_CLUSTER_SERVICE_HOST")
        natsPort := os.Getenv("NATS_CLUSTER_SERVICE_PORT")

        var eventSink om.LinkManagerEvents
        if natsHostname != "" {
                natsUrl := natsHostname + ":" + natsPort
                eventSink, err = nats.NewEventSender(natsUrl)
                if err != nil {
                        log.Fatal(err)
                }
        } else {
                eventSink = &EventSink{}
        }

        svc, err := lm.NewLinkManager(store, socialGraphClient, eventSink,
maxLinksPerUser)
```

```
if err != nil {
        log.Fatal(err)
}
```

At this point, whenever a new link is added or updated for a user, `LinkManager` will invoke the `OnLinkAdded()` or `OnLinkUpdated()` method for each of the followers, which will result in that event being sent to the NATS server on the `link-events` topic, where all the subscribers will receive it and can handle it. The next step is for the news service to subscribe to these events.

Subscribing to link events with NATS

The news service uses the `Listen()` function from `pkg/link_manager_events/listener.go`. It accepts the NATS server URL and an event sink that implements the `LinkManagerEvents` interface. It connects to the NATS server and then subscribes to the `link-events` subject. This is the same subject that the event sender is sending those events to:

```
package link_manager_events

import (
        om "github.com/the-gigi/delinkcious/pkg/object_model"
)

func Listen(url string, sink om.LinkManagerEvents) (err error) {
        conn, err := connect(url)
        if err != nil {
                return
        }

        conn.Subscribe(subject, func(e *Event) {
                switch e.EventType {
                case om.LinkAdded:
                        {
                                sink.OnLinkAdded(e.Username, e.Link)
                        }
                case om.LinkUpdated:
                        {
                                sink.OnLinkAdded(e.Username, e.Link)
                        }
                default:
                        // Ignore other event types
                }
        })
```

```
        return
}
```

Now, let's look at the `nats.go` file that defines the `link-events` subject, as well as the `connect()` function that's used by both the event sender and the `Listen()` function. The connect function uses the `go-nats` client to establish a connection and then wraps it with a JSON encoder, which allows it to send and receive Go structs that get serialized automatically. This is pretty neat:

```
package link_manager_events

import "github.com/nats-io/go-nats"


const subject = "link-events"

func connect(url string) (encodedConn *nats.EncodedConn, err error) {
        conn, err := nats.Connect(url)
        if err != nil {
                return
        }

        encodedConn, err = nats.NewEncodedConn(conn, nats.JSON_ENCODER)
        return
}
```

The news service calls the `Listen()` function in its `NewNewsManager()` factory function. First, it instantiates the news manager object that implements `LinkManagerEvents`. Then, if composes a NATS server URL if a NATS hostname was provided and calls the `Listen()` function, thereby passing the news manager object as the sink:

```
func NewNewsManager(natsHostname string, natsPort string) (om.NewsManager,
error) {
        nm := &NewsManager{eventStore: NewInMemoryNewsStore()}
        if natsHostname != "" {
                natsUrl := natsHostname + ":" + natsPort
                err := link_manager_events.Listen(natsUrl, nm)
                if err != nil {
                        return nil, err
                }
        }

        return nm, nil
}
```

The next step is to do something with the incoming events.

Handling link events

The news manager was subscribed to link events by the `NewNewsManager()` function, and the result is that those events will arrive as calls on `OnLinkAdded()` and `OnlinkUpdated()` (delete link events are ignored). The news manager creates an `Event` object that's defined in the abstract object model, populates it with `EventType`, `Username`, `Url`, and `Timestamp`, and then calls the event store's `AddEvent()` function. Here is the `OnLinkAdded()` method:

```
func (m *NewsManager) OnLinkAdded(username string, link *om.Link) {
        event := &om.Event{
                EventType: om.LinkAdded,
                Username:  username,
                Url:       link.Url,
                Timestamp: time.Now().UTC(),
        }
        m.eventStore.AddEvent(username, event)
}
```

Here is the `OnLinkUpdated()` method:

```
func (m *NewsManager) OnLinkUpdated(username string, link *om.Link) {
        event := &om.Event{
                EventType: om.LinkUpdated,
                Username:  username,
                Url:       link.Url,
                Timestamp: time.Now().UTC(),
        }
        m.eventStore.AddEvent(username, event)
}
```

Let's see what the store does in its `AddEvent()` method. It's pretty simple: the subscribed user is located in the `userEvents` map. If they don't exist yet, then an empty entry is created and the new event added. If the target user calls `GetNews()`, they'll receive the events that have been collected for them:

```
func (m *InMemoryNewsStore) AddEvent(username string, event *om.Event) (err
error) {
        if username == "" {
                err = errors.New("user name can't be empty")
                return
        }
        if event == nil {
                err = errors.New("event can't be nil")
                return
        }
```

```
        if m.userEvents[username] == nil {
                m.userEvents[username] = []*om.Event{}
        }
        m.userEvents[username] = append(m.userEvents[username], event)
        return
}
```

That concludes our coverage of the news service and its interactions with the link manager via the NATS service. This is an application of the **command query responsibility segregation** (**CQRS**) pattern we discussed in Chapter 2, *Getting Started with Microservices*. Here is what the Delinkcious system looks like now:

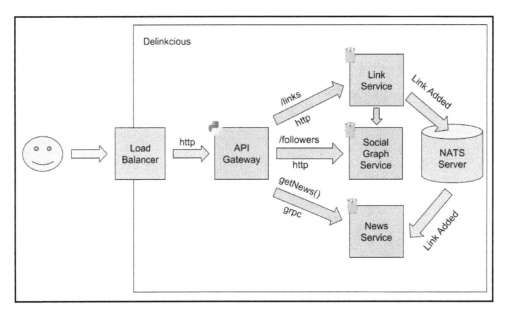

Now that we understand how events are handled in Delinkcious, let's take a quick look at service meshes.

Understanding service meshes

A service mesh is another layer of management that's running in your cluster. We will look into service meshes and Istio in particular in Chapter 13, *Service Mesh – Working with Istio*. At this point, I just want to mention that a service mesh often takes the role of the ingress controller too.

One of the primary reasons to use a service mesh for ingress is that the built-in ingress resource, being very generic, is limited and suffers from multiple issues, such as the following:

- No good way to validate the rules
- Ingress resources can conflict with one other
- Working with specific ingress controllers is often complicated and requires custom annotations

Summary

In this chapter, we accomplished many tasks and connected all the dots. In particular, we implemented two microservices design patterns (API gateway and CQRS), added a whole new service implemented in Python (including a split Docker base image), added a gRPC service, added an open source message queue system (NATS) to our cluster and integrated it with pub-sub message passing, and, finally, opened up our cluster to the world and demonstrated end-to-end interaction by adding and fetching links from Delinkcious.

At this point, Delinkcious can be considered Alpha-grade software. It's functional, but not even close to production ready. In the next chapter, we will start making Delinkcious more robust by taking care of the most valuable commodity of any software system – the data. Kubernetes provides many facilities for managing data and stateful services that we will put to good use.

Further reading

You can refer to the following sources for more information regarding what was covered in this chapter:

- **The Kubernetes service**: `https://kubernetes.io/docs/concepts/services-networking/service/`
- **Exposing your app as a service**: `https://kubernetes.io/docs/tutorials/kubernetes-basics/expose/expose-intro/`
- **Building Oauth apps**: `https://developer.github.com/apps/building-oauth-apps/`
- **High-performance gRPC**: `https://grpc.io/`
  `http://www.devx.com/architect/high-performance-services-with-grpc.html`
- **NATS message broker**: `https://nats.io/`

Working with Stateful Services

8

So far, everything was fun and games. We built services, deployed them to Kubernetes, and ran commands and queries against these services. We enabled Kubernetes to have those services up and running by scheduling pods on deployment or if anything went wrong. This works great for stateless services that can just run anywhere. In the real world, distributed systems manage important data. If a database stores its data on the host filesystem and that host goes down, you (or Kubernetes) can't just start a fresh instance of the database on a new node because the data will be lost.

In general, you keep your data from getting lost by redundancy; you keep multiple copies, store backups, utilize append-only logs, and more. Kubernetes assists by providing a whole storage model with concepts and related resources, such as volumes, volume claims, and StatefulSets.

In this chapter, we will dive deeper into the Kubernetes storage model. We will also extend the Delinkcious news service to store its data in Redis instead of in memory. We will cover the following topics:

- Abstracting storage
- Storing data outside your Kubernetes cluster
- Storing data inside your Kubernetes cluster with StatefulSets
- Achieving high performance with local storage
- Using relational databases in Kubernetes
- Using non-relational data stores in Kubernetes

Technical requirements

In this chapter, we will examine a number of Kubernetes manifests, work with different storage options, and extend Delinkcious to support a new data store. There is no need to install anything new.

The code

The code is split between two Git repositories, as follows:

- You can find the code samples at `https://github.com/PacktPublishing/Hands-On-Microservices-with-Kubernetes/tree/master/Chapter08`
- You can find the updated Delinkcious application at `https://github.com/the-gigi/delinkcious/releases/tag/v0.6`

Abstracting storage

At its core, Kubernetes is an orchestration engine used for managing containerized workloads. Note that, here, the keyword is *containerized*. Kubernetes doesn't care what the workloads are as long as they are packaged in containers; it knows how to handle them. Initially, Kubernetes only supported Docker images, and then, later, it added support for other runtimes. Then, Kubernetes 1.5 introduced the **Container Runtime Interface** (**CRI**), and gradually pushed the explicit support for other runtimes out of tree. Here, Kubernetes no longer cared about which container runtime was actually deployed on the nodes and just needed to work with the CRI.

A similar story unfolded with networking, where the **Container Networking Interface** (**CNI**) was defined early. The life of Kubernetes was simple. It was left to different networking solutions to provide their CNI plugins. Storage, however, was different (until it wasn't). In the following subsections, we'll go over the Kubernetes storage model, understand the differences between in-tree and out-of-tree storage plugins, and, finally, learn about the **Container Storage Interface** (**CSI**), which provides a neat solution for storage in Kubernetes.

The Kubernetes storage model

The Kubernetes storage model consists of several concepts: storage classes, volumes, persistent volumes, and persistent volume claims. Let's examine how these concepts interact to allow containerized workloads access to storage during execution.

Storage classes

The storage class is a way of describing the available types of storage that can be provisioned. Often, there is a default storage class that is used when provisioning a volume without specifying a particular storage class. Here is the standard storage class in Minikube, which stores data on the host (that is, the hosting node):

```
$ kubectl get storageclass
NAME PROVISIONER AGE
standard (default) k8s.io/minikube-hostpath 65d
```

Different storage classes have different parameters tied to the actual backing storage. Volume provisioners know how to use the parameters of their storage classes. The storage class metadata includes the provisioner, as follows:

```
$ kubectl get storageclass -o jsonpath='{.items[0].provisioner}'
k8s.io/minikube-hostpath
```

Volumes, persistent volumes, and provisioning

A volume in Kubernetes has an explicit lifetime that coincides with its pod. When the pod goes away, so does the storage. There are many types of volumes that are very useful. We've already seen a few examples, such as ConfigMap and secret volumes. But there are other volume types that are used for reading and writing.

 You can take a look at the full list of volume types here: `https://kubernetes.io/docs/concepts/storage/volumes/#types-of-volumes`.

Kubernetes also supports the concept of persistent volumes. These volumes must be provisioned by system administrators, and they are not managed by Kubernetes itself. When you want to store data persistently, then you use persistent volumes. Administrators can statically provision persistent volumes ahead of time. The process involves administrators provisioning external storage and creating a `PersistentVolume` Kubernetes object that users can consume.

Dynamic provisioning is the process of creating volumes on the fly. Users request storage and this is created dynamically. Dynamic provisioning depends on storage classes. Users can specify a particular storage class, otherwise, the default storage class (if it exists) will be used. All Kubernetes cloud providers support dynamic provisioning. Minikube supports it too (the backing store is the localhost filesystem).

Persistent volume claims

So, the cluster administrator either provisions some persistent volumes or, alternatively, the cluster supports dynamic provisioning. We can now claim some storage for our workload by creating a persistent volume claim. But, first, it's important to understand the difference between ephemeral and persistent storage. We'll create an ephemeral file in a pod, restart the pod, and check that the file vanished. Then, we'll do the same thing again, but, this time, write the file to the persistent storage and check that the file still exists once the pod is restarted.

Before we start, let me share some convenient shell functions and aliases that I created in order to quickly launch an interactive session in specific pods. A Kubernetes deployment generates random pod names. For example, for the `trouble` deployment, the current pod name is `trouble-6785b4949b-84x22`:

```
$ kubectl get po | grep trouble
trouble-6785b4949b-84x22     1/1 Running   1     2h
```

This is not a very memorable name, and it also changes whenever the pod is restarted (automatically by the deployment). Unfortunately, the `kubectl exec` command requires an exact pod name to run commands. I created a little shell function called `get_pod_name_by_label()`, which returns a pod name based on a label. Since labels from the pod template don't change, this is a good way to discover pod names. However, there may be multiple pods from the same deployment with the same labels. We just need any kind of pod, so we can simply pick the first. Here is the function, and I aliased it to `kpn` so that it's easier to use:

```
get_pod_name_by_label ()
 {
 kubectl get po -l $1 -o custom-columns=NAME:.metadata.name | tail +2 |
uniq
 }

alias kpn='get_pod_name_by_label'
```

For example, the `trouble` deployment pods can have a label called `run=trouble`. Here is how to find the actual pod name:

```
$ get_pod_name_by_label run=trouble
trouble-6785b4949b-84x22
```

Using this function, I created an alias called `trouble`, which launches an interactive bash session in the `trouble` pod:

```
$ alias trouble='kubectl exec -it $(get_pod_name_by_label run=trouble)
bash'
```

Now, we can connect to the `trouble` pod and start working in it:

```
$ trouble
root@trouble-6785b4949b-84x22:/#
```

This was a long digression, but it's a very useful technique. Now, let's get back to our plan and create an ephemeral file, as follows:

```
root@trouble-6785b4949b-84x22:/# echo "life is short" > life.txt
root@trouble-6785b4949b-84x22:/# cat life.txt
life is short
```

Now, let's kill the pod. The `trouble` deployment will schedule a new `trouble` pod, as follows:

```
$ kubectl delete pod $(get_pod_name_by_label run=trouble)
pod "trouble-6785b4949b-84x22" deleted

$ get_pod_name_by_label run=trouble
trouble-6785b4949b-n6cmj
```

When we access the new pod, we discover that `life.txt` vanished as expected:

```
$ trouble
root@trouble-6785b4949b-n6cmj:/# cat life.txt
cat: life.txt: No such file or directory
```

That's understandable because it was stored in the filesystem of the container. The next step is to have the `trouble` pod claim some persistent storage. Here is a persistent volume claim that provisions one gibibyte dynamically:

```
apiVersion: v1
kind: PersistentVolumeClaim
metadata:
  name: some-storage
spec:
  accessModes:
  - ReadWriteOnce
  resources:
    requests:
      storage: 1Gi
  volumeMode: Filesystem
```

Here is the YAML manifest for the entire `trouble` deployment that consumes this claim as a volume and mounts it to the container:

```
---
apiVersion: apps/v1
kind: Deployment
metadata:
  name: trouble
  labels:
     run: trouble
spec:
  replicas: 1
  selector:
    matchLabels:
       run: trouble
  template:
    metadata:
      labels:
         run: trouble
    spec:
      containers:
      - name: trouble
        image: g1g1/py-kube:0.2
        imagePullPolicy: Always
        command: ["/bin/bash", "-c", "while true ; do sleep 10 ; done"]
        volumeMounts:
        - name: keep-me
          mountPath: "/data"
      imagePullSecrets:
      - name: private-dockerhub
      volumes:
      - name: keep-me
        persistentVolumeClaim:
           claimName: some-storage
```

The `keep-me` volume is based on the `some-storage` persistent volume claim:

```
volumes:
- name: keep-me
  persistentVolumeClaim:
    claimName: some-storage
```

The volume is mounted to the `/data` directory inside the container:

```
volumeMounts:
- name: keep-me
  mountPath: "/data"
```

Now, let's write something to `/data`, as follows:

```
$ trouble
root@trouble-64554479d-tszlb:/# ls /data
root@trouble-64554479d-tszlb:/# cd /data/
root@trouble-64554479d-tszlb:/data# echo "to infinity and be-yond!" >
infinity.txt
root@trouble-64554479d-tszlb:/data# cat infinity.txt
to infinity and beyond!
```

The final state is to delete the pod and, when a new pod is created, verify whether the `infinity.txt` file is still in `/data`:

```
$ kubectl delete pod trouble-64554479d-tszlb
pod "trouble-64554479d-tszlb" deleted

$ trouble
root@trouble-64554479d-mpl24:/# cat /data/infinity.txt
to infinity and beyond!
```

Yay, it works! A new pod was created and the persistent storage with the `infinity.txt` file was mounted to the new container.

Persistent volumes can also be used to share information directly between multiple instances of the same image because the same persistence storage will be mounted to all containers using the same persistent storage claim.

In-tree and out-of-tree storage plugins

There are two types of storage plugins: in-tree and out-of-tree. In-tree means that these storage plugins are part of Kubernetes itself. In the volume clause, you refer to them by name. For example, here, a **Google Compute Engine** (**GCE**) persistent disk is configured by name. Kubernetes explicitly knows that such a volume has fields such as `pdName` and `fsType`:

```
volumes:
  - name: test-volume
    gcePersistentDisk:
      pdName: my-data-disk
      fsType: ext4
```

Take a look at the complete list of in-tree storage plugins at: `https://kubernetes.io/docs/concepts/storage/persistent-volumes/#types-of-persistent-volumes`.

There are several other specialized volume types, such as `emptyDir`, `local`, `downwardAPI`, and `hostPath`, that you can read more about. The concept of in-tree plugins is somewhat cumbersome. It bloats Kubernetes and requires changing Kubernetes itself whenever a provider wants to improve their storage plugin or introduce a new one.

This is where out-of-tree plugins come into the picture. The idea is that Kubernetes defines a standard storage interface and a standard way of providing plugins to implement the interface in a running cluster. Then, it's the job of the cluster administrator to make sure that the proper out-of-tree plugins are available.

There are two types of out-of-tree plugins that Kubernetes supports: FlexVolume and CSI. FlexVolume is old and deprecated. I will not go into detail about FlexVolume, except to recommend that you don't use it.

 For more detail, you can refer to the following link: `https://kubernetes.io/docs/concepts/storage/volumes/#flexVolume`

The big star of storage is the CSI. Let's drill down and understand how CSI works and what a huge improvement it is.

Understanding CSI

CSI was designed to address all the issues with in-tree plugins and the cumbersome aspects of FlexVolume plugins. What makes CSI so enticing to storage providers is that it is not a Kubernetes-only standard, but an industry-wide standard. It allows storage providers to write a single driver for their storage solution and become immediately compatible with a broad range of container orchestration platforms such as Docker, Cloud Foundry, Mesos, and, of course, Kubernetes.

 You can find the official specification at `https://github.com/container-storage-interface/spec`.

The Kubernetes team provides three components that are sidecar containers and provide generic CSI support for any CSI storage provider. These components are as follows:

- Driver registrar
- External provisioner
- External attacher

Their job is to interface with the kubelet as well as the API server. The storage provider will typically package these sidecar containers along with their storage driver implementation in a single pod that can be deployed as a Kubernetes DaemonSet on all nodes.

Here is a diagram that demonstrates the interaction between all the pieces:

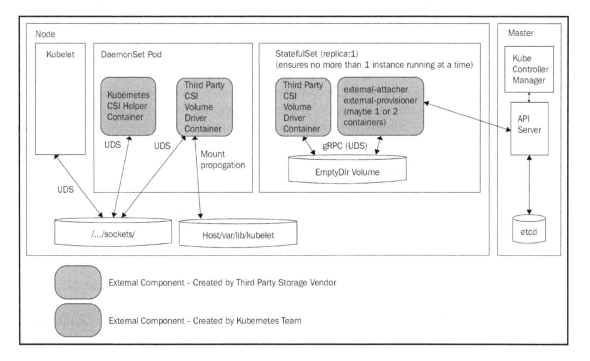

It is pretty complicated, but this complication is necessary to separate concerns, allow the Kubernetes team to do a lot of the heavy lifting, and leave storage providers to focus on their storage solution. As far as users and developers are concerned, this is all completely transparent. They continue to interact with storage through the same Kubernetes storage abstractions of storage classes, volumes, and persistent volume claims.

Standardizing on CSI

CSI is superior to in-tree plugins (and FlexVolume plugins). However, the current situation of a hybrid, where you can use either in-tree plugins (or FlexVolume plugins) or CSI plugins is suboptimal. The Kubernetes team has a detailed plan to migrate in-tree plugins to CSI.

 You can find out more about this detailed plan at `https://github.com/` `kubernetes/community/blob/master/contributors/design-proposals/` `storage/csi-migration.md`.

Storing data outside your Kubernetes cluster

Kubernetes is not a closed system. Workloads running inside a Kubernetes cluster can access storage running outside the cluster. This is most appropriate when you migrate an existing application that is already in storage, and configured and operated outside of Kubernetes. In this case, it is a wise move to do it gradually. First, move the workloads to run as containers managed by Kubernetes. These containers will be configured with endpoints to data stores that live outside the cluster. Later, you can consider whether it is worth the effort to bring this external storage into the fold.

There are some other use cases where it makes sense to use out-of-cluster storage, such as the following:

- Your storage cluster uses some exotic hardware, or the networking doesn't have a mature in-tree or CSI plugin (hopefully, as CSI becomes the gold standard, this will become rare).
- You run Kubernetes through a cloud provider and it's going to be too expensive, too risky, and/or too slow to migrate all the data.
- Other applications in your organization use the same storage cluster and it is often impractical and non-economical to migrate all the applications and systems in your organization to Kubernetes.
- Due to regulatory requirements, you must retain control of your data.

There are several downsides to managing storage outside of Kubernetes:

- Security (you need to provide network access from your workloads to a separate storage cluster).
- You must implement the scaling, availability, monitoring, and configuration of your storage cluster.
- When things change on the storage cluster side, you often need to make corresponding configuration changes on the Kubernetes side.
- You might suffer performance or latency overhead due to extra network hops and/or authentication, authorization, or encryption.

Storing data inside your cluster with StatefulSets

It's best to store data within your Kubernetes cluster. This provides a uniform one-stop shop to manage your workloads and all the resources they depend on (excluding third-party external services). Additionally, you get to integrate your storage with your streamlined monitoring, which is very important. We will discuss monitoring in depth in a future chapter. However, running out of disk space is the bane of many system administrators. But there is a problem if you store data on a node and your data store pods get rescheduled to a different node, and the data it expects to be available is not there. The Kubernetes designers realized that the ephemeral pod philosophy doesn't work for storage. You could try to manage it yourself using pod-node affinity and other mechanisms that Kubernetes provides, but it's much better to use StatefulSet, which is a specific solution for managing storage-aware services in Kubernetes.

Understanding a StatefulSet

At its core, a StatefulSet is a controller that manages a set of pods with some extra properties, such as ordering and uniqueness. The StatefulSet allows its set of pods to be deployed and scaled, while preserving their special properties. StatefulSets reached **general availability** (**GA**) status in Kubernetes 1.9. You can think of a StatefulSet as a souped-up deployment. Let's take a look at a sample StatefulSet for the user service, which uses a relational PostgresDB as its data store:

```
apiVersion: apps/v1
kind: StatefulSet
metadata:
  name: user-db
```

```
    spec:
      selector:
        matchLabels:
          svc: user
          app: postgres
      serviceName: user-db
      replicas: 1
      template:
        metadata:
          labels:
            svc: user
            app: postgres
        spec:
          terminationGracePeriodSeconds: 10
          containers:
          - name: nginx
            image: postgres:11.1-alpine
            ports:
            - containerPort: 5432
            env:
            - name: POSTGRES_DB
              value: user_manager
            - name: POSTGRES_USER
              value: postgres
            - name: POSTGRES_PASSWORD
              value: postgres
            - name: PGDATA
              value: /data/user-db

            volumeMounts:
            - name: user-db
              mountPath: /data/user-db
      volumeClaimTemplates:
      - metadata:
          name: user-db
        spec:
          accessModes: [ "ReadWriteOnce" ]
          # storageClassName: <custom storage class>
          resources:
            requests:
              storage: 1Gi
```

There is a lot going on here, but it's all a composition of familiar concepts. Let's break it down into its components.

StatefulSet components

The StatefulSet is comprised of three main parts, as follows:

- **StatefulSet metadata and definition**: The StatefulSet metadata and definition are pretty similar to a deployment. You have the standard API version, kind, and metadata name; then, `spec`, which includes a selector for the pods (which must match the pod template selectors that will come next), the number of replicas (just one, in this case), and the major difference compared with a deployment, that is, `serviceName`:

```
apiVersion: apps/v1
kind: StatefulSet
metadata:
  name: user-db
spec:
  selector:
    matchLabels:
      svc: user
      app: postgres
  replicas: 1
  serviceName: user-db
```

  A StatefulSet *must* have a headless service associated with the StatefulSet to manage the network identity of the pods. The service name is `user-db` in this case; here it is for completeness:

```
apiVersion: v1
kind: Service
metadata:
  name: user-db
spec:
  ports:
  - port: 5432
  clusterIP: None
  selector:
    svc: user
    app: postgres
```

- **A pod template**: The next part is a standard pod template. The PGDATA environment variable (`/data/user-db`), which tells postgres where to read and write its data, must be the same as the mount path of the `user-db` volume (`/data/user-db`) or a subdirectory. This is where we wire up the data store with the underlying storage:

```
template:
  metadata:
    labels:
      svc: user
      app: postgres
  spec:
    terminationGracePeriodSeconds: 10
    containers:
    - name: nginx
      image: postgres:11.1-alpine
      ports:
      - containerPort: 5432
      env:
      - name: POSTGRES_DB
        value: user_manager
      - name: POSTGRES_USER
        value: postgres
      - name: POSTGRES_PASSWORD
        value: postgres
      - name: PGDATA
        value: /data/user-db
      volumeMounts:
      - name: user-db
        mountPath: /data/user-db
```

- **Volume claim templates**: The last part is the volume claim templates. Note that this is plural; some data stores may require multiple types of volumes (for example, for logging or caching) that require their own persistent claims. In this case, one persistent claim is enough:

```
volumeClaimTemplates:
- metadata:
    name: user-db
  spec:
    accessModes: [ "ReadWriteOnce" ]
    # storageClassName: <custom storage class>
    resources:
      requests:
        storage: 1Gi
```

Now is a good time to dive deeper and gain an understanding of the special properties of StatefulSets and why they are important.

Pod identity

StatefulSet pods have a stable identity that includes the following triplet: a stable network identity, an ordinal index, and stable storage. These always go together; the name of each pod is `<statefulset name>-<ordinal>`.

The headless service associated with the StatefulSet provides the stable network identity. The service DNS name will be as follows:

```
<service name>.<namespace>.svc.cluster.local
```

Each pod, *X*, will have a stable DNS name as follows:

```
<statefulset name>-<ordinal>.<service name>.<namespace>.svc.cluster.local
```

For example, the first pod of the `user-db` StatefulSet will be called the following:

```
user-db-0.user-db.default.svc.cluster.local
```

Additionally, StatefulSet pods automatically get assigned a label, as follows:

```
statefulset.kubernetes.io/pod-name=<pod-name>
```

Orderliness

Each pod in a StatefulSet gets an ordinal index. But, what is this for? Well, some data stores rely on the orderly sequence of initialization. The StatefulSet ensures that when the StatefulSet pods are initialized, scaled up, or scaled down, it is always done in order.

In Kubernetes 1.7, the orderliness restriction was relaxed. For data stores that don't require orderliness, it makes sense to allow for parallel operations on multiple pods in the StatefulSet. This can be specified in the `podPolicy` field. The values allowed are `OrderedReady` for the default orderly behavior, or *parallel* for the relaxed parallel mode, where pods can be launched or terminated while other pods are still launching or terminating.

When should you use a StatefulSet?

You should use a StatefulSet when you manage your data store yourself in the cloud and require good control over the storage your data store uses. The primary use case is for distributed data stores, but a StatefulSet is useful even if your data store has just one instance or pod. The stable pod identity with the stable attached storage is well worth it, although orderliness, of course, is not required. If your data store is backed up by a shared storage layer such as NFS, then a StatefulSet might not be necessary.

Additionally, this may be common sense, but if you don't manage the data store yourself, then you don't need to worry about the storage layer and you don't need to define your own StatefulSets. For example, if you run your system on AWS and use S3, RDS, DynamoDB, and Redshift, then you don't really need a StatefulSet.

Comparing deployment and StatefulSets

Deployments are designed to manage any sets of pods. They can also be used to manage the pods of a distributed data store. StatefulSets were specifically designed to support the needs of distributed data stores. However, the special properties of ordering and uniqueness are not always necessary. Let's compare deployments to StatefulSets and see for ourselves:

- Deployments don't have associated storage, whereas StatefulSets do.
- Deployments have no associated service, whereas StatefulSets do.
- Deployment pods have no DNS name, whereas StatefulSet pods do.
- Deployments launch and terminate pods in any order, whereas StatefulSets follow a prescribed order (by default).

I recommend that you stick to deployments unless your distributed data store requires the special properties of StatefulSets. If you just need a stable identity, and not an ordered launch and shutdown, then use `podPolicy=Parallel`.

Reviewing a large StatefulSet example

Cassandra (`https://cassandra.apache.org/`) is an interesting distributed data store that I have a lot of experience with. It is very powerful, but it requires a lot of knowledge to operate properly and develop against. It is also a great use case for StatefulSets. Let's quickly review Cassandra and learn how to deploy it in Kubernetes. Note that we will not use Cassandra in Delinkcious.

A quick introduction to Cassandra

Cassandra is an Apache open source project. It's a columnar data store and is very well suited for managing time series data. I've used it to collect and manage data from a network of thousands of air quality sensors for more than three years.

Cassandra has an interesting modeling approach, but, here, we care about storage. Cassandra is highly available, linearly scalable, and very reliable (no SPOF) via redundancy. Cassandra nodes share responsibility for the data (which is partitioned through the **distributed hash table**, or **DHT**). Multiple copies of the data are spread across multiple nodes (this is typically three or five).

In this way, if a Cassandra node goes down, then there are two other nodes that have the same data and can respond to queries. All nodes are the same; there are no masters and no slaves. The nodes constantly chat with each other through a gossip protocol and, when new nodes join the cluster, Cassandra redistributes the data among all the nodes. Here is a diagram that shows how data is distributed across the Cassandra cluster:

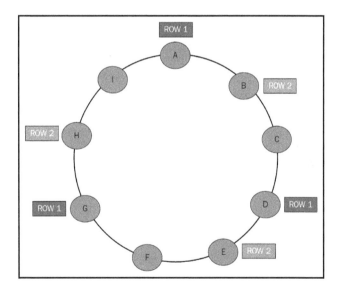

You can think of the nodes as a ring and the DHT algorithm hashes each wide row (the unit of work) and assigns it to the *N* nodes (depending on the replication factor of the cluster). With that kind of precise placement of individual rows in specific nodes, you can see how the stable identity and, potentially, the ordering properties of a StatefulSet can come in handy.

Let's explore what it takes to deploy a Cassandra cluster as a StatefulSet in Kubernetes.

Deploying Cassandra on Kubernetes using StatefulSets

Here is a truncated version that includes the parts we should focus on.

The first part includes `apiVersion`, `kind`, `metadata`, and `spec`, as we've seen before. The name is `cassandra`, and the label is `app: cassandra`. In `spec`, the `serviceName` name is also `cassandra`, and there are three replicas:

```
apiVersion: apps/v1
kind: StatefulSet
metadata:
  name: cassandra
  labels:
    app: cassandra
  spec:
    serviceName: cassandra
    replicas: 3
    selector:
      matchLabels:
        app: cassandra
```

The pod template has a matching label of `app: cassandra`. The container is named `cassandra`, too, and uses a Google sample image with the always pull policy. Here, `terminationGraceInSeconds` is set to 1,800 seconds (that is, 30 minutes). That's the time that the StatefulSet will allow the pod to try and recover if it becomes unresponsive. Cassandra has a lot of redundancy built in, so it's okay to let a node attempt recovery for 30 minutes. I removed a lot of ports, environment variables, and readiness checks (the ellipses). The volume mount is called `cassandra-data`, and its path is `/cassandra_data`. That's where Cassandra stores its data files:

```
template:
  metadata:
    labels:
      app: cassandra
  spec:
    terminationGracePeriodSeconds: 1800
    containers:
    - name: cassandra
      image: gcr.io/google-samples/cassandra:v13
      imagePullPolicy: Always
      ...
      volumeMounts:
      - name: cassandra-data
        mountPath: /cassandra_data
```

Finally, the volume claim template defines the persistent storage that matches the volume mounted in the container with the name `cassandra-data`. The storage class, `fast`, is not shown here, but it is typically local storage on the same node that runs the Cassandra pod. The storage size is one gibibyte:

```
volumeClaimTemplates:
- metadata:
    name: cassandra-data
  spec:
    accessModes: [ "ReadWriteOnce" ]
    storageClassName: fast
    resources:
      requests:
        storage: 1Gi
```

This should all look very familiar to you at this point. However, there's more successful Cassandra deployment to discover. If you recall, Cassandra has no master; Cassandra nodes talk to each other constantly using the gossip protocol.

But how do Cassandra nodes find each other? Enter the seed provider; whenever a new node is added to the cluster, it is configured with the IP addresses of some seed nodes (in this case, `10.0.0.1`, `10.0.0.2`, and `10.0.0.3`). It starts exchanging messages with these seed nodes, which inform the new node of other Cassandra nodes in the cluster, as well as notifying all the other existing nodes that a new node has joined the cluster. In this way, each node in the cluster can very quickly know about every other node in the cluster.

Here is a section from a typical Kubernetes config file (`cassandra.yaml`) that defines the seed provider. In this case, it's just a simple list of IP addresses:

```
seed_provider:
    - class_name: SEED_PROVIDER
      parameters:
      # seeds is actually a comma-delimited list of addresses.
      # Ex: "<ip1>,<ip2>,<ip3>"
      - seeds: "10.0.0.1,10.0.0.2,10.0.0.3,"
```

The seed provider can be a custom class, too. This is a very nice extensible design. In Kubernetes, it is necessary because the original seed nodes may be moved around and get new IP addresses.

To address this, there is a custom `KubernetesSeedProvider` class that talks to the Kubernetes API server and can always return the IP addresses of the seed nodes at the time of the query. Cassandra is implemented in Java, and so is the custom seed provider that implements the `SeedProvider` Java interface.

We're not going to dissect this code in detail. The main thing to note is that it interfaces with a native Go library called `cassandra-seed.so`, and then it uses it to get the Kubernetes endpoints of the Cassandra service:

```
package io.k8s.cassandra;

import java.io.IOException;
import java.net.InetAddress;
import java.util.Collections;
import java.util.List;
import java.util.Map;

...

 /**
 * Create new seed provider
 *
 * @param params
 */
 public KubernetesSeedProvider(Map<String, String> params) {
 }

...
 }
 }

private static String getEnvOrDefault(String var, String def) {
 String val = System.getenv(var);
...
 static class Endpoints {
 public List<InetAddress> ips;
 }
 }
```

 The complete source code can be found at `https://github.com/kubernetes/examples/blob/master/cassandra/java/src/main/java/io/k8s/cassandra/KubernetesSeedProvider.java`.

That's the magic that connects Cassandra to Kubernetes and allows them to work together. Now that we've seen how a complicated distributed data store can be deployed in Cassandra, let's take a look at local storage, which graduated to GA in Kubernetes 1.14.

Achieving high performance with local storage

Let's now discuss the affinity between compute and storage. There is an interesting relationship between speed, capacity, persistence, and cost. When your data lives near your processor, you can start working on it immediately, as opposed to fetching it over the network. That's the promise of local storage.

There are two primary ways to store your data locally: in memory and on local drives. However, there are nuances; memory is the fastest, SSD drives are about 4 times slower than memory, and spinning disks are roughly 20 times slower than SSD drives (`https://gist.github.com/jboner/2841832`).

Let's consider both of these following options:

- Storing your data in memory
- Storing your data on a local SSD

Storing your data in memory

The highest performance, as far as read and write latency and throughput is concerned, is when you keep your data in memory. There are different memory types and caches, but the bottom line is that memory is super fast. However, memory has significant downsides too, such as the following:

- A node has much more limited memory compared to disks (that is, it requires more machines to store the same amount of data).
- Memory is very expensive.
- Memory is ephemeral.

There are some use cases where you require your entire dataset in memory. In these cases, either the dataset is very small, or you can split it across multiple machines. If the data is important and can't be easily generated, then you can address the ephemeral nature of memory in the following two ways:

- Keep a persistent copy.
- Redundancy (that is, keep data in memory across multiple machines and potentially geodistributed).

Storing your data on a local SSD

A local SSD is not as fast as memory, but it is very fast. Of course, you can always combine in-memory caching too (any respectable data store will use memory caching to its advantage). Using an SSD is appropriate when you require fast performance, but your working set doesn't fit in memory or, alternatively, you don't want to pay the premium of large memory when you can get by with a much cheaper, yet still very fast, SSD. For example, Cassandra recommends using local SSD storage as the backing store for its data.

Using relational databases in Kubernetes

So far, we've used a relational database in all our services, but, as we will soon discover, we didn't have real persistence. First, we'll look at where the data is stored, and then we'll explore how durable it is. Finally, we'll migrate one of the databases to use a StatefulSet for proper persistence and durability.

Understanding where the data is stored

For PostgreSQL, there is a `data` directory; this directory can be set using the `PGDATA` environment variable. By default, it is set to `/var/lib/postgresql/data`:

```
$ kubectl exec -it link-db-6b9b64db5-zp59g env | grep PGDATA
PGDATA=/var/lib/postgresql/data
```

Let's take a look at what this directory contains:

```
$ kubectl exec -it link-db-6b9b64db5-zp59g ls /var/lib/postgresql/data
PG_VERSION pg_multixact pg_tblspc
base pg_notify pg_twophase
global pg_replslot pg_wal
pg_commit_ts pg_serial pg_xact
pg_dynshmem pg_snapshots post-gresql.auto.conf
pg_hba.conf pg_stat postgresql.conf
pg_ident.conf pg_stat_tmp postmaster.opts
pg_logical pg_subtrans postmaster.pid
```

However, the `data` directory can be ephemeral or persistent depending on how it was mounted to the container.

Using a deployment and service

With a service fronting your database pods, you can easily access the data. When a database pod is killed, it will be restarted by the deployment. However, since the pod can be scheduled on a different node, it is up to you to make sure that it has access to the storage where the actual data is. Otherwise, it will just start empty and you'll lose all the data. This is a development-only setup, and how most Delinkcious services keep their data – by running a PostgresDB container that is only as persistent as its pod. It turns out that the data is stored in the Docker container itself running inside the pod.

In Minikube, I can inspect the Docker container directly by first SSH-ing into the node, finding the ID of the postgres container, and then inspecting it (that is, only if the relevant information is displayed):

```
$ minikube ssh

    _ _
 _ _ ( ) ( )
___ ___ (_) ___ (_)| |/') _ _ | |_ __
/' _ ` _ `\| |/' _ `\| || , < ( ) ( )| '_`\ /'__`\
| ( ) ( ) || || ( ) || || |\`\ | (_) || |_) )( ___/
(_) (_) (_)(_)(_) (_)(_)(_) (_)`\___/'(_,__/'`\____)

$ docker ps -f name=k8s_postgres_link-db -q
409d4a52a7f5

$ docker inspect -f "{{json .Mounts}}" 409d4a52a7f5 | jq .[1]
{
"Type": "volume",
"Name": "f9d090d6defba28f0c0bfac8ab7935d189332478d0bf03def6175f5c0a2e93d7",
 "Source":
"/var/lib/docker/volumes/f9d090d6defba28f0c0bfac8ab7935d189332478d0bf03def6
175f5c0a2e93d7/_data",
"Destination": "/var/lib/postgresql/data",
"Driver": "local",
"Mode": "",
"RW": true,
"Propagation": ""
}
```

This means that, if the container goes away (for example, if we upgrade to a new version) and certainly if the node goes away, then all our data disappears.

Using a StatefulSet

With a StatefulSet, the situation is different. The data directory is mounted to the container, but the storage itself is managed externally. As long as the external storage is reliable and redundant, our data is safe, regardless of what happens to specific containers, pods, and nodes. We've previously mentioned how to define a StatefulSet for the user database using a headless service. However, consuming the storage of the StatefulSet can be a little challenging. The headless service attached to a StatefulSet has no cluster IP. So, how would the user service connect to its database? Well, we will have to help it.

Helping the user service locate StatefulSet pods

The headless `user-db` service has no cluster IP, as follows:

```
$ kubectl get svc user-db
NAME TYPE CLUSTER-IP EXTERNAL-IP PORT(S) AGE
user-db ClusterIP None <none> 5432/TCP 4d
```

However, it does have endpoints, which are the IP addresses in the cluster of all the pods that back the service:

```
$ kubectl get endpoints user-db
NAME ENDPOINTS AGE
user-db 172.17.0.25:5432 4d
```

This is a good option; endpoints are not exposed through environment variables, such as a service with a cluster IP (`<service name>_SERVICE_HOST and <service name>_SERVICE_PORT`). So, for a service to find the endpoints of a headless service, they'll have to query the Kubernetes API directly. While that's possible, it adds unnecessary coupling between the service and Kubernetes. We won't be able to run the service outside of Kubernetes for testing because it relies on the Kubernetes API. However, we can trick the user service and populate `USER_DB_SERVICE_HOST` and `USER_DB_SERVICE_PORT` using a config map.

The idea is that StatefulSet pods have a stable DNS name. For the user database, there is one pod whose DNS name is `user-db-0.user-db.default.svc.cluster.local`. Inside the troubleshooter container shell, we can verify that the DNS name indeed resolves to the user database endpoint, `172.17.0.25`, by running the `dig` command:

```
root@trouble-64554479d-zclxc:/# dig +short us-er-db-0.user-
db.default.svc.cluster.local
172.17.0.25
```

Now, we can take this stable DNS name and assign it to USER_DB_SERVICE_HOST in a config map for the user-manager service:

```
apiVersion: v1
kind: ConfigMap
metadata:
  name: user-manager-config
  namespace: default
data:
  USER_DB_SERVICE_HOST: "us-er-db-0.user-db.default.svc.cluster.local"
  USER_DB_SERVICE_PORT: "5432"
```

Once this config map is applied, the user service will be able to locate the user database pod of the StatefulSet through the environment variables. Here is the code that uses these environment variables from pkg/db_util/db_util.go:

```
func GetDbEndpoint(dbName string) (host string, port int, err error) {
 hostEnvVar := strings.ToUpper(dbName) + "_DB_SERVICE_HOST"
 host = os.Getenv(hostEnvVar)
 if host == "" {
 host = "localhost"
 }

 portEnvVar := strings.ToUpper(dbName) + "_DB_SERVICE_PORT"
 dbPort := os.Getenv(portEnvVar)
 if dbPort == "" {
 dbPort = "5432"
 }

 port, err = strconv.Atoi(dbPort)
 return
 }
```

The user service calls it in its Run() function to initialize its database store:

```
func Run() {
 dbHost, dbPort, err := db_util.GetDbEndpoint("user")
 if err != nil {
 log.Fatal(err)
 }

 store, err := sgm.NewDbUserStore(dbHost, dbPort, "postgres", "postgres")
 if err != nil {
 log.Fatal(err)
 }
 ...
 }
```

Now, let's take a look at how to address the problem of managing schema changes.

Managing schema changes

One of the most challenging topics when working with relational databases is managing the SQL schema. When the schema changes, the change may be backward compatible (by adding a column) or non-backward compatible (by splitting a table into two separate tables). When the schema changes, we need to migrate our database, but also migrate the code that is affected by the schema change.

If you can afford a short downtime, then the process can be very simple, as follows:

1. Shut down all the impacted services and perform DB migration.
2. Deploy a new code that knows how to work with the new schema.
3. Everything just works.

However, if you need to keep the system running, you'll have to go through a more complicated process by breaking the schema change into multiple backward-compatible changes, including corresponding code changes.

For example, when splitting a table into two tables, the following process can be performed:

1. Keep the original table.
2. Add the two new tables.
3. Deploy code that writes both to the old table and the new tables and can read from all of the tables.
4. Migrate all the data from the old table to the new tables.
5. Deploy a code change that reads only from the new tables (which have all the data now).
6. Delete the old table.

Relational databases are very useful; however, sometimes, the correct solution is a non-relational data store.

Using non-relational data stores in Kubernetes

Kubernetes and StatefulSets are not limited or even geared toward relational data stores. Non-relational (also known as NoSQL) data stores are very useful for many use cases. One of the most versatile and popular in-memory data stores is Redis. Let's get to know Redis and examine how to migrate the Delinkcious news service to use Redis instead of storing events in ephemeral memory.

An introduction to Redis

Redis is often described as a data structure server. Since it keeps the entire data store in memory, it can perform many advanced operations on the data efficiently. The price you pay, of course, is that you have to keep *all* of the data in memory. This is possible only for small datasets and, even then, it's expensive. If you don't access most of your data, keeping it in memory is a huge waste. Redis can be used as a fast, distributed cache for hot data; so, even if you can't use it as a distributed cache for your entire dataset in memory, you can still use Redis for the hot data (which is frequently used). Redis also supports clusters where the data is shared across multiple nodes, so it's able to handle very large datasets too. Redis has an impressive list of features, including the following:

- It provides multiple data structures such as lists, hashes, sets, sorted sets, bitmaps, streams, and geospatial indexes.
- It provides atomic operations on many data structures.
- It supports transactions.
- It supports auto-eviction with TTL.
- It supports LRU eviction.
- It enables pub/sub.
- It allows optional persistence to the disk.
- It allows optional appending of operations to the journal.
- It provides Lua scripting.

Now, let's take a look at how Delinkcious uses Redis.

Persisting events in the news service

The news service provisions a Redis instance as a StatefulSet, as follows:

```
apiVersion: apps/v1
kind: StatefulSet
metadata:
  name: news-manager-redis
spec:
  serviceName: news-manager-redis
  replicas: 1
  selector:
    matchLabels:
      app: redis
      svc: news-manager
  template:
    metadata:
      labels:
        app: redis
        svc: news-manager
    spec:
      containers:
      - name: redis-primary
        image: redis:5.0.3-alpine
        imagePullPolicy: Always
        ports:
        - containerPort: 6379
          name: redis
        volumeMounts:
        - name: news-manager-redis
          mountPath: /data
  volumeClaimTemplates:
  - metadata:
      name: news-manager-redis
    spec:
      accessModes: [ "ReadWriteOnce" ]
      resources:
        requests:
          storage: 1Gi
```

It is supported by a headless service:

```
apiVersion: v1
kind: Service
metadata:
  name: news-manager-redis
  labels:
    app: redis
```

```
      svc: news-manager
spec:
  selector:
    app: redis
    svc: news-manager
  type: None
  ports:
  - port: 6379
    name: redis
```

We can use the same trick of injecting the DNS name of the Redis pod through environment variables using a config map:

```
apiVersion: v1
kind: ConfigMap
metadata:
  name: news-manager-config
  namespace: default
data:
  PORT: "6060"
  NEWS_MANAGER_REDIS_SERVICE_HOST: "news-manager-redis-0.news-manager-
redis.default.svc.cluster.local"
  USER_DB_SERVICE_PORT: "6379"
```

With the provisioning out of the way, let's take a look at how the code is accessing Redis. In the Run() function of the news service, if the environment variables for Redis are not empty, then it will create a new Redis store:

```
redisHostname := os.Getenv("NEWS_MANAGER_REDIS_SERVICE_HOST")
redisPort := os.Getenv("NEWS_MANAGER_REDIS_SERVICE_PORT")

var store nm.Store
if redisHostname == "" {
store = nm.NewInMemoryNewsStore()
} else {
address := fmt.Sprintf("%s:%s", redisHostname, redisPort)
store, err = nm.NewRedisNewsStore(address)
if err != nil {
log.Fatal(err)
}
}
```

The `NewRedisNewStore()` function is defined in
`pkg/new_manager/redis_news_store`. It creates a new Redis client (from the `go-redis`
library). It also calls the client's `Ping()` method to ensure that Redis is up and running and
is reachable:

```
package news_manager

import (
 "github.com/go-redis/redis"
 "github.com/pelletier/go-toml"
 om "github.com/the-gigi/delinkcious/pkg/object_model"
 )

// RedisNewsStore manages a UserEvents data structure
 type RedisNewsStore struct {
 redis *redis.Client
 }

func NewRedisNewsStore(address string) (store Store, err error) {
 client := redis.NewClient(&redis.Options{
 Addr: address,
 Password: "", // use empty password for simplicity. should come from a
secret in production
 DB: 0, // use default DB
 })

 _, err = client.Ping().Result()
 if err != nil {
 return
 }

 store = &RedisNewsStore{redis: client}
 return
 }
```

`RedisNewsStore` stores the events in a Redis list, which is serialized to TOML. This is all
implemented in `AddEvent()`, as follows:

```
func (m *RedisNewsStore) AddEvent(username string, event *om.Event) (err
error) {
 t, err := toml.Marshal(*event)
 if err != nil {
 return
 }
 err = m.redis.RPush(username, t).Err()
 return
 }
```

`RedisNewsStore` implements the `GetNews()` method to fetch events in order. First, it calculates the start and end indexes to query the event list based on the starting index and the maximum page size. Then, it gets the results, which are serialized to TOML, unmarshals them into the `om.Event` struct, and appends them to the result list of events. Finally, it computes the next index to fetch (−1 if there are no more events):

```
const redisMaxPageSize = 10

func (m *RedisNewsStore) GetNews(username string, startIndex int) (events
[]*om.Event, nextIndex int, err error) {
 stop := startIndex + redisMaxPageSize - 1
 result, err := m.redis.LRange(username, int64(startIndex),
int64(stop)).Result()
 if err != nil {
 return
 }

 for _, t := range result {
 var event om.Event
 err = toml.Unmarshal([]byte(t), &event)
 if err != nil {
 return
 }

 events = append(events, &event)
 }

 if len(result) == redisMaxPageSize {
 nextIndex = stop + 1
 } else {
 nextIndex = -1
 }

 return
 }
```

At this point, you should have a good grasp of a non-relational data store, including when to use them and how to integrate Redis as a data store for your services.

Summary

In this chapter, we dealt with the very important topic of storage and real-world data persistence. We learned about the Kubernetes storage model, the common storage interface, and StatefulSets. Then, we discussed how to manage relational and non-relational data in Kubernetes and migrated several Delinkcious services to use proper persistent storage through StatefulSets, including how to provide data store endpoints for StatefulSet pods. Finally, we implemented a non-ephemeral data store for the news service using Redis. At this point, you should have a clear idea of how Kubernetes manages storage and is able to choose the proper data stores for your system, as well as integrate them into your Kubernetes cluster and with your services.

In the next chapter, we will explore the exciting domain of serverless computing. We'll consider when the serverless model is useful, discuss current solutions for Kubernetes, and extend Delinkcious with some serverless tasks.

Further reading

You can refer to the following references for more information:

- **CSI**: https://medium.com/google-cloud/understanding-the-container-storage-interface-csi-ddbeb966a3b
- **StatefulSet**: https://kubernetes.io/docs/concepts/workloads/controllers/statefulset/
- **Cassandra**: https://cassandra.apache.org/
- **Redis**: http://redis.io/
- **Latency numbers every programmer should know**: https://gist.github.com/jboner/2841832

Running Serverless Tasks on Kubernetes

9

In this chapter, we will dive into one of the hottest trends in cloud-native systems: serverless computing (also known as **Function as a Service**, or **FaaS**). We will explain what serverless means (spoiler alert: it means more than one thing) and how it compares to microservices. We will implement and deploy a cool new feature for Delinkcious, known as link checking, using the Nuclio serverless framework. Finally, we'll briefly cover other ways to do serverless computing in Kubernetes.

The following topics will be covered in this chapter:

- Serverless in the cloud
- Link checking with Delinkcious
- Serverless link checking with Nuclio

Technical requirements

In this chapter, we'll install a serverless framework called Nuclio. First, let's create a dedicated namespace as follows:

```
$ kubectl create namespace nuclio
```

This is a good security practice because Nuclio will not interfere with the rest of your cluster. Next, we'll apply some **role-based access control** (**RBAC**) permissions. If you take a look at the file (you should always check Kubernetes manifests before running them on your cluster), you'll see that most of the permissions are limited to the Nuclio namespace and there are a few cluster-wide permissions regarding **custom resource definitions** (**CRDs**) that Nuclio itself creates; this is an excellent hygiene:

```
$ kubectl apply -f
https://raw.githubusercontent.com/nuclio/nuclio/master/hack/k8s/resources/n
uclio-rbac.yaml
```

Let's now deploy Nuclio itself; it creates a few CRDs, and deploys a controller and a dashboard service. This is very economical and straightforward, as follows:

```
$ kubectl apply -f
https://raw.githubusercontent.com/nuclio/nuclio/master/hack/k8s/resources/n
uclio.yaml
```

Now, let's verify the installation by checking that the controller and the dashboard pods are running successfully:

```
$ kubectl get pods --namespace nuclio
NAME                                  READY   STATUS    RESTARTS   AGE
nuclio-controller-556774b65-mtvmm     1/1     Running   0          22m
nuclio-dashboard-67ff7bb6d4-czvxp     1/1     Running   0          22m
```

The dashboard is nice, but it is more appropriate for ad hoc exploration. For more serious production use, it is better to use the `nuctl` CLI. The next step is to download and install `nuctl` from `https://github.com/nuclio/nuclio/releases`.

Then, copy the executable to your path to create `symlink nuctl`, as follows:

```
$ cd /usr/local/bin
$ curl -LO
https://github.com/nuclio/nuclio/releases/download/1.1.2/nuctl-1.1.2-darwin
-amd64
$ ln -s nuctl-1.1.2-darwin-amd64 nuctl
```

Finally, let's create an image pull secret so that Nuclio can deploy functions to our cluster:

```
$ kubectl create secret docker-registry registry-credentials -n nuclio \
    --docker-username g1g1 \
    --docker-password $DOCKERHUB_PASSWORD \
    --docker-server registry.hub.docker.com \
    --docker-email the.gigi@gmail.com

secret "registry-credentials" created
```

You can also use other registries with the proper credentials; in Minikube, you can even use a local registry. However, we'll use the Docker Hub registry for consistency.

The code

The code is split between two Git repositories, as follows:

- You can find the code samples at `https://github.com/PacktPublishing/Hands-On-Microservices-with-Kubernetes/tree/master/Chapter09`
- You can find the updated Delinkcious application at `https://github.com/the-gigi/delinkcious/releases/tag/v0.7`

Serverless in the cloud

People have two different definitions for serverless in the cloud, especially in the context of Kubernetes. The first meaning is that you don't have to manage the nodes for your cluster. Some good examples of this concept include AWS Fargate (`https://aws.amazon.com/fargate/`) and **Azure Container Instances** (**ACI**) (`https://azure.microsoft.com/en-us/services/container-instances/`). The second meaning of serverless is that your code is not deployed as a long-running service, but is packaged as a function that can be invoked or triggered in different ways on demand. Some good examples of this concept include AWS Lambda, and Google Cloud Functions.

Let's understand the commonalities and differences between services and serverless functions.

Microservices and serverless functions

The same code can often run either as a microservice or as a serverless function. The difference is mostly operational. Let's compare the operational attributes of microservices and serverless functions, as follows:

Microservices	Serverless functions
• Always running (it can scale down to at least one). • Can expose multiple endpoints (such as HTTP and gRPC). • Requires that you implement the request handling and routing yourself. • Can listen to events. • Service instances can maintain in-memory caches, long-term connections, and sessions. • In Kubernetes, microservices are represented directly by the service object.	• Runs on demand (theoretically; it can scale down to zero). • Exposes a single endpoint (usually HTTP). • Can be triggered by events or get an automatic endpoint. • Often has severe limitations on resource usage and maximum runtime. • Sometimes, it might have a cold start (that is, when scaling up from zero). • In Kubernetes, there is no native serverless function concept (Jobs and CronJobs come close).

This should provide you with some relatively good guidance on when to use microservices and when to use serverless functions. A microservice is the right choice in the following cases:

- Your workload needs to run non-stop, or almost non-stop.
- Each request runs for a long time and can't be supported by serverless function limitations.
- The workload uses a local state between invocations that can't be easily moved to an external data store.

However, if you have workloads that run infrequently for a relatively short time, then you may prefer to use a serverless function.

There are a few other engineering considerations to bear in mind. For example, services are more familiar and often have various support libraries. Developers may be more comfortable with services and prefer to have a single paradigm for deploying code to your system. In particular, in Kubernetes, there is a large selection of serverless functions options and it can be difficult to choose the right one. On the other hand, serverless functions often support agile and lightweight deployment models, where developers can just put some code together and it magically starts running on the cluster because the serverless function solution takes care of all the business of packaging and deploying it.

Modeling serverless functions in Kubernetes

At the end of the day, Kubernetes runs containers, so you know your serverless function will be packaged as a container. However, there are two primary ways to represent serverless functions in Kubernetes. The first one is just as code; here, developers, essentially, provide a function in some form (as a file or by pushing to a Git repository). The second one is to build it as an actual container. The developer builds a regular container and the serverless framework takes care of scheduling it and running it as a function.

Functions as code

The benefit of this approach is that, as a developer, you completely sidestep the whole business of building images, tagging them, pushing them to a registry, and deploying them to the cluster with all the Kubernetes ceremony around it (that is, deployment, service, ingress, and NetworkPolicy). It's great for ad hoc exploration and one-off jobs too.

Functions as containers

Here, as a developer, you are on familiar ground. You build a container using your regular process and you just deploy it later to the cluster as a serverless function. It is still more lightweight than a regular service because you only need to implement a function in your container and not a fully-fledged HTTP or gRPC server or register to listen for some events. You get all that for the serverless functions solution.

Building, configuring, and deploying serverless functions

You have implemented your serverless function and now you want to deploy it to the cluster. Regardless of whether you build your serverless function (if it's a container) or whether you provide it as a function, you typically also need to configure it in some way. The configuration may contain information such as scaling limits, where the function code is located, and how to invoke and trigger it. Then, the next step is to deploy the function to the cluster. It may be a one-time deployment through a CLI or web UI, or, alternatively, it may be integrated with your CI/CD pipeline. This depends mostly on whether your serverless function is part of your main application or whether it is something you launch in an ad hoc manner for troubleshooting or manual cleanup tasks.

Invoking serverless functions

Once a serverless function is deployed in the cluster, it will be dormant. There will be a controller that runs constantly ready to invoke or trigger functions. The controller should take very few resources and just listen for incoming requests or events to trigger functions. In Kubernetes, if you need to invoke functions from outside the cluster, there will probably be some additional ingress configuration. However, the most common use case is to invoke functions internally and expose a fully-fledged service to the world.

Now that we understand what serverless functions are all about, let's add some serverless function capabilities to Delinkcious.

Link checking with Delinkcious

Delinkcious is a link management system. Links – or, as they are known officially, **uniform resource identifiers** (**URIs**) – are really just a pointer to a particular resource. There could be two issues with links, such as the following:

- They may be broken (that is, they point to a non-existent resource).
- They may point to a *bad* resource (such as a phishing or virus-injecting site, hate speech, or child pornography).

Checking links and maintaining the status of each link is an important aspect of link management. Let's start by designing the way Delinkcious will perform link checking.

Designing link checks

Let's consider link checking in the context of Delinkcious. We should consider the current state as a future improvement. Here are some assumptions:

- Links can be temporarily or permanently broken.
- Link checking may be a heavyweight operation (especially if analyzing content).
- The status of a link may change at any time (that is, a valid link can suddenly break if the resource that it's pointing to is deleted).

Specifically, Delinkcious links are stored redundantly per user. If two users add the same link, it will be stored for each user separately. This means that, if link checking happens when a link is added, and if N users add the same link, then it will be checked each time. This is not very efficient, especially for popular links that many users may add and that can all benefit from a single check.

Consider the following case, which is even worse:

- *N* users add the link, *L*.
- The link check for *L* passed for all those *N* users.
- Another user, *N+1*, adds the same link, *L*, which is now broken (for example, the hosting company removed the page).
- Only the last user, *N+1*, will have the correct status of the link, *L*, as invalid.
- All previous *N* users will still assume that the link is valid.

Since we want, in this chapter, to focus on serverless functions, we will accept these limitations in the way in which Delinkcious stores links for each user. A more efficient and robust design in the future could be as follows:

- Store all the links independent of the users.
- Users that add a link will have an association to that link.
- Link checking will automatically reflect the latest status of a link for all users.

When it comes to designing a link check, let's consider some of the following options for checking links when adding a new link:

- When adding a link, just run the link checking code in the link service.
- When adding a link, call a separate link checking service.
- When adding a link, invoke a link checking serverless function.
- When adding a link, keep it in pending status, which periodically runs checks on all recently added links.

Additionally, since links can break at anytime, it may be useful to run link checks periodically for existing links.

Let's consider the first option, that is, running the link check inside the link manager. While it has the benefit of simplicity, it also suffers from several problems, such as the following:

- If link checking takes too long (for example, if the target is unreachable or the content takes a long time to classify), then it will delay the response to the user adding the link or it can even time out.
- Even if the actual link checking is done asynchronously, it still ties up resources of the link service in unpredictable ways.
- There is no easy way to schedule periodic checks or ad hoc checks of links without making serious changes to the link manager.
- Conceptually, link checking is a separate responsibility to link management and shouldn't live in the same microservice.

Let's consider the second option, that is, implementing a dedicated link checking service. This option addresses most of the issues as the first option, but it may be overkill. That said, it is not the best option when there is no need to check links very often; for example, if the majority of added links are checked or if link checking happens only periodically. Additionally, for implementing a service for a single operation, checking links seems like overkill for a service.

This leaves us with the third and fourth options, and both can be implemented effectively using a serverless function solution, as shown in the following diagram.

Let's start with the following simple design:

- The link manager will invoke a serverless function when adding a new link.
- The new link will initially be in a pending state.
- The serverless function will only check whether the link is reachable.
- The serverless function will send an event through the NATS system, which the link manager will subscribe to.
- The link manager will update the link status from *pending* to *valid* or *invalid* when it receives the event.

Here is a diagram that describes this flow:

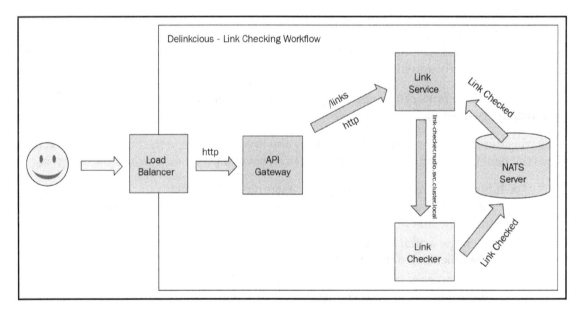

With a solid design in place, let's go ahead and implement and integrate it with Delinkcious.

Implementing link checks

At this stage, we will implement the link checking functionality independent of serverless functions. Let's start with our object model and add the `Status` field to our link object with the possible values of `pending`, `valid`, and `invalid`. We define an `alias` type here called `LinkStatus`, and constants for the values. However, note that it is not a strongly typed `enum` like other languages; it is really just a string:

```
const (
    LinkStatusPending = "pending"
    LinkStatusValid   = "valid"
    LinkStatusInvalid = "invalid"
)

type LinkStatus = string

type Link struct {
    Url         string
    Title       string
    Description string
    Status      LinkStatus
    Tags        map[string]bool
    CreatedAt   time.Time
    UpdatedAt   time.Time
}
```

Let's also define a `CheckLinkRequest` object that will come in handy later. Note that each request is per specific user and includes the link's URL:

```
type CheckLinkRequest struct {
    Username string
    Url      string
}
```

Now, let's define an interface that `LinkManager` will implement to get notified when a link has been checked. The interface is very simple and has a single method that informs the receiver (`LinkManager`, in our case) of the user, the URL, and the link status:

```
type LinkCheckerEvents interface {
    OnLinkChecked(username string, url string, status LinkStatus)
}
```

Let's create a new package, `pkg/link_checker`, to isolate this functionality. It has a single `CheckLink()` function that accepts a URL and uses the built-in Go HTTP client to call its HEAD HTTP method.

If the result is less than 400, it is considered a success, otherwise, it returns the HTTP status as an error:

```
package link_checker

import (
    "errors"
    "net/http"
)

// CheckLinks tries to get the headers of the target url and returns error
if it fails
func CheckLink(url string) (err error) {
    resp, err := http.Head(url)
    if err != nil {
        return
    }
    if resp.StatusCode >= 400 {
        err = errors.New(resp.Status)
    }
    return
}
```

The HEAD method, which just returns a few headers, is an effective way to check whether a link is reachable because, even for very large resources, the headers will be a small amount of data. Obviously, this is not good enough if we want to extend link checks to scanning and analyzing the content, but it will do for now.

According to our design, when the link checking is complete, `LinkManager` should receive an event through NATS with the check result. This is very similar to the news service listening to link events (such as the link added and the link updated events). Let's implement another package, `link_checker_events`, for the NATS integration, which will allow us to send and subscribe to link checking events. First, we need an event object that contains the username, the URL, and the link status:

```
package link_checker_events

import (
    om "github.com/the-gigi/delinkcious/pkg/object_model"
)

type Event struct {
    Username  string
    Url       string
    Status    om.LinkStatus
}
```

Then, we need to be able to send events through NATS. The eventSender object implements the LinkCheckerEvents interface. Whenever it receives a call, it creates link_checker_events.Event and publishes it to NATS:

```
package link_checker_events

import (
    "github.com/nats-io/go-nats"
    om "github.com/the-gigi/delinkcious/pkg/object_model"
    "log"
)

type eventSender struct {
    hostname string
    nats       *nats.EncodedConn
}

func (s *eventSender) OnLinkChecked(username string, url string, status
om.LinkStatus) {
    err := s.nats.Publish(subject, Event{username, url, status})
    if err != nil {
        log.Fatal(err)
    }
}

func NewEventSender(url string) (om.LinkCheckerEvents, error) {
    ec, err := connect(url)
    if err != nil {
        return nil, err
    }
    return &eventSender{hostname: url, nats: ec}, nil
}
```

The reason the event is defined in the link_checker_events package and not in the general Delinkcious object model is that this event is just created for the purpose of interfacing though NATS with the link checker listener that is also implemented in this package. There is no need to expose this event outside the package (except for letting NATS serialize it). In the Listen() method, the code connects to the NATS server and subscribes to NATS in a queue (which means that only one listener will handle each event, even if multiple subscribers subscribe to the same queue).

When the listener function that is subscribed to the queue receives an event from NATS, it forwards it to the event sink that implements om.LinkCheckerEvents (while ignoring the link deletion events):

```
package link_manager_events

import (
    om "github.com/the-gigi/delinkcious/pkg/object_model"
)

func Listen(url string, sink om.LinkManagerEvents) (err error) {
    conn, err := connect(url)
    if err != nil {
        return
    }

    conn.QueueSubscribe(subject, queue, func(e *Event) {
        switch e.EventType {
        case om.LinkAdded:
            {
                sink.OnLinkAdded(e.Username, e.Link)
            }
        case om.LinkUpdated:
            {
                sink.OnLinkUpdated(e.Username, e.Link)
            }
        default:
            // Ignore other event types
        }
    })

    return
}
```

If you followed closely, you may have noticed that there is one key piece missing, which we described in our design, that is, invoking the link checking. Everything is wired up and ready to check links, but nobody is actually calling the link checker. This is where LinkManager comes in to invoke the serverless function.

Serverless link checking with Nuclio

Before we dive into LinkManager and close the loop of link checking in Delinkcious, let's get familiar with Nuclio (https://nuclio.io/) and explore how it provides a serverless function solution that works very well for Delinkcious.

A quick introduction to Nuclio

Nuclio is a polished, open source platform for high-performance serverless functions. It was developed by Iguazio and supports multiple platforms, such as Docker, Kubernetes, GKE, and Iguazio itself. We obviously care about Kubernetes, but it's interesting to note that Nuclio can be used on other platforms too. It has the following features:

- It can build functions from the source code or provide your own container.
- It is a very clean, conceptual model.
- It has great integration with Kubernetes.
- It uses a CLI called `nuctl`.
- It has a web dashboard if you want to play with it interactively.
- It has a slew of methods to deploy, manage, and invoke your serverless functions.
- It offers GPU support.
- It is a managed solution with 24/7 support (this is paid).

Finally, it has a super cool logo! You can view the logo here:

Let's now build and deploy our link checking capability into Delinkcious using Nuclio.

Creating a link checker serverless function

The first step is creating a serverless function; there are two components here:

- The function code
- The function configuration

Let's create a dedicated directory called `fun` for storing serverless functions. Serverless functions don't really fit into any of our existing categories; that is, they are not plain packages, they are not services, and they are not commands. We can put the function code and its configuration as a YAML file under the `link_checker` subdirectory. Later, if we decide to model additional capabilities as serverless functions, then we can create additional subdirectories for each function as follows:

```
$ tree fun
fun
└── link_checker
    ├── function.yaml
    └── link_checker.go
```

The function itself is implemented in `link_checker.go`. The `link_checker` function is responsible for checking a link when triggered and publishing an event to NATS with the results. Let's break it down piece by piece, starting with the imports and constants. Our function will utilize the Nuclio GO SDK, which provides a standard signature that we will look at later. It also imports our Delinkcious packages: the `object_model`, the `link_checker`, and the `link_checker_events` packages.

Here, we also define the NATS URL based on the well-known Kubernetes DNS name. Note that the `natsUrl` constant includes the namespace (by default). The `link_checker` serverless function will run in the Nuclio namespace, but will send events to the NATS server running in the default namespace.

This is not a problem; namespaces are not isolated from each other at the network level (unless you explicitly create a network policy):

```
package main

import (
    "encoding/json"
    "errors"
    "fmt"
    "github.com/nuclio/nuclio-sdk-go"
    "github.com/the-gigi/delinkcious/pkg/link_checker"
    "github.com/the-gigi/delinkcious/pkg/link_checker_events"
    om "github.com/the-gigi/delinkcious/pkg/object_model"
```

```
)
```

```
const natsUrl = "nats-cluster.default.svc.cluster.local:4222"
```

Implementing a Nuclio serverless function (in Go) means implementing a handler function with a certain signature. The function accepts a Nuclio context and a Nuclio event object. Both are defined in the Nuclio GO SDK. The handler function returns an empty interface (which can pretty much return anything). However, there is a standard Nuclio response object for the HTTP-invoked functions that we use here. The Nuclio event has a GetBody() message that can be used to get the input to the function.

Here, we unmarshal it using the standard JSON encoder in CheckLinkRequest from the Delinkcious object model. This is the contract between whoever invokes the link_checker function and the function itself. Since Nuclio provides a generic signature, we must validate the input that was provided in the body. If it wasn't, then the json.Unmarshal() call will fail and the function will return a 400 (that is, a bad request) error:

```
func Handler(context *nuclio.Context, event nuclio.Event) (interface{},
error) { r := nuclio.Response{ StatusCode: 200, ContentType:
"application/text", }

body := event.GetBody()
 var e om.CheckLinkRequest
 err := json.Unmarshal(body, &e)
 if err != nil {
     msg := fmt.Sprintf("failed to unmarshal body: %v", body)
     context.Logger.Error(msg)

     r.StatusCode = 400
     r.Body = []byte(fmt.Sprintf(msg))
     return r, errors.New(msg)

}
```

Additionally, if the unmarshaling succeeded but the resulting CheckLinkRequest has an empty username or empty URL, it is still an invalid input and the function will return a 400 error as well:

```
username := e.Username
 url := e.Url
 if username == "" || url == "" {
     msg := fmt.Sprintf("missing USERNAME ('%s') and/or URL ('%s')",
username, url)
     context.Logger.Error(msg)

     r.StatusCode = 400
```

```
    r.Body = []byte(msg)
    return r, errors.New(msg)
}
```

At this point, the function validated the input, we got a username and a URL, and it's ready to check whether the link itself is valid. All it takes is to call the CheckLink() function of the pkg/link_checker package that we implemented earlier. The status is initialized to LinkStatusValid and, if the check returns an error, then the status is set to LinkStatusInvalid as follows:

```
status := om.LinkStatusValid
err = link_checker.CheckLink(url)
if err != nil {
status = om.LinkStatusInvalid
    }
```

However, don't get confused! The pkg/link_checker package is a package that implements the CheckLink() function. In comparison, fun/link_checker is a Nuclio serverless function that calls CheckLink().

The link was checked and we have its status; it's now time to publish the result through NATS. Again, we've already done all the hard work in pkg/link_checker_events. The function creates a new event sender using the natsUrl constant. If it failed, then the function returns an error. If the sender was created properly, it invokes its OnLinkChecked() method with the username, the URL, and the status. Finally, it returns the Nuclio response (initialized to 200 OK) and no error, as follows:

```
sender, err := link_checker_events.NewEventSender(natsUrl)
if err != nil {
    context.Logger.Error(err.Error())

    r.StatusCode = 500
    r.Body = []byte(err.Error())
    return r, err
}

sender.OnLinkChecked(username, url, status)
return r, nil
```

The code is only half the story, however. Let's review the function configuration in fun/link_checker/function.yaml. It looks just like a standard Kubernetes resource and this is no coincidence.

You can take a look at the full specification at `https://nuclio.io/docs/latest/reference/function-configuration-reference/`.

In the following code block, we specify the API version, the kind (`NuclioFunction`), and then the spec. We have a description filled, the runtime field says Golang, and the handler defines the package and function name that implements the handler function. We also specify the minimum and maximum replicas, which, in this case, are both 1. Note that Nuclio doesn't provide a way to scale to zero. There will always be at least one replica of each deployed function waiting to be triggered. The only custom part of the configuration is the `build` command to install the `ca-certificates` package. This uses the **Alpine Linux Package Manager** (**APK**) system. This is necessary because the link checker needs to check HTTPS links too, and that requires root CA certificates:

```
apiVersion: "nuclio.io/v1beta1"
 kind: "NuclioFunction"
 spec:
   description: >
     A function that connects to NATS, checks incoming links and publishes
LinkValid or LinkInvalid events.
   runtime: "golang"
   handler: main:Handler
   minReplicas: 1
   maxReplicas: 1
   build:
     commands:
     - apk --update --no-cache add ca-certificates
```

All right! We created a link checker serverless function and a configuration; let's now deploy it to our cluster.

Deploying the link checker function with nuctl

When Nuclio deploys a function, it actually builds a Docker image and pushes it to a registry. Here, we'll use the Docker Hub registry; so, first, let's log in:

```
$ docker login
Login with your Docker ID to push and pull images from Docker Hub. If you
don't have a Docker ID, head over to https://hub.docker.com to create one.
 Username: g1g1
 Password:
 Login Succeeded
```

The function name must follow DNS naming rules, so the `""` marks in `link_checker` are not acceptable. Instead, we'll name the function `link-checker` and run the `nuctl deploy` command, as follows:

```
$ cd fun/link_checker
$ nuctl deploy link-checker -n nuclio -p . --registry g1g1


   nuctl (I) Deploying function {"name": "link-checker"}
   nuctl (I) Building {"name": "link-checker"}
   nuctl (I) Staging files and preparing base images
   nuctl (I) Pulling image {"imageName": "quay.io/nuclio/handler-builder-
   golang-onbuild:1.1.2-amd64-alpine"}
   nuctl (I) Building processor image {"imageName": "processor-link-
   checker:latest"}
   nuctl (I) Pushing image {"from": "processor-link-checker:latest", "to":
   "g1g1/processor-link-checker:latest"}
   nuctl (I) Build complete {"result": {"Image":"processor-link-
   checker:latest"...}}
   nuctl (I) Function deploy complete {"httpPort": 31475}
```

Note that the documentation for deploying a function with `nuctl` to the Docker Hub registry is incorrect at the time of writing. I opened a GitHub issue (`https://github.com/nuclio/nuclio/issues/1181`) for the Nuclio team. Hopefully, it will be fixed by the time you read this.

The function was deployed to the Nuclio namespace, as follows:

```
$ kubectl get nucliofunctions -n nuclio
NAME            AGE
link-checker    42m
```

The best way to see all the configuration is to use `nuctl` again:

```
$ nuctl get function -n nuclio -o yaml
metadata:
name: link-checker
namespace: nuclio
spec:
alias: latest
build:
path: .
registry: g1g1
timestamp: 1554442452
description: |
A function with a configuration that connects to NATS, listens to LinkAdded
events, check the links and send LinkValid or LinkInvalid events.
```

```
handler: main:Handler
image: g1g1/processor-link-checker:latest
imageHash: "1554442427312071335"
maxReplicas: 1
minReplicas: 1
platform: {}
readinessTimeoutSeconds: 30
replicas: 1
resources: {}
runRegistry: g1g1
runtime: golang
serviceType: NodePort
targetCPU: 75
version: -1
```

As you can see, it borrows a lot from our `function.yaml` configuration file.

We have successfully deployed our function using the `nuctl` CLI, which is great for developers and CI/CD systems. Let's now take a look at how to deploy a function using the Nuclio web UI.

Deploying a function using the Nuclio dashboard

Nuclio has a cool web UI dashboard. The Nuclio dashboard is very well done; it is installed as a service in our cluster. First, we need to do a little port forwarding before we can access it:

```
$ kubectl port-forward -n nuclio $(kubectl get pods -n nuclio -l
nuclio.io/app=dashboard -o jsonpath='{.items[0].metadata.name}') 8070
```

Next, we can browse to `localhost:8070` and play with the dashboard. The dashboard allows you to view, deploy, and test (or invoke) serverless functions directly from a single screen. This is great for ad hoc exploration.

Here, I slightly modified the `hello` example function (in Python) and even tested it with the text, `Yeah, it works!`:

Once the function is deployed in the cluster, we can invoke it in different ways.

Invoking the link-checker function directly

Invoking the function using `nuctl` is very simple. We need to provide the function name (`link-checker`), the namespace, the cluster IP address, and the body, which is the input to the function:

```
nuctl invoke link-checker -n nuclio --external-ips $(mk ip)
```

Triggering link checking in LinkManager

Using `nuctl` is nice when you develop your functions and want a quick edit-deploy-debug
cycle. However, in production, you will want to either invoke the function by using an
HTTP endpoint or one of the triggers. For Delinkcious, the simplest way is by having
`LinkManager` directly hit the HTTP endpoint. This happens when a new link is added to
the `AddLink()` method of `LinkManager`. It simply calls `triggerLinkCheck` with the
username and URL, as follows:

```
func (m *LinkManager) AddLink(request om.AddLinkRequest) (err error) {
    ...


    // Trigger link check asynchronously (don't wait for result)
    triggerLinkCheck(request.Username, request.Url)
    return
}
```

It's important that the `AddLink()` method doesn't have to wait for the link check to
complete. If you remember, the link will be stored immediately with a *pending* status. Later,
when the check is complete, the status will be changed to either *valid* or *invalid*. To
accomplish this, the `triggerLinkCheck()` function runs a goroutine that returns control
immediately.

The goroutine, in the meantime, prepares `om.CheckLinkRequest`, which the handler of
the `link_checker` serverless function is expecting. It serializes it into JSON
via `json.Marshal()` and, using the Go built-in HTTP client, it sends a POST request to the
link checker function URL in the Nuclio namespace (it has no problem hitting HTTP
endpoints in another namespace). Here, we just ignore any errors; if something goes wrong,
then the link will stay in the *pending* state and we can decide what to do about it later:

```
// Nuclio functions listen by default on port 8080 of their service IP
 const link_checker_func_url =
"http://link-checker.nuclio.svc.cluster.local:8080"


func triggerLinkCheck(username string, url string) {
    go func() {
        checkLinkRequest := &om.CheckLinkRequest{Username: username, Url:
url}
        data, err := json.Marshal(checkLinkRequest)
        if err != nil {
            return
        }
```

```
        req, err := http.NewRequest("POST", link_checker_func_url,
    bytes.NewBuffer(data))
        req.Header.Set("Content-Type", "application/json")
        client := &http.Client{}
        resp, err := client.Do(req)
        if err != nil {
            return
        }
        defer resp.Body.Close()
    }()
}
```

We did a lot of work here, but we kept everything loosely coupled and ready for extension. It would be very easy to add more sophisticated link checking logic in order to trigger link checking as a NATS event instead of directly hitting an HTTP endpoint, or even replace the Nuclio serverless function with a completely different serverless function solution. Let's briefly take a look at the other options in the following section.

Other Kubernetes serverless frameworks

AWS Lambda functions made serverless functions in the cloud very popular. Kubernetes is not a fully-fledged serverless function primitive, but it gets pretty close with the Job and CronJob resources. In addition to this, a plethora of serverless function solutions were developed by the community (Nuclio being one of them). Here are some of the more popular and mature options that we will see in the following subsections:

- Kubernetes Jobs and CronJobs
- KNative
- Fission
- Kubeless
- OpenFaas

Kubernetes Jobs and CronJobs

Kubernetes deployments and services are all about creating a set of long-running pods that are supposed to run indefinitely. A Kubernetes Job is all about running one or more pods until one of them completes successfully. When you create a Job, it looks very much like a deployment, except that the restart policy should be `Never`.

Here is a Kubernetes Job that prints `Yeah, it works in a Job!!!` from Python:

```
apiVersion: batch/v1
kind: Job
metadata:
  name: yeah-it-works
spec:
  template:
    spec:
      containers:
      - name: yeah-it-works
        image: python:3.6-alpine
        command: ["python", "-c", "print('Yeah, it works in a Job!!!')"]
      restartPolicy: Never
```

I can now run this Job, watch it complete, and check the logs, as follows:

```
$ kubectl create -f job.yaml
  job.batch/yeah-it-works created

$ kubectl get po | grep yeah-it-works
yeah-it-works-flz15              0/1       Completed   0           116s

$ kubectl logs yeah-it-works-flz15
Yeah, it works in a Job!!!
```

This is almost a serverless function. Of course, it doesn't come with all the bells and whistles, but the core functionality is there: launch a container, run it to completion, and get back the results.

A Kubernetes CronJob is similar to a Job, except that it gets triggered on a schedule. If you don't want to incur additional dependencies on a third-party serverless function framework, then you can build a basic solution on top of the Kubernetes Job and CronJob objects.

KNative

KNative (`https://cloud.google.com/knative/`) is a relative newcomer to the serverless functions scene, but I actually predict that it will become the mainstream go-to solution, and there are several reasons for this, such as the following:

- It is a strong solution that can scale to zero (unlike Nuclio).
- It can build images in-cluster (using Kaniko).
- It is Kubernetes-specific.

- It has the cloud of Google behind it and is available on GKE via Cloud Run (`https://cloud.google.com/blog/products/serverless/announcing-cloud-run-the-newest-member-of-our-serverless-compute-stack`).
- It uses the Istio service mesh as a foundation, and Istio is becoming very important (more on that in `Chapter 13`, *Service Mesh – Working with Istio*).

KNative has three separate components, as follows:

- Building
- Serving
- Eventing

It is designed to be very pluggable so that you bring your own builder or event sources. The build component is in charge of going from the source to the image. The serving component is responsible for scaling the number of containers needed to handle the load. It can scale up as more load is generated, or down, including all the way to zero. The eventing component is related to producing and consuming events in your serverless functions.

Fission

Fission (`https://fission.io/`) is an open source serverless framework from Platform9 that supports multiple languages, such as Python, NodeJS, Go, C#, and PHP. It can be extended to support other languages. It keeps a pool of containers ready to go, so new function invocations have very low latency at the expense of not scaling to zero when there is no load. What makes Fission special is its ability to compose and chain functions through Fission workflows (`https://fission.io/workflows/`). This is similar to AWS step functions; other interesting features of Fission include the following:

- It can integrate with Istio for monitoring.
- It can incorporate logs into the CLI through Fluentd integration (Fluentd is automatically installed as a DaemonSet).
- It offers Prometheus integration for metrics collection and dashboard visibility.

Kubeless

Kubeless is another Kubernetes-native framework from Bitnami. It uses a conceptual model of functions, triggers, and runtimes, which are implemented using Kubernetes CRDs that are configured through ConfigMaps. Kubeless uses Kubernetes deployments for function pods, and **Horizontal Pod Autoscaler** (**HPA**) for autoscaling.

This means that Kubeless doesn't scale to zero because HPA doesn't scale to zero at the moment. One of Kubeless's primary claims to fame is its excellent UI.

OpenFaas

OpenFaas (`https://www.openfaas.com/`) is one of the earliest FaaS projects. It can run on Kubernetes or Docker Swarm. Since it's cross-platform, it does a lot of things in a generic and non-Kubernetes way. For example, it can scale to zero by using its own management for function containers. It also supports many languages and even plain binaries as functions.

It also has the OpenFaaS Cloud project, which is a complete GitOps-based CI/CD pipeline to manage your serverless functions. Similar to other serverless function projects, OpenFaas has its own CLI and UI for management and deployment.

Summary

In this chapter, we introduced link checking to Delinkcious and we did it in style! We discussed the serverless scene, including its two common meanings; that is, not dealing with instances, nodes, or servers, and cloud functions as a service. We then implemented a loosely coupled solution within Delinkcious for link checking, which took advantage of our NATS messaging system to distribute events when links are checked. Then, we covered Nuclio in some detail and used it to close the loop and let the `LinkManager` initiate link checks on a serverless function and get notified later to update the link status.

Finally, we surveyed many other solutions and frameworks for serverless functions on Kubernetes. At this point, you should have a solid understanding of what serverless computing and serverless functions are all about. You should be able to make an informed decision about whether your systems and projects can benefit from serverless functions and which solution is the best. It's clear that the benefits are real, and that it's not a fad that will disappear. I anticipate that the serverless solutions in Kubernetes will consolidate (possibly around KNative) and become a cornerstone of most Kubernetes deployments, even if they are not part of core Kubernetes.

In the next chapter, we will go back to the basics and explore one of my favorite subjects, that is, testing. Testing can make or break large projects and there are many lessons to apply in the context of microservices and Kubernetes.

Further reading

You can refer to the following references for more information:

- **Nuclio documentation**: https://nuclio.io/docs/latest
- **Kubernetes (Jobs – Run to Completion)**: https://kubernetes.io/docs/concepts/workloads/controllers/jobs-run-to-completion/
- **CronJob**: https://kubernetes.io/docs/concepts/workloads/controllers/cron-jobs/
- **KNative**: https://cloud.google.com/knative/
- **Fission**: https://fission.io/
- **Kubeless**: https://kubeless.io/
- **OpenFaas**: https://www.openfaas.com

10
Testing Microservices

Software is the most complex thing humans create. Most programmers can't write 10 lines of code without any errors occurring. Now, take this common knowledge and consider what it takes to write a distributed system made of tens, hundreds, or thousands of interacting components that have been designed and implemented by large teams using lots of third-party dependencies, lots of data-driven logic, and lots of configuration. Over time, many of the original architects and engineers that built the system might have left the organization or moved to a different role. Requirements change, new technologies are reintroduced, and better practices are discovered. The system must evolve to meet all of these changes.

The bottom line is that you have zero chance of building a working non-trivial system without rigorous testing. Proper tests are the skeleton that ensures that your system works as expected and immediately identifies problems when you introduce a breaking change before it makes in into production. A microservices-based architecture introduces some unique challenges for testing since many of the workflows touch upon multiple microservices and it may be difficult to control the test conditions across all the relevant microservices and data stores. Kubernetes introduces its own testing challenges since it does so much under the covers, which takes more work to create predictable and repeatable tests.

We will demonstrate all these types of tests within Delinkcious. In particular, we will focus on local testing with Kubernetes. Then, we'll discuss the important issue of isolation, which allows us to run end-to-end tests without impacting our production environments. Finally, we'll see how to deal with data-intensive tests.

The following topics will be covered in this chapter:

- Unit testing
- Integration testing
- Local testing with Kubernetes
- Isolation
- End to end testing
- Managing test data

Technical requirements

The code is split between two Git repositories:

- You can find the code samples here: `https://github.com/PacktPublishing/Hands-On-Microservices-with-Kubernetes/tree/master/Chapter10`
- You can find the updated Delinkcious application here: `https://github.com/the-gigi/delinkcious/releases/tag/v0.8`

Unit testing

Unit testing is the easiest type of testing to incorporate into your codebase, yet it brings a lot of value. When I say it's the easiest, I take it for granted that you can use best practices such as proper abstraction, separation of concerns, dependency injection, and so on. There is nothing easy about trying to test a spaghetti codebase!

Let's talk briefly about unit testing in Go, the Ginkgo test framework, and then review some unit tests in Delinkcious.

Unit testing with Go

Go is a modern language and recognizes the importance of testing. Go encourages that for each `foo.go` file you have, to have `foo_test.go`. It also provides the testing package, and the Go tool has a `test` command. Let's look at a simple example. Here is a `foo.go` file that contains the `safeDivide()` function. This function divides integers and returns a result and an error.

If the denominator is non-zero, it returns no error, but if the denominator is zero, it returns a `division by zero` error:

```
package main

import "errors"

func safeDivide(a int, b int) (int, error) {
        if b == 0 {
                return 0, errors.New("division by zero")
        }

        return a / b, nil
}
```

Note that Go division uses integer division when both operands are integers. This is done so that the result of dividing two integers is always the whole part (the fractional part is discarded). For example, 6/4 returns 1.

Here is a Go unit test in a file called `foo_test.go` that tests both non-zero and zero denominators and uses the `testing` package. Each `test` function accepts a pointer to the `testing.T` object. When a test fails, it calls the `Errorf()` method of the `T` object:

```
package main

import (
        "testing"
)

func TestExactResult(t *testing.T) {
        result, err := safeDivide(8, 4)
        if err != nil {
                t.Errorf("8 / 4 expected 2,  got error %v", err)
        }

        if result != 2 {
         t.Errorf("8 / 4 expected 2,  got %d", result)
        }
}

func TestIntDivision(t *testing.T) {
        result, err := safeDivide(14, 5)
        if err != nil {
                t.Errorf("14 / 5 expected 2,  got error %v", err)
        }

        if result != 2 {
```

```
                    t.Errorf("14 / 5 expected 2,  got %d", result)
        }
}

func TestDivideByZero(t *testing.T) {
        result, err := safeDivide(77, 0)
        if err == nil {
                t.Errorf("77 / 0 expected 'division by zero' error,  got
result %d", result)
        }

        if err.Error() != "division by zero" {
                t.Errorf("77 / 0 expected 'division by zero' error,  got
this error instead %v", err)
        }
}
```

Now, to run the tests, we can use the `go test -v` command. It is part of the standard Go tool:

```
$ go test -v
=== RUN    TestExactResult
--- PASS: TestExactResult (0.00s)
=== RUN    TestIntDivision
--- PASS: TestIntDivision (0.00s)
=== RUN    TestDivideByZero
--- PASS: TestDivideByZero (0.00s)
PASS
ok      github.com/the-gigi/hands-on-microservices-with-kubernetes-
code/ch10    0.010s
```

Nice – all the tests pass. We can also see how long it took to run the tests. Let's introduce an intentional bug. Now, `safeDivide` subtracts instead of divides:

```
package main

import "errors"

func safeDivide(a int, b int) (int, error) {
        if b == 0 {
                return 0, errors.New("division by zero")
        }

        return a - b, nil
}
```

We only expect the divide by zero test to pass:

```
$ go test -v
=== RUN    TestExactResult
--- FAIL: TestExactResult (0.00s)
    foo_test.go:14: 8 / 4 expected 2,   got 4
=== RUN    TestIntDivision
--- FAIL: TestIntDivision (0.00s)
    foo_test.go:25: 14 / 5 expected 2,   got 9
=== RUN    TestDivideByZero
--- PASS: TestDivideByZero (0.00s)
FAIL
exit status 1
FAIL    github.com/the-gigi/hands-on-microservices-with-kubernetes-
code/ch10    0.009s
```

We got exactly what we expected.

There is a lot more to the `testing` package. The `T` object has additional methods you can use. There are facilities for benchmarks and for common setups. However, overall, due to the ergonomics of the testing package, it's not ideal to have call methods on the `T` object. It can also be difficult to manage a complex and hierarchical set of tests using the `testing` package without additional tooling on top of it. This is exactly where Ginkgo comes into the picture. Let's get to know Ginkgo. Delinkcious uses Ginkgo for its unit tests.

Unit testing with Ginkgo and Gomega

Ginkgo (`https://github.com/onsi/ginkgo`) is a **behavior-driven development** (BDD) testing framework. It still uses the testing package under the covers, but allows you to write tests using a much nicer syntax. It also pairs well with Gomega (`https://github.com/onsi/gomega`), which is an excellent assertions library. Here is what you get with Ginkgo and Gomega:

- Write BDD-style tests
- Arbitrary nested blocks (`Describe`, `Context`, `When`)
- Good setup/teardown support (`BeforeEach`, `AfterEach`, `BeforeSuite`, `AfterSuite`)
- Focus on one test only or match by regex
- Skip tests by regex
- Parallelism
- Integration with coverage and benchmarking

Let's see how Delinkcious uses Ginkgo and Gomega for its unit tests.

Delinkcious unit testing

We'll use `LinkManager` from the `link_manager` package as an example. It has pretty sophisticated interactions: it allows you to manage a data store, hit another microservice (social graph service), trigger a serverless function (link checker), and respond to link check events. This sounds like a very diverse set of dependencies, but as you'll see, by designing for testability, it is possible to achieve a high level of testing without too much complexity.

Designing for testability

Proper testing starts a long time before you write your test. Even if you practice **test-driven design** (**TDD**) and you write your tests before the implementation, you still need to design the interface of the code you want to test before you write the test (otherwise what functions or methods will the test invoke?). With Delinkcious, we took a very deliberate approach with abstractions, layers, and separation of concerns. All our hard work is going to pay off now.

Let's look at `LinkManager` and just consider its dependencies:

```
package link_manager

import (
    "bytes"
    "encoding/json"
    "errors"
    "github.com/the-gigi/delinkcious/pkg/link_checker_events"
    om "github.com/the-gigi/delinkcious/pkg/object_model"
    "log"
    "net/http"
)
```

As you can see, `LinkManager` depends on the Delinkcious object model abstract package, `link_checker_events`, and standard Go packages. `LinkManager` doesn't depend on the implementation of any other Delinkcious component or on any third-party dependency. During testing, we can provide alternative (mock) implementations for all the dependencies and have total control of the test environment and the result. We'll see how we can go about doing this in the next section.

The art of mocking

Ideally, an object should have all its dependencies injected when it is created. Let's look at the `NewLinkManager()` function:

```
func NewLinkManager(linkStore LinkStore,
    socialGraphManager om.SocialGraphManager,
    natsUrl string,
    eventSink om.LinkManagerEvents,
    maxLinksPerUser int64) (om.LinkManager, error) {
    ...
}
```

This is almost the ideal situation. We get interfaces to the link store, social graph manager, and to the event sink. However, there are two dependencies that are not injected here: `link_checker_events` and the built-in `net/http` package. Let's start with mocking the link store, the social graph manager, and the link manager event sink, and then consider the more difficult cases.

`LinkStore` is an interface that's defined internally:

```
package link_manager

import (
    om "github.com/the-gigi/delinkcious/pkg/object_model"
)

type LinkStore interface {
    GetLinks(request om.GetLinksRequest) (om.GetLinksResult, error)
    AddLink(request om.AddLinkRequest) (*om.Link, error)
    UpdateLink(request om.UpdateLinkRequest) (*om.Link, error)
    DeleteLink(username string, url string) error
    SetLinkStatus(username, url string, status om.LinkStatus) error
}
```

In the `pkg/link_manager/mock_social_graph_manager.go` file, we can find a mock social graph manager that implements `om.SocialGraphManager` and always returns the followers that were provided to the `newMockSocialGraphManager()` function from the `GetFollowers()` method. This is a great way to reuse the same mock for different tests that require different canned responses from `GetFollowers()`. The reason the other methods just return nil is that they are not called by `LinkManager`, so there's no need to provide an actual response:

```
package link_manager
type mockSocialGraphManager struct { followers map[string]bool }
```

```
func (m *mockSocialGraphManager) Follow(followed string, follower string)
error { return nil }

func (m *mockSocialGraphManager) Unfollow(followed string, follower string)
error { return nil }

func (m *mockSocialGraphManager) GetFollowing(username string)
(map[string]bool, error) { return nil, nil }

func (m *mockSocialGraphManager) GetFollowers(username string)
(map[string]bool, error) { return m.followers, nil }

func newMockSocialGraphManager(followers []string) *mockSocialGraphManager
{ m := &mockSocialGraphManager{ map[string]bool{}, } for _, f := range
followers { m.followers[f] = true }

return m

}
```

The event sink is a little different. We are interested in verifying that when various
operations, such as `AddLink()`, are called, `LinkManager` properly notifies the event sink.
In order to do that, we can create a test event sink that implements the
`om.LinkManagerEvents` interface and keeps track of events coming its way. Here is the
code in the `pkg/link_manager/test_event_sink.go` file. The `testEventSink` struct
keeps a map for each event type, where the keys are username and the values are a list of
links. It updates these maps in response to the various events:

```
package link_manager

import ( om "github.com/the-gigi/delinkcious/pkg/object_model" )

type testEventsSink struct { addLinkEvents map[string][]om.Link
updateLinkEvents map[string][]om.Link deletedLinkEvents map[string][]string
}

func (s testEventsSink) OnLinkAdded(username string, link om.Link) { if
s.addLinkEvents[username] == nil { s.addLinkEvents[username] = []*om.Link{}
} s.addLinkEvents[username] = append(s.addLinkEvents[username], link) }

func (s testEventsSink) OnLinkUpdated(username string, link om.Link) { if
s.updateLinkEvents[username] == nil { s.updateLinkEvents[username] =
[]*om.Link{} } s.updateLinkEvents[username] =
append(s.updateLinkEvents[username], link) }

func (s *testEventsSink) OnLinkDeleted(username string, url string) { if
s.deletedLinkEvents[username] == nil { s.deletedLinkEvents[username] =
```

```
[]string{} } s.deletedLinkEvents[username] =
append(s.deletedLinkEvents[username], url) }

func newLinkManagerEventsSink() testEventsSink { return &testEventsSink{
map[string][]om.Link{}, map[string][]*om.Link{}, map[string][]string{}, } }
```

Now that we've got our mocks in place, let's create the Ginkgo test suite.

Bootstrapping your test suite

Ginkgo builds on top of Go's testing package, which is convenient because you can run your Ginkgo tests with just `go test`, although Ginkgo also provides a CLI called Ginkgo with more options. To bootstrap a test suite for a package, run the `ginkgo bootstrap` command. It will generate a file called `<package>_suite_test.go`. The file wires up all the Ginkgo tests to the standard Go testing, and also imports the `ginkgo` and `gomega` packages. Here is the test suite file for the `link_manager` package:

```
package link_manager
import ( "testing"
. "github.com/onsi/ginkgo"
. "github.com/onsi/gomega"
)
func TestLinkManager(t *testing.T) { RegisterFailHandler(Fail) RunSpecs(t,
"LinkManager Suite") }
```

With the test suite file in place, we can start writing some unit tests.

Implementing the LinkManager unit tests

Let's look at the test for getting and adding links. There is a lot going on there. This is all in the `pkg/link_manager/in_memory_link_manager_test.go` file. First, let's set the scene by importing `ginkgo`, `gomega`, and the `delinkcious` object model:

```
package link_manager
import ( . "github.com/onsi/ginkgo" . "github.com/onsi/gomega" om
"github.com/the-gigi/delinkcious/pkg/object_model" )
```

The Ginkgo `Describe` block describes all the tests in the file and defines variables that will be used by multiple tests:

```
var _ = Describe("In-memory link manager tests", func() { var err error var
linkManager om.LinkManager var socialGraphManager mockSocialGraphManager
var eventSink testEventsSink
```

The `BeforeEach()` function is called before each test. It creates a fresh mock social graph manager with `liat` as the only follower, a new event sink, and initializes the new `LinkManager` with these dependencies, as well as an in-memory link store, thus utilizing the dependency injection practice:

```
BeforeEach(func() {
    socialGraphManager = newMockSocialGraphManager([]string{"liat"})
    eventSink = newLinkManagerEventsSink()
    linkManager, err = NewLinkManager(NewInMemoryLinkStore(),
        socialGraphManager,
        "",
        eventSink,
        10)
    Ω(err).Should(BeNil())
})
```

Here is the actual test. Note the BDD style of defining tests that read like English, *It should add and get link*. Let's break it down piece by piece; first, the test makes sure that there are no existing links for the `"gigi"` user by calling `GetLinks()` and asserting that the result is empty by using Gomega's Ω operator:

```
It("should add and get links", func() {
    // No links initially
    r := om.GetLinksRequest{
        Username: "gigi",
    }
    res, err := linkManager.GetLinks(r)
    Ω(err).Should(BeNil())
    Ω(res.Links).Should(HaveLen(0))
```

The next part is about adding a link and just making sure that no errors occurred:

```
// Add a link
r2 := om.AddLinkRequest{
    Username: "gigi",
    Url:      "https://golang.org/",
    Title:    "Golang",
    Tags:     map[string]bool{"programming": true},
}
err = linkManager.AddLink(r2)
Ω(err).Should(BeNil())
```

Now, the test calls `GetLinks()` and expects the link that was just added to be returned:

```
res, err = linkManager.GetLinks(r)
Ω(err).Should(BeNil())
Ω(res.Links).Should(HaveLen(1))
```

```
link := res.Links[0]
Ω(link.Url).Should(Equal(r2.Url))
Ω(link.Title).Should(Equal(r2.Title))
```

Finally, the test makes sure that the event sink recorded the `OnLinkAdded()` call for follower `"liat"`:

```
// Verify link manager notified the event sink about a single added
event for the follower "liat"
    Ω(eventSink.addLinkEvents).Should(HaveLen(1))
    Ω(eventSink.addLinkEvents["liat"]).Should(HaveLen(1))
    Ω(*eventSink.addLinkEvents["liat"][0]).Should(Equal(link))
    Ω(eventSink.updateLinkEvents).Should(HaveLen(0))
    Ω(eventSink.deletedLinkEvents).Should(HaveLen(0))
})
```

This is a pretty typical unit test that performs the following tasks:

- Controls the test environment
- Mocks dependencies (social graph manager)
- Provides recording placeholders for outgoing interactions (test event sink records link manager events)
- Executes the code under test (get links and add links)
- Verifies the responses (no links at first; one link is returned after it is added)
- Verifies any outgoing interactions (the event sink received the `OnLinkAdded()` event)

We didn't test error cases here, but it's easy to add. You add bad inputs and check the code under the test that returned the expected error.

Should you test everything?

The answer is no! Testing provides a lot of value, but has costs too. The marginal value of adding tests is decreasing. Testing *everything* is difficult, if not impossible. Considering that testing takes time to develop, it can slow down changes to the system (you need to update the tests), and the tests might need to change when dependencies change. Testing also takes time and resources to run, which can slow down the edit-test-deploy cycle. Also, tests can have bugs too. Finding the sweet spot of how much testing you need is a judgement call.

Unit tests are very valuable, but they are not enough. This is especially true for microservice-based architectures where there are a lot of small components that may work independently, but fail to work together to accomplish the goals of the system. This is where integration tests come in.

Integration testing

Integration testing is a test that includes multiple components that interact with each other. Integration tests means testing complete subsystems without or very little mocking. Delinkcious has several integration tests focused on particular services. These tests are not automated Go tests. They don't use Ginkgo or the standard Go testing. They are executable programs that panic on error. These programs are designed to test cross-service interaction and how a service integrates with third-party components such as actual data stores. For example, the link_manager_e2e test performs the following steps:

1. Starts the social graph service and the link service as local processes
2. Starts a Postgres DB in a Docker container
3. Runs the test against the link service
4. Verifies the results

Let's see how it all plays out. The list of imports includes the Postgres Golang driver (lib/pq), several Delinkcious packages, and a couple of standard Go packages (context, log, and os). Note that pq is imported as a dash. This means that the pq name is unavailable. The reason to import a library in such an unnamed mode is that it just needs to run some initialization code and is not accessed externally. Specifically, pq registers a Go driver with the standard Go database/sql library:

```
package main
import ( "context" _ "github.com/lib/pq" "github.com/the-
gigi/delinkcious/pkg/db_util" "github.com/the-
gigi/delinkcious/pkg/link_manager_client" om "github.com/the-
gigi/delinkcious/pkg/object_model" . "github.com/the-
gigi/delinkcious/pkg/test_util" "log" "os" )
```

Let's look at some of the functions that are used to set up the test environments, starting with initializing the database.

Initializing a test database

The `initDB()` function calls the `RunLocalDB()` function by passing the name of the database (`link_manager`). This is important because if you're starting from fresh, it needs to create the database too. Then, to make sure that the test always runs from scratch, it deletes the `tags` and `links` tables, as follows:

```
func initDB() { db, err := db_util.RunLocalDB("link_manager") Check(err)
tables := []string{"tags", "links"}
 for _, table := range tables {
    err = db_util.DeleteFromTableIfExist(db, table)
    Check(err)
 }
}
```

Running services

The test has two separate functions to run the services. These functions are very similar. They set environment variables and call the `RunService()` function, which we will dive into soon. Both services depend on the value of the `PORT` environment variable, and it needs to be different for each of the services. This means that it is imperative that we launch the services sequentially and not in parallel. Otherwise, a service might end up listening on the wrong port:

```
func runLinkService(ctx context.Context) {
    // Set environment
    err := os.Setenv("PORT", "8080")
    Check(err)

    err = os.Setenv("MAX_LINKS_PER_USER", "10")
    Check(err)

    RunService(ctx, ".", "link_service")
}

func runSocialGraphService(ctx context.Context) {
    err := os.Setenv("PORT", "9090")
    Check(err)

    RunService(ctx, "../social_graph_service", "social_graph_service")
}
```

Running the actual test

The `main()` function is the driver of the entire test. It turns on the mutual authentication between the link manager and the social graph manager, initializes the database, and runs the services (as long as the RUN_XXX_SERVICE environment variable is `true`):

```
func main() {
    // Turn on authentication
    err := os.Setenv("DELINKCIOUS_MUTUAL_AUTH", "true")
    Check(err)

    initDB()

    ctx := context.Background()
    defer KillServer(ctx)

    if os.Getenv("RUN_SOCIAL_GRAPH_SERVICE") == "true" {
        runSocialGraphService(ctx)
    }

    if os.Getenv("RUN_LINK_SERVICE") == "true" {
        runLinkService(ctx)
    }
```

Now it's ready to actually run the test. It uses the link manager client to connect to port `8080` on the localhost, which is where the link service is running. Then, it calls the `GetLinks()` method, prints the result (should be empty), adds a link by calling `AddLink()`, calls `GetLinks()` again, and prints the results (should be one link):

```
// Run some tests with the client
    cli, err := link_manager_client.NewClient("localhost:8080")
    Check(err)

    links, err := cli.GetLinks(om.GetLinksRequest{Username: "gigi"})
    Check(err)
    log.Print("gigi's links:", links)

    err = cli.AddLink(om.AddLinkRequest{Username: "gigi",
        Url:   "https://github.com/the-gigi",
        Title: "Gigi on Github",
        Tags:  map[string]bool{"programming": true}})
    Check(err)

    links, err = cli.GetLinks(om.GetLinksRequest{Username: "gigi"})
    Check(err)
    log.Print("gigi's links:", links)
```

This integration test is not automated. It is designed for interactive use where the developer can run and debug individual services. If an error occurs, it immediately bails out. The results of each operation are simply printed to the screen.

The rest of the test checks the `UpdateLink()` and `DeleteLink()` operations:

```
    err = cli.UpdateLink(om.UpdateLinkRequest{Username: "gigi",
        Url:          "https://github.com/the-gigi",
        Description: "Most of my open source code is here"},
    )

    Check(err)
    links, err = cli.GetLinks(om.GetLinksRequest{Username: "gigi"})
    Check(err)
    log.Print("gigi's links:", links)

    err = cli.DeleteLink("gigi", "https://github.com/the-gigi")
    Check(err)
    Check(err)
    links, err = cli.GetLinks(om.GetLinksRequest{Username: "gigi"})
    Check(err)
    log.Print("gigi's links:", links)
}
```

The fact that the test is conducted through the link manager client library ensures that the entire chain is working from client to service to dependent services and their data stores.

Let's review some test helper functions, which are very useful when we are trying to test and debug complex interactions between microservices locally.

Implementing database test helpers

Before diving into the code, let's consider what we want to accomplish. We want a local empty database to be created. We want to launch it as a Docker container, but only if it's not running already. In order to do that, we need to check whether a Docker container is running already, if we should restart it, or if we should run a new one. Then, we will try to connect to the target database and create it if it doesn't exist. The service will be responsible for creating the schema if needed because the generic DB utilities know nothing about the database schema of specific services.

The db_util.go file in the db_util package contains all the helpers functions. First, let's review the imports that include the standard Go database/sql package and squirrel – a fluent-style Go library to generate SQL (but not an ORM). The Postgres driver library – pq – is imported as well:

```
package db_util

import (
    "database/sql"
    "fmt"
    sq "github.com/Masterminds/squirrel"
    _ "github.com/lib/pq"
    "log"
    "os"
    "os/exec"
    "strconv"
    "strings"
)
```

The dbParams struct contains the information that's needed to connect to the database, and the defaultDbParams() function is convenient for getting a struct that's populated with default values:

```
type dbParams struct {
    Host     string
    Port     int
    User     string
    Password string
    DbName   string
}

func defaultDbParams() dbParams {
    return dbParams{
        Host:     "localhost",
        Port:     5432,
        User:     "postgres",
        Password: "postgres",
    }
}
```

You can call the connectToDB() function by passing the information from the dbParams struct. If everything goes OK, you'll get back a handle to the database (*sql.DB) that you can then use to access the database later:

```
func connectToDB(host string, port int, username string, password string,
dbName string) (db *sql.DB, err error) {
    mask := "host=%s port=%d user=%s password=%s dbname=%s
```

```
sslmode=disable"
    dcn := fmt.Sprintf(mask, host, port, username, password, dbName)
    db, err = sql.Open("postgres", dcn)
    return
}
```

With all the preliminaries out of the way, let's see how the `RunLocalDB()` function works. First, it runs a `docker ps -f name=postgres` command, which lists the running Docker containers named `postgres` (there can only be one):

```
func RunLocalDB(dbName string) (db *sql.DB, err error) {
    // Launch the DB if not running
    out, err := exec.Command("docker", "ps", "-f", "name=postgres", "--
format", "{{.Names}}").CombinedOutput()
    if err != nil {
        return
    }
```

If the output is empty, it means there is no such container running, so it tries to restart the container in case it has stopped. If that fails too, it just runs a new container of the `postgres:alpine` image, exposing the standard `5432` port to the local host. Note the `-z` flag. It tells Docker to run the container in detached (non-blocking) mode, which allows the function to continue. If it fails to run the new container for any reason, it gives up and returns an error:

```
    s := string(out)
    if s == "" {
        out, err = exec.Command("docker", "restart",
"postgres").CombinedOutput()
        if err != nil {
            log.Print(string(out))
            _, err = exec.Command("docker", "run", "-d", "--name",
"postgres",
                "-p", "5432:5432",
                "-e", "POSTGRES_PASSWORD=postgres",
                "postgres:alpine").CombinedOutput()

        }
        if err != nil {
            return
        }
    }
```

At this point, we are running a Postgres DB running in a container. We can use the `defaultDBParams()` function and call the `EnsureDB()` function, which we will examine next:

```
p := defaultDbParams()
  db, err = EnsureDB(p.Host, p.Port, p.User, p.Password, dbName)
  return
}
```

To ensure that the DB is ready, we need to connect to the Postgres DB of the postgres instance. Each postgres instance has several built-in databases, including the `postgres` database. The Postgres DB of the postgres instance can be used to get information and metadata about the instance. In particular, we can query the `pg_database` table to check if the target database exists. If it doesn't exist, we can create it by executing the `CREATE database <db name>` command. Finally, we connect to the target database and return its handle. As usual, if anything goes wrong, we return an error:

```
// Make sure the database exists (creates it if it doesn't)

func EnsureDB(host string, port int, username string, password string,
dbName string) (db *sql.DB, err error) { // Connect to the postgres DB
postgresDb, err := connectToDB(host, port, username, password, "postgres")
if err != nil { return }

// Check if the DB exists in the list of databases
  var count int
  sb := sq.StatementBuilder.PlaceholderFormat(sq.Dollar)
  q := sb.Select("count(*)").From("pg_database").Where(sq.Eq{"datname":
dbName})
  err = q.RunWith(postgresDb).QueryRow().Scan(&count)
  if err != nil {
      return
  }

// If it doesn't exist create it
if count == 0 {
      _, err = postgresDb.Exec("CREATE database " + dbName)
      if err != nil {
          return
      }
  }

  db, err = connectToDB(host, port, username, password, dbName)
  return
}
```

That was a deep dive into automatically setting up a database for local tests. It's very handy in many situations, even beyond microservices.

Implementing service test helpers

Let's look at some of the helper functions for testing services. The `test_util` package is very basic and uses Go standard packages as dependencies:

```
package test_util

import ( "context" "os" "os/exec" )
```

It provides an error checking function and two functions to run and stop services.

Checking errors

One of the annoying things about Go is the explicit error checking you have to do all time. The following snippet is very common; we call a function that returns a result and an error, check the error, and if it's not nil, we do something (often, we just return):

```
. . .
  result, err := foo()
  if err != nil {
      return err
  }
. . .
```

The `Check()` function makes this a little more concise by deciding that it will just panic and exit the program (or the current Go routine). This is an acceptable choice in a testing scenario where you want to bail out once any failure is encountered:

```
func Check(err error) { if err != nil { panic(err) } }
```

The previous snippet can be shortened to the following:

```
. . .
  result, err := foo()
  Check(err)
. . .
```

If you have code that needs to check many errors, then these small savings accumulate.

Running a local service

One of the most important helper functions is `RunService()`. Microservices often depend on other microservices. When testing a service, the test code often needs to run the dependent services. Here, the code builds a Go service in its `target` directory and executes it:

```
// Build and run a service in a target directory
func RunService(ctx context.Context, targetDir string, service string) {
    // Save and restore later current working dir
    wd, err := os.Getwd()
    Check(err)
    defer os.Chdir(wd)

    // Build the server if needed
    os.Chdir(targetDir)
    _, err = os.Stat("./" + service)
    if os.IsNotExist(err) {
        _, err := exec.Command("go", "build", ".").CombinedOutput()
        Check(err)
    }

    cmd := exec.CommandContext(ctx, "./"+service)
    err = cmd.Start()
    Check(err)
}
```

Running a service is important, but cleaning up at the end of the test by stopping all the services that were started by the test is important too.

Stopping a local service

Stopping a service is as simple as calling the `Done()` method of the context. It can be used to signal completion to any code that uses contexts:

```
func StopService(ctx context.Context) { ctx.Done() }
```

As you can see, there is a lot of work involved in running Delinkcious, or even just a few parts of Delinkcious locally without the help of Kubernetes. When Delinkcious is running, it's great for debugging and troubleshooting, but creating and maintaining this setup is tedious and error-prone.

Also, even if all the integration tests work, they don't fully replicate the Kubernetes cluster, and there may be many failure modes that are not captured. Let's see how we can do local testing with Kubernetes itself.

Local testing with Kubernetes

One of the hallmarks of Kubernetes is that the same cluster can run anywhere. For real-world systems, it's not always trivial if you use services that are not available locally or are prohibitively slow or expensive to access locally. The trick is to find a good spot between high fidelity and convenience.

Let's write a smoke test that takes Delinkcious through the primary workflow of getting links, adding links, and checking their status.

Writing a smoke test

The Delinkcious smoke test is not an automated one. It can be, but it will require special setup to make it work in the CI/CD environment. For real-world production systems, I highly recommend that you have an automated smoke test (and other tests, too).

The code is in the `cmd/smoke_test` directory and consists of a single file, `smoke.go`. It exercises Delinkcious though the REST API that's exposed by the API gateway. We could write this test in any language because there is no client library. I chose to use Go for consistency and to highlight how to consume a raw REST API from Go, working directly with URLs, query strings, and JSON payload serialization. I also used the Delinkcious object model link as a convenient serialization target.

The test expects a local Minikube cluster where Delinkcious is installed to be up and running. Here is the flow of the test:

1. Delete our test link to start fresh.
2. Get links (and print them).
3. Add a test link.
4. Get links again (the new link should have a *pending* status).
5. Wait a couple of seconds.
6. Get links one more time (the new link should have a *valid* status now).

This simple smoke test goes through a significant portion of Delinkcious functionality, such as the following:

- Hitting the API gateway for multiple endpoints (GET links, POST new link, DELETE link).
- Verifying the caller identity (via access token).
- The API gateway will forward the requests to the link manager service.

- The link manager service will trigger the link checker serverless function.
- The link checker will notify the link manager via NATS about the status of the new link.

Later, we can extend the test to create social relationships, which will involve the social graph manager, as well as checking the news service. This will establish a comprehensive end-to-end test. For smoke test purposes, the aforementioned workflow is just fine.

Let's start with the list of imports, which includes a lot of standard Go libraries, as well as the Delinkcious object_model (for the Link struct) package and the test_util package (for the Check() function). We could easily avoid these dependencies, but they are familiar and convenient:

```
package main

import ( "encoding/json" "errors" "fmt" om "github.com/the-
gigi/delinkcious/pkg/object_model" . "github.com/the-
gigi/delinkcious/pkg/test_util" "io/ioutil" "log" "net/http" net_url
"net/url" "os" "os/exec" "time" )
```

The next part defines a few variables. delinkciousUrl will be initialized later. delinkciousToken should be available in the environment, and httpClient is the standard Go HTTP client that we will use to call the Delinkcious REST API:

```
var ( delinkciousUrl string delinkciousToken =
os.Getenv("DELINKCIOUS_TOKEN") httpClient = http.Client{} )
```

With the preliminaries out of the way, we can focus on the test itself. It is surprisingly simple and looks pretty much like the high-level description of the smoke test. It gets the Delinkcious URL from Minikube using the following command:

```
$ minikube service api-gateway --url http://192.168.99.161:30866
```

Then, it calls the DeleteLink(), GetLinks(), and AddLink() functions, as follows:

```
func main() { tempUrl, err := exec.Command("minikube", "service", "api-
gateway", "--url").CombinedOutput() delinkciousUrl =
string(tempUrl[:len(tempUrl)-1]) + "/v1.0" Check(err)

// Delete link
 deleteLink("https://github.com/the-gigi")

 // Get links
 getLinks()

 // Add a new link
```

```
addLink("https://github.com/the-gigi", "Gigi on Github")

// Get links again
getLinks()

// Wait a little and get links again
time.Sleep(time.Second * 3)
getLinks()

}
```

The GetLinks() function constructs the proper URL, creates a new HTTP request, adds the authentication token as a header (as required by the API gateway social login authentication), and hits the /links endpoint. When the response comes back, it checks the status code and bails out if there was an error. Otherwise, it deserializes the response's body into the om.GetLinksResult struct and prints the links:

```
func getLinks() { req, err := http.NewRequest("GET",
string(delinkciousUrl)+"/links", nil) Check(err)

req.Header.Add("Access-Token", delinkciousToken)
 r, err := httpClient.Do(req)
 Check(err)

 defer r.Body.Close()

 if r.StatusCode != http.StatusOK {
     Check(errors.New(r.Status))
 }

 var glr om.GetLinksResult
 body, err := ioutil.ReadAll(r.Body)

 err = json.Unmarshal(body, &glr)
 Check(err)

 log.Println("======= Links =======")
 for _, link := range glr.Links {
     log.Println(fmt.Sprintf("title: '%s', url: '%s', status: '%s'",
link.Title, link.Url, link.Status))
 }

}
```

The `addLink()` function is very similar except that it uses the POST method and just checks that the response has an OK status. The function takes a URL and a title and constructs a URL (including encoding the query string) to comply with the API gateway specification. If the status is not OK, it will use the contents of the body as an error message:

```
func addLink(url string, title string) { params := net_url.Values{}
params.Add("url", url) params.Add("title", title) qs := params.Encode()

log.Println("===== Add Link ======")
 log.Println(fmt.Sprintf("Adding new link - title: '%s', url: '%s'", title,
url))

 url = fmt.Sprintf("%s/links?%s", delinkciousUrl, qs)
 req, err := http.NewRequest("POST", url, nil)
 Check(err)

 req.Header.Add("Access-Token", delinkciousToken)
 r, err := httpClient.Do(req)
 Check(err)
 if r.StatusCode != http.StatusOK {
     defer r.Body.Close()
     bodyBytes, err := ioutil.ReadAll(r.Body)
     Check(err)
     message := r.Status + " " + string(bodyBytes)
     Check(errors.New(message))
 }

 }
```

Great! Now, let's see the test in action.

Running the test

Before running the test, we should export `DELINKCIOUS_TOKEN` and make sure that Minikube is running:

```
$ minikube status host: Running kubelet: Running apiserver: Running
kubectl: Correctly Configured: pointing to minikube-vm at 192.168.99.160
```

To run the test, we just type the following:

```
$ go run smoke.go
```

The results are printed to the console. There was already one invalid link, that is, `http://gg.com`. Then, the test added the new link, that is, `https://github.com/the-gigi`. The new link's status was initially pending and then, after a couple of seconds when the link check succeeded, it became valid:

```
2019/04/19 10:03:48 ======= Links ======= 2019/04/19 10:03:48 title: 'gg',
url: 'http://gg.com', status: 'invalid' 2019/04/19 10:03:48 ===== Add Link
====== 2019/04/19 10:03:48 Adding new link - title: 'Gigi on Github', url:
'https://github.com/the-gigi' 2019/04/19 10:03:49 ======= Links =======
2019/04/19 10:03:49 title: 'gg', url: 'http://gg.com', status: 'invalid'
2019/04/19 10:03:49 title: 'Gigi on Github', url:
'https://github.com/the-gigi', status: 'pending' 2019/04/19 10:03:52
======= Links ======= 2019/04/19 10:03:52 title: 'gg', url:
'http://gg.com', status: 'invalid' 2019/04/19 10:03:52 title: 'Gigi on
Github', url: 'https://github.com/the-gigi', status: 'valid'
```

Telepresence

Telepresence (`https://www.telepresence.io/`) is a special tool. It lets you run a service locally as if it's running inside your Kubernetes cluster. Why is that interesting? Consider the smoke test we just implemented. If we detect a failure, we would like to do the following three things:

- Find the root cause.
- Fix it.
- Verify that the fix works.

Since we discovered the failure only when running the smoke test on our Kubernetes cluster, it is probably a failure that is not detected by our local unit tests. The normal way to find the root cause (other than reviewing the code offline) is to add a bunch of logging statements, add experimental debug code, comment out irrelevant sections and deploy the modified code, rerun the smoke test, and try to get a sense about what's broken.

Deploying modified code to a Kubernetes cluster typically involves the following steps:

1. Modifying the code
2. Pushing the modified code to a Git repository (pollute your Git history with changes that are only used for debugging)
3. Building an image (often requires running various tests)
4. Pushing the new image to an image registry
5. Deploying the new image to the cluster

This process is cumbersome and doesn't encourage ad hoc exploration and quick edit-debug-fix cycles. There are tools we will explore in Chapter 11, *Deploying Microservices*, that can skip pushing to the Git repository and automatically building your images for you, but the image is still built and deployed to the cluster.

With Telepresence, you just make changes to the code locally, and Telepresence makes sure that your local service becomes a full-fledged member of your cluster. It sees the same environment and Kubernetes resources, it can communicate with other services though the internal network, and for all intents and purposes it is part of the cluster.

Telepresence accomplishes this by installing a proxy inside the cluster that reaches out and talks to your local service. This is pretty ingenious. Let's install Telepresence and start playing with it.

Installing Telepresence

The installation of Telepresence requires the FUSE filesystem:

```
brew cask install osxfuse
```

Then, we can install Telepresence itself:

```
brew install datawire/blackbird/telepresence
```

Running a local link service via Telepresence

Let's run the link manager service locally via Telepresence. First, to demonstrate that it is really the local service that is running, we can modify the service code. For example, we can print a message when getting links, that is, "**** Local link service here! calling GetLinks() ****".

Let's add it to the GetLinks endpoint in svc/link_service/service/transport.go:

```
func makeGetLinksEndpoint(svc om.LinkManager) endpoint.Endpoint { return
func(_ context.Context, request interface{}) (interface{}, error) {
fmt.Println("**** Local link service here! calling GetLinks() ****") req :=
request.(om.GetLinksRequest) result, err := svc.GetLinks(req) res :=
getLinksResponse{} for _, link := range result.Links { res.Links =
append(res.Links, newLink(link)) } if err != nil { res.Err = err.Error()
return res, err } return res, nil } }
```

Now, we can build the local link service (with flags recommended by Telepresence) and swap the `link-manager` deployment with the local service:

```
$ cd svc/service/link_service
$ go build -gcflags "all=-N -l" .

$ telepresence --swap-deployment link-manager --run ./link_service
T: How Telepresence uses sudo:
https://www.telepresence.io/reference/install#dependencies
T: Invoking sudo. Please enter your sudo password.
Password:
T: Starting proxy with method 'vpn-tcp', which has the following
limitations: All processes are affected, only one telepresence can run per
machine, and you can't use other VPNs. You may need to add cloud hosts and
headless services with --also-proxy.
T: For a full list of method limitations see
https://telepresence.io/reference/methods.html
T: Volumes are rooted at $TELEPRESENCE_ROOT. See
https://telepresence.io/howto/volumes.html for details.
T: Starting network proxy to cluster by swapping out Deployment link-
manager with a proxy
T: Forwarding remote port 8080 to local port 8080.

T: Guessing that Services IP range is 10.96.0.0/12. Services started after
this point will be inaccessible if are outside this range; restart
telepresence if you can't access a new Service.
T: Setup complete. Launching your command.
2019/04/20 01:17:06 DB host: 10.100.193.162 DB port: 5432
2019/04/20 01:17:06 Listening on port 8080...
```

Note that Telepresence requires `sudo` privileges when you swap a deployment for the following tasks:

- Modifying your local network (via `sshuttle` and `pf/iptables`) for the `vpn-tcp` method that's used for Go programs
- Running the `docker` command (for some configurations on Linux)
- Mounting the remote filesystem for access in a Docker container

To test our new changes, let's run the `smoke` test again:

```
$ go run smoke.go
2019/04/21 00:18:50 ======= Links ======= 2019/04/21 00:18:50 ===== Add
Link ====== 2019/04/21 00:18:50 Adding new link - title: 'Gigi on Github',
url: 'https://github.com/the-gigi' 2019/04/21 00:18:50 ======= Links
======= 2019/04/21 00:18:50 title: 'Gigi on Github', url:
'https://github.com/the-gigi', status: 'pending' 2019/04/21 00:18:54
======= Links ======= 2019/04/21 00:18:54 title: 'Gigi on Github', url:
'https://github.com/the-gigi', status: 'valid'
```

Looking at the our local service output, we can see that it was indeed invoked when the `smoke` test ran:

```
**** Local link service here! calling GetLinks() ****
**** Local link service here! calling GetLinks() ****
```

As you may recall, the smoke test exercises the API gateway in the cluster, so the fact that our local service was invoked shows that it is indeed running in the cluster. One interesting fact is that the output of our local service is NOT captured by Kubernetes logs. If we search the logs, we find nothing. The following command generates no output:

```
$ kubectl logs svc/link-manager | grep "Local link service here"
```

Now, let's see what it takes to attach the GoLand debugger to the running local service.

Attaching to the local link service with GoLand for live debugging

This is the holy grail of debugging! We will be connecting to our local link service using the GoLand interactive debugger while it's running as part of the Kubernetes cluster. It doesn't get better than that. Let's get started:

1. First, follow the instructions here to get ready for attaching to a local Go process with GoLand: `https://blog.jetbrains.com/go/2019/02/06/debugging-with-goland-getting-started/#debugging-a-running-application-on-the-local-machine`.

2. Then, click the **Run** | **Attach to Process** menu option in GoLand, which will bring the following dialog box:

Unfortunately, when GoLand attaches to the process (successfully), Telepresence mistakenly thinks that the local service has exited and tears down the tunnel to the Kubernetes cluster and its own control process.

The local link service keeps running, but it's not connected to the cluster anymore. I opened a GitHub issue for the Telepresence team: `https://github.com/telepresenceio/telepresence/issues/1003`.

I later contacted the Telepresence developers, dived into the code, and contributed a fix that was merged recently.

See the following PR (Adding support for attaching a debugger to processes under Telepresence): `https://github.com/telepresenceio/telepresence/pull/1005`.

If you're using VS Code for Go programming, you can try your luck by following the information here: `https://github.com/Microsoft/vscode-go/wiki/Debugging-Go-code-using-VS-Code`.

So far, we have written a standalone smoke test and used Telepresence to be able to debug locally services that are part of our Kubernetes cluster. It doesn't get any better for interactive development. The next section will deal with test isolation.

Isolating tests

Isolation is a key topic with tests. The core idea is that, in general, your tests should be isolated from your production environment, or even isolated from other shared environments. If tests are not isolated, then changes the tests make can impact these environments and vice versa (external changes to these environments can break tests that make assumptions). Another level of isolation is between tests. If your tests run in parallel and make changes to the same resources, then various race conditions can occur and tests can interfere with each other and cause false negatives.

This can happen if tests don't run in parallel, but neglecting to clean up test A can make changes that break test B. Another case where isolation can help is when multiple teams or developers want to test incompatible changes. If two developers make incompatible changes to a shared environment, at least one of them will experience failures. There are various levels of isolation and they often have inverse relation to cost – more isolated tests are more expensive to set up.

Let's consider the following isolation approaches:

- Test clusters
- Test namespaces
- Cross namespace/ cluster

Test clusters

Cluster-level isolation is the highest form of isolation. You run your tests in clusters that are totally independent of your production cluster. The challenge with this approach is how to keep your test cluster/clusters in sync with your production cluster. On the software side, this may not be too difficult with a good CI/CD system, but populating and migrating data is often pretty complicated.

There are two forms of test clusters:

- Each developer gets their own cluster.
- Dedicated clusters for performing system tests.

Cluster per developer

Creating a cluster per developer is the ultimate level of isolation. The developer doesn't have to worry about breaking other people's code or being impacted by other people's code. However, there are some significant downsides for this approach, such as the following:

- It is often too expensive to provision a full-fledged cluster for each developer.
- The provisioned cluster often doesn't have high fidelity with the production system.
- You will generally still need another integration environment to reconcile changes from multiple teams/developers.

With Kubernetes, it may be possible to utilize Minikube as a local cluster per developer and avoid many of the downsides.

Dedicated clusters for system tests

Creating dedicated clusters for system tests is a great way to consolidate changes and test them one more time before deploying to production. The test cluster can run more rigorous tests, depend on external resources, and interact with third-party services. Such test clusters are expensive resources, and you must manage them carefully.

Test namespaces

Test namespaces are a lightweight form of isolation. They can run side-by-side next to the production system and reuse some of the resources of the production environment (for example, the control plane). It can be much easier to sync data, and on Kubernetes, in particular, writing a custom controller to sync and audit the test namespace against the production namespace is a good option.

The downside of test namespaces is the reduced level of isolation. By default, services in different namespaces can still talk to each other. If your system is already using multiple namespaces, then you have to be extremely careful to keep tests isolated from production.

Writing multi-tenant systems

Multi-tenant systems are systems where totally isolated entities share the same physical or virtual resources. Kubernetes namespaces provide several mechanisms to support this. You can define network policies that prevent connectivity between namespaces (except for interaction with the Kubernetes API server). You can define resource quotas and limits per namespace to prevent rogue namespaces from hogging all the cluster resources. If your system is already set up for multi-tenancy, you can treat a test namespace as just another tenant.

Cross namespace/cluster

Sometimes, your system is deployed into multiple coordinated namespaces or even multiple clusters. Under these circumstances, you'll need to pay more attention on how to design tests that mimic the same architecture, yet be careful that tests don't interact with production namespaces or clusters.

End-to-end testing

End-to-end tests are very important for complex distributed systems. The smoke test we wrote for Delinkcious is one example of an end-to-end test, but there are several other categories. End-to-end tests often run against a dedicated environment such as a staging environment, but in some cases they run against the production environment itself (with a lot of attention). Since end-to-end tests typically take a long time to run and may be slow and expansive to set up, it is not common to run them for every commit. Instead, it is common to run them periodically (every night, every weekend, or every month) or ad hoc (for example, before an important release). There are several categories of end-to-end tests.

We will explore some of the most important categories in the following sections, such as the following:

- Acceptance testing
- Regression testing
- Performance testing

Acceptance testing

Acceptance testing is a form of testing that verifies that the system behaves as expected. It is up to the system stakeholder to decide what is considered as acceptable. It could be as simple as a smoke test or as elaborate as testing all the possible paths through the code, all failure modes, and all side effects (for example, which messages are written to log files). One of the main benefits of a good battery of acceptance tests is that it is a forcing function for describing your system in terms that make sense for non-engineer stakeholders, such as product managers and top management. The ideal situation (I've never seen in it practice) is that business stakeholders will be able to write and maintain acceptance tests themselves.

This is close in spirit to visual programming. I personally believe that all automated testing should be written and maintained by the developers, but your mileage may vary. Delinkcious currently exposes just a REST API and doesn't have a user facing web application. Most systems these days have web applications that become the acceptance test boundary. It is common to run acceptance tests in the browser. There are many good frameworks. If you prefer to stay with Go, Agouti (`https://agouti.org/`) is a great choice. It has tight integration with Ginkgo and Gomega and can drive the browser though PhantomJS, Selenium, or ChromeDriver.

Regression testing

Regression testing is a good option when you just want to make sure that the new system doesn't deviate from the behavior of the current system. If you have comprehensive acceptance tests, then you just have to make sure that the new version of your system passes all the acceptance tests, just like the previous version did. However, if your acceptance tests coverage is lacking, you can get some form of confidence by bombarding the current system and the new system with the same inputs and verify that the outputs are identical. This can be done with fuzz testing too, where you generate random inputs.

Performance testing

Performance testing is a large topic. Here, the goal is to measure the performance of the system and not the correctness of its responses. That being said, errors can significantly influence performance. Consider the following error handling options:

- Return immediately when an error is encountered
- Retry five times and sleep for one second between tries

Now, given these two strategies, consider a request that usually takes about two seconds to process. A large number of errors for this request on a naive performance test will increase performance when using the first strategy (because requests will not be processed and return immediately), but will reduce performance when using the second strategy (requests will be retried for five seconds before failing).

Microservices architectures often utilize asynchronous processing, queues, and other mechanisms that can make it challenging to measure the actual performance of the system. In addition, a lot of networking calls are involved, which might be volatile.

In addition, performance is not just about response time. It can include CPU and memory utilization, a number of external API calls, access to network storage, and so on. Performance is also tightly related to availability and cost. In a complex cloud-native distributed system, performance tests can often inform and guide architectural decisions.

As you can see, end-to-end testing is quite a complicated issue and must be considered with great care, because both the value and the costs of end-to-end tests are not trivial. One of the most difficult resources to manage with end-to-end tests is the test data.

Let's take a look at some of the approaches for managing test data, their pros, and their cons.

Managing test data

With Kubernetes, it is relatively easy to deploy a lot of software, including software made of many components, as in typical microservice architectures. However, data is much less dynamic. There are different ways to generate and maintain test data. Different tactics of test data management are appropriate for different types of end-to-end tests. Let's look into synthetic data, manual test data, and production snapshots.

Synthetic data

Synthetic data is test data that you generate programmatically. The pros and cons are as follows:

- **Pros:**
  - Easy to control and update because it is generated programmatically
  - Easy to create bad data to test error handling
  - Easy to create a lot of data

- **Cons:**
  - You have to write code to generate it.
  - It can get out of sync with the format of actual data.

Manual test data

Manual test data is similar to synthetic data, but you create it manually. The pros and cons are as follows:

- **Pros:**
  - Ultimate control, including verifying what the out should be
  - Can be based on example data and tweaked lightly
  - Easy to start quickly (no need to write and maintain code)
  - No need to filter or deanonymize

- **Cons:**
  - Tedious and error-prone
  - Difficult to generate a lot of test data
  - Difficult to generate related data across multiple microservices
  - Have to manually update when the data format changes

Production snapshot

A production snapshot is literally recording real data and using it to populate your test system. The pros and cons are as follows:

- **Pros**:
    - High fidelity to real data
    - Recollection ensures test data is always in sync with production data
- **Cons**:
    - Need to filter and anonymize sensitive data
    - Data might not support all testing scenarios (for example, error handling)
    - Might be difficult to collect all relevant data

Summary

In this chapter, we covered the topic of testing and its various flavors: unit testing, integration testing, and all kinds of end-to-end testing. We also dived deep into how Delinkcious tests are structured. We explored the link manager unit tests, added a new smoke test, and introduced Telepresence for expediting the edit-test-debug life cycle against a real Kubernetes cluster while modifying the code locally.

That being said, testing is a spectrum that has costs, and just blindly adding more and more tests doesn't make your system better or higher quality. There are many important trade-offs between quantity and quality of tests, such as the time it takes to develop and maintain the tests, the time and resources it takes to run the tests, and the number and complexity of problems that tests detect early. You should have enough context to make those tough decisions for your system and choose the testing strategies that will work best for you.

It's also important to remember that testing evolves with the system, and the level of testing often has to be ratcheted up when the stakes are higher, even for the same organization. If you're a hobbyist developer that has a Beta product out there with a few users that just play with it at home, you may not be as rigorous in your testing (unless it saves you development time). However, as your company grows and gathers more users that use your product for mission-critical applications, the impact of problems in your code might require much more stringent testing.

In the next chapter, we will look at various deployment use cases and situations for Delinkcious. Kubernetes and its ecosystem provides many interesting options and tools. We will consider both robust deployment to production as well as quick developer-focused scenarios.

Further reading

You can refer to the following references for more information regarding what was covered in this chapter:

- **The Go Programming Language Package testing**: `https://golang.org/pkg/testing/`
- **Ginkgo**: `http://onsi.github.io/ginkgo/`
- **Gomega**: `http://onsi.github.io/gomega/`
- **Agouti**: `https://agouti.org/`
- **Telepresence**: `https://telepresence.io`

11
Deploying Microservices

In this chapter, we will deal with two related, yet separate themes: production deployments and development deployments. The concerns, processes, and tools that are used for these two areas are very different. In both cases, the goal is to deploy new software to the cluster, but everything else is different. With production deployments, it's desirable to keep the system stable, be able to have a predictable build and deployment experience, and most importantly, to identify and be able to roll back bad deployments. With development deployments, it's desirable to have isolated deployments for each developer, a fast turnaround, and the ability to avoid cluttering source control or the **continuous integration** / **continuous deployment** (**CI/CD**) system (including image registries) with temporary development versions. Due to this, divergent emphasis is beneficial to isolate production deployments from development deployments.

In this chapter, we will cover the following topics:

- Kubernetes deployments
- Deploying to multiple environments
- Understanding deployment strategies (rolling updates, blue-green deployment, canary deployment)
- Rolling back deployments
- Managing versions and upgrades
- Local development deployments

Technical requirements

In this chapter, we will install many tools, including the following:

- KO
- Ksync
- Draft
- Skaffold
- Tilt

There is no need to install them ahead of time.

The code

The code is split between two Git repositories:

- You can find the code samples here: `https://github.com/PacktPublishing/Hands-On-Microservices-with-Kubernetes/tree/master/Chapter11`
- You can find the updated Delinkcious application here: `https://github.com/the-gigi/delinkcious/releases/tag/v0.9`

Kubernetes deployments

We talked about deployments briefly in `Chapter 1`, *Introduction to Kubernetes for Developers*, and we've used Kubernetes deployments in almost every chapter. However, before diving into more sophisticated patterns and strategies, it will be useful to review the basic building blocks and the relationships between Kubernetes deployments, Kubernetes services, and scaling or autoscaling.

Deployments are Kubernetes resources that manage pods via a ReplicaSet. A Kubernetes ReplicaSet is a group of pods that are identified by a common set of labels with a certain number of replicas. The connection between the ReplicaSet to its pods is the `ownerReferences` field in the pod's metadata. The ReplicaSet controller ensures that the correct number of replicas are always running. If a pod dies for whatever reason, the ReplicaSet controller will schedule a new pod in its place. The following diagram illustrates this relationship:

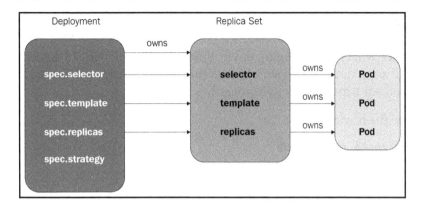

Deployment and ReplicaSet

We can also observe the ownership chain in the metadata with kubectl. First, let's get the name of the social graph manager pod and find the name of its ReplicaSet owner from the `ownerReferences` metadata:

```
$ kubectl get po -l svc=social-graph,app=manager
NAME READY STATUS RESTARTS AGE
social-graph-manager-7d84ffc5f7-bst7w 1/1 Running 53 20d

 $ kubectl get po social-graph-manager-7d84ffc5f7-bst7w -o
jsonpath="{.metadata.ownerReferences[0]['name']}"
 social-graph-manager-7d84ffc5f7

 $ kubectl get po social-graph-manager-7d84ffc5f7-bst7w -o
jsonpath="{.metadata.ownerReferences[0]['kind']}"
 ReplicaSet
```

Next, we'll get the name of the deployment that owns the ReplicaSet:

```
 $ kubectl get rs social-graph-manager-7d84ffc5f7 -o
jsonpath="{.metadata.ownerReferences[0]['name']}"
 graph-manager

 $ kubectl get rs social-graph-manager-7d84ffc5f7 -o
jsonpath="{.metadata.ownerReferences[0]['kind']}"
 Deployment
```

So, if the ReplicaSet controller takes care of managing the number of pods, what does the `Deployment` object add? The `Deployment` object encapsulates the concept of a deployment, including a deployment strategy and rollout history. It also provides deployment-oriented operations such as updating a deployment and rolling back a deployment, which we will look at later.

Deploying to multiple environments

In this section, we will create a staging environment for Delinkcious in a new staging namespace. The `staging` namespace will be a full-fledged copy of the default namespace that will serve as our production environment.

First, let's create the namespace:

```
$ kubectl create ns staging
namespace/staging created
```

Then, in Argo CD, we can create a new project called `staging`:

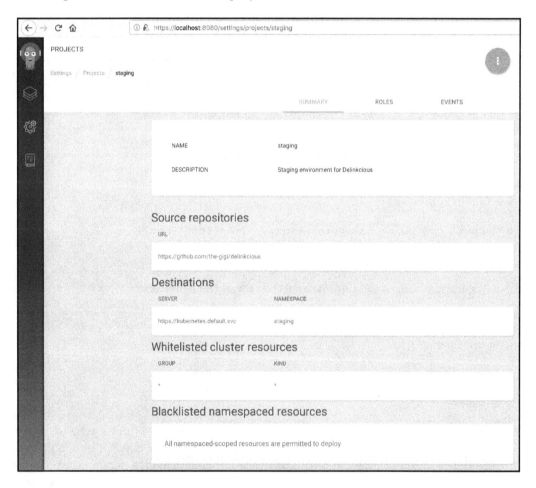

Argo CD staging project

Now, we need to configure all our services so that Argo CD can sync them to the staging environment. This can be a little tedious to do in the UI now that we have a substantial amount of services. Instead, we will use the Argo CD CLI and a Python 3 program called bootstrap_staging.py to automate the process. The program expects the following:

- The staging namespace has been created.
- The Argo CD CLI is installed and in the path.
- The Argo CD service is available through the localhost on port 8080.
- The Argo CD admin password is configured as the environment variable.

To expose Argo CD on the localhost at port 80, we can run the following command:

```
kubectl port-forward -n argocd svc/argocd-server 8080:443
```

Let's break down the program and understand how it works. This is a good foundation where you can develop your own custom CI/CD solutions by automating CLI tools. The only dependencies are Python's standard library modules: subprocess (allows you to run command-line tools) and os (for accessing environment variables). Here, we only need to run the Argo CD CLI.

The run() function hides all the implementation details and provides a convenient interface where you just need to pass the arguments as a string. The run() function will prepare a proper command list that can be passed to the subprocess module's check_output() function, capture the output, and decode it from bytes to a string:

```
import os
 import subprocess

def run(cmd):
    cmd = ('argocd ' + cmd).split()
    output = subprocess.check_output(cmd)
    return output.decode('utf-8')
```

The login() function utilizes run(), gets the admin password from the environment, and constructs the proper command string with all the necessary flags so that you can log in as the admin user to Argo CD:

```
def login():
    host = 'localhost:8080'
    password = os.environ['ARGOCD_PASSWORD']
    cmd = f'login {host} --insecure --username admin --password
{password}'
    output = run(cmd)
    print(output)
```

The `get_apps()` function takes a namespace and returns the relevant fields of the Argo CD apps in it. This function will be used both on the `default` namespace and the `staging` namespace. The function invokes the `app list` command, parses the output, and populates a Python dictionary with the relevant information:

```
def get_apps(namespace):
    """ """
    output = run(f'app list -o wide')
    keys = 'name project namespace path repo'.split()
    apps = []
    lines = output.split('\n')
    headers = [h.lower() for h in lines[0].split()]
    for line in lines[1:]:
        items = line.split()
        app = {k: v for k, v in zip(headers, items) if k in keys}
        if app:
            apps.append(app)
    return apps
```

The `create_project()` function takes all the necessary information to create a new Argo CD project. Note that multiple Argo CD projects can coexist in the same Kubernetes namespace. It also allows access to all cluster resources, which is necessary to create applications. Since we have already created the project in the Argo CD UI, there is no need to use it in this program, but it's good to have it around in case we need to create more projects in the future:

```
def create_project(project, cluster, namespace, description, repo):
    """ """
    cmd = f'proj create {project} --description {description} -d
{cluster},{namespace} -s {repo}'
    output = run(cmd)
    print(output)

    # Add access to resources
    cmd = f'proj allow-cluster-resource {project} "*" "*"'
    output = run(cmd)
    print(output)
```

The last generic function is called `create_app()`, and takes all the necessary information for creating an Argo CD application. It assumes that Argo CD is running inside the destination cluster, so `--dest-server` is always `https://kubernetes.default.svc`:

```
def create_app(name, project, namespace, repo, path):
    """ """
    cmd = f"""app create {name}-staging --project {project} --dest-server
https://kubernetes.default.svc
```

```
                    --dest-namespace {namespace} --repo {repo} --path {path}"""
    output = run(cmd)
    print(output)
```

The `copy_apps_from_default_to_staging()` function uses some of the functions we declared earlier. It gets all the apps from the default namespace, iterates over them, and creates the same app in the staging project and namespace:

```
def copy_apps_from_default_to_staging():
    apps = get_apps('default')

    for a in apps:
        create_app(a['name'], 'staging', 'staging', a['repo'], a['path'])
```

Finally, here's the `main` function:

```
def main():
    login()
    copy_apps_from_default_to_staging()

    apps = get_apps('staging')
    for a in apps:
        print(a)

if __name__ == '__main__':
    main()
```

Now that we have two environments, let's consider some workflows and promotion strategies. Whenever a change is pushed, GitHub CircleCI will detect it. If all the tests pass, it will bake a new image for each service and push it to Docker Hub. The question is, what should happen on the deployment side? Argo CD has sync policies, and we can configure them to automatically sync/deploy whenever a new image is available on Docker Hub. For example, a common practice is to automatically deploy to staging, deploying to production only after various tests (for example, the `smoke` test) have passed on staging. The promotion from staging to production may be automated or manual.

There is no one-size-fits-all answer. Even within the same organization, different deployment policies and strategies are often employed for projects or services with different sets of requirements.

Let's look at some of the more common deployment strategies and what use cases they enable.

Understanding deployment strategies

A deployment of a new version of a service in Kubernetes means replacing the *N* backing pods of the service, which run version *X* with *N* backing pods running version *X+1*. There are multiple ways to get from N pods running version *X*, to zero pods running version *X* and *N* pods running version *X+1*. Kubernetes deployments support two strategies out of the box: `Recreate` and `RollingUpdate` (the default strategy). Blue-green deployments and canary deployments are two other popular strategies. Before diving into the various deployment strategies, as well as their pros and cons, it's important to understand the process of updating a deployment in Kubernetes.

A rollout of a new set of pods for a deployment happens if and only if the deployment spec's pod template has changed. This typically happens when you change the image version of the pod template or the set of labels for a container. Note that scaling a deployment (increasing or decreasing its number of replicas) is *not* an update, so the deployment strategy is not used. The same version of the image as the current running pods will be used in any new pods that are added.

Recreating deployment

A trivial yet naive way to do this is to terminate all the pods running version *X*, and then create a new deployment where the image version in the pod template spec is set to *X+1*. There are a couple of problems with this approach:

- The service will be unavailable until the new pods come online.
- If the new version has issues, the service will be unavailable until the process is reversed (ignoring errors and data corruption).

The `Recreate` deployment strategy is appropriate for development, or when you prefer to have a short outage, but ensure that there is no mix of versions that are live at the same time. The short outage may be acceptable, for example, if the service pulls its work from a queue and there are no adverse consequences if the service is briefly down while upgrading to a new version. Another situation is if you want to change the public API of the service or one of its dependencies in a non-backward compatible way. In this case, the current pods must be terminated in one fell swoop, and the new pods must be deployed. There are solutions for multi-phase deployments of incompatible changes, but in some cases, it is easier and acceptable to just cut the cord and pay the cost of a short outage.

To enable this strategy, edit the deployment's manifest, change the strategy type to be `Recreate`, and remove the `rollingUpdate` section (this is only allowed when the type is `RollingUpdate`):

```
$ kubectl edit deployment user-manager
 deployment.extensions/user-manager edited

$ kubectl get deployment user-manager -o yaml | grep strategy -A 1
   strategy:
     type: Recreate
```

For most services, it is desirable to have service continuity and zero downtime when upgrading, as well as an instant rollback in case a problem is detected. The `RollingUpdate` strategy addresses these situations.

Rolling updates

The default deployment strategy is `RollingUpdate`:

```
$ kubectl get deployment social-graph-manager -o yaml | grep strategy -A 4
   strategy:
     rollingUpdate:
       maxSurge: 25%
       maxUnavailable: 25%
     type: RollingUpdate
```

Rolling updates work as follows: the total number of pods (old and new) is going to be the current replica count, plus the max surge. The deployment controller will start replacing old pods with new pods, making sure not to exceed the limit. The max surge can be an absolute number, such as 4, or a percentage, such as 25%. For example, if the number of replicas for the deployment is 4 and the max surge is 25%, then an additional new pod can be added, and one of the old pods can be terminated. `maxUnavailable` is the number of pods that are below the replica count during a deployment.

The following diagram illustrates how rolling updates work:

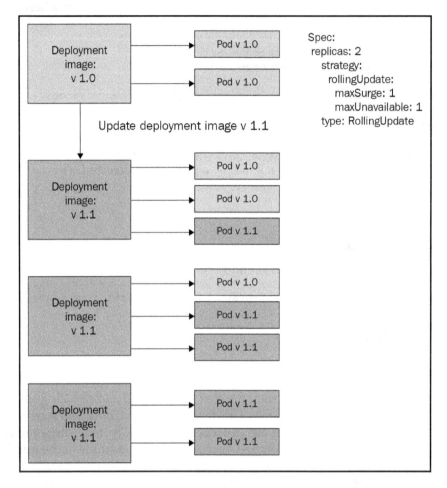

Rolling update

Rolling updates make sense when the new version is compatible with the current version. The number of active pods that are ready to handle requests remains within a reasonable range of the replica count that you specify using maxSurge and maxUnavailable, and gradually, all the current pods are replaced with new pods. The overall service is not disrupted.

Sometimes, however, you must replace all the pods at once, and for critical services that must remain available, the Recreate strategy doesn't work. This is where blue-green deployments come in.

Blue-green deployment

Blue-green deployment is a well-known pattern. The idea is that you don't update the existing deployment; instead, you create a brand new deployment with the new version. Initially, your new version doesn't service traffic. Then, when you verify that the new deployment is up and running (you can even run some `smoke` tests against it), you switch all the traffic in one fell swoop from the current version to the new version. If you encounter any problems after you switch to the new version, you can instantly switch all the traffic back to the previous deployment, which is still up and running. When you are confident that the new deployment is doing well, you can destroy the previous deployment.

One of the greatest advantages of blue-green deployments is that they don't have to operate at the level of a single Kubernetes deployment. This can be critical in a microservice architecture where you must update multiple interacting services at the same time. If you tried to do it just by updating multiple Kubernetes deployments at the same time, there could be some services that have already been replaced and some that weren't (even if you accept the cost of the `Recreate` strategy). If a single service experiences problems during deployment, you now have to roll back all the other services. With blue-green deployments, you are safe from these issues and are in total control of when you want to switch to the new version across all services at once.

How do you switch from blue (current) to green (new)? The traditional approach that works with Kubernetes is to do it at the load balancer level. Most systems that require such a sophisticated deployment strategy will have a load balancer. When you use the load balancer to switch traffic, your green deployment includes both a green Kubernetes deployment and a green Kubernetes service, as well as any other resources if anything needs to change, such as secrets and config maps. If you need to update multiple services, then you'll have a collection of green resources that all refer to each other.

If you have an Ingress controller such as contour, then it can often be used to switch traffic from blue to green and back, if necessary.

The following diagram illustrates how blue-green deployments work:

Blue-green deployment

Let's do a single-service blue-green deployment for the link manager service. We'll call our starting point *blue*, and we want to deploy the *green* version of link manager without disruption. Here's the plan:

1. Add the `deployment: blue` label to the current `link-manager` deployment.
2. Update the `link-manager` service selector to match the `deployment: blue` label.
3. Implement the new version of `LinkManager` that prefixes the description of each link with the `[green]` string.

4. Add the `deployment: green` label to the deployment's pod template spec.
5. Bump the version number.
6. Let CircleCI create a new version.
7. Deploy the new version as a separate deployment called `green-link-manager`.
8. Update the `link-manager` service selector to match the `deployment: green` label.
9. Verify the description of the returned links from the service and include the `[green]` prefix.

This may sound complicated, but just like many CI/CD processes, once you establish a pattern, you can automate and build tooling around it. This lets you execute complex workflows without human involvement, or inject human review and approval at important junctures (for example, before really deploying to production). Let's go over the steps in detail.

Adding deployment – the blue label

We can just edit the deployment and manually add `deployment: blue`, in addition to the existing `svc: link` and `app: manager` labels:

```
$ kubectl edit deployment link-manager
deployment.extensions/link-manager edited
```

This will trigger a redeployment of the pods because we changed the labels. Let's verify that the new pods have the `deployment: blue` label. Here is a pretty fancy `kubectl` command that uses custom columns to display the name, the deployment label, and the IP addresses of all the pods that match `svc=link` and `app=manager`.

As you can see, all three pods have the `deployment:blue` label, as expected:

```
$ kubectl get po -l svc=link,app=manager
  -o custom
columns="NAME:.metadata.name,DEPLOYMENT:.metadata.labels.deployment,IP:.sta
tus.podIP"
NAME                            DEPLOYMENT IP
link-manager-65d4998d47-chxpj   blue       172.17.0.37
link-manager-65d4998d47-jwt7x   blue       172.17.0.36
link-manager-65d4998d47-rlfhb   blue       172.17.0.35
```

We can even verify that the IP addresses match the endpoints of the `link-manager` service:

```
$ kubectl get ep link-manager
NAME ENDPOINTS AGE
link-manager 172.17.0.35:8080,172.17.0.36:8080,172.17.0.37:8080 21d
```

Now that the pods are labeled with the `blue` label, we need to update the service.

Updating the link-manager service to match blue pods only

The service, as you may recall, matches any pods with the `svc: link` and `app: manager` labels:

```
$ kubectl get svc link-manager -o custom-columns=SELECTOR:.spec.selector
SELECTOR
map[app:manager svc:link]
```

By adding the `deployment: blue` label, we didn't interfere with the matching. However, in preparation for our green deployment, we should make sure that the service only matches the pods of the current blue deployment.

Let's add the `deployment: blue` label to the service's `selector`:

```
selector: app: manager svc: link deployment: blue
```

We can verify that it worked by using the following command:

```
$ kubectl get svc link-manager -o custom-columns=SELECTOR:.spec.selector
SELECTOR
map[app:manager deployment:blue svc:link]
```

Before we switch to the green version, let's make a change in the code to make it clear that's it's a different version.

Prefixing the description of each link with [green]

Let's do this in the transport layer of the link service.

The target file is https://github.com/the-gigi/delinkcious/blob/master/svc/link_service/service/transport.go#L26.

The change is very minimal. In the newLink() function, we will prefix the description with the [green] string:

```
func newLink(source om.Link) link {
return link{
Url: source.Url,
Title: source.Title,
Description: "[green] " + source.Description,
Status: source.Status,
Tags: source.Tags,
CreatedAt: source.CreatedAt.Format(time.RFC3339),
UpdatedAt: source.UpdatedAt.Format(time.RFC3339), } }
```

In order to deploy our new green version, we need to create a new image. This requires bumping the Delinkcious version number.

Bumping the version number

The Delinkcious version is maintained in the [build.sh] file at (https://github.com/the-gigi/delinkcious/blob/master/build.sh#L6) that CircleCI is invoked from, that is, the [.circleci/config.yml] file at (https://github.com/the-gigi/delinkcious/blob/master/.circleci/config.yml#L28) file.

The STABLE_TAG variable controls the version numbers. The current version is 0.3. Let's bump it up to 0.4:

```
#!/bin/bash
set -eo pipefail
IMAGE_PREFIX='g1g1' STABLE_TAG='0.4'
TAG="{CIRCLE_BUILD_NUM}" ...
```

OK. We bumped the version and we're ready to have CircleCI build a new image.

Letting CircleCI build the new image

Thanks to GitOps and our CircleCI automation, this step just involves pushing our changes to GitHub. CircleCI detects the change, builds the new code, creates a new Docker image, and pushes it to the Docker Hub registry. Here it is:

Docker Hub link service 0.4

Now that the new image has been built and pushed to the Docker Hub registry, we can deploy it to the cluster as the green deployment.

Deploying the new (green) version

OK – we've got our new `delinkcious-link:0.4` image on Docker Hub. Let's deploy it to the cluster. Remember that we want to deploy it side by side with our current (blue) deployment, which is called `link-manager`. Let's create a new deployment called `green-link-manager`. The differences it has to our blue deployment are as follows:

- The name is `green-link-manager`.
- The pod template spec has the `deployment: green` label.
- The image version is `0.4`.

```
apiVersion: apps/v1
kind: Deployment
metadata:
  name: green-link-manager
  labels:
    svc: link
    app: manager
    deployment: green
spec:
  replicas: 3
  selector:
    matchLabels:
      svc: link
      app: manager
      deployment: green
  template:
    metadata:
      labels:
        svc: link
        app: manager
        deployment: green
    spec:
      serviceAccount: link-manager
      containers:
      - name: link-manager
        image: g1g1/delinkcious-link:0.4
        imagePullPolicy: Always
        ports:
        - containerPort: 8080
        envFrom:
        - configMapRef:
            name: link-manager-config
        volumeMounts:
        - name: mutual-auth
          mountPath: /etc/delinkcious
```

```
            readOnly: true
        volumes:
        - name: mutual-auth
          secret:
            secretName: link-mutual-auth
```

Now, it's time to deploy:

```
$ kubectl apply -f green_link_manager.yaml
deployment.apps/green-link-manager created
```

Before we update the service to use the green deployment, let's review the cluster. As you can see, we have the blue and green deployments running side by side:

```
$ kubectl get po -l svc=link,app=manager -o custom-
columns="NAME:.metadata.name,DEPLOYMENT:.metadata.labels.deployment"
NAME                                   DEPLOYMENT
green-link-manager-5874c6cd4f-21dfn    green
green-link-manager-5874c6cd4f-mvm5v    green
green-link-manager-5874c6cd4f-vcj9s    green
link-manager-65d4998d47-chxpj          blue
link-manager-65d4998d47-jwt7x          blue
link-manager-65d4998d47-rlfhb          blue
```

Updating the link-manager service to use the green deployment

First, let's make sure that the service is still using the blue deployment. When we get a link description, there shouldn't be any [green] prefix:

```
$ http "${DELINKCIOUS_URL}/v1.0/links" "Access-Token:
${DELINKCIOUS_TOKEN}"'
HTTP/1.0 200 OK
Content-Length: 214
Content-Type: application/json
Date: Tue, 30 Apr 2019 06:02:03 GMT
Server: Werkzeug/0.14.1 Python/3.7.2

{
    "err": "",
    "links": [
        {
            "CreatedAt": "2019-04-30T06:01:47Z",
            "Description": "nothing to see here...",
            "Status": "invalid",
            "Tags": null,
```

```
            "Title": "gg",
            "UpdatedAt": "2019-04-30T06:01:47Z",
            "Url": "http://gg.com"
        }
    ]
}
```

The description is `nothing to see here....` This time, instead of interactively editing the service using `kubectl edit`, we will use the `kubectl patch` command to apply a patch that will switch the deployment label from `blue` to `green`. Here is the patch file – `green-patch.yaml`:

```
spec:
  selector:
    deployment: green
```

Let's apply the patch:

```
$ kubectl patch service/link-manager --patch "$(cat green-patch.yaml)"
  service/link-manager patched
```

The last step is to verify that the service now uses the green deployment.

Verifying that the service now uses the green pods to serve requests

Let's do this methodically, starting with the selector in the service:

```
$ kubectl get svc link-manager -o jsonpath="{.spec.selector.deployment}"
  green
```

OK – the selector is green. Let's get the links again and see if the `[green]` prefix shows up:

```
$ http "${DELINKCIOUS_URL}/v1.0/links" "Access-Token:
${DELINKCIOUS_TOKEN}"'

HTTP/1.0 200 OK
Content-Length: 221
Content-Type: application/json
Date: Tue, 30 Apr 2019 06:19:43 GMT
Server: Werkzeug/0.14.1 Python/3.7.2

{
  "err": "",
  "links": [
  {
```

```
  "CreatedAt": "2019-04-30T06:01:47Z",
  "Description": "[green] nothing to see here...",
  "Status": "invalid",
  "Tags": null,
  "Title": "gg",
  "UpdatedAt": "2019-04-30T06:01:47Z",
  "Url": "http://gg.com"
  }
  ]
}
```

Yes! The description is now `[green] nothing to see here...`

Now, we can get rid of the blue deployment and our service will continue running against the green deployment:

```
$ kubectl delete deployment link-manager
 deployment.extensions "link-manager" deleted


$ kubectl get po -l svc=link,app=manager
NAME                                      READY   STATUS    RESTARTS   AGE
green-link-manager-5874c6cd4f-21dfn       1/1     Running   5          1h
green-link-manager-5874c6cd4f-mvm5v       1/1     Running   5          1h
green-link-manager-5874c6cd4f-vcj9s       1/1     Running   5          1h
```

We have successfully performed a blue-green deployment on Delinkcious. Let's discuss the last pattern, that is, canary deployments.

Canary deployments

Canary deployments are another sophisticated deployment pattern. Consider the situation of a massive distributed system with lots of users. You want to introduce a new version of the service. You have tested this change to the best of your ability, but the production system is too complex to mimic completely in a staging environment. As a result, you can't be sure that your new version will not cause some problems. What do you do? You use canary deployments. The idea is that some changes must be tested in production before you can be reasonably sure they work as expected. The canary deployment patterns allow you to limit the damage the new version might cause if something goes wrong.

Basic canary deployments on Kubernetes work by running the current version on most of your pods, and just a small number of pods with the new version. Most of the requests will be processed by the current version, and only a small proportion will be processed by the new version.

This assumes a round-robin load balancing algorithm (the default), or any other algorithm that distributes requests more or less uniformly across all pods.

The following diagram illustrates what canary deployments look like:

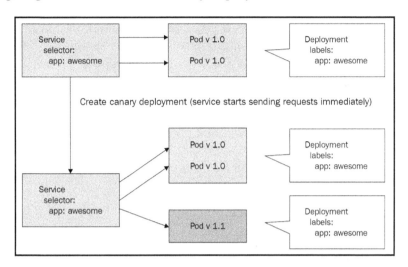

Canary deployment

Note that canary deployments require that your current version and your new version can coexist. For example, if your change involved a schema change, then your current and new versions are incompatible, and naive canary deployment will not work.

The nice thing about the basic canary deployment is that it works using existing Kubernetes objects and can be configured by an operator from the outside. There's no need for custom code or installing additional components into your cluster. However, the basic canary deployment has several limitations:

- The granularity is K/N (the worst case is singletons where N = 1).
- Can't control different percentages for different requests to the same service (for example, canary deployments of read requests only).
- Can't control all requests for a user who goes to the same version.

In some cases, these limitations are too severe and another solution is needed. Sophisticated canary deployments typically utilize application-level knowledge. This can be done through Ingress objects, a service mesh, or a dedicated application-level traffic shaper. We will look at an example of this in `Chapter 13`, *Service Mesh – Working with Istio*.

It's time for a hands-on canary deployment of the link service.

Employing a basic canary deployment for Delinkcious

Creating a canary deployment is very similar to blue-green deployment. Our `link-manager` service currently runs the green deployment. This means that it has a selector with `deployment: green`. Canaries are yellow, so we will create a new version of the code that prefixes the link description with `[yellow]`. Let's aim for 10% of requests going to the new version. In order to achieve this, we will scale the current versions to nine replicas and add a deployment with one pod with the new version. Here is the canary trick – we will drop the deployment label from the service selector. This means that it will select both pods; that is, `deployment: green` and `deployment: yellow`. We could also drop the labels from the deployments (because nobody is selecting based on this label), but it's good to keep them around as metadata, and also in case we want to do another blue-green deployment.

Here is the plan:

1. Build a new version of the code.
2. Create a deployment with a replica count of one for the new version, which is labeled as `deployment: yellow`.
3. Scale the current green deployment to nine replicas.
4. Update the service to select for `svc: link` and `app: manager` (ignore `deployment: <color>`).
5. Run multiple queries against the service and verify that the ratio of requests that are being served by the canary deployment is 10%.

The code change is `trivial: [green] -> [yellow]`:

```
func newLink(source om.Link) link {
    return link{
        Url:         source.Url,
        Title:       source.Title,
        Description: "[green] " + source.Description,
        Status:      source.Status,
        Tags:        source.Tags,
        CreatedAt:   source.CreatedAt.Format(time.RFC3339),
        UpdatedAt:   source.UpdatedAt.Format(time.RFC3339),
    }
}
```

Then, we need to bump the version in `build.sh` from `0.4` to `0.5`:

```
#!/bin/bash

set -eo pipefail

IMAGE_PREFIX='g1g1'
STABLE_TAG='0.4'

TAG="${STABLE_TAG}.${CIRCLE_BUILD_NUM}"
...
```

Once we push these changes to GitHub, CircleCI will build and push a new image to DockerHub: `g1g1/delinkcious-link:0.5`.

At this point, we can create a deployment with the new `0.5` version, a single replica, and updated labels. Let's call it `yellow_link_manager.yaml`:

```yaml
---
apiVersion: apps/v1
kind: Deployment
metadata:
  name: yellow-link-manager
  labels:
    svc: link
    app: manager
    deployment: yellow
spec:
  replicas: 1
  selector:
    matchLabels:
      svc: link
      app: manager
      deployment: yellow
  template:
    metadata:
      labels:
        svc: link
        app: manager
        deployment: yellow
    spec:
      serviceAccount: link-manager
      containers:
      - name: link-manager
        image: g1g1/delinkcious-link:0.5
        imagePullPolicy: Always
        ports:
        - containerPort: 8080
```

```
        envFrom:
        - configMapRef:
            name: link-manager-config
        volumeMounts:
        - name: mutual-auth
          mountPath: /etc/delinkcious
          readOnly: true
      volumes:
      - name: mutual-auth
        secret:
          secretName: link-mutual-auth
```

The next step is deploying our canary:

```
$ kubectl apply -f yellow_link_manager.yaml
deployment.apps/yellow-link-manager created
```

Before changing the service to include the canary deployment, let's scale the green deployment to 9 replicas so that it can receive 90% of the traffic once we activate our canary:

```
$ kubectl scale --replicas=9 deployment/green-link-manager
deployment.extensions/green-link-manager scaled
```

```
$ kubectl get po -l svc=link,app=manager
NAME                                         READY   STATUS    RESTARTS   AGE
green-link-manager-5874c6cd4f-21dfn          1/1     Running   10         15h
green-link-manager-5874c6cd4f-9csxz          1/1     Running   0          52s
green-link-manager-5874c6cd4f-c5rqn          1/1     Running   0          52s
green-link-manager-5874c6cd4f-mvm5v          1/1     Running   10         15h
green-link-manager-5874c6cd4f-qn4zj          1/1     Running   0          52s
green-link-manager-5874c6cd4f-r2jxf          1/1     Running   0          52s
green-link-manager-5874c6cd4f-rtwsj          1/1     Running   0          52s
green-link-manager-5874c6cd4f-sw27r          1/1     Running   0          52s
green-link-manager-5874c6cd4f-vcj9s          1/1     Running   10         15h
yellow-link-manager-67847d6b85-n97b5         1/1     Running   4          6m20s
```

Alright, we have nine green pods and one yellow (canary) pod running. Let's update the service to select just based on the svc: link and app: manager labels, which will include all ten pods. We need to remove the deployment: green label.

The YAML patch file method we've used before doesn't work here, because it can only add or update a label. We'll use a JSON patch this time with the *remove* operation and specify the path to the *deployment* key in the selector.

Note that before the patch, the selector had `deployment: green`, and that after the patch, only `svc: link` and `app: manager` remain:

```
$ kubectl get svc link-manager -o custom-
columns=NAME:.metadata.name,SELECTOR:.spec.selector
 NAME            SELECTOR
 link-manager    map[app:manager deployment:green svc:link]


 $ kubectl patch svc link-manager --type=json -p='[{"op": "remove", "path":
"/spec/selector/deployment"}]'
 service/link-manager patched

 $ kubectl get svc link-manager -o custom-
columns=NAME:.metadata.name,SELECTOR:.spec.selector
 NAME            SELECTOR
 link-manager    map[app:manager svc:link]
```

It's showtime. We'll send 30 GET requests to Delinkcious and check the description:

```
$ for i in {1..30}
> do
>    http "${DELINKCIOUS_URL}/v1.0/links" "Access-Token:
${DELINKCIOUS_TOKEN}" | jq .links[0].Description
> done

 "[green] nothing to see here..."
 "[yellow] nothing to see here..."
 "[green] nothing to see here..."
 "[green] nothing to see here..."
 "[green] nothing to see here..."
 "[green] nothing to see here..."
 "[green] nothing to see here..."
 "[green] nothing to see here..."
 "[green] nothing to see here..."
 "[yellow] nothing to see here..."
 "[green] nothing to see here..."
 "[green] nothing to see here..."
 "[green] nothing to see here..."
 "[green] nothing to see here..."
 "[green] nothing to see here..."
 "[yellow] nothing to see here..."
 "[green] nothing to see here..."
 "[yellow] nothing to see here..."
 "[yellow] nothing to see here..."
 "[green] nothing to see here..."
 "[green] nothing to see here..."
 "[green] nothing to see here..."
```

```
"[green] nothing to see here..."
"[yellow] nothing to see here..."
"[green] nothing to see here..."
"[green] nothing to see here..."
"[green] nothing to see here..."
"[green] nothing to see here..."
"[green] nothing to see here..."
"[green] nothing to see here..."
```

Interesting – we've got 24 green responses and 6 yellow responses. This is much higher than expected (three yellow responses on average). I ran it a couple more times and got six yellow responses again for the second run, and just one yellow response for the third run. This is all running on Minikube, so load balancing may be a little special. Let's declare victory.

Using canary deployments for A/B testing

Canary deployments can also be used to support A/B testing. We can deploy as many versions as we want, as long as we have enough pods to juggle the load. Each version could include special code to log the relevant data, and then you can gain insights and correlate user behavior with specific versions. This is possible, but you'll probably have to build a lot of tooling and conventions to make it usable. If A/B testing is an important part of your design workflow, I recommend going with one of the established A/B testing solutions. The A/B testing wheel is not worth reinventing, in my opinion.

Let's consider what to do when things go wrong and we need to get back to a working state as soon as possible.

Rolling back deployments

When things go wrong in production after a deployment, the best-practice response is to roll back the changes and get back to the last previous version known to work. The way you go about this depends on the deployment pattern you've employed. Let's consider them one by one.

Rolling back standard Kubernetes deployments

Kubernetes deployments keep a history. For example, if we edit the user manager deployment and set the image version to 0.5, then we can see that there are two revisions now:

```
$ kubectl get po -l svc=user,app=manager -o
jsonpath="{.items[0].spec.containers[0].image}"
 g1g1/delinkcious-user:0.5

$ kubectl rollout history deployment user-manager
deployment.extensions/user-manager
REVISION   CHANGE-CAUSE
1          <none>
2          <none>
```

The CHANGE-CAUSE column is not recorded by default. Let's make another change to version 0.4, but using the --record=true flag:

```
$ kubectl edit deployment user-manager --record=true
 deployment.extensions/user-manager edited

$ kubectl rollout history deployment user-manager
deployment.extensions/user-manager
REVISION   CHANGE-CAUSE
1          <none>
2          <none>
3          kubectl edit deployment user-manager --record=true
```

OK. Let's roll back to the original 0.3 version. That would be revision 1. We can look at this by using the rollout history command at specific revisions, too:

```
$ kubectl rollout history deployment user-manager --revision=1
 deployment.extensions/user-manager with revision #1
 Pod Template:
   Labels:     app=manager
     pod-template-hash=6fb9878576
     svc=user
   Containers:
    user-manager:
     Image:     g1g1/delinkcious-user:0.3
     Port:      7070/TCP
     Host Port:    0/TCP
     Limits:
       cpu:     250m
       memory:     64Mi
     Requests:
```

```
    cpu:      250m
    memory:      64Mi
  Environment Variables from:
    user-manager-config    ConfigMap    Optional: false
  Environment:      <none>
  Mounts:      <none>
Volumes:      <none>
```

As you can see, revision 1 has version 0.3. The command to roll back is as follows:

```
$ kubectl rollout undo deployment user-manager --to-revision=1
  deployment.extensions/user-manager rolled back

$ kubectl get deployment user-manager -o
jsonpath="{.spec.template.spec.containers[0].image}"
  g1g1/delinkcious-user:0.3
```

Rolling back will use the same mechanics of a rolling update, gradually replacing pods until all the running pods have the correct version.

Rolling back blue-green deployments

Blue-green deployments are not supported directly by Kubernetes. Switching back from green to blue (assuming that the blue deployment's pods are still running) is very simple. You just change the `Service` selector and select `deployment: blue` instead of `deployment: green`. The instant switch from blue to green and vice versa is the main motivation for the blue-green deployment pattern, so it's no wonder that it's that easy. Once you've switched back to blue, you can delete the green deployment and figure out what went wrong.

Rolling back canary deployments

Canary deployments are arguably even simpler to roll back. The majority of your pods run the tried and true version. The canary deployment's pods serve just a small amount of requests. If you detect that something is wrong with the canary deployment, simply delete the deployment. Your main deployment will keep serving incoming requests. If necessary (for example, your canary deployment served a small but significant amount of traffic), you can scale up your main deployment to make up for the canary pods that are no longer there.

Dealing with a rollback after a schema, API, or payload change

The deployment strategy you choose often depends on the nature of the change the new version introduces. For example, if your change involved a breaking database schema change, such as splitting table A into two tables, B and C, then you can't simply deploy the new version that reads to/writes from B and C. The database needs to be migrated first. However, if you run into problems and want to roll back to the previous version, then you'll have the same problem in the reverse direction. Your old version will try and read from/write to table A, which doesn't exist anymore. The same issue can happen if you change the format of a configuration file or payload on some network protocol. API changes can break clients if you don't coordinate them.

The way to address those compatibility issues is to perform those changes across multiple deployments, where each deployment is fully compatible with the previous deployment. This takes some planning and work. Let's consider the case of splitting table A into tables B and C. Suppose we're on version 1.0 and eventually want to end up with version 2.0.

Our first change will be marked as version 1.1. It will perform the following:

- Create tables B and C (but leave table A in place).
- Change the code to write to B and C.
- Change the code to read from both A, B, and C and merge the results (old data comes from A, while new data comes from B and C).
- If data needs to be deleted, it is just marked as deleted instead.

We deploy version 1.1 and if we see that something is wrong, we will roll back to version 1.0. All our old data is still in table A, which version 1.0 is fully compatible with. We might have lost or corrupted a small amount of data in tables B and C, but that's the price we have to pay for not testing properly earlier. Version 1.1 could have been a canary deployment, so only a small amount of requests have been lost.

Then, we discover the issues, fix them, and deploy version 1.2, which is just like how version 1.1 writes to B and C, but reads from A, B, and C and doesn't delete data from A.

We observe for a while until we're confident that version 1.2 works as expected.

The next step is to migrate the data. We write the data in table A into tables B and C. The active deployment, version 1.2, keeps reading from B and C and only merges missing data from A. We still keep all the old data in A until we finish all code changes.

At this point, all the data is in tables B and C. We deploy version 1.3, which ignores table A and works fully against tables B and C.

We observe again, and can go back to version 1.2 if we encounter any problems with 1.3 and release version 1.4, 1.5, and so on. However, at some point, our code will work as expected and then we can rename/retag the final version as 2.0, or just cut a new version that is identical except for the version number.

The last step is to delete table A.

This can be a slow process that requires running a lot of tests whenever deploying a new version, but it is necessary when you're making dangerous changes that have the potential to corrupt your data.

Of course, you'll back up your data before starting, but for high-throughput systems, even short outages during bad upgrades can be very costly.

The bottom line is that updates that include schema changes are complicated. The way to manage it is to perform a multi-phase upgrade, where each phase is compatible with the previous phase. You move forward only when you have proved that the current phase works correctly. The benefit of the principle of a single microservice owning each data store is that at least DB schema changes are constrained to a single service, and don't require coordination across multiple services.

Managing versions and dependencies

Managing versions is a tricky topic. In microservice-based architecture, your microservices may have many dependencies, as well as many clients, both internal and external. There are several categories of versioned resources, and they all require different management strategies and versioning schemes.

Managing public APIs

Public APIs are network APIs that are used outside the cluster, often by a large number of users and/or developers who may or may not have a formal relationship with your organization. Public APIs may require authentication, but sometimes may be anonymous. The versioning scheme for public APIs typically involves just a major version, such as V1, V2, and so on. The Kubernetes API is a good example of such a versioning scheme, although it also has the concept of API groups and uses alpha and beta qualifiers because it caters to developers.

Delinkcious has a single public API that used the `<major>.<minor>` versioning scheme up to this point:

```
api = Api(app)
resource_map = (
    (Link, '/v1.0/links'),
    (Followers, '/v1.0/followers'),
    (Following, '/v1.0/following'),
)
```

This is overkill, and a major version only is enough. Let's change it (and all the impacted tests, of course):

```
api = Api(app)
resource_map = (
    (Link, '/v1/links'),
    (Followers, '/v1/followers'),
    (Following, '/v1/following'),
)
```

Note that we keep the same version, even when we make breaking changes during this book. This is fine because there are no external users so far, so we have the liberty to change our public API. However, once we officially release our application, we are obligated to consider the burden on our users if we make breaking changes without changing the API version. This is is a pretty bad anti-pattern.

Managing cross-service dependencies

Cross-service dependencies are often well defined and documented as internal APIs. However, subtle changes to the implementation and/or to the contract can significantly impact other services. For example, if we change the structs in `object_model/types.go`, a lot of code might have to be modified. In a well-tested mono-repo, this is less of a problem because the developer who makes the changes can ensure that all the relevant consumers and tests were updated. Many systems are built out of multiple repositories, and it might be challenging to identify all the consumers. In these cases, breaking changes can remain and be discovered after deployment.

Delinkcious is a mono-repo, and it is actually not using any versioning scheme at all in the URLs of its endpoints. Here is the social graph manager's API:

```
r := mux.NewRouter()
r.Methods("POST").Path("/follow").Handler(followHandler)
r.Methods("POST").Path("/unfollow").Handler(unfollowHandler)
```

```
r.Methods("GET").Path("/following/{username}").Handler(getFollowingHandler)

r.Methods("GET").Path("/followers/{username}").Handler(getFollowersHandler)
```

This approach is acceptable if you never intend to run multiple versions of the same service. In large systems, this is not a scalable approach. There will always be some consumers that don't want to upgrade to the latest and greatest immediately.

Managing third-party dependencies

There are three flavors of third-party dependencies:

- Libraries and packages you build your software against (as discussed in Chapter 2, *Getting Started with Microservices*)
- Third-party services that are accessed through an API by your code
- Services you use to operate and run your system

For example, if you run your system in the cloud, then your cloud provider is a huge dependency (Kubernetes can help mitigate risk). Another great example is using a third-party service as your CI/CD solution.

When choosing a third-party dependency, you relinquish some (or a lot) control. You should always consider what happens if the third-party dependency suddenly becomes unavailable or unacceptable. There are many reasons why this can happen:

- Open source project abandoned or loses steam
- Third-party provider shuts down
- Library has too many security vulnerabilities
- Service has too many outages

Assuming that you've picked your dependencies wisely, let's consider two cases:

- Upgrading to a new version of a library
- Upgrading to a new API version of a third-party service

Every such upgrade requires the corresponding upgrade of any component (a library or service) in your system that uses these dependencies. Typically, these upgrades shouldn't modify the API of any of your services, nor the public interfaces of your libraries. They may change the operational profile of your services (hopefully for the better, as in less memory, more performance).

Upgrading your services is a simple matter. You just deploy the new version of your service that depends on the new third-party dependency and you're good to go. Changes to third-party libraries can be a little more involved. You need to identify all of your libraries that depend on this third-party library. Upgrade your libraries and then identify every service that uses any of your (now-upgraded) libraries and upgrade those services too.

It is highly recommended to use semantic versioning for your libraries and packages.

Managing your infrastructure and toolchain

Your infrastructure and toolchain must be managed carefully too, and even versioned. In a large system, your CI/CD pipeline will typically invoke various scripts that automate important tasks, such as migrating databases, preprocessing data, and provisioning cloud resources. These internal tools can change dramatically. Another important category in container-based systems are the versions of your base images. The infrastructure of code approach, combined with GitOps, advocates versioning and storing those aspects of your system in your source control system (Git) as well.

So far, we've covered a lot of dark corners and difficult use cases regarding real-world deployments and how to evolve and upgrade large systems safely and reliably. Let's get back to the individual developer. There is a very different set of requirements and concerns for developers that need a quick edit-test-debug cycle in the cluster.

Local development deployments

Developers want fast iterations. When I make a code change to some code, I want to run the tests as soon as possible, and if something is wrong, to fix it as soon as possible. We've seen how well this works with unit tests. However, when the system uses a microservice architecture packaged as containers and deployed to a Kubernetes cluster, this is not enough. To truly evaluate the impact of a change, we often have to build an image (which may include updating Kubernetes manifests like Deployments, Secrets, and ConfigMaps) and deploy it to the cluster. Developing locally against Minikube is awesome, but even deploying to a local Minikube cluster takes time and effort. In `Chapter 10`, *Testing Microservices*, we used Telepresence to great effect for interactive debugging. However, Telepresence has its own quirks and downsides, and it's not always the best tool for the job. In the following subsections, we'll cover several other alternatives that may be a better choice in certain circumstances.

Ko

Ko (`https://github.com/google/ko`) is a very interesting Go-specific tool. Its goal is to streamline and hide the process of building images. The idea is that, in your Kubernetes deployment, you replace the image path from the registry with a Go import path. Ko will read this import path, build a Docker image for you, publish it to a registry (or locally if using Minikube), and deploy it to your cluster. Ko provides ways to specify a base image and include static data in the generated image.

Let's give it a try and discuss the experience later.

You can install Ko through the standard `go get` command:

```
go get github.com/google/ko/cmd/ko
```

Ko requires that you work in `GOPATH`. I don't typically work inside `GOPATH` for various reasons (Delinkcious use Go modules that don't require `GOPATH`). To accommodate Ko, I used the following code:

```
$ export GOPATH=~/go
$ mkdir -p ~/go/src/github.com/the-gigi
$ cd ~/go/src/github.com/the-gigi
$ ln -s ~/git/delinkcious delinkcious
$ cd delinkcious
$ go get -d ./...
```

Here, I have replicated the directory structure Go expects under `GOPATH`, including replicating the path on GitHub to Delinkcious. Then, I got all the dependencies of Delinkcious recursively using `go get -d ./...`.

The last preparatory step is to set Ko for local development. When Ko builds an image, we shouldn't push it to Docker Hub or any remote registry. We want a fast local loop. Ko allows you to do this in various ways. One of the simplest ways is as follows:

```
export KO_DOCKER_REPO=ko.local
```

Other ways include a configuration file or passing the `-L` flag when running Ko.

Now, we can go ahead and use Ko. Here is the `ko-link-manager.yaml` file where the image is replaced with the Go import path to the link manager service (`github.com/the-gigi/delinkcious/svc/link_service`). Note that I changed `imagePullPolicy` from `Always` to `IfNotPresent`.

The `Always` policy is the secure and production-ready policy, but when working locally, it will ignore the local Ko images and will instead pull from Docker Hub:

```
---
apiVersion: apps/v1
kind: Deployment
metadata:
  name: ko-link-manager
  labels:
    svc: link
    app: manager
spec:
  replicas: 1
  selector:
    matchLabels:
      svc: link
      app: manager
  template:
    metadata:
      labels:
        svc: link
        app: manager
    spec:
      serviceAccount: link-manager
      containers:
      - name: link-manager
        image: "github.com/the-gigi/delinkcious/svc/link_service"
        imagePullPolicy: IfNotPresent
        ports:
        - containerPort: 8080
        envFrom:
        - configMapRef:
            name: link-manager-config
        volumeMounts:
        - name: mutual-auth
          mountPath: /etc/delinkcious
          readOnly: true
      volumes:
      - name: mutual-auth
        secret:
          secretName: link-mutual-auth
```

The next step is running Ko on this modified deployment manifest:

```
$ ko apply -f ko_link_manager.yaml
 2019/05/01 14:29:31 Building github.com/the-
gigi/delinkcious/svc/link_service
 2019/05/01 14:29:34 Using base gcr.io/distroless/static:latest for
```

```
github.com/the-gigi/delinkcious/svc/link_service
 2019/05/01 14:29:34 No matching credentials were found, falling back on
anonymous
 2019/05/01 14:29:36 Loading
ko.local/link_service-1819ff5de960487aed3f9074cd43cc03:1c862ed08cf571c6a82a
3e4a1eb2d79dbe122fc4901e73f88b51f0731d4cd565
 2019/05/01 14:29:38 Loaded
ko.local/link_service-1819ff5de960487aed3f9074cd43cc03:1c862ed08cf571c6a82a
3e4a1eb2d79dbe122fc4901e73f88b51f0731d4cd565
 2019/05/01 14:29:38 Adding tag latest
 2019/05/01 14:29:38 Added tag latest
 deployment.apps/ko-link-manager configured
```

To test the deployment, let's run our `smoke` test:

```
$ go run smoke.go
2019/05/01 14:35:59 ======= Links =======
2019/05/01 14:35:59 ===== Add Link ======
2019/05/01 14:35:59 Adding new link - title: 'Gigi on Github', url:
'https://github.com/the-gigi'
2019/05/01 14:36:00 ======= Links =======
2019/05/01 14:36:00 title: 'Gigi on Github', url:
'https://github.com/the-gigi', status: 'pending', description: '[yellow] '
2019/05/01 14:36:04 ======= Links =======
2019/05/01 14:36:04 title: 'Gigi on Github', url:
'https://github.com/the-gigi', status: 'valid', description: '[yellow] '
```

Everything looks good. The link description contains the `[yellow]` prefix from our canary deployment work. Let's change it to `[ko]` and see how fast Ko can redeploy:

```
func newLink(source om.Link) link {
    return link{
        Url:         source.Url,
        Title:       source.Title,
        Description: "[ko] " + source.Description,
        Status:      source.Status,
        Tags:        source.Tags,
        CreatedAt:   source.CreatedAt.Format(time.RFC3339),
        UpdatedAt:   source.UpdatedAt.Format(time.RFC3339),
    }
}
```

Running Ko again on the modified code takes just 19 seconds, all the way to deployment in the cluster. That's impressive:

```
$ ko apply -f ko_link_manager.yaml
 2019/05/01 14:39:37 Building github.com/the-
gigi/delinkcious/svc/link_service
```

```
2019/05/01 14:39:52 Using base gcr.io/distroless/static:latest for
github.com/the-gigi/delinkcious/svc/link_service
2019/05/01 14:39:52 No matching credentials were found, falling back on
anonymous
2019/05/01 14:39:54 Loading
ko.local/link_service-1819ff5de960487aed3f9074cd43cc03:1af7800585ca70a390da
7e68e6eef506513e0f5d08cabc05a51c453e366ededf
2019/05/01 14:39:56 Loaded
ko.local/link_service-1819ff5de960487aed3f9074cd43cc03:1af7800585ca70a390da
7e68e6eef506513e0f5d08cabc05a51c453e366ededf
2019/05/01 14:39:56 Adding tag latest
2019/05/01 14:39:56 Added tag latest
deployment.apps/ko-link-manager configured
```

The `smoke` test works and the description now contains the `[ko]` prefix instead of
`[yellow]`, which proves that Ko works as advertised and indeed built a Docker container
very quickly and deployed it to the cluster:

```
$ go run smoke.go
2019/05/01 22:12:10 ======= Links =======
2019/05/01 22:12:10 ===== Add Link ======
2019/05/01 22:12:10 Adding new link - title: 'Gigi on Github', url:
'https://github.com/the-gigi'
2019/05/01 22:12:10 ======= Links =======
2019/05/01 22:12:10 title: 'Gigi on Github', url:
'https://github.com/the-gigi', status: 'pending', description: '[ko] '
2019/05/01 22:12:14 ======= Links =======
2019/05/01 22:12:14 title: 'Gigi on Github', url:
'https://github.com/the-gigi', status: 'valid', description: '[ko] '
```

Let's take a look at the image that Ko built. In order to do that, we will `ssh` into the
Minikube node and check the Docker images:

```
$ mk ssh

               _                 _
         _    ( )               ( )
  __   __( )   __   (_)| |/')    _    _ | |_        __
/' _ `_ `\| |/'  _ `\| | | , <  ( ) ( )| '_`\   /'_`\
| ( ) ( ) || || ( ) || | | |\`\ | (_) || |_) ) (  ___/
(_) (_) (_)(_)(_) (_)(_) (_)`\___/'(_,__/''`\____)


$ docker images | grep ko
ko.local/link_service-1819ff5de960487aed3f9074cd43cc03
1af7800585ca70a390da7e68e6eef506513e0f5d08cabc05a51c453e366ededf
9188384722a5         49 years ago         14.1MB
ko.local/link_service-1819ff5de960487aed3f9074cd43cc03                       latest
9188384722a5         49 years ago         14.1MB
```

The image appears to have a creation date of the beginning of the Unix epoch (1970) for some reason. Other than that, everything looks good. Note that the image is larger than our normal link manager because Ko uses `gcr.io/distroless/base:latest` as a base image by default, while Delinkcious uses the SCRATCH image. You can override the base image if you want, using a `.ko.yaml` configuration file.

In short, Ko is easy to install, configure, and it works very well. Still, I find it too limited:

- It is a Go-only tool.
- You must have your code in `GOPATH` and use the standard Go directory structure (obsolete with Go 1.11+ modules).
- You have to modify your manifests (or create a copy with the Go import path).

It may be a good option to test new Go services before integrating them into your CI/CD system.

Ksync

Ksync is a very interesting tool. It doesn't build images at all. It syncs files directly between a local directory, and a remote directory inside a running container in your cluster. It doesn't get more streamlined than that, especially if you sync to a local Minikube cluster. This awesomeness comes with a price, though. Ksync works especially well for services that are implemented using dynamic languages, such as Python and Node, that can hot-reload the application when changes are synced. If your application doesn't do hot reloading, Ksync can restart the container after each change. Let's get to work:

1. Installing Ksync is very simple, but remember to check what you are installing before just piping it to `bash`!

   ```
   curl https://vapor-ware.github.io/gimme-that/gimme.sh | bash
   ```

   If you prefer, you can install it with a `go` command:

   ```
   go get github.com/vapor-ware/ksync/cmd/ksync
   ```

2. We also need to start the cluster-side component of Ksync, which will create a DaemonSet on every node to listen for changes and reflect them into running containers:

   ```
   ksync init
   ```

3. Now, we can tell Ksync to watch for changes. This is a blocking operation and Ksync will watch forever. We can run it in a separate Terminal or tab:

```
ksync watch
```

4. The last part of the setup is to establish a mapping between a local directory and a remote directory on a target pod or pods. As usual, we identify the pods via a label selector. The only Delinkcious service that uses a dynamic language is the API gateway, so we'll use this here:

```
cd svc/api_gateway_service ksync create --selector=svc=api-gateway
$PWD /api_gateway_service
```

5. We can test that Ksync works by modifying our API gateway. Let's add a Ksync message to our get() method:

```
def get(self):
    """Get all links
    """
    username, email = _get_user()
    parser = RequestParser()
    parser.add_argument('url_regex', type=str, required=False)
    parser.add_argument('title_regex', type=str, required=False)
    parser.add_argument('description_regex', type=str,
required=False)
    parser.add_argument('tag', type=str, required=False)
    parser.add_argument('start_token', type=str, required=False)
    args = parser.parse_args()
    args.update(username=username)
    r = requests.get(self.base_url, params=args)

    if not r.ok:
        abort(r.status_code, message=r.content)

    result = r.json()
    result.update(ksync='Yeah, it works!')
    return result
```

6. A few seconds later, we will see the Yeah, it works! message from Ksync. This is a great success:

```
$ http "${DELINKCIOUS_URL}/v1/links" "Access-Token:
${DELINKCIOUS_TOKEN}"'
HTTP/1.0 200 OK Content-Length: 249 Content-Type: application/json
Date: Thu, 02 May 2019 17:17:07 GMT Server: Werkzeug/0.14.1
Python/3.7.2
{ "err": "", "ksync": "Yeah, it works!", "links": [ { "CreatedAt":
```

```
"2019-05-02T05:12:10Z", "Description": "[ko] ", "Status": "valid",
"Tags": null, "Title": "Gigi on Github", "UpdatedAt":
"2019-05-02T05:12:10Z", "Url": "https://github.com/the-gigi" } ] }
```

To recap, Ksync is extremely streamlined and fast. I really like the fact that it doesn't bake images, push them to a registry, and then deploy to the cluster. If all your workloads use a dynamic language, then using Ksync is a no-brainer.

Draft

Draft is another tool from Microsoft (originally from Deis) that lets you quickly build images without a Dockerfile. It uses standard buildpacks for various languages. It doesn't seem like you can provide your own base image. This is a problem for two reasons:

- Your service may be more than just code, and may depend on things that you set up in the Dockerfile.
- The base images that Draft uses are pretty big.

Draft depends on Helm, so you must have Helm installed on your cluster. The installation is very versatile and supports many methods.

You can be sure that Draft works well on Windows, unlike many other tools in the cloud-native area where Windows is a second-class citizen. This mindset is starting to change since Microsoft, Azure, and AKS are prominent contributors to the Kubernetes ecosystem. OK, let's take Draft for a test drive:

1. Installing `draft` on macOS (assuming you've installed Helm already) is as simple as doing the following:

   ```
   brew install azure/draft/draft
   ```

2. Let's configure Draft to push its images directly to Minikube (the same as Ko):

   ```
   $ draft init
   $ draft init Installing default plugins... Installation of default
   plugins complete Installing default pack repositories...
   Installation of default pack repositories complete $DRAFT_HOME has
   been configured at /Users/gigi.sayfan/.draft. Happy Sailing!
   $ eval $(minikube docker-env)
   ```

As usual, let's add a prefix, `[draft]`, to the description:

```
func newLink(source om.Link) link { return link{ Url: source.Url,
Title: source.Title, Description: "[draft]" + source.Description,
Status: source.Status, Tags: source.Tags, CreatedAt:
source.CreatedAt.Format(time.RFC3339), UpdatedAt:
source.UpdatedAt.Format(time.RFC3339), } }
```

3. Next, we let draft prepare by calling the `draft create` command and also choosing the Helm release name using `--app`:

```
$ draft create --app draft-link-manager --> Draft detected Go
(67.381270%) --> Ready to sail
```

4. Finally, we can deploy to the cluster:

```
$ draft up
Draft Up Started: 'draft-link-manager': 01D9XZD650WS93T46YE4QJ3V70
draft-link-manager: Building Docker Image: SUCCESS (9.0060s) draft-
link-manager: Pushing Docker Image
```

Unfortunately, draft hung in the `Pushing Docker Image` stage. It worked for me in the past, so perhaps it's a new issue with the latest versions.

Overall, draft is pretty simple, but too limited. The big images it creates and the inability to provide your own base images are deal breakers. The documentation is very sparse, too. I recommend using it only if you're on Windows and the other tools don't work well enough.

Skaffold

Skaffold (`https://skaffold.dev/`) is a very complete solution. It is very flexible, supports both local development and integration with CI/CD, and has excellent documentation. Here are some of the features of Skaffold:

- Detect code changes, build image, push, and deploy.
- Can sync source files to pods directly (just like Ksync).
- It has a sophisticated conceptual model with builders, testers, deployers, tag polices, and push strategies.

- You can customize every aspect.
- Integrate with your CI/CD pipeline by running Skaffold from end to end, or use specific stages as building blocks.
- Per-environment configuration via profiles, user-level config, environment variables, or command-line flags.
- It is a client-side tool – there is no need to install anything in your cluster.
- Automatically forward container ports to the local machine.
- Aggregate logs from the deployed pods.

Here is a diagram that illustrates the workflow of Skaffold:

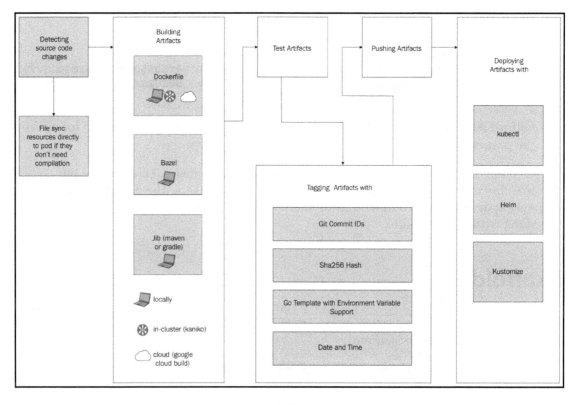

Skaffold

Let's install Skaffold and take it for a ride:

```
$ brew install skaffold
```

Next, let's create a configuration file in the `link_service` directory. Skaffold will ask us some questions about which Dockerfile to use for different elements, such as the database and the service itself:

```
$ skaffold init ? Choose the dockerfile to build image postgres:11.1-alpine
None (image not built from these sources) ? Choose the dockerfile to build
image g1g1/delinkcious-link:0.6 Dockerfile WARN[0014] unused dockerfiles
found in repository: [Dockerfile.dev] apiVersion: skaffold/v1beta9 kind:
Config build: artifacts: - image: g1g1/delinkcious-link:0.6 deploy:
kubectl: manifests: - k8s/configmap.yaml - k8s/db.yaml -
k8s/link_manager.yaml - k8s/secrets.yaml
Do you want to write this configuration to skaffold.yaml? [y/n]: y
Configuration skaffold.yaml was written You can now run [skaffold build] to
build the artifacts or [skaffold run] to build and deploy or [skaffold dev]
to enter development mode, with auto-redeploy.
```

Let's try to build an image with Skaffold:

```
$ skaffold build Generating tags... - g1g1/delinkcious-link:0.6 ->
g1g1/delinkcious-link:0.6:v0.6-79-g6b178c6-dirty Tags generated in
2.005247255s Starting build... Found [minikube] context, using local docker
daemon. Building [g1g1/delinkcious-link:0.6]... Sending build context to
Docker daemon 10.75kB Complete in 4.717424985s FATA[0004] build failed:
building [g1g1/delinkcious-link:0.6]: build artifact: docker build: Error
response from daemon: invalid reference format
```

Oh, no – it fails. I did some searching and there is an open issue:

```
https://github.com/GoogleContainerTools/skaffold/issues/1749
```

Skaffold is a big solution. It does much more than just local development. It has a non-trivial learning curve, too (for example, syncing files requires manually setting up each directory and file type). If you like its model and you use it in your CI/CD solution, then it makes sense to use it for local development as well. Definitely check it out and make up your own mind. The fact that it can build images as well as directly sync files is a big plus if you have a hybrid system similar to Delinkcious.

Tilt

Last, but absolutely not least, is Tilt. Tilt is my favorite development tool by far. Tilt is also very comprehensive and flexible. It is centered around a Tiltfile written in a language called Starlark (`https://github.com/bazelbuild/starlark/`), which is a subset of Python. I was hooked right way. What's special about Tilt is that it goes beyond just building an image automatically and deploying it to the cluster or syncing files. It actually gives you a complete live development environment that presents a lot of information, highlights events and errors, and lets you drill down and understand what's happening in your cluster. Let's get started.

Let's install Tilt and then get to business:

```
brew tap windmilleng/tap brew install windmilleng/tap/tilt
```

I wrote a Tiltfile for the link service that's very generic.

```
# Get all the YAML files
script = """python -c 'from glob import glob;
print(",".join(glob("k8s/*.yaml")))'""" yaml_files =
str(local(script))[:-1] yaml_files = yaml_files.split(',') for f in
yaml_files: k8s_yaml(f)

# Get the service name
script = """import os; print('-
'.join(os.getcwd().split("/")[-1].split("_")[:-1])""" name =
str(local(script))[:-1]
docker_build('g1g1/delinkcious-' + name, '.', dockerfile='Dockerfile.dev')
```

Let's break this down and analyze it. First, we need all the YAML files under the k8s subdirectory. We could just hard code them, but where's the fun in that? Also, there will be a different list of YAML files for different services. Skylark is Python-like, but you can't use Python libraries. For example, the glob library is great for enumerating files with wildcards. Here is the Python code to list all files with the `.yaml` suffix in the `k8s` subdirectory:

```
Python 3.7.3 (default, Mar 27 2019, 09:23:15) [Clang 10.0.1
(clang-1001.0.46.3)] on darwin Type "help", "copyright", "credits" or
"license" for more information. >>> from glob import glob >>>
glob("k8s/*.yaml") ['k8s/db.yaml', 'k8s/secrets.yaml',
'k8s/link_manager.yaml', 'k8s/configmap.yaml']
```

We can't do that directly in Starlark, but we can use the `local()` function, which allows us to run any command and capture the output. Therefore, we can execute the previous Python code by running the Python interpreter with a little script through Tilt's `local()` function:

```
script = """python -c 'from glob import glob;
print(",".join(glob("k8s/*.yaml")))'""" yaml_files =
str(local(script))[:-1]
```

There are a few extra details here. First, we convert the list of files returned from glob into a comma-separated string. However, the `local()` function returns a Tilt object called Blob. We just want a plain string, so we convert the blob into a string by wrapping the `local()` call with the `str()` function. Finally, we remove the last character (the final `[:-1]`), which is a newline (because we used Python's `print()` function).

The end result is that, in the `yaml_files` variable, we have a string that is a comma-separated list of all the YAML manifests.

Next, we split this comma-separated string back into a Python/Starlark list of file names:

```
yaml_files = yaml_files.split(',')
```

For each of these files, we call Tilt's `k8s_yaml()` function. This function tells Tilt to monitor these files for changes:

```
for f in yaml_files: k8s_yaml(f)
```

Next, we repeat the same trick as before and execute a Python one-liner that extracts the service name from the current directory name. All the Delinkcious service directories follow the same naming convention, that is, `<service name>_service`. This one-liner splits the current directory, disposes of the last component (which is always `service`), and joins the components back via - as a separator.

Now, we need to get the service name:

```
script = """import os; print('-
'.join(os.getcwd().split("/")[-1].split("_")[:-1]),""" name =
str(local(script))[:-1]
```

Now that we have the service name, the final step is to build the image by calling Tilt's `docker_build()` function. Remember that the naming convention for Docker images that Delinkcious uses is `g1g1/delinkcious-<service name>`. I am also using a special `Dockerfile.dev` here, which is different than the production Dockerfile, and is more convenient for debugging and troubleshooting. If you don't specify a Docker file, then the default is `Dockerfile`:

```
docker_build('g1g1/delinkcious-' + name, '.', dockerfile='Dockerfile.dev')
```

This may seem very complicated and convoluted, but the benefit is that I can drop this file in any service directory and it will work as is.

For the link service, the equivalent hardcoded file would be as follows:

```
k8s_yam('k8s/db.yaml') k8s_yam('k8s/secrets.yaml')
k8s_yam('k8s/link_manager.yaml') k8s_yam(''k8s/configmap.yaml'')
docker_build('g1g1/delinkcious-link, '.', dockerfile='Dockerfile.dev')
```

That's not too bad, but every time you add a new manifest, you have to remember to update your Tiltfile, and you'll need to keep a separate Tiltfile for each service.

Let's see Tilt in action. When we type `tilt up`, we will see the following text UI:

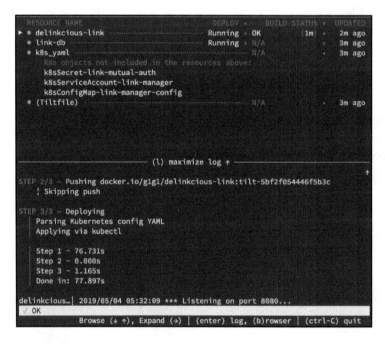

Tilt

There are many things you can do in the Tilt console, including checking logs and exploring errors. Tilt constantly displays updates and the status of the system, and always attempts to surface the most useful information.

It's interesting to see that Tilt build images with its own tag:

```
$ kubectl get po link-manager-654959fd78-9rnnh -o
jsonpath="{.spec.containers[0].image}"
docker.io/g1g1/delinkcious-link:tilt-2b1afed5db0064f2
```

Let's make our standard change and see how Tilt reacts:

```
func newLink(source om.Link) link { return link{ Url: source.Url, Title:
source.Title, Description: "[tilt] " + source.Description, Status:
source.Status, Tags: source.Tags, CreatedAt:
source.CreatedAt.Format(time.RFC3339), UpdatedAt:
source.UpdatedAt.Format(time.RFC3339), } }
```

Tilt detected the change and built a new image, then promptly deployed it to the cluster:

```
$ http "${DELINKCIOUS_URL}/v1/links" "Access-Token: ${DELINKCIOUS_TOKEN}"
HTTP/1.0 200 OK Content-Length: 221 Content-Type: application/json Date:
Sat, 04 May 2019 07:38:32 GMT Server: Werkzeug/0.14.1 Python/3.7.2
{ "err": "", "links": [ { "CreatedAt": "2019-05-04T07:38:28Z",
"Description": "[tilt] nothing to see here...", "Status": "pending",
"Tags": null, "Title": "gg", "UpdatedAt": "2019-05-04T07:38:28Z", "Url":
"http://gg.com" } ] }
```

Let's try our hand at some file syncing. We must run Flask in debug mode for hot reloading to work. This is as simple as adding FLASK_DEBUG=1 to ENTRYPOINT in the Dockerfile:

```
FROM g1g1/delinkcious-python-flask-grpc:0.1 MAINTAINER Gigi Sayfan
"the.gigi@gmail.com" COPY . /api_gateway_service WORKDIR
/api_gateway_service EXPOSE 5000 ENTRYPOINT FLASK_DEBUG=1 python run.py
```

It's up to you to decide if you want a separate Dockerfile.dev file to use with Tilt, as we used for the link service. Here is a Tiltfile for the API gateway service that uses the live update facilities of Tilt:

```
# Get all the YAML files
yaml_files = str(local("""python -c 'from glob import glob;
print(",".join(glob("k8s/*.yaml")))'"""))[:-1] yaml_files =
yaml_files.split(',') for f in yaml_files: k8s_yaml(f)
```

```
# Get the service name
script = """python -c 'import os; print("-
".join(os.getcwd().split("/")[-1].split("_")[:-1]))'""" name =
str(local(script))[:-1]
docker_build('g1g1/delinkcious-' + name, '.', live_update=[ # when
requirements.txt changes, we need to do a full build
fall_back_on('requirements.txt'), # Map the local source code into the
container under /api_gateway_service sync('.', '/api_gateway_service'), ])
```

At this point, we can run tilt up and hit the /links endpoint:

```
$ http "${DELINKCIOUS_URL}/v1/links" "Access-Token: ${DELINKCIOUS_TOKEN}"
HTTP/1.0 200 OK
Content-Length: 221
Content-Type: application/json
Date: Sat, 04 May 2019 20:39:42 GMT
Server: Werkzeug/0.14.1 Python/3.7.2
{
"err": "",
"links": [ {
"CreatedAt": "2019-05-04T07:38:28Z",
"Description": "[tilt] nothing to see here...",
"Status": "pending",
"Tags": null,
"Title": "gg",
"UpdatedAt": "2019-05-04T07:38:28Z",
"Url": "http://gg.com"
} ]
}
```

Tilt will show us the request and the successful 200 response:

Tilt API gateway

Let's make a little change and see if tilt picks it up and syncs the code in the container. In the `resources.py` file, let's add to the result of the GET links the key-value pair - `tilt`: `Yeah, sync works!!`.

```
class Link(Resource): host = os.environ.get('LINK_MANAGER_SERVICE_HOST',
'localhost') port = os.environ.get('LINK_MANAGER_SERVICE_PORT', '8080')
base_url = 'http://{}:{}/links'.format(host, port)
def get(self):
    """Get all links
    """
    username, email = _get_user()
    parser = RequestParser()
    parser.add_argument('url_regex', type=str, required=False)
    parser.add_argument('title_regex', type=str, required=False)
    parser.add_argument('description_regex', type=str, required=False)
    parser.add_argument('tag', type=str, required=False)
    parser.add_argument('start_token', type=str, required=False)
    args = parser.parse_args()
    args.update(username=username)
    r = requests.get(self.base_url, params=args)

    if not r.ok:
        abort(r.status_code, message=r.content)
    r['tilt'] = 'Yeah, sync works!!!'
    return r.json()
```

As you can see in the following screenshot, Tilt detected the code change in `resources.py` and copied the new file into the container:

```
RESOURCE NAME                                                    CONTAINER  .  UPDATE STATUS  .      AS OF
► ● (Tiltfile)                                                              .  N/A            .   13m ago
  ● api-gateway                                               Running ● OK                  (0.1s)  . 7m ago
  ● k8s_yaml                                                            ● OK                (4.6s)  . 13m ago
       K8s objects not included in the resources above:
       k8sSecret-github-creds
       k8sServiceAccount-api-gateway
       k8sConfigMap-api-gateway-config




 1: ALL LOGS  | 2: build log | 3: pod log |                                                    X: expand
                                                                                                      ↑
 ┤ Rebuilding: api-gateway ├──────────────────────────────────────
  → Updating container…
 Copying 1 file(s) to container: c94f8bed64
 - '/Users/gigi.sayfan/git/delinkcious/svc/api_gateway_service/api_gateway_service/resources.py' -->
 '/api_gateway_service/api_gateway_service/resources.py'
  → Container updated!
 ✓ OK
                            Browse (↓ ↑), Expand (→)  | (enter) log, (b)rowser | (ctrl-C) quit
```

Tilt API gateway 2

Let's invoke the endpoint again and observe the results. It works as intended. We got the expected key-value after the links in the result:

```
$ http "${DELINKCIOUS_URL}/v1/links" "Access-Token:
${DELINKCIOUS_TOKEN}"

HTTP/1.0 200 OK
Content-Length: 374
Content-Type: application/json
Date: Sat, 04 May 2019 21:06:13 GMT
Server: Werkzeug/0.14.1 Python/3.7.2
{
  "err": "",
"links":
[ {
"CreatedAt": "2019-05-04T07:38:28Z",
"Description": "[tilt] nothing to see here...",
"Status": "pending",
"Tags": null,
"Title": "gg", "UpdatedAt":
"2019-05-04T07:38:28Z",
```

```
"Url": "http://gg.com"
} ],
"tilt": "Yeah,
sync works!!!"
}
```

Overall, Tilt is extremely well done. It's based on a solid conceptual model, is very well executed, and it addresses the problems of local development better than any of the other tools. Tiltfile and Starlark are powerful and concise. It supports both full-fledged Docker builds and file syncing for dynamic languages.

Summary

In this chapter, we covered a broad swatch of topics related to deployments to Kubernetes. We started with a deep dive into the Kubernetes deployment object and considered and implemented deployments to multiple environments (for example, staging and production). We delved into advanced deployment strategies like rolling updates, blue-green deployments, and canary deployments, and experimented with all of them on Delinkcious. Then, we looked at rolling back failed deployments and the crucial topic of managing dependencies and versions. Later on, we switched gears into local development, and surveyed multiple tools for fast iterations where you make changes to your code, and they are automatically deployed to your cluster. We covered Ko, Ksync, Draft, Skaffold, and my personal favorite, Tilt.

At this point, you should have a deep understanding of the various deployment strategies, when to employ them on your system, and good hands-on experience with local development tools for Kubernetes that you can integrate into your workflow.

In the next chapter, we will take it to the next level and get serious about monitoring our system. We will look into failure modes, how to design self-healing systems, autoscaling, provisioning, and performance. Then, we will consider logging, collecting metrics, and distributed tracing.

Further reading

Refer to the following links if you want to find out more about what was covered in this chapter:

- **KO**: https://github.com/google/ko
- **Ksync**: https://vapor-ware.github.io/ksync/
- **Draft**: https://draft.sh/
- **Skaffold**: https://skaffold.dev/
- **Tilt**: https://docs.tilt.dev

12
Monitoring, Logging, and Metrics

In this chapter, we will focus on the operational side of running a large-scale distributed system on Kubernetes, as well as on how to design the system and what to take into account to ensure top-notch operational posture. That being said, things will always go south and you must be ready to detect, troubleshoot, and respond as soon as possible. The operational best practices that Kubernetes provides out of the box include the following:

- Self-healing
- Auto scaling
- Resource management

However, the cluster administrator and the developers must understand how these capabilities work, configure, and interact in order to understand them properly. There is always a balancing act between high availability, robustness, performance, security, and cost. It's also important to realize that all of these factors and the relationships between them change over time and must be revisited and evaluated regularly.

This is where monitoring comes in. Monitoring is all about understanding what's going on with your system. There are several sources of information that are relevant for different purposes:

- **Logging**: You explicitly log relevant information in your application code (and libraries you use may log too).
- **Metrics**: Collect detailed information about your system such as CPU, memory, disk usage, disk I/O, network, and custom application metrics.
- **Tracing**: Attach an ID to follow a request across multiple microservices.

In this chapter, we will see how Go-kit, Kubernetes, and the ecosystem enable and support all the relevant use cases.

The following topics are covered in this chapter:

- Self-healing with Kubernetes
- Autoscaling a Kubernetes cluster
- Provisioning resources with Kubernetes
- Getting performance right
- Logging
- Collecting metrics on Kubernetes
- Alerting
- Distributed tracing

Technical requirements

In this chapter, we will install several components into the cluster:

- **Prometheus**: A metrics and alerting solution
- **Fluentd**: A central logging agent
- **Jaeger**: A distributed tracing system

The code

The code is split between two Git repositories:

- You can find the code samples here: `https://github.com/PacktPublishing/Hands-On-Microservices-with-Kubernetes/tree/master/Chapter12`
- You can find the updated Delinkcious application here: `https://github.com/the-gigi/delinkcious/releases/tag/v0.10`

Self-healing with Kubernetes

Self-healing is a very important property of large-scale systems made up of a myriad of physical and virtual components. Microservice-based systems running on large Kubernetes clusters are a prime example. Components can fail in multiple ways. The premise of self-healing is that the overall system will not fail and will be able to automatically heal itself, even if this causes it to operate in a reduced capacity temporarily.

The building blocks of such reliable systems are as follows:

- Redundancy
- Observability
- Auto-recovery

The basic premise is that every component might fail – machines crash, disks get corrupted, network connections drop, configuration may get out of sync, new software releases have bugs, third-party services have outages, and so on. Redundancy means there are no **single point of failures** (**SPOFs**). You can run multiple replicas of many components, like nodes and pods, write data to multiple data stores, and deploy your system in multiple data centers, availability zones, or regions. You are even able to deploy your system on multiple cloud platforms (especially if you use Kubernetes). There is a limit to redundancy, of course. Total redundancy is very expansive. For example, running a complete redundant system on both AWS and GKE is probably a luxury that very few companies can afford or even need.

Observability is the ability to detect when things go wrong. You must monitor your system and understand the signals you observe in order to detect abnormal situations. This is the first step before remediation and recovery can take place.

The automated part of auto healing and recovery is not needed in theory. You could have a team of operators watching a dashboard all day and take corrective action when they identify a problem. In practice, this approach doesn't scale. Humans are slow to respond, interpret, and act – not to mention that they are much more error-prone. That being said, most automated solutions start with manual processes that get automated later as the cost of repeated manual intervention becomes clear. If some issues happen only once in a blue moon, then it may be OK to address those with manual intervention.

Let's discuss several failure modes and see how Kubernetes helps with all the pillars of self-healing.

Container failures

Kubernetes runs containers inside pods. If a container dies for whatever reason, Kubernetes will detect it and restart it right away by default. The behavior of Kubernetes can be controlled by the `restartPolicy` file of the pod spec. The possible values are `Always` (default), `OnFailure`, and `Never`. Note that the restart policy applies to all the containers in the pod. There is no way to specify a restart policy per container. This seems a little short-sighted as you may have multiple containers in a pod that require a different restart policy.

If a container keeps failing, it will enter a `CrashOff`. Let's see this in action by introducing an intentional error to our API gateway:

```python
import os
from api_gateway_service.api import app
def main():
    port = int(os.environ.get('PORT', 5000))
    login_url = 'http://localhost:{}/login'.format(port)
    print('If you run locally, browse to', login_url)
    host = '0.0.0.0'
    app.run(host=host, port=port)

if __name__ == "__main__":
    raise RuntimeError('Failing on purpose to demonstrate
CrashLoopBackOff')
    main()
```

After performing a tilt up, we can see that the API gateway enters a `CrashLoopBackOff` state. This means that it keeps failing and Kubernetes keep restarting it. The backoff part is the delay between restart attempts. Kubernetes uses an exponential backoff delay starting at 10 seconds and doubling every time, up to a maximum delay of 5 minutes:

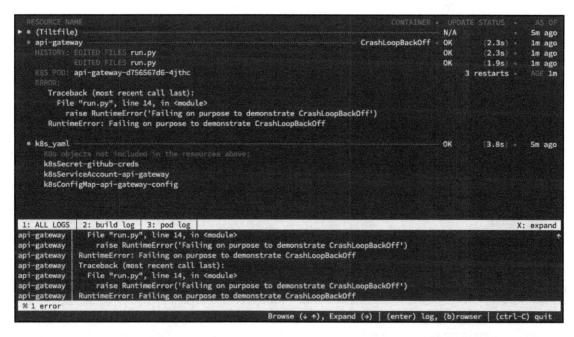

Crash loop backoff

This approach is very useful because if the failure was transient, then Kubernetes would self-heal by restarting the container until the transient issue went away. However, if the problem were to persist, then the container status and the error logs are around and provide observability that can be used by higher-level recovery processes or as a last resort by a human operator or developer.

Node failure

When a node fails, all the pods on the node will become unavailable and Kubernetes will schedule them to run on other nodes in the cluster. Assuming you design your system with redundancy in place and the failed node is not a SPOF, the system should recover automatically. If the cluster has just a few nodes, then the loss of a node can be significant to the cluster's ability to handle traffic.

Systemic failures

Sometimes, systemic failures take place. Some of these are as follows:

- Total networking failure (entire cluster is unreachable)
- Data center outage
- Availability zone outage
- Region outage
- Cloud provider outage

In these situations, you may not have redundancy by design (the cost-benefit ratio is not economical). The system will be down. Users will experience an outage. The important thing is not to lose or corrupt any data and be able to come back online as soon as the root cause is addressed. However, if it is important for your organization to stay online at all costs, Kubernetes will have options for you. The operative word is *will*, as in the future. The work on this is conducted under a project called federation v2, (v1 was deprecated as it suffered from too many problems.)

You will be able to bring up a complete Kubernetes cluster or even a set of clusters in a different data center, a different availability zone, a different region, or even a different cloud provider. You will be able to run, manage, and treat those physically distributed clusters as a single logical cluster and, hopefully, fail over between those clusters seamlessly.

If you want to implement this kind of cluster-level redundancy, you may consider building it using the gardener (`https://gardener.cloud/`) project.

Autoscaling a Kubernetes cluster

Autoscaling is all about adapting your system to demand. This can mean adding more replicas to a deployment, expanding the capacity of existing nodes, or adding new nodes. While scaling your cluster up or down is not a failure, it follows the same pattern as self-healing. You can consider a cluster that is misaligned with demand as unhealthy. If the cluster is underprovisioned, then requests are not handled or wait too long, which can lead to timeouts or just poor performance. If the cluster is overprovisioned, then you're paying for resources you don't need. In both cases, you can consider the cluster as unhealthy, even if the pods and services themselves are up and running.

Just like with self-healing, you first need to detect that you need to scale your cluster, and then you can take the correct action. There are several ways to scale your cluster capacity: you can add more pods, you can add new nodes, and you can increase the capacity of existing nodes. Let's review them in detail.

Horizontal pod autoscaling

The horizontal pod autoscaler is a controller that is designed to adjust the number of pods in a deployment to match the load on those pods. The decision of whether a deployment should be scaled up (add pods) or down (remove pods) is based on metrics. Out of the box, the horizontal pod autoscaler supports CPU utilization, but custom metrics can be added too. The cool thing about the horizontal autoscaler is that it sits on top of the standard Kubernetes deployment and just adjusts its replica count. The deployment itself and the pods are blissfully unaware that they are being scaled:

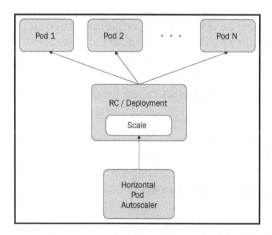

Horizontal pod autoscaler

The preceding diagram illustrates how the horizontal autoscaler works.

Using the horizontal pod autoscaler

We can use kubectl for autoscaling. Since the autoscaler relies on Heapster and the metrics server, we need to enable them using the `minikube addons` command. We have already enabled Heapster, so this should be good enough:

```
$ minikube addons enable metrics-server
  metrics-server was successfully enabled
```

We must also specify a CPU request in the pod spec of the deployment:

```
resources:
   requests:
      cpu: 100m
```

As you may recall, a resource request is what Kubernetes promises it can provide to the container if it is ever scheduled. This way, the horizontal pod autoscaler can ensure that it will start a new pod only if it can provide this requested minimum of CPU to the new pod.

Let's introduce some code that will cause the social graph manager to waste a lot of CPU:

```
func wasteCPU() {
    fmt.Println("wasteCPU() here!")
    go func() {
        for {
            if rand.Int() % 8000 == 0 {
                time.Sleep(50 * time.Microsecond)
            }
        }
    }()
}
```

Here, we are scaling the social graph manager between 1 and 5 pods based on CPU utilization of 50%:

```
$ kubectl autoscale deployment social-graph-manager --cpu-percent=50 --
min=1 --max=5
```

After running a tilt up and deploying the CPU wasting code, the CPU utilization increased, and more and more pods were created up to the maximum of five. Here is a screenshot of the Kubernetes dashboard that shows the CPU, the pods, and the horizontal pod autoscaler:

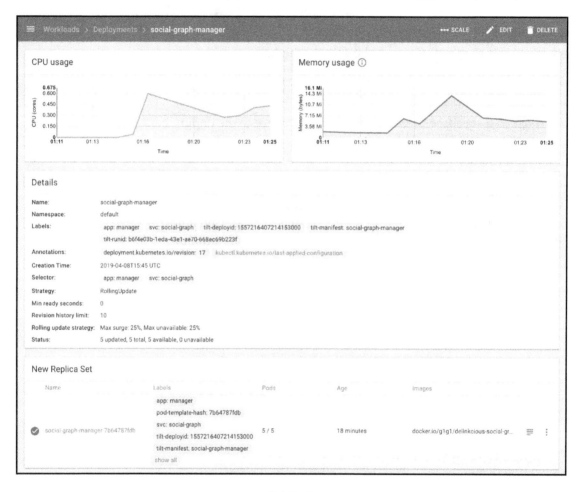

Hp dashboard

Let's review the horizontal pod autoscaler itself:

```
$ kubectl get hpa
NAME      REFERENCE    TARGETS    MINPODS    MAXPODS    REPLICAS    AGE
social-graph-manager    Deployment/social-graph-manager    138%/50%    1
5          5            12h
```

As you can see, the current load is `138%` of CPU utilization, which means that more than one CPU core is needed, which is greater than the 50%. Therefore, the social graph manager will keep running five pods (the maximum that's allowed).

The horizontal pod autoscaler is a universal mechanism that has been part of Kubernetes for a long time. It depends on internal components only for collecting metrics. We've demonstrated the default CPU-based autoscaling here, but it can be configured to work based on multiple custom metrics, too. Now is a good time to look at some other autoscaling methods.

Cluster autoscaling

Pod autoscaling is a gift to developers and operators – there's no need for them to manually scale services up and down or write their own half-based autoscaling scripts. Kubernetes provides a robust solution that is well-designed, well-implemented, and battle tested. However, that leaves the question of cluster capacity. If Kubernetes tries to add more pods to your cluster, but the cluster is running at maximum capacity, then the pod autoscaler will fail. On the other hand, if you over-provision your cluster just in case the pod autoscaler needs to add a few more pods, then you're wasting money.

Enter the `auto-scaler` cluster (`https://github.com/kubernetes/autoscaler/tree/master/cluster-autoscaler`).

It is a Kubernetes project that has been generally available since Kubernetes 1.8. It works with GCP, AWS, Azure, AliCloud, and BaiduCloud. If GKE, EKS, and AKS give you a managed control plane (they take care of managing Kubernetes itself), then the cluster autoscaler gives you a managed data plane. It will add or remove nodes from your cluster based on your needs and your configuration.

The trigger for adjusting the size of the cluster is when Kubernetes can't schedule pods due to insufficient resources. This works really well with the horizontal pod autoscaler. Together, the combination gives you a truly elastic Kubernetes cluster that can grow and shrink automatically (within bounds) to match the current load.

The cluster autoscaler is essentially very simple. It doesn't care why pods can't be scheduled. It will add nodes to the cluster as long as pods can't be scheduled. It will remove empty nodes or nodes that their pods can be rescheduled on other nodes. That being said, it is not a completely mindless mechanism.

It is aware of several Kubernetes concepts and takes them into account when deciding to grow or shrink the cluster:

- PodDisruptionBudgets
- Overall resource constraints
- Affinity and anti-affinity
- Pod priorities and preemption

For example, if pods with best effort priority can't be scheduled, the cluster autoscaler will not grow the cluster. In particular, it will not remove nodes that have one or more of these properties:

- Use local storage
- Annotated with `"cluster-autoscaler.kubernetes.io/scale-down-disabled": "true"`
- Host pods annotated `"cluster-autoscaler.kubernetes.io/safe-to-evict": "false"`
- Host nodes with restrictive `PodDisruptionBudget`

The total time for adding a node is typically less than 5 minutes. The cluster autoscaler scans for unscheduled pods every ten seconds and immediately provisions a new node if necessary. However, the cloud provider takes 3-4 minutes to provide and attach the node to the cluster.

Let's move on to another form of autoscaling: vertical pod autoscaling.

Vertical pod autoscaling

The vertical pod autoscaler is currently (Kubernetes 1.15) in its Beta stages. It takes on a different task related to autoscaling – fine-tuning your CPU and memory requests. Consider a pod that doesn't really do much and needs 100 MiB of memory, but it currently requests 500 MiB. First of all, it's a net waste of 400 MiB of memory that is always allocated to the pod and is never used. However, the impact can be much greater. Because the pod is chunkier, it can prevent other pods from getting scheduled alongside it.

The vertical autoscaler addresses this problem by monitoring the actual CPU and memory usage of pods and adjusting their requests automatically. It also requires that you install the metrics server.

This is very cool. The vertical pod autoscaler works in several modes:

- **Initial**: Assigns resource requests when the pod is created
- **Auto**: Assigns resource requests when the pod is created and also updates them during the pod's lifetime
- **Recreate**: Similar to Auto, the pod always restarts when its resource requests need to be updated
- **updatedOff**: Doesn't modify the resource requests, but recommendations can be viewed

At the moment, Auto works just like Recreate and restarts the pods on every change. In the future, it will use an in-place update. Let's take the vertical autoscaler for a spin. The installation is pretty rough and requires cloning the Git repository and running a shell script (that runs many other shell scripts):

```
$ git clone https://github.com/kubernetes/autoscaler.git
$ cd autoscaler/vertical-pod-autoscaler/hack/
$ ./vpa-up.sh
```

It installs a service, two CRDs, and three pods:

```
$ kubectl -n kube-system get svc | grep vpa
vpa-webhook    ClusterIP    10.103.169.18    <none>        443/TCP

$ kubectl -n kube-system get po | grep vpa
vpa-admission-controller-68c748777d-92hbg 1/1  Running  0   72s
vpa-recommender-6fc8c67d85-shh8g               1/1  Running  0   77s
vpa-updater-786b96955c-8mcrc                   1/1  Running  0   78s

$ kubectl get crd | grep vertical
verticalpodautoscalercheckpoints.autoscaling.k8s.io  2019-05-08T04:58:24Z
verticalpodautoscalers.autoscaling.k8s.io            2019-05-08T04:58:24Z
```

Let's create a VPA configuration file for the link manager deployment. We'll set the mode to Off so that it only recommends on proper values of CPU and memory requests, but doesn't actually set them:

```
apiVersion: autoscaling.k8s.io/v1beta2
kind: VerticalPodAutoscaler
metadata:
  name: link-manager
spec:
  targetRef:
    apiVersion: "extensions/v1beta1"
    kind:       Deployment
    name:       link-manager
```

```
      updatePolicy:
        updateMode: "Off"
```

We can create it and examine the recommendations:

```
$ kubectl create -f link-manager-vpa.yaml
  verticalpodautoscaler.autoscaling.k8s.io/link-manager created

$ kubectl get vpa link-manager -o
jsonpath="{.status.recommendation.containerRecommendations[0].lowerBound}"
  map[cpu:25m memory:262144k]

$ kubectl get vpa link-manager -o
jsonpath="{.status.recommendation.containerRecommendations[0].target}"
  map[cpu:25m memory:262144k]
```

I don't recommend letting the vertical pod autoscaler loose on your system at this point. It is still in flux and has some serious limitations. The biggest one is that it can't run side by side with the horizontal pod autoscaler.

An interesting approach, if you want to utilize it to fine-tune your resource requests, is to run it for a while on a test cluster that mimics your production cluster, turn off the horizontal pod autoscaler, and see how well it does.

Provisioning resources with Kubernetes

Provisioning resources has traditionally been an operator or system administrator job. However, with the DevOps approach, developers are often tasked with self-provisioning. If the organization has a traditional IT department, they are often more concerned with what permissions developers should have for provisioning and what global limits should they set. In this section, we will look at the problem of resource provisioning from both viewpoints.

What resources should you provision?

It's important to distinguish between Kubernetes resources and the underlying infrastructure resources they depend on. For Kubernetes resources, the Kubernetes API is the way to go. How you interact with the API is up to you, but I recommend that you generate YAML files and run them through `kubectl create` or `kubectl apply` as part of your CI/CD pipeline.

Commands like `kubectl run` and `kubectl scale` are useful for interactive exploration of your cluster and running ad hoc tasks, but they go against the grain of declarative infrastructure as code.

You could also directly hit the REST endpoints of the Kubernetes API or use a client library if you have a very complex CI/CD workflow that you implement using some higher-level programming language like Python. Even there, you can consider just invoking `kubectl`.

Let's move on to the infrastructure layer that your cluster is running on. The primary resources are compute, memory, and storage. Nodes combine compute, memory, and local storage. Shared storage is provisioned separately. In the cloud, you may use pre-provisioned cloud storage. This means that your primary concern is to provision nodes and external storage for your cluster. But that's not all. You also need to connect all these nodes via a networking layer and consider permissions. The networking in a Kubernetes cluster is taken care of most of the time by a CNI provider. The famous flat networking model where each pod gets its own IP is one of the best features of Kubernetes and simplifies so many things for developers.

Permissions and access are usually handled by **role-based access control** (**RBAC**) on Kubernetes, as we discussed at length in `Chapter 6`, *Securing Microservices with Kubernetes*.

It's very important to impose reasonable quotas and limits on resources given that we strive for automatic provisioning.

Defining container limits

On Kubernetes, we can define limits on CPU and memory per container. These ensure that the container will not use more than the limit. It serves two primary purposes:

- Prevents containers and pods on the same node from cannibalizing each other
- Helps Kubernetes schedule pods in the most efficient way by knowing the maximum amount of resources a pod will use

We've looked at limits from a security lens in `Chapter 6`, *Securing Microservices on Kubernetes*. The emphasis was on controlling the blast radius. If a container is compromised, it can utilize more than the limit of resources configured for it.

Here is an example of setting CPU and memory limits for the `user-manager` service. It follows the best practice of setting both resource limits and resource requests to the same values:

```
apiVersion: apps/v1
kind: Deployment
metadata:
  name: user-manager
  labels:
    svc: user
    app: manager
spec:
  replicas: 1
  selector:
    matchLabels:
      svc: user
      app: manager
  template:
    metadata:
      labels:
        svc: user
        app: manager
    spec:
      containers:
      - name: user-manager
        image: g1g1/delinkcious-user:0.3
        imagePullPolicy: Always
        ports:
        - containerPort: 7070
        resources:
          requests:
            memory: 64Mi
            cpu: 250m
          limits:
            memory: 64Mi
            cpu: 250m
```

Setting container limits is very useful, but it doesn't help with the problem of runaway allocation of many pods or other resources. This is where resource quotas come in.

Specifying resource quotas

Kubernetes lets you specify quotas per namespace. There are different types of quotas you can set, for example, CPU, memory, and counts of various objects, including persistent volume claims. Let's set some quotas for the default namespace of Delinkcious:

```
apiVersion: v1
kind: List
items:
- apiVersion: v1
  kind: ResourceQuota
  metadata:
    name: awesome-quota
  spec:
    hard:
      cpu: "1000"
      memory: 200Gi
      pods: "100"
```

Here is the command to apply to `quota`:

```
$ kubectl create -f resource-quota.yaml
resourcequota/awesome-quota created
```

Now, we can check the resource quota objects for the actual usage and compare it to the quota to see how close we are:

```
$ kubectl get resourcequota awesome-quota -o yaml | grep status -A 8
status:
  hard:
    cpu: 1k
    memory: 200Gi
    pods: "100"
  used:
    cpu: 350m
    memory: 64Mi
    pods: "10"
```

Obviously, this resource quota is far beyond the current utilization of the cluster. That's fine. It doesn't allocate or reserve any resources. It just means that the quota is not very restricting.

There are many more nuances and options for resource quotas. There are scopes that apply the resource quota for resources with certain conditions or states (`Terminating`, `NotTerminating`, `BestEffort`, and `NotBestEffort`). There are resources that are quota-specific to certain priority classes. The gist is that you can get pretty granular and provide resource quota policies to control the resource allocation in your cluster, even in the face of mistakes in configuration or attacks.

At this point, we have got our bases covered with resource quotas and can move on to actually provisioning resources. There are several ways to do this, and we may want to employ some, if not all of them, for complicated systems.

Manual provisioning

Manual provisioning sounds like an anti-pattern, but in practice it is useful in several situations; for example, if you are managing on-premises cluster where you physically have to provision servers, wire them together, and install storage too. Another common use case is during development when you want to develop your automated provisioning, but you have an interactive experiment (probably not in production). However, even in production, if you discover some misconfiguration or another issue, you may need to respond by manually provisioning some resources to address the crisis.

Utilizing autoscaling

On the cloud, it is highly recommended to use the autoscaling solutions we discussed earlier. The horizontal pod autoscaler is a no-brainer. The cluster autoscaler is great too, if your cluster deals with a very dynamic workload and you don't want to overprovision on a regular basis. The vertical autoscaler is probably best for fine-tuning your resource requests at this point.

Rolling your own automated provisioning

If you have more sophisticated needs, you can always roll your own. Kubernetes encourages both running your own controllers that can watch for different events and respond by provisioning some resources or even running some tools locally, or as part of your CI/CD pipeline, that check the state of the cluster and make some provisioning decisions.

Once your cluster is properly provisioned, you should start thinking about performance. Performance is interesting because there are so many trade-offs you need to take into account.

Getting performance right

Performance is important for many reasons, which we will delve into soon. It is very important to understand when is the right time to try and improve performance. My guiding principle is: make it work, make it right, make it fast. That is, first, just get the system to do whatever it needs to do, however slow and clunky. Then, clean up the architecture and the code. Now, you are ready to take on performance and consider refactoring, changes, and many other factors that can impact performance.

But there is a preliminary step for performance improvements, and that's profiling and benchmarking. Trying to improve performance without measuring what you try to improve is just like trying to make your code work correctly without writing any tests. Not only is it futile, but, even if you actually got lucky and improved the performance, how would you know without measurements?

Let's understand something about performance. It makes everything complicated. However, it is often a necessary evil. Improving performance is important when it affects the user experience or cost. To make things worse, improving the user experience often comes at a cost. Finding the sweet spot is difficult. Unfortunately, the sweet spot doesn't stay put. Your system evolves, the number of users grow, technologies change, and the costs of your resources change. For example, a small social media startup has no business building its own data centers, but a social media giant like Facebook now designs their own custom servers to squeeze a little bit more performance and save costs. Scale changes a lot.

The bottom line is, that in order to make those decisions, you must understand how your system works and be able to measure every component and the impact on the performance of changes that have been made to your system.

Performance and user experience

The user experience is all about perceived performance. How fast do I see pretty pictures on my screen after I click a button? Obviously, you can improve the real performance of your system, buy faster hardware, run things in parallel, improve your algorithms, upgrade your dependencies to newer and more performant versions, and so on. But, very often, it is more about smarter architecture and doing less work by adding caches, providing approximate results, and pushing work to the client. Then, there are methods like pre-fetching, where you try to do work before it is needed in order to anticipate the user's needs.

User experience decisions can significantly impact performance. Consider a chat program where the clients constantly poll the server every second for every keystroke versus just checking once every minute for new messages. That's a different user experience with a 60x performance price tag.

Performance and high availability

One of the worst routine things that can happen on a system is a timeout. A timeout means that the user will not get an answer on time. A timeout means that you did a lot of work that is now wasted. You may have retry logic and the user will eventually get their answer, but performance will take a hit. When your system and all its components are highly available (as well as not overloaded), you can minimize the occurrence of timeouts. If your system is very redundant, you can even send the same request multiple times to different backends and, whenever one of them responds, you have the answer.

On the other hand, a highly available and redundant system sometimes requires syncing with all the shards/backends (or at least a quorum) to make sure you have the latest, most up-to-date answer. Of course, inserting or updating data is also more complicated and often takes longer on a highly available system. If the redundancy is across multiple availability zones, regions, or continents, it can add orders of magnitude to the response time.

Performance and cost

Performance and cost have a very interesting relationship. There are many ways to improve performance. Some of them reduce costs, like optimizing your code, compressing the data you send, or pushing computation to the client. However, other ways to improve performance increase the cost, like running on stronger hardware, replicating your data to multiple locations close to your client, and pre-fetching unrequested data.

In the end, this is a business decision. Even win-win performance improvements are not always like improving your algorithms is, at the high-priority. For example, you can invest a lot of time in coming up with an algorithm that runs 10x faster than the previous algorithm. But the computation time might be negligible in the overall time to process a request because it's dominated by access to the database, serializing the data, and sending it to the client. In this case, you just wasted time that could have been used for developing something more useful, you potentially destabilized your code and introduced bugs, and made your code harder to understand. Again, good metrics and profiling will help you identify the hot spots in your system that are worth improvement performance-wise and cost-wise.

Performance and security

Performance and security are generally at odds. Security typically pushes toward encryption across the board, outside and inside the cluster. There are strong authentication and authorization methods, may be necessary, but has performance overhead. However, security sometimes indirectly helps performance by advocating to cut unnecessary features and reduce the surface area of the system. This spartan approach that produces tighter systems allows you to focus on a smaller target to improve performance. Typically, secure systems don't just add arbitrary features that can hurt performance without careful consideration.

Later, we will explore how to collect and use metrics with Kubernetes, but first let's take a look at logging, which is another pillar of monitoring your system.

Logging

Logging is the ability to record messages during the operation of your system. Log messages are typically structured and timestamped. They are often indispensable when trying to diagnose problems and troubleshoot your system. They are also critical when doing post-mortems and discovering root causes after the fact. In a large-scale distributed system, there will be many components that log messages. Collecting, organizing, and sifting through them is a non-trivial task. But first, let's consider what information is useful to log.

What should you log?

This is the million dollar question. A simplistic approach is to log *everything*. You can never have too much data, and it's difficult to predict what data you'll need when trying to figure out what's wrong with your system. However, what does everything mean exactly? You can obviously go too far. For example, you can log every call to every little function in your code, including all the parameters, as well as the current state, or log the payload of every network call. Sometimes, there are security and regulatory restrictions that prevent you from logging certain data, like **protected health information** (**PHI**) and **personally identifiable information** (**PII**). You'll need to understand your system well enough to decide what kind of information is relevant for you. A good starting point is logging any incoming requests and interactions between your microservices and between your microservices and third-party services.

Logging versus error reporting

Errors are a special kind of information. There are errors that your code can handle (for example, with retries or using some alternative). However, there are also errors that must be handled as soon as possible or the system will suffer partial or complete outage. But even errors that are not urgent sometimes require that you record a lot of information. You could log errors just like any other information, but it is often worthwhile to record errors to a dedicated error reporting service like Rollbar or Sentry. One of the crucial pieces of information with errors is a stack trace that includes the state (local variables) of each frame in the stack. For a production system, I recommend that you use a dedicated error reporting service, in addition to just logging.

The quest for the perfect Go logging interface

Delinkcious is primarily implemented with Go, so let's talk about logging in Go. There is a standard library Logger, which is a struct and not an interface. It is configurable, and you can pass an `io.Writer` object when you create it. However, the methods of the `Logger` struct are rigid and don't support log levels or structured logging. Also, the fact that there is just one output writer may be a limitation in some cases. Here is the specification for the standard Logger:

```
type Logger struct { ... } // Not an interface!

func New(out io.Writer, prefix string, flag int) *Logger

// flag controls date, time, µs, UTC, caller
```

```
// Log
func (l *Logger) Print(v ...interface{})
func (l *Logger) Printf(format string, v ...interface{})
func (l *Logger) Println(v ...interface{})

// Log and call os.Exit(1)
func (l *Logger) Fatal(v ...interface{})
func (l *Logger) Fatalf(format string, v ...interface{})
func (l *Logger) Fatalln(v ...interface{})

// Log and panic
func (l *Logger) Panic(v ...interface{})
func (l *Logger) Panicf(format string, v ...interface{})
func (l *Logger) Panicln(v ...interface{})

func (l *Logger) Output(calldepth int, s string) error
```

If you need those capabilities, you need to use another library that sits on top of the standard library `Logger`. There are several packages that provide various flavors:

- `glog`: https://godoc.org/github.com/golang/glog
- `logrus`: https://github.com/Sirupsen/logrus
- `loggo`: https://godoc.org/github.com/juju/loggo
- `log15`: https://github.com/inconshreveable/log15

They address the interface, comparability, and playability in different ways. However, we're using Go-kit, which has its own take on logging.

Logging with Go-kit

Go-kit has the simplest interface ever. There is just one method, `Log()`, that accepts a list of keys and values that can be of any type:

```
type Logger interface {
  Log(keyvals ...interface{}) error
}
```

The basic idea here is that Go-kit has no opinions about how you log your messages. Do you always add a timestamp? Do you have logging levels? What levels? The answers to all these questions are up to you. You get a totally generic interface and you decide what key-values you want to log.

Setting up a logger with Go-kit

OK. The interface is generic, but we need an actual logger object to work with. Go-kit supports several writers and logger objects that generate familiar log formats like JSON, logfmt, or logrus out of the box. Let's set up a logger with JSON formatter and a sync writer. A sync writer is safe to use from multiple Go routines, and a JSON formatter formats the key values into a JSON string. In addition, we can add some default fields, such as the service name, which is where the log message is coming from in the source code and the current timestamp. Since we may want to use the same logger specification from multiple services, let's put it in a package all the services can use. One last thing is to add also a `Fatal()` function that will forward to the standard `log.Fatal()` function. This allows code that currently uses `Fatal()` to continue working without changes. Here is the Delinkcious log package that contains a factory function for the logger and the `Fatal()` function:

```
package log

import (
  kit_log "github.com/go-kit/kit/log"
  std_log "log"
  "os"
)

func NewLogger(service string) (logger kit_log.Logger) {
  w := kit_log.NewSyncWriter(os.Stderr)
  logger = kit_log.NewJSONLogger(w)
  logger = kit_log.With(logger, "service", service)
  logger = kit_log.With(logger, "timestamp", kit_log.DefaultTimestampUTC)
  logger = kit_log.With(logger, "called from", kit_log.DefaultCaller)

  return
}

func Fatal(v ... interface{}) {
  std_log.Fatal(v...)
}
```

The writer just writes to the standard error stream, which will be captured and sent to the container logs on Kubernetes.

To see our logger in action, let's attach it to our link service.

Using a logging middleware

Let's think about where we want to instantiate our logger and then where we want to use it and log messages. This is important because we need to make sure that the logger is available to all the places in the code that need to log messages. A trivial approach is to just add a logger parameter to all our interfaces and propagate the logger in this way. However, this is very disruptive and will violate our clean object model. Logging is really an implementation and operational detail. Ideally, it should not appear in our object model types or interfaces. Also, it is a Go-kit type and, so far, we've managed to keep our object model and even our domain packages totally oblivious to the fact that they are wrapped by Go-kit. The Delinkcious services under SVC are the only part of the code that is Go-kit aware.

Let's try to keep it this way. Go-kit provides the middleware concept, which allows us to chain multiple middleware components in a loosely coupled way. All the middleware components for a service implement the service interface, and a little shim allows Go-kit to call them one after the other. Let's begin with the shim, which is just a function type that accepts a `LinkManager` interface and returns a `LinkManager` interface:

```
type linkManagerMiddleware func(om.LinkManager) om.LinkManager
```

The `logging_middleware.go` file has a factory function called `newLoggingMiddlware()` that takes a logger object and returns a function that matches `linkManagerMiddleware`. That function, in turn, instantiates the `loggingMiddleware` struct, passing it the next component in the chain and the logger:

```
// implement function to return ServiceMiddleware
func newLoggingMiddleware(logger log.Logger) linkManagerMiddleware {
  return func(next om.LinkManager) om.LinkManager {
    return loggingMiddleware{next, logger}
  }
}
```

This may be very confusing, but the basic idea is having the ability to chain arbitrary middleware components that do some work and let the rest of the computation go on. The reason that we have all these layers of indirection is that Go-kit doesn't know anything about our types and interfaces, so we have to assist by writing this boilerplate code. As I mentioned earlier, all of it can, and should be, auto-generated. Let's examine the loggingMiddleware struct and its methods. The struct itself has a linkManager interface, which is the next component in the chain and the logger object:

```
type loggingMiddleware struct {
  next om.LinkManager
  logger log.Logger
}
```

As a LinkManager middleware component, it must implement the LinkManager interface methods. Here is the implementation of GetLinks(). It uses the logger to log a few values, specifically, the method name, that is, GetLinks, the request object, the result, and the duration. Then, it calls the GetLinks() method on the next component in the chain:

```
func (m loggingMiddleware) GetLinks(request om.GetLinksRequest) (result
om.GetLinksResult, err error) {
  defer func(begin time.Time) {
    m.logger.Log(
      "method", "GetLinks",
      "request", request,
      "result", result,
      "duration", time.Since(begin),
    )
  }(time.Now())
  result, err = m.next.GetLinks(request)
  return
}
```

For simplicity, the other methods just call the next component in the chain doing anything:

```
func (m loggingMiddleware) AddLink(request om.AddLinkRequest) error {
  return m.next.AddLink(request)
}

func (m loggingMiddleware) UpdateLink(request om.UpdateLinkRequest) error {
  return m.next.UpdateLink(request)
}

func (m loggingMiddleware) DeleteLink(username string, url string) error {
  return m.next.DeleteLink(username, url)
}
```

The middleware chain concept is very powerful. The middleware can preprocess inputs before passing them on to the next component, it can short circuit and return immediately without calling the next component, or it can postprocess the result coming from the next component.

Let's see the log output from the link service when running our smoke test. It looks a bit messy for humans, but all the necessary information is there, clearly marked and ready for large-scale analysis if needed. It's easy to grep and it's easy to use tools like `jq` to dig deeper:

```
$ kubectl logs svc/link-manager
{"called from":"link_service.go:133","msg":"*** listening on
***","port":"8080","service":"link
manager","timestamp":"2019-05-13T02:44:42.588578835Z"}
{"called
from":"logging_middleware.go:25","duration":"1.526953ms","method":"GetLinks
","request":{"UrlRegex":"","TitleRegex":"","DescriptionRegex":"","Username"
:"Gigi
Sayfan","Tag":"","StartToken":""},"result":{"Links":[],"NextPageToken":""},
"service":"link manager","timestamp":"2019-05-13T02:45:05.302342532Z"}
{"called
from":"logging_middleware.go:25","duration":"591.148µs","method":"GetLinks"
,"request":{"UrlRegex":"","TitleRegex":"","DescriptionRegex":"","Username":
"Gigi
Sayfan","Tag":"","StartToken":""},"result":{"Links":[{"Url":"https://github
.com/the-gigi","Title":"Gigi on
Github","Description":"","Status":"pending","Tags":null,"CreatedAt":"2019-0
5-13T02:45:05.845411Z","UpdatedAt":"2019-05-13T02:45:05.845411Z"}],"NextPag
eToken":""},"service":"link
manager","timestamp":"2019-05-13T02:45:06.134842509Z"}
{"called
from":"logging_middleware.go:25","duration":"911.499µs","method":"GetLinks"
,"request":{"UrlRegex":"","TitleRegex":"","DescriptionRegex":"","Username":
"Gigi
Sayfan","Tag":"","StartToken":""},"result":{"Links":[{"Url":"https://github
.com/the-gigi","Title":"Gigi on
Github","Description":"","Status":"pending","Tags":null,"CreatedAt":"2019-0
5-13T02:45:05.845411Z","UpdatedAt":"2019-05-13T02:45:05.845411Z"}],"NextPag
eToken":""},"service":"link
manager","timestamp":"2019-05-13T02:45:09.438915897Z"}
```

Thanks to Go-kit, we have a strong and flexible logging mechanism in place. However, manually fetching logs with `kubectl logs` doesn't scale. For real-world systems, we need centralized log management.

Centralized logging with Kubernetes

In Kubernetes, containers write to the standard output and standard error streams. Kubernetes makes those logs available (for example, via `kubectl logs`). You can even get logs of the previous run of a container if it crashed by using `kubectl logs -p`, but, if the pod is rescheduled, then its containers and their logs disappear. If the node itself crashes, you'll lose the logs too. Even when all the logs are available for a cluster with a lot of services, it is a non-trivial task to sift through the container logs and try to make sense of the state of the system. Enter centralized logging. The idea is to have a log agent running, either as a side container in each pod, or as daemon set on each node, listen to all the logs, and ship them in real time to a centralized location where they can be aggregated, filtered, and sorted. Of course, you can explicitly log from your containers directly to the centralized logging service too.

The simplest and most robust approach in my opinion is the demon set. The cluster admin makes sure that a log agent is installed on each node and that's it. There's no need to change your pod spec to inject side containers, no need to depend on special libraries to communicate with remote logging services. Your code writes to standard output and standard error, and you're done. Most other services you may use, like web servers and databases, can be configured to write to the standard output and standard error, too.

One of the most popular log agents on Kubernetes is Fluentd (`https://www.fluentd.org`). It is also a CNCF graduated project. You should use Fluentd unless you have a very good reason to use another logging agent. Here is a diagram that illustrates how Fluentd fits into Kubernetes as a DaemonSet that is deployed into each node, pulls all the logs of all the pods, and sends them to a centralized log management system:

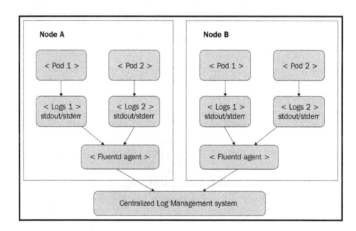

Fluentd

Let's talk about the log management system. In the open source world, the ELK stack – ElasticSearch, LogStash, and Kibana – are a very popular combination. ElasticSearch stores the logs and provides various ways to slice and dice them. LogStash is the log ingest pipeline and Kibana is a powerful visualization solution. Fluentd can replace LogStash as the logging agent, and you get the EFK stack – ElasticSearch. Fluentd and Kibana work very well on Kubernetes. There's also Helm charts and the GitHub repository, which can install EFK on your Kubernetes cluster in one click. However, you should also consider out of cluster logging service. As we discussed previously, logs are very helpful for troubleshooting and post mortems. If your cluster is in trouble, you might not be able to access your logs at the time you need them the most. Fluentd can integrate with a plethora of data outputs. Check the full list here: `https://www.fluentd.org/dataoutputs`. We've got logging covered, so now it's time to talk about metrics.

Collecting metrics on Kubernetes

Metrics are a key component that enables many interesting use cases like self-healing, autoscaling, and alerting. Kubernetes, as a distributed platform, has a very strong offering around metrics, with a powerful yet generic and flexible metrics API.

Kubernetes always had support for metrics via cAdvisor (integrated into kube-proxy) and Heapster (`https://github.com/kubernetes-retired/heapster`). However, cAdvisor was removed in Kubernetes 1.12 and Heapster was removed in Kubernetes 1.13. You can still install them (like we did earlier on minikube using the Heapster add-on), but they aren't part of Kubernetes and aren't recommended anymore. The new way to do metrics on Kubernetes is by using the metrics API and the metrics server (`https://github.com/kubernetes-incubator/metrics-server`).

Introducing the Kubernetes metrics API

The Kubernetes metrics API is very generic. It supports node and pod metrics, as well as custom metrics. A metric has a usage field, a timestamp, and a window (the time range the metric was collected in). Here is the API definition for node metrics:

```
// resource usage metrics of a node.
type NodeMetrics struct {
  metav1.TypeMeta
  metav1.ObjectMeta

  // The following fields define time interval from which metrics were
  // collected from the interval [Timestamp-Window, Timestamp].
```

```
    Timestamp metav1.Time
    Window metav1.Duration

    // The memory usage is the memory working set.
    Usage corev1.ResourceList
}

// NodeMetricsList is a list of NodeMetrics.
type NodeMetricsList struct {
  metav1.TypeMeta
  // Standard list metadata.
  // More info:
https://git.k8s.io/community/contributors/devel/api-conventions.md#types-ki
nds
  metav1.ListMeta

  // List of node metrics.
  Items []NodeMetrics
}
```

The usage field type is `ResourceList`, but it's actually a map of a resource name to a
quantity:

```
// ResourceList is a set of (resource name, quantity) pairs.
type ResourceList map[ResourceName]resource.Quantity
```

There are two other metrics-related APIs: the external metrics API and the custom metrics
API. They are designed for extending the Kubernetes metrics with arbitrary custom metrics
or metrics coming from outside Kubernetes, such as cloud providers monitoring. You can
annotate those additional metrics and use them for autoscaling.

Understanding the Kubernetes metrics server

The Kubernetes metric server is a modern replacement for Heapster and cAdvisor. It
implements the metrics API and provides the nodes and pods metrics. Those metrics are
used by the various autoscalers and by the Kubernetes scheduler itself when dealing with
best effort scenarios. Depending on your Kubernetes distribution, the metrics server may or
may not be installed. If you need to install it, you can use helm. For example, on AWS EKS,
you have to install the metrics server yourself using the following command (you can
choose any namespace):

```
helm install stable/metrics-server \
  --name metrics-server \
  --version 2.0.4 \
  --namespace kube-system
```

Typically, you don't interact with the metrics server directly. You can access the metrics using the `kubectl get --raw` command:

```
$ kubectl get --raw "/apis/metrics.k8s.io/v1beta1/nodes" | jq .
{
  "kind": "NodeMetricsList",
  "apiVersion": "metrics.k8s.io/v1beta1",
  "metadata": {
    "selfLink": "/apis/metrics.k8s.io/v1beta1/nodes"
  },
  "items": [
    {
      "metadata": {
        "name": "ip-192-168-13-100.ec2.internal",
        "selfLink":
"/apis/metrics.k8s.io/v1beta1/nodes/ip-192-168-13-100.ec2.internal",
        "creationTimestamp": "2019-05-17T20:05:29Z"
      },
      "timestamp": "2019-05-17T20:04:54Z",
      "window": "30s",
      "usage": {
        "cpu": "85887417n",
        "memory": "885828Ki"
      }
    }
  ]
}
```

In addition, you can use the very useful `kubectl` command, that is, `kubectl top`, which gives you a quick overview of the performance of your nodes or pods:

```
$ kubectl top nodes
NAME                              CPU(cores)  CPU%  MEMORY(bytes)  MEMORY%
ip-192-168-13-100.ec2.internal    85m         4%    863Mi          11%

$ kubectl top pods
NAME                                   CPU(cores)  MEMORY(bytes)
api-gateway-795f7dcbdb-ml2tm           1m          23Mi
link-db-7445d6cbf7-2zs2m               1m          32Mi
link-manager-54968ff8cf-q94pj          0m          4Mi
nats-cluster-1                         1m          3Mi
nats-operator-55dfdc6868-fj5j2         2m          11Mi
news-manager-7f447f5c9f-c4pc4          0m          1Mi
news-manager-redis-0                   1m          1Mi
social-graph-db-7565b59467-dmdlw       1m          31Mi
social-graph-manager-64cdf589c7-4bjcn  0m          1Mi
user-db-0                              1m          32Mi
user-manager-699458447-6lwjq           1m          1Mi
```

Note that as of Kubernetes 1.15 (current version at the time of writing) the Kubernetes dashboard doesn't integrate with the metrics server for performance yet. It still requires Heapster. I'm sure you will be able to work with the metrics-server soon.

The metrics-server is the standard Kubernetes metrics solution for CPU and memory, but, if you want to go further and consider custom metrics, there is one obvious choice: Prometheus. Unlike most things Kubernetes, where you have a plethora of options in the metrics arena, Prometheus stands head and shoulders above all the other free and open source options.

Using Prometheus

Prometheus (`https://prometheus.io/`) is an open source and CNCF graduated project (the second after Kubernetes itself). It is the de facto standard metrics collection solution for Kubernetes. It has an impressive set of features, a large installation base on Kubernetes, and an active community. Some of the prominent features are as follows:

- A generic multi-dimensional data model where each metric is modeled as a time series of key-value pairs
- A powerful query language, called PromQL, that lets you generate reports, graphs, and tables
- A built-in alerting engine where alerts are defined and triggered by PromQL queries
- Powerful visualization – Grafana, console template language, and more
- Many integrations with other infrastructure components beyond Kubernetes

Let's look at the following references:

- **Monitoring your Kubernetes Deployments with Prometheus**: `https://supergiant.io/blog/monitoring-your-kubernetes-depl oyments-with-prometheus/`
- **Configure Kubernetes Autoscaling With Custom Metrics**: `https://docs. bitnami.com/kubernetes/how-to/configure-autoscaling-custom-metrics/`

Deploying Prometheus into the cluster

Prometheus is a large project with many capabilities, options, and integrations. Deploying it and managing it is not a trivial task. There a couple of projects that can help. The Prometheus operator (`https://github.com/coreos/prometheus-operator`) provides a way to deeply configure Prometheus using Kubernetes resources.

The operator concept (`https://coreos.com/blog/introducing-operators.html`) was introduced in 2016 by CoreOS (who was acquired by RedHat, who was acquired by IBM). A Kubernetes operator is a controller that is responsible for managing stateful applications inside a cluster using Kubernetes CRDs. Operators, in practice, extend the Kubernetes API to provide a seamless experience when managing foreign components like Prometheus. Actually, the Prometheus operator was the first operator (along with the Etcd operator):

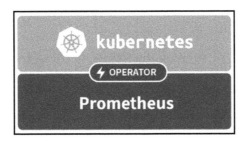

Prometheus operator

The kube-promethus (`https://github.com/coreos/kube-prometheus`) project is built on top of the Prometheus operator and adds the following:

- Grafana visualization
- A highly available Prometheus cluster
- A highly available `Alertmanager` cluster
- An adapter for the Kubernetes Metrics APIs
- Kernel and OS metrics via the Prometheus node exporter
- Various metrics on the state of Kubernetes objects via `kube-state-metrics`

The Prometheus operator brings the ability to launch a Prometheus instance into a Kubernetes namespace, configure it, and target services via labels to the table.

For now, we'll just use helm to deploy a full-fledged installation of Prometheus:

```
$ helm install --name prometheus stable/prometheus
 This will create service accounts, RBAC roles, RBAC bindings, deployments,
services and even a daemon set. In addition it will print the following
information to connect to different components:
```

The Prometheus server can be accessed via port `80` on the following DNS name from within your cluster: `prometheus-server.default.svc.cluster.local`.

Get the Prometheus server URL by running the following commands in the same shell:

```
   export POD_NAME=$(kubectl get pods --namespace default -l
 "app=prometheus,component=server" -o jsonpath="{.items[0].metadata.name}")
   kubectl --namespace default port-forward $POD_NAME 9090
```

The Prometheus `alertmanager` can be accessed via port `80` on the following DNS name from within your cluster:

```
   prometheus-alertmanager.default.svc.cluster.local
```

Get the `Alertmanager` URL by running the following commands in the same shell:

```
   export POD_NAME=$(kubectl get pods --namespace default -l
   "app=prometheus,component=alertmanager" -o
   jsonpath="{.items[0].metadata.name}")
     kubectl --namespace default port-forward $POD_NAME 9093
```

The Prometheus `pushgateway` can be accessed via port 9091 on the following DNS name from within your cluster:

```
   prometheus-pushgateway.default.svc.cluster.local
```

Get the `PushGateway` URL by running the following commands in the same shell:

```
   export POD_NAME=$(kubectl get pods --namespace default -l
 "app=prometheus,component=pushgateway" -o
 jsonpath="{.items[0].metadata.name}")
   kubectl --namespace default port-forward $POD_NAME 9091
```

Let's see what services were installed:

```
$ kubectl get svc -o name | grep prom
service/prometheus-alertmanager
service/prometheus-kube-state-metrics
service/prometheus-node-exporter
service/prometheus-pushgateway
service/prometheus-server
```

Everything seems in order. Let's follow the instructions and check out the Prometheus web UI:

```
$ export POD_NAME=$(kubectl get pods --namespace default -l
 "app=prometheus,component=server" -o jsonpath="{.items[0].metadata.name}")

$ kubectl port-forward $POD_NAME 9090
Forwarding from 127.0.0.1:9090 -> 9090
Forwarding from [::1]:9090 -> 9090
```

We can now browse to `localhost:9090` and do some checks. Let's check the number of goroutines in the cluster:

Prometheus web UI

The number of metrics that have been collected by Prometheus is mind-numbing. There are hundreds of different built-in metrics. Check out how small the scroll thumb on the right is when opening the metric selection dropdown:

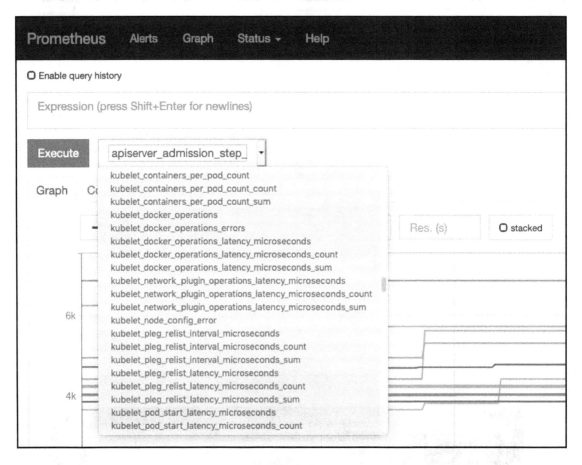

Prometheus dropdown

There are way more metrics than you will ever need, but each one of them can be important for some specific troubleshooting task.

Recording custom metrics from Delinkcious

OK: Prometheus is installed and collecting standard metrics automatically, but we want to record our own custom metrics too. Prometheus works in pull mode. A service that want to provide metrics needs to expose a /metrics endpoint (it is possible to push metrics to Prometheus too, using its Push Gateway). Let's utilize the middleware concept of Go-kit and add a metrics middleware that's similar to the logging middleware. We will take advantage of the Go client library provided by Prometheus.

The client library provides several primitives like counter, summary, histogram, and gauge. For the purpose of understanding how to record metrics from a Go service, we will instrument each endpoint of the link service to record the number of requests (a counter), as well as a summary of all requests (a summary). Let's start by providing factory functions in a separate library called pkg/metrics. The library provides a convenient wrapper around the Prometheus Go client. Go-kit has its own abstraction layer on top of the Prometheus Go client, but it doesn't provide a lot of value, unless you plan to switch to another metrics provider like statsd. This is unlikely for Delinkcious and probably for your system too. The service name, metric name, and help string will be used to construct the fully qualified metric name later:

```
package metrics

import (
  "github.com/prometheus/client_golang/prometheus"
  "github.com/prometheus/client_golang/prometheus/promauto"
)

func NewCounter(service string, name string, help string)
prometheus.Counter {
  opts := prometheus.CounterOpts{
    Namespace: "",
    Subsystem: service,
    Name: name,
    Help: help,
  }
  counter := promauto.NewCounter(opts)
  return counter
}

func NewSummary(service string, name string, help string)
prometheus.Summary {
  opts := prometheus.SummaryOpts{
    Namespace: "",
    Subsystem: service,
    Name: name,
    Help: help,
```

```
    }

    summary := promauto.NewSummary(opts)
    return summary
}
```

The next step is to construct the middleware. It should look very familiar, as it is almost identical to the logging middleware. The newMetricsMiddleware() function creates a counter and a summary metrics for each endpoint and returns it as the generic linkManagerMiddleware function we defined earlier (a function that accepts the next middleware and returns itself to assemble a chain of components that all implement the om.LinkManager interface):

```
package service

import (
    "github.com/prometheus/client_golang/prometheus"
    "github.com/the-gigi/delinkcious/pkg/metrics"
    om "github.com/the-gigi/delinkcious/pkg/object_model"
    "strings"
    "time"
)


// implement function to return ServiceMiddleware
func newMetricsMiddleware() linkManagerMiddleware {
    return func(next om.LinkManager) om.LinkManager {
        m := metricsMiddleware{next,
            map[string]prometheus.Counter{},
            map[string]prometheus.Summary{}}
        methodNames := []string{"GetLinks", "AddLink", "UpdateLink",
"DeleteLink"}
        for _, name := range methodNames {
            m.requestCounter[name] = metrics.NewCounter("link",
strings.ToLower(name)+"_count",
                                                        "count # of requests")
            m.requestLatency[name] = metrics.NewSummary("link",
strings.ToLower(name)+"_summary",
                                                        "request summary in
milliseconds")

        }
        return m
    }
```

The `metricsMiddleware` struct stores the next middleware and two maps. One map is a mapping of method names to Prometheus counters, while the other map is a mapping of method names to Prometheus summaries. They are used by the `LinkManager` interface methods to record metrics separately for each method:

```
type metricsMiddleware struct {
  next om.LinkManager
  requestCounter map[string]prometheus.Counter
  requestLatency map[string]prometheus.Summary
}
```

The middleware methods use the pattern of performing an action, which, in this case, is recording metrics and then calling the next component. Here is the `GetLinks()` method:

```
func (m metricsMiddleware) GetLinks(request om.GetLinksRequest) (result
om.GetLinksResult, err error) {
  defer func(begin time.Time) {
    m.recordMetrics("GetLinks", begin)
  }(time.Now())
  result, err = m.next.GetLinks(request)
  return
}
```

The actual metric recording is done by the `recordMetrics()` method, which takes the method name (`GetLinks` here) and beginning time. It is deferred until the end of the `GetLinks()` method, which allows it to calculate the duration of the `GetLinks()` method itself. It uses the counter and summary from the maps that match the method name:

```
func (m metricsMiddleware) recordMetrics(name string, begin time.Time) {
  m.requestCounter[name].Inc()
  durationMilliseconds := float64(time.Since(begin).Nanoseconds() *
1000000)
  m.requestLatency[name].Observe(durationMilliseconds)
}
```

At this point, we have our metrics middleware ready to go, but we still need to hook it up to the middleware chain and expose it as the `/metrics` endpoint. Since we've done all the preliminary work, these are just two lines in the link service's `Run()` method:

```
// Hook up the metrics middleware
svc = newMetricsMiddleware()(svc)

...

// Expose the metrics endpoint
r.Methods("GET").Path("/metrics").Handler(promhttp.Handler())
```

Now, we can query the /metrics endpoint and see our metrics being returned. Let's run the smoke test three times and check the metrics of the GetLinks() and AddLink() methods. As expected, the AddLink() method was called once per smoke test (three times total) and the GetLinks() method was called three times per test and nine times total. We can also see the help strings.

The summary quantiles are very useful when dealing with large datasets:

```
$ http http://localhost:8080/metrics | grep 'link_get\|add'

# HELP link_addlink_count count # of requests
# TYPE link_addlink_count counter
link_addlink_count 3
# HELP link_addlink_summary request summary in milliseconds
# TYPE link_addlink_summary summary
link_addlink_summary{quantile="0.5"} 2.514194e+12
link_addlink_summary{quantile="0.9"} 2.565382e+12
link_addlink_summary{quantile="0.99"} 2.565382e+12
link_addlink_summary_sum 7.438251e+12
link_addlink_summary_count 3
# HELP link_getlinks_count count # of requests
# TYPE link_getlinks_count counter
link_getlinks_count 9
# HELP link_getlinks_summary request summary in milliseconds
# TYPE link_getlinks_summary summary
link_getlinks_summary{quantile="0.5"} 5.91539e+11
link_getlinks_summary{quantile="0.9"} 8.50423e+11
link_getlinks_summary{quantile="0.99"} 8.50423e+11
link_getlinks_summary_sum 5.710272e+12
link_getlinks_summary_count 9
```

Custom metrics are great. However, beyond looking at a lot of numbers and graphs and histograms and admiring your handiwork, the real value of metrics is to inform an automated system or you about changes in the state of the system. That's where alerting comes in.

Alerting

Alerting is super important for critical systems. You can plan and build resiliency features as much as you want, but you will never build a failproof system. The right mindset for building robust and reliable systems is to try to minimize failures, but also acknowledge that failures will happen. When failures do happen, you need quick detection and have to alert the right people so that they can investigate and address the problem. Note that I said explicitly *alerting people*. If your system has self-healing capabilities, then you may be interested in viewing a report of the issues that the system was able to rectify itself. I don't consider those failures, because the system is designed to handle them. For example, containers can crash as much as they want; the kubelet will keep restarting them. A container crash is not considered a failure from a Kubernetes point of view. If your application running inside the container is not designed to handle such crashes and restarts, then you may want to configure an alert for this case, but that's your decision.

The main point I want to raise is that failure is a big word. Many things that could be considered failures are processes running out of memory, a server crashing, a corrupted disk, an intermittent or prolonged network outage, and a data center going offline. However, if you design for it and put mitigating measures in place, they are not failures of the system. The system will keep running as designed, possibly in a reduced capacity, but still running. If those incidents happen a lot and degrade to the total throughput of the system or the user experience in a significant way, you may want to investigate the root causes and address them. This is all part of defining **service-level objectives** (**SLOs**) and **service-level agreements** (**SLAs**). As long as you operate within your SLAs, the system is not failing, even if multiple components are failing and even if a service doesn't meet its SLO.

Embracing component failure

Embracing failure means recognizing that components will fail all the time in a large system. This is not an unusual situation. You want to minimize component failures because each failure has various costs, even if the system as a whole continues to work. But it will happen. Most component failures can be handled either automatically or without urgency by having redundancy in place. However, systems evolve all the time and most systems are not in the perfect position where every component failure has mitigation in place for each type of failure. As a result, theoretically preventable component failures might become system failures. For example, if you write your logs to a local disk and you don't rotate your log files, then, eventually, you'll run out of disk space (very common failure), and, if the server using this disk is running some critical component with no redundancy, then you've got a system failure on your hands.

Grudgingly accepting system failure

So, system failures will happen. Even the largest cloud providers have outages from time to time. There are different levels of system failures, ranging from temporary short failure of a non-critical subsystem, through to total outage of the entire system for a prolonged time, all the way to massive data loss. An extreme example is when malicious attackers target a company and all its backups, which can put it out of business. This is more related to security, but it's good to understand the full spectrum of system failures.

Common approaches for dealing with system failures are redundancy, backups, and compartmentalization. These are solid approaches, but are expensive, and, as we mentioned earlier, will not prevent all failures. The next step after minimizing the likelihood and impact of system failures is to plan for quick disaster recovery.

Taking human factors into account

Now, we're strictly in the domain of people responding to an actual incident. Some critical systems may have 24/7 live monitoring by people watching the system state diligently and ready to act. Most companies will have alerts based on various triggers. Note that, even if you have live 24/7 monitoring for complex systems, you still need to surface alerts to the people monitoring the system because, for such systems, there is typically a huge amount of data and information that describe the current state.

Let's look at several aspects of a reasonable alerting plan that work well for people.

Warnings versus alerts

Let's consider our out of disk space situation again. This is a case were the state gets worse over time. The disk space is gradually reduced as more and more data is logged to the log files. If you've got nothing in place, you will discover that you've ran out of disk space when an application starts to issue strange errors, often downstream from the actual failure, and you'll have to trace it back to the source. I've been there and done that; it's no fun. A better approach is to check the disk space regularly and raise an alert when it exceeds a certain threshold (for example, 95%). But why wait until the situation becomes critical? In such gradually worsening situations, it is much better to detect the problem early (for example, 75%) and issue a warning through some mechanism. This will give the system operator ample time to respond without causing an unnecessary crisis.

Considering severity levels

This brings us to alert severity levels. Different severity levels deserve different responses. Different organizations may define their own levels. For example, PagerDuty has a 1-5 scale that follows the DEFCON ladder. I personally prefer two levels for alerts: *wake me up at 3 AM* and *it can wait to the morning*. I like to think of severity levels in practical terms. What kind of response or follow up do you perform for each severity level? If you always do the same thing for severity levels 3 -5, then what's the benefits of classifying them as 3, 4, and 5 as opposed to just grouping them together into a single low-priority severity level?

Your situation may be different, so make sure that you consider all stakeholders. Production incidents are not fun.

Determining alert channels

Alert channels are tightly coupled to severity levels. Let's consider the following options:

- Wake-up call to on-call engineer
- Instant message to a public channel
- Email

Often, the same incident will be broadcasted to multiple channels. Obviously, the wake-up call is the most intrusive, the instant message (for example, slack) may pop up as a notification, but someone has to be around and look at it. The email is often more informative in nature. It is common to combine multiple channels. For example, the on-call engineer gets the wake up call, the team incident channel gets a message, and the group manager gets and email.

Fine-tuning noisy alerts

Noisy alerts are a problem. If there are too many alerts – especially low-priority ones – then there are two major problems:

- It is distracting to all the people that get notified (especially to the poor engineer being woke up in the middle of the night).
- It might lead to people ignoring alerts.

You don't want to miss an important alert because of a lot of noisy low-priority alerts. Fine-tuning your alerts is an art and an ongoing process.

I recommend reading and adopting *My Philosophy on Alerting* (`https://docs.google.com/document/d/199PqyG3UsyXlwieHaqbGiWVa8eMWi8zzAn0YfcApr8Q/edit`) by Rob Ewaschuk (ex-Google site reliability engineer).

Utilizing the Prometheus alert manager

Alerts naturally feed off metrics. Prometheus, in addition to being a fantastic metrics collector, also provides an alert manager. We've already installed it as part of the overall Prometheus installation:

```
$ kubectl get svc prometheus-alertmanager
NAME                       TYPE        CLUSTER-IP EXTERNAL-IP PORT(S) AGE
prometheus-alertmanager    ClusterIP   10.100.109.90 <none>  80/TCP   24h
```

We're not going to configure any alerts because I don't want to be on call for Delinkcious.

The Alert manager has a conceptual model that includes the following:

- Groupings
- Integrations
- Inhibition
- Silences

Grouping deals with consolidating multiple signals into a single notification. For example, if many of your services use AWS S3 and it suffers an outage, then a lot of services might trigger alerts. But with grouping, you can configure the alert manager to send just one notification.

Integrations are notification targets. The alert manager supports many targets out of the box like email, PagerDuty, Slack, HipChat, PushOver, OpsGenie, VictoOps, and WeChat. For all other integrations, the recommendation is to use the generic HTTP webhook integration.

Inhibition is an interesting concept where you can skip sending notifications for alerts if other alerts are already firing. This is another way on top of grouping to avoid sending multiple notifications for the same high-level problem.

Silences are just a mechanism to temporarily mute some alerts. This is useful if your alerting rules are not neatly configured with grouping and inhibitions, or even if some valid alerts keep firing, but you are already handling the situation and you don't need more notifications at the moment. You can configure silences in the web UI.

Configuring alerts in Prometheus

You can raise alerts by configuring rules in the Prometheus server configuration file. Those alerts are handled by the alert manager which decides, based on its configuration, what to do about them. Here is an example:

```
groups:
- name: link-manager
  rules:
  - alert: SlowAddLink
    expr: link_addlink_summary{quantile="0.5"} > 5
    for: 1m
    labels:
      severity: critical
    annotations:
      description: the AddLink() method takes more than 5 seconds for more
than half of the request in the last minute
      summary: the AddLink() method takes too long
```

The rule has an expression, which, if true, triggers the alert. There is a period of time (1 minute here) where the condition must be true, so that you can avoid triggering one-off anomalies (if you so choose). There is severity associated with the alert and some annotations.

With metrics and alerts covered, let's move on and see what to do when an alert fires and we get notified of a problem.

Distributed tracing

The notifications that alert you that something is wrong can be as vague as *Something is wrong with the website*. Well, that's not very useful for troubleshooting, detecting the root cause, and fixing it. This is especially true for microservice-based architectures where every user request can be handled by a large number of microservices and each component might fail in interesting ways. There are several ways to try and narrow down the scope:

- Look at recent deployments and configuration changes.
- Check whether any of your third-party dependencies suffered an outage.
- Consider similar issues if the root cause hasn't been fixed yet.

If you're lucky, you can just diagnose the problem right away. However, when debugging large-scale distributed systems, you don't really want to rely on luck. It's much better to have a methodical approach in place. Enter distributed tracing.

We will use the Jaeger (`https://www.jaegertracing.io/`) distributed tracing system. It is yet another CNCF project that started as an Uber open source project. The problems Jaeger can help with are as follows:

- Distributed transaction monitoring
- Performance and latency optimization
- Root cause analysis
- Service dependency analysis
- Distributed context propagation

Before we can use Jaeger, we need to install it into the cluster.

Installing Jaeger

The best way to install Jaeger is using the Jaeger-operator, so let's install the operator first:

```
$ kubectl create -f
https://raw.githubusercontent.com/jaegertracing/jaeger-operator/master/depl
oy/crds/jaegertracing_v1_jaeger_crd.yaml
customresourcedefinition.apiextensions.k8s.io/jaegers.jaegertracing.io
created
$ kubectl create -f
https://raw.githubusercontent.com/jaegertracing/jaeger-operator/master/depl
oy/service_account.yaml
serviceaccount/jaeger-operator created
$ kubectl create -f
https://raw.githubusercontent.com/jaegertracing/jaeger-operator/master/depl
oy/role.yaml
clusterrole.rbac.authorization.k8s.io/jaeger-operator created
$ kubectl create -f
https://raw.githubusercontent.com/jaegertracing/jaeger-operator/master/depl
oy/role_binding.yaml
clusterrolebinding.rbac.authorization.k8s.io/jaeger-operator created
$ kubectl create -f
https://raw.githubusercontent.com/jaegertracing/jaeger-operator/master/depl
oy/operator.yaml
deployment.apps/jaeger-operator created
```

Once the operator has been installed, we can create a Jaeger instance using the following manifest:

```
apiVersion: jaegertracing.io/v1
kind: Jaeger
metadata:
  name: jaeger-in-memory
spec:
  agent:
    strategy: DaemonSet
```

This is a simple in-memory instance. You can also create instances that are backed up by Elasticsearch and Cassandra:

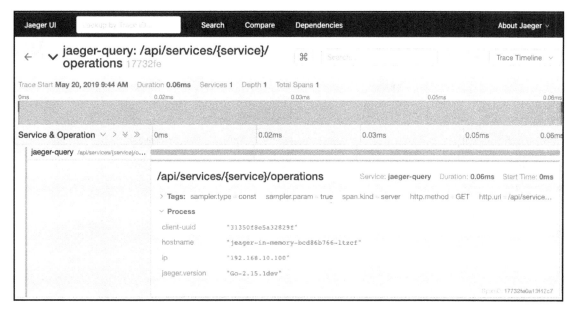

Jaeger UI

Jaeger has a very slick web UI that lets you drill down and explore distributed workflows.

Integrating tracing into your services

There are several steps here, but the gist of it is that you can think of tracing as another form of middleware. The core abstraction is a span. A request spans multiple microservices, and you record those spans and associate logs with them.

Here is the tracing middleware, which is similar to the logging middleware, except that it starts a span for the `GetLinks()` method instead of logging. As usual, there is the factory function that returns a `linkManagerMiddleware` function that calls the next middleware in the chain. The factory function accepts a tracer, which can start and finish a span:

```
package service

import (
  "github.com/opentracing/opentracing-go"
  om "github.com/the-gigi/delinkcious/pkg/object_model"
)

func newTracingMiddleware(tracer opentracing.Tracer) linkManagerMiddleware
{
  return func(next om.LinkManager) om.LinkManager {
    return tracingMiddleware{next, tracer}
  }
}

type tracingMiddleware struct {
  next om.LinkManager
  tracer opentracing.Tracer
}

func (m tracingMiddleware) GetLinks(request om.GetLinksRequest) (result
om.GetLinksResult, err error) {
  defer func(span opentracing.Span) {
    span.Finish()
  }(m.tracer.StartSpan("GetLinks"))
  result, err = m.next.GetLinks(request)
  return
}
```

Let's add the following function to create a Jaeger tracer:

```
// createTracer returns an instance of Jaeger Tracer that samples
// 100% of traces and logs all spans to stdout.
func createTracer(service string) (opentracing.Tracer, io.Closer) {
  cfg := &jaegerconfig.Configuration{
    ServiceName: service,
    Sampler: &jargerconfig.SamplerConfig{
      Type: "const",
      Param: 1,
    },
    Reporter: &jaegerconfig.ReporterConfig{
      LogSpans: true,
    },
  }
  logger := jaegerconfig.Logger(jaeger.StdLogger)
  tracer, closer, err := cfg.NewTracer(logger)
  if err != nil {
    panic(fmt.Sprintf("ERROR: cannot create tracer: %v\n", err))
  }
  return tracer, closer
}
```

Then, the `Run()` function creates a new tracer and a tracing middleware that it hooks up to the chain of middlewares:

```
// Create a tracer
 tracer, closer := createTracer("link-manager")
 defer closer.Close()

 ...

 // Hook up the tracing middleware
 svc = newTracingMiddleware(tracer)(svc)
```

After running the smoke test, we can search the logs for reports of spans. We expect three spans since the smoke test calls `GetLinks()` three times:

```
$ kubectl logs svc/link-manager | grep span
2019/05/20 16:44:17 Reporting span 72bce473b1af5236:72bce473b1af5236:0:1
2019/05/20 16:44:18 Reporting span 6e9f45ce1bb0a071:6e9f45ce1bb0a071:0:1
2019/05/20 16:44:21 Reporting span 32dd9d1edc9e747a:32dd9d1edc9e747a:0:1
```

There is much more to tracing and Jaeger. This is barely starting to scratch the surface. I encourage you to read more on it, experiment with it, and integrate it into your systems.

Summary

In this chapter, we covered a large number of topics, including self-healing, autoscaling, logging, metrics, and distributed tracing. Monitoring a distributed system is tough. Just installing and configuring the various monitoring services like Fluentd, Prometheus, and Jaeger is a non-trivial project. Managing the interactions between them and how your services support logging, instrumentation, and tracing adds another level of complexity. We've seen how Go-kit, with its middleware concept, makes it somewhat easier to add those operational concerns in a decoupled way from the core business logic. Once you have all the monitoring for those systems in place, there's a new set of challenges to take into account – how do you gain insights from all the data? How can you integrate it into your alerting and incident response process? How can you continuously improve your understanding of the system and improve your processes? These are all hard questions that you'll have to answer for yourself, but you may find some guidance in the *Further reading* section that follows.

In the next chapter, we will look at the exciting world of service meshes and Istio. Service meshes are a true innovation that can really offload many operational concerns from the services and let them focus on their core domain. However, a service mesh like Istio has a large surface area and there is a significant learning curve to overcome. Do the benefits of the service mesh compensate for the added complexity? We'll find out soon.

Further reading

Refer to the following links to find out more about what was covered in this chapter:

- **Kubernetes federation**: https://github.com/kubernetes-sigs/federation-v2
- **Kubernetes autoscaler**: https://github.com/kubernetes/autoscaler
- **The hunt for a logger interface**: https://go-talks.appspot.com/github.com/ChrisHines/talks/structured-logging/structured-logging.slide#1
- **Gradener**: https://gardener.cloud
- **Prometheus**: https://prometheus.io/docs/introduction/overview/
- **Fluentd**: https://www.fluentd.org/
- **Cluster-level logging**: https://kubernetes.io/docs/concepts/cluster-administration/logging/#cluster-level-logging-architectures
- **Monitoring best practices**: https://docs.google.com/document/d/199PqyG3UsyXlwieHaqbGiWVa8eMWi8zzAn0YfcApr8Q/edit#
- **Jaeger**: https://github.com/jaegertracing/jaeger

13
Service Mesh - Working with Istio

In this chapter, we will review the hot topic of service meshes and, in particular, Istio. This is exciting because service meshes are a real game changer. They remove many complicated tasks from services into independent proxies. This is a huge win, especially in a polyglot environment, where different services are implemented in different programming languages or if you need to migrate some legacy applications into your cluster.

We will cover the following topics in this chapter:

- What a service mesh is
- What Istio brings to the table
- Delinkcious on Istio
- Alternatives to Istio

Technical requirements

In this chapter, we will work with Istio. I chose to use **Google Kubernetes Engine** (**GKE**) in this chapter because Istio can be enabled on GKE as an add-on and doesn't require you to install it. This has the following two benefits:

- It saves time on installation
- It demonstrates that Delinkcious can run in the cloud and not just locally

To install Istio, you simply have to enable it in the GKE console and select an mTLS mode, which is the mutual authentication between services. I chose permissive, which means that the internal communication inside the cluster is not encrypted by default, and the services will accept both encrypted and non-encrypted connections. You can override it per service. For production clusters, I recommend using the strict mTLS mode, where all connections must be encrypted:

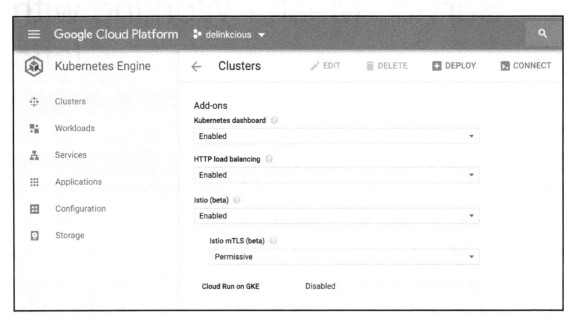

Istio gets installed in its own `istio-system` namespace, as follows:

```
$ kubectl -n istio-system get po

NAME READY STATUS RESTARTS AGE
istio-citadel-6995f7bd9-69qhw 1/1 Running 0 11h
istio-cleanup-secrets-6xkjx 0/1 Completed 0 11h
istio-egressgateway-57b96d87bd-81ld5 1/1 Running 0 11h
istio-galley-6d7dd498f6-pm8zz 1/1 Running 0 11h
istio-ingressgateway-ddd557db7-b4mqq 1/1 Running 0 11h
istio-pilot-5765d76b8c-19n5n 2/2 Running 0 11h
istio-policy-5b47b88467-tfq4b 2/2 Running 0 11h
istio-sidecar-injector-6b9fbbfcf6-vv2pt 1/1 Running 0 11h
istio-telemetry-65dcd9ff85-dxrhf 2/2 Running 0 11h
promsd-7b49dcb96c-cn491 2/2 Running 1 11h
```

The code

You can find the updated Delinkcious application at `https://github.com/the-gigi/delinkcious/releases/tag/v0.11.`

What is a service mesh?

Let's start by reviewing the problems microservices face compared to monoliths, see how service mesh addresses them, and then you'll see why I'm so excited about them. When designing and writing Delinkcious, the application code was fairly simple. We keep track of users, their links, and their follower/following relationships. We also do some link checking and store recent links in the news service. Finally, we expose all of this functionality through an API.

Comparing monoliths to microservices

It would have been pretty easy to implement all this functionality in a single monolith. It would also be pretty simple to deploy, monitor, and debug a Delinkcious monolith. However, as Delinkcious grows in functionality, as well as users and the team developing it, the downsides of monolith applications become much more pronounced. That's why we embarked on this journey with the microservice-based approach. However, along the way, we had to write a lot of code, install a lot of additional tools, and configure many components that have nothing to do with the Delinkcious application itself. We wisely took advantage of Kubernetes and Go kit to cleanly separate all of these additional concerns from the Delinkcious domain code, but it was a lot of hard work.

For example, if security is a high priority, you would want to authenticate and authorize inter-service calls in your system. We have done this in Delinkcious by introducing a mutual secret between the link service and the social graph service. We have to configure a secret, make sure it is accessible only to these two services, and add code to verify that each call is coming from the correct service. Maintaining (for example, rotating secrets) and evolving this across many services is not an easy task.

Another example of this is distributed tracing. In a monolith, the entire chain of calls can be captured by a stack trace. In Delinkcious, you have to install a distributed tracing service, such as Jaeger, and modify the code to record spans.

Centralized logging in a monolith is trivial since the monolith is already a single centralized entity.

The bottom line is that microservices bring a lot of benefits, but they are much harder to manage and reign in.

Using a shared library to manage the cross-cutting concerns of microservices

One of the most common approaches is to implement all these concerns in a library or a set of libraries. All the microservices include or depend on the shared library that takes care of all these cross-cutting aspects, such as configuration, logging, secret management, tracing, rate limiting, and fault tolerance. This sounds great in theory; let the services deal with the application domain and let a shared library or libraries deal with the common concerns. Hystrix from Netflix is a great example of a Java library that takes care of managing latency and fault tolerance. Finagle from Twitter is another good example of a Scala library (targeting the JVM). Many organizations use a collection of such libraries and often write their own.

In practice, however, this approach has severe downsides. The first issue is that, being a programming language library, it is naturally implemented in a specific language (for example, Java, in the case of Hystrix). Your system may have microservices in multiple languages (even Delinkcious has both Go and Python services). Having microservices implemented in different programming languages is one of the greatest benefits. A shared library (or libraries) significantly hinders this aspect. This is because you end up with several unappealing options, as follows:

- You restrict all your microservices to a single programming language.
- You maintain cross-language shared libraries for each programming language you use that behaves the same.
- You accept that different services will interact differently with your centralized services (for example, different logging formats or missing tracing).

All of these options are pretty bad. But that's not the end of it; let's say you've picked a combination of the preceding options. This will very likely include a significant amount of custom code, because no off-the-shelve library will provide you with everything that you need. Now, you want to update your shared code library. Since it's shared by all or most of your services, this means you have to do an across-the-board upgrade of all your services. However, it's likely that you can't just shut down your system and upgrade all the services at once.

Instead, you'll have to do it in the form of a rolling update. Even blue-green deployment can't be done instantly across multiple services. The problem is that, often, the shared code is related to how you manage mutual secrets or authentication between services. For example, if service A upgrades to the new version of the shared library and service B is still on the previous version, they might not be able to communicate. This results in an outage, which can cascade and impact many services. You can find a way to introduce changes in a backward-compatible way, but this is more difficult and error-prone.

Okay, so shared libraries across all services are useful but hard to manage. Let's take a look at how a service mesh can help.

Using a service mesh to manage the cross-cutting concerns of microservices

A service mesh is a set of intelligent proxies and additional control infrastructure components. The proxies are deployed on every node in your cluster. The proxies intercept all communication between the services and can do a lot of work on your behalf that previously had to be done by the service (or a shared library used by the service). Some of the responsibilities of a service mesh are as follows:

- Reliable delivery of requests between services through retries and automatic failovers
- Latency-aware load balancing
- Route requests based on flexible and dynamic routing rules (this is also known as traffic shaping)
- Circuit breaking through deadlines
- Service-to-service authentication and authorization
- Report metrics and support for distributed tracing

All of these capabilities are important for many large-scale cloud-native applications. Offloading them from the services is a huge win. Features such as smart traffic shaping require building dedicated and reliable services without a service mesh.

The following diagram illustrates how a service mesh is embedded into a Kubernetes cluster:

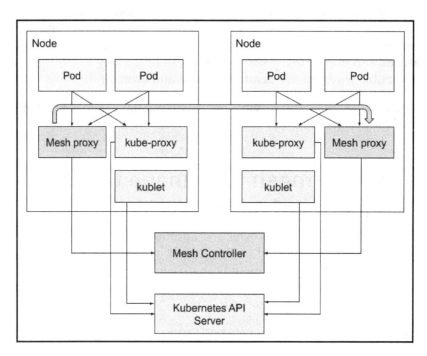

Service meshes sound revolutionary indeed. Let's take a look at how they fit into Kubernetes.

Understanding the relationship between Kubernetes and a service mesh

At first glance, the service mesh sounds very similar to Kubernetes itself. Kubernetes deploys the kubelet and the kube-proxy into each node and the service mesh deploys its own proxy. Kubernetes has a control plane that kubelet/kube-proxy interacts with, and the service mesh has its own control plane that the mesh proxies interact with.

I like to think of a service mesh as a complement to Kubernetes. Kubernetes is primarily in charge of scheduling pods and providing it with the flat networking model and service discovery, so different pods and services can communicate with each other. This is where the service mesh takes over and manages this service-to-service communication in a much more fine-grained way. There is a thin layer of overlap in responsibilities around load balancing and network policies but, overall, the service mesh is a great complement to Kubernetes.

It's also important to realize that these two amazing technologies don't depend on each other. Obviously, you can run a Kubernetes cluster without a service mesh. Additionally, many service meshes can work with other non-Kubernetes platforms, such as Mesos, Nomad, Cloud Foundry, and Consul-based deployments.

Now that we understand what a service mesh is, let's take a look at a specific example.

What does Istio bring to the table?

Istio is a service mesh that was originally developed by Google, IBM, and Lyft. It was introduced in mid-2017 and took off like a rocket. It brings a coherent model with a control and data plane, is built around the Envoy proxy, has a lot of momentum, and already serves as the foundation for additional projects. It is, of course, open source and a **Cloud Native Computing Foundation** (**CNCF**) project. In Kubernetes, each Envoy proxy is injected as a sidecar container to each pod that participates in the mesh.

Let's explore the Istio architecture, and then dive into the services that it provides.

Getting to know the Istio architecture

Istio is a large framework that provides a lot of capabilities, and it has multiple parts that interact with each other and with Kubernetes components (mostly indirectly and unobtrusively). It is divided into a control plane and a data plane. The data plane is a set of proxies (one per pod). Their control plane is a set of components that are responsible for configuring the proxies and collecting telemetry of data.

The following diagram illustrates the different parts of Istio, how they are related to each other, and what information is exchanged between them:

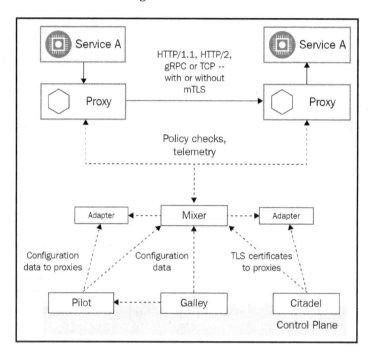

Let's go a little deeper into each component, starting with the Envoy proxy.

Envoy

Envoy is a high-performance proxy that's implemented in C++. It was developed by Lyft and functions as the data plane of Istio, but it is also an independent CNCF project and can be used on its own. For each pod in the service mesh, Istio injects (either automatically or through the `istioctl` CLI) an Envoy side container that does the heavy lifting:

- Proxy HTTP, HTTP/2, and gRPC traffic between pods
- Sophisticated load balancing
- mTLS termination
- HTTP/2 and gRPC proxies
- Providing service health
- Circuit breaking for unhealthy services

- Percent-based traffic shaping
- Injecting faults for testing
- Detailed metrics

The Envoy proxy controls all the incoming and outgoing communication to its pod. It is, by far, the most important component of Istio. The configuration of Envoy is not trivial, and this is a large part of what the Istio control plane deals with.

The next component is Pilot.

Pilot

Pilot is responsible for platform-agnostic service discovery, dynamic load balancing, and routing. It translates high-level routing rules and resiliency from its own rules API into an Envoy configuration. This abstraction layer allows Istio to run on multiple orchestration platforms. Pilot takes all the platform-specific information, converts it into the Envoy data plane configuration format, and propagates it to each Envoy proxy with the Envoy data plane API. Pilot is stateless; in Kubernetes, all the configuration is stored as **custom resources definitions** (**CRDs**) on etcd.

Mixer

Mixer is responsible for abstracting the metrics collection and policies. These aspects are typically implemented in services by accessing APIs directly for specific backends. This has the benefit of offloading this burden from service developers and putting the control into the hands of the operators that configure Istio. It also allows you to switch backends easily without code changes. The types of backends that Mixer can work with include the following:

- Logging
- Authorization
- Quota
- Telemetry
- Billing

The interaction between the Envoy proxy and Mixer is straightforward – before each request, the proxy calls Mixer for precondition checks, which might cause the request to be rejected; after each request, the proxy reports the metrics to Mixer. Mixer has an adapter API to facilitate extensions for arbitrary infrastructure backends. It is a major part of its design.

Citadel

Citadel is responsible for certificate and key management in Istio. It integrates with various platforms and aligns with their identity mechanisms. For example, in Kubernetes, it uses service accounts; on AWS, it uses AWS IAM; and on GCP/GKE, it can use GCP IAM. The Istio PKI is based on Citadel. It uses X.509 certificates in SPIFEE format as a vehicle for service identity.

Here is the workflow in Kubernetes:

- Citadel creates certificates and key pairs for existing service accounts.
- Citadel watches the Kubernetes API server for new service accounts to provision with a certificate a key pair.
- Citadel stores the certificates and keys as Kubernetes secrets.
- Kubernetes mounts the secrets into each new pod that is associated with the service account (this is standard Kubernetes practice).
- Citadel automatically rotates the Kubernetes secrets when the certificates expire.
- Pilot generates secure naming information that associates a service account with an Istio service. Pilot then passes the secure naming information to the Envoy proxy.

The final major component that we will cover is Galley.

Galley

Galley is a relatively simple component. Its job is to abstract away the user configuration on different platforms. It provides the ingested configuration to Pilot and Mixer.

Now that we have broken down Istio into its major components, let's take a look at how it accomplishes its duties as a service mesh. The number one capability is traffic management.

Managing traffic with Istio

Istio operates at the network level inside the cluster between your services, as well as managing how you expose your services to the world. It provides many capabilities, such as request routing, load balancing, automatic retries, and fault injection. Let's review all of these, starting with routing requests.

Routing requests

Istio introduces its own virtual services as a CRD. Istio services have a concept of a version that doesn't exist for Kubernetes services. The same image can be deployed as different versions of a virtual service. For example, you can represent the production or staging environment as different versions of the same service. Istio allows you to configure rules that determine how to route traffic to different versions of a service.

The way this works is that Pilot sends ingress and egress rules to the proxies that determine where requests should be handled. You then define the rules as a CRD in Kubernetes. Here is a simple example that defines a virtual service for the `link-manager` service:

```
apiVersion: networking.istio.io/v1alpha3
kind: VirtualService
metadata:
 name: link-manager
spec:
  hosts:
  - link-manager # same as link-manager.default.svc.cluster.local
  http:
  - route:
    - destination:
        host: link-manager
```

Let's take a look at how Istio does load balancing.

Load balancing

Istio has its own platform-independent service discovery with adapters for the underlying platform (for example, Kubernetes). It relies on the existence of a service registry that the underlying platform manages, and removes unhealthy instances in order to update its load balancing pools. There are currently three supported load balancing algorithms:

- Round robin
- Random
- Weighted least request

Envoy has a few more algorithms, such as Maglev, ring hash, and weighted round robin, that Istio doesn't support yet.

Istio also performs periodic health checks to verify that instances in the pool are actually healthy, and can remove them from load balancing temporarily if they fail the configured health check threshold.

You can configure load balancing through the destination rules in a separate
`DestinationRule` CRD, as follows:

```
apiVersion: networking.istio.io/v1alpha3
kind: DestinationRule
metadata:
  name: link-manager
spec:
  host: link-manager
  trafficPolicy:
    loadBalancer:
      simple: ROUND_ROBIN
```

You can specify different algorithms by the port, as follows:

```
apiVersion: networking.istio.io/v1alpha3
kind: DestinationRule
metadata:
  name: link-manager
spec:
  host: link-manager
  trafficPolicy:
    portLevelSettings:
    - port:
        number: 80
      loadBalancer:
        simple: LEAST_CONN
    - port:
        number: 8080
      loadBalancer:
        simple: ROUND_ROBIN
```

Now, let's take a look at how Istio can help us deal with failures automatically.

Handling failures

Istio provides many mechanisms to deal with failure, including the following:

- Timeouts
- Retries (including backoff and jitter)
- Rate limiting
- Health checks
- Circuit breakers

All of these can be configured through Istio CRDs.

For example, the following code demonstrates how to set the connection limits and timeout for the `link-manager` service at the TCP level (HTTP is supported too):

```
apiVersion: networking.istio.io/v1alpha3
kind: DestinationRule
metadata:
    name: link-manager
spec:
  host: link-manager
  trafficPolicy:
      connectionPool:
        tcp:
          maxConnections: 200
          connectTimeout: 45ms
          tcpKeepalive:
            time: 3600s
            interval: 75s
```

Circuit breaking is done by explicitly checking for application errors (for example, the 5XX HTTP status code) within a given time period. This is done in an `outlierDetection` section. The following example checks for 10 consecutive errors every 2 minutes. If the service crosses this threshold, the instance will be ejected from the pool for a period of 5 minutes:

```
apiVersion: networking.istio.io/v1alpha3
kind: DestinationRule
metadata:
  name: link-manager
spec:
  host: link-manager
  trafficPolicy:
      outlierDetection:
        consecutiveErrors: 10
        interval: 2m
        baseEjectionTime: 5m
```

Note that, as far as Kubernetes is concerned, the service may be fine because the container is running.

It's great that Istio provides so many ways to deal with errors and failures at the operational level. When testing distributed systems, it is important to test the behavior when certain components fail. Istio supports this use case by allowing you to inject faults on purpose.

Injecting faults for testing

The failure handling mechanisms of Istio don't magically fix errors. Automatic retries can automatically address intermittent failures, but some failures need to be handled by the application or even a human operator. In fact, the misconfiguration of Istio failure handling can itself cause failures (for example, configuring timeouts that are too short). Testing how the system behaves in the presence of failures can be done by artificially injecting faults. There are two types of faults that Istio can inject: aborts and delays. You can configure fault injection at the virtual service level.

Here is an example of where a delay of 5 seconds is added to 10% of all requests to the `link-manager` service in order to simulate a heavy load on the system:

```
apiVersion: networking.istio.io/v1alpha3
kind: VirtualService
metadata:
   name: link-manager
 spec:
   hosts:
   - link-manager
   http:
   - fault:
       delay:
         percent: 10
         fixedDelay: 5s
```

Testing under stress and in the presence of faults is a tremendous boon, but all testing is incomplete. When it's time to deploy the new version, you may want to deploy it to a small percentage of users or have the new version handle just a small percentage of all requests. This is where canary deployments come in.

Doing canary deployments

We previously discovered how to perform canary deployments in Kubernetes. If we want to divert 10% of requests to our canary version, we have to deploy nine pods of the current version and one canary pod to get the correct ratio. Kubernetes' load balancing is tightly coupled to deployed pods. This is suboptimal. Istio has a better load balancing approach since it operates at the network level. You can simply configure two versions of your service and decide what percentage of requests go to each version, regardless of how many pods run each version.

Here is an example of where Istio will split the traffic and send 95% to v1 of the service and 5% to v2 of the service:

```
apiVersion: networking.istio.io/v1alpha3
kind: VirtualService
metadata:
  name: link-service
spec:
  hosts:
    - reviews
  http:
  - route:
    - destination:
        host: link-service
        subset: v1
      weight: 95
    - destination:
        host: reviews
        subset: v2
      weight: 5
```

The subsets named v1 and v2 are defined in a destination rule based on labels. In this case, the label are `version: v1` and `version: v2`:

```
apiVersion: networking.istio.io/v1alpha3
 kind: DestinationRule
 metadata:
   name: link-manager
 spec:
   host: link-manager
   subsets:
   - name: v1
     labels:
       version: v1
   - name: v2
     labels:
       version: v2
```

This was a pretty comprehensive coverage of the traffic management capabilities of Istio, but there is much more to discover. Let's turn our attention to security.

Securing your cluster with Istio

The security model of Istio revolves around three themes: identity, authentication, and authorization.

Understanding Istio identity

Istio manages its own identity model, which can represent human users, services, or groups of services. In Kubernetes, Istio uses Kubernetes' service account to represent identity. Istio uses its PKI (through Citadel) to create a strong cryptographic identity for each pod that it manages. It creates a x.509 certificate (in SPIFEE format) and a key pair for each service account and injects them as secrets to the pod. Pilot manages a map between the DNS service names and the identities that are allowed to run them. When clients call into services, they can verify that the services are indeed run by allowed identities and can detect rogue services. With a strong identity in place, let's take a look at how authentication works with Istio.

Authenticating users with Istio

Istio authentication is based on policies. There are two kinds of policies: namespace policies and mesh policies. A namespace policy applies to a single namespace. A mesh policy applies to the entire cluster. There can be only one mesh policy with a kind of MeshPolicy and it must be named default. Here is an example of a mesh policy that requires all services to use mTLS:

```
apiVersion: "authentication.istio.io/v1alpha1"
 kind: "MeshPolicy"
 metadata:
   name: "default"
 spec:
   peers:
   - mtls: {}
```

Namespace policies have a kind of Policy. If you don't specify a namespace, then it will apply to the default namespace. There can be only one policy per namespace and it must be called default too. The following policy uses the targets selector to apply only to the api-gateway service and port 8080 of the link service:

```
apiVersion: "authentication.istio.io/v1alpha1"
 kind: "Policy"
 metadata:
   name: "default"
   namespace: "some-ns"
 spec:
   targets:
     - name: api-gateway
     - name: link-manager
       ports:
       - number: 8080
```

The idea is to avoid ambiguity; policies are resolved from a service to a namespace to a mesh. If a narrow policy exists, it takes precedence.

Istio provides either peer authentication through mTLS or origin authentication through JWT.

You can configure peer authentication through the `peers` section, as follows:

```
peers:
   - mtls: {}
```

You can configure the origin through the `origins` section, as follows:

```
origins:
 - jwt:
     issuer: "https://accounts.google.com"
     jwksUri: "https://www.googleapis.com/oauth2/v3/certs"
     trigger_rules:
     - excluded_paths:
       - exact: /healthcheck
```

As you can see, origin authentication can be configured for specific paths (through the include or exclude paths). In the preceding example, the `/healthcheck` path is exempt from authentication, which makes sense for a health check endpoint that often needs to be called from a load balancer or remote monitoring service.

By default, peer authentication is used if there is a peers section. If not, then authentication will not be set. To force origin authentication, you can add the following to the policy:

```
principalBinding: USE_ORIGIN
```

Now that we've discovered how Istio authenticates requests, let's take a look at how it does authorization.

Authorizing requests with Istio

Services usually expose multiple endpoints. Service A may be allowed to call only specific endpoints of service B. Service A must first authenticate against service B, and then the specific request must be authorized as well. Istio supports this by extending the **role-based access control** (**RBAC**) that Kubernetes uses to authorize requests to its API server.

It's important to note that authorization is turned off by default. To turn it on, you can create a `ClusterRbacConfig` object. The mode controls how authorization is enabled, as follows:

- `OFF` means authorization is disabled (the default).
- `ON` means authorization is enabled for all the services in the entire mesh.
- `ON_WITH_INCLUSION` means authorization is enabled for all the included namespaces and services.
- `ON_WITH_EXCLUSION` means authorization is enabled for all namespaces and services except the excluded ones.

Here is an example of when authorization is enabled on all the namespaces except `kube-system` and `development`:

```
apiVersion: "rbac.istio.io/v1alpha1"
 kind: ClusterRbacConfig
 metadata:
   name: default
 spec:
   mode: 'ON_WITH_EXCLUSION'
   exclusion:
     namespaces: ["kube-system", "development"]
```

The actual authorization operates at the service level and is very similar to the RBAC model of Kubernetes. Where in Kubernetes there is `Role`, `ClusterRole`, `RoleBinding`, and `ClusterRoleBinding`, in Istio, there is `ServiceRole` and `ServiceRoleBinding`.

The basic level of granularity is `namespace/service/path/method`. You can use wildcards for grouping. For example, the following role grants GET and HEAD access to all the Delinkcious managers and the API gateway in the default namespace:

```
apiVersion: "rbac.istio.io/v1alpha1"
 kind: ServiceRole
 metadata:
   name: full-access-reader
   namespace: default
 spec:
   rules:
   - services: ["*-manager", "api-gateway"]
     paths:
     methods: ["GET", "HEAD"]
```

However, Istio offers even further control with constraints and properties. You can limit a rule by the source namespace or the IP, labels, request headers, and other attributes.

You can refer to `https://istio.io/docs/reference/config/authorization/constraints-and-properties/` for more details.

Once you have a `ServiceRole`, you need to associate it with a list of subjects (such as service accounts or human users) that will be allowed to perform the requested operations. Here is how you can define `ServiceRoleBinding`:

```
apiVersion: "rbac.istio.io/v1alpha1"
 kind: ServiceRoleBinding
 metadata:
   name: test-binding-products
   namespace: default
 spec:
   subjects:
   - user: "service-account-delinkcious"
   - user: "istio-ingress-service-account"
     properties:
        request.auth.claims[email]: "the.gigi@gmail.com"
   roleRef:
     kind: ServiceRole
     name: "full-access-reader"
```

You can make a role publicly available to authenticated or unauthenticated users by setting the subject user to `*`.

There is much to Istio authorization that we can cover here. You can read up on the following topics:

- Authorization for TCP protocols
- Permissive mode (experimental)
- Debugging authorization problems
- Authorization through Envoy filters

Once a request is authorized there, it may still be rejected if it fails to comply with policy checks.

Enforcing policies with Istio

Istio policy enforcement is similar to the way admission controllers work in Kubernetes. Mixer has a set of adapters that are invoked before and after a request is processed. Before we dive in further, it's important to note that policy enforcement is disabled by default. If you install Istio using helm, you can enable it by providing the following flag:

```
--set global.disablePolicyChecks=false.
```

On GKE, it is enabled; here is how to check this:

```
$ kubectl -n istio-system get cm istio -o jsonpath="{@.data.mesh}" | grep
disablePolicyChecks
disablePolicyChecks: false
```

If the result is `disablePolicyChecks: false`, then it's already enabled. Otherwise, enable it by editing the Istio ConfigMap and setting it to false.

One common type of policy is rate limiting. You can enforce rate limits by configuring quota objects, binding them to specific services, and defining mixer rules. A good example from the Istio demo application can be found at `https://raw.githubusercontent.com/istio/istio/release-1.1/samples/bookinfo/policy/mixer-rule-productpage-ratelimit.yaml`.

You can also add your own policies by creating a Mixer adapter. There are three built-in types of adapters, as follows:

- Check
- Quota
- Report

This is not trivial; you'll have to implement a gRPC service that can handle the data specified in a dedicated template. Now, let's take a look at the metrics Istio collects for us.

Collecting metrics with Istio

Istio collects metrics after each request. The metrics are sent to Mixer. Envoy is the primary producer of metrics, but you can add your own metrics if you wish. The configuration model for metrics is based on multiple Istio concepts: attributes, instances, templates, handlers, rules, and Mixer adapters.

Here is a sample instance that counts all the requests and reports them as the `request-count` metric:

```
apiVersion: config.istio.io/v1alpha2
 kind: instance
 metadata:
   name: request-count
   namespace: istio-system
 spec:
   compiledTemplate: metric
   params:
     value: "1" # count each request
     dimensions:
       reporter: conditional((context.reporter.kind | "inbound") ==
"outbound", "client", "server")
       source: source.workload.name | "unknown"
       destination: destination.workload.name | "unknown"
       message: '"counting requests..."'
     monitored_resource_type: '"UNSPECIFIED"'```
```

Now, we can configure a Prometheus handler to receive the metrics. Prometheus is a compiled adapter (which is part of Mixer), so we can just use it in the spec. The `spec | params | metrics` section has a kind of `COUNTER`, a Prometheus metric name (`request_count`), and, most importantly, the instance name that we just defined, which is the source of the metrics:

```
apiVersion: config.istio.io/v1alpha2
 kind: handler
 metadata:
   name: request-count-handler
   namespace: istio-system
 spec:
   compiledAdapter: prometheus
   params:
     metrics:
     - name: request_count # Prometheus metric name
       instance_name: request-count.instance.istio-system # Mixer instance
name (fully-qualified)
       kind: COUNTER
       label_names:
       - reporter
       - source
       - destination
       - message
```

Finally, we tie it all together with a rule, as follows:

```
apiVersion: config.istio.io/v1alpha2
 kind: rule
 metadata:
   name: prom-request-counter
   namespace: istio-system
 spec:
   actions:
   - handler: request-count-handler
     instances: [ request-count ]
```

Okay, so Istio is amazingly powerful. But are there any situations where you shouldn't use Istio?

When should you avoid Istio?

Istio provides a lot of value. However, this value is not without a cost. The intrusive nature of Istio and its complexity have some significant downsides. You should consider these downsides before you adopt Istio:

- Additional concepts and management systems on top of the already complex Kubernetes make the learning curve very steep.
- Troubleshooting configuration issues is challenging.
- Integration with other projects might be missing or partial (for example, NATS and Telepresence).
- The proxies add latency and consume CPU and memory resources.

If you're just starting with Kubernetes, I recommend waiting until you get the hang of it before you even consider using Istio.

Now that we understand what Istio is all about, let's explore how Delinkcious can benefit from Istio.

Delinkcious on Istio

With Istio, Delinkcious can potentially shed a lot of extra baggage. So, why is it a good idea to move this functionality from Delinkcious services or Go kit middleware to Istio?

Well, the reason is that this functionality is often unrelated to the application domain. We invested a lot of work to carefully separate concerns and isolate the Delinkcious domain from the way they are deployed and managed. However, as long as all of those concerns are addressed by the microservices themselves, we will need to make changes to the code and rebuild them every time we want to make an operational change. Even if a lot of this is data-driven, it can make it difficult to troubleshoot and debug issues because, when a failure happens, it's not always easy to determine whether it was due to a bug in the domain code or the operational code.

Let's take a look at some specific examples where Istio can simplify Delinkcious.

Removing mutual authentication between services

As you may recall, in Chapter 6, *Securing Microservices on Kubernetes*, we created a mutual secret between the `link-manager` service and the `social-graph-manager` service:

```
$ kubectl get secret | grep mutual
link-mutual-auth              Opaque              1       9d
  social-graph-mutual-auth    Opaque              1       5d19h
```

It required a lot of coordination and explicit work to encode the secrets, and then mount the secrets into the containers:

```
spec:
  containers:
  - name: link-manager
    image: g1g1/delinkcious-link:0.3
    imagePullPolicy: Always
    ports:
    - containerPort: 8080
    envFrom:
    - configMapRef:
        name: link-manager-config
    volumeMounts:
    - name: mutual-auth
      mountPath: /etc/delinkcious
      readOnly: true
```

```
        volumes:
        - name: mutual-auth
          secret:
            secretName: link-mutual-auth
```

Then, the link manager had to get the secret through the `auth_util` package we had to implement, and inject it as a header to the request:

```
// encodeHTTPGenericRequest is a transport/http.EncodeRequestFunc that
// JSON-encodes any request to the request body. Primarily useful in a
client.
func encodeHTTPGenericRequest(_ context.Context, r *http.Request, request
interface{}) error {
    var buf bytes.Buffer
    if err := json.NewEncoder(&buf).Encode(request); err != nil {
        return err
    }
    r.Body = ioutil.NopCloser(&buf)

    if os.Getenv("DELINKCIOUS_MUTUAL_AUTH") != "false" {
        token := auth_util.GetToken(SERVICE_NAME)
        r.Header["Delinkcious-Caller-Token"] = []string{token}
    }

    return nil
}
```

Finally, the social graph manager has to be aware of this scheme and explicitly check whether the caller is allowed:

```
func decodeGetFollowersRequest(_ context.Context, r *http.Request)
(interface{}, error){
    if os.Getenv("DELINKCIOUS_MUTUAL_AUTH") != "false" {
        token := r.Header["Delinkcious-Caller-Token"]
        if len(token) == 0 || token[0] == "" {
            return nil, errors.New("Missing caller token")
        }
        if !auth_util.HasCaller("link-manager", token[0]) {
         return nil, errors.New("Unauthorized caller")
        }
    }
  ...
}
```

That's a lot of work that has nothing to do with the service itself. Imagine managing access to hundreds of interacting microservices with thousands of methods. This approach is cumbersome, error-prone, and requires code changes being made to two services whenever you add or remove an interaction.

With Istio, we can externalize this completely as a role and a role binding. Here is a role that allows you to call the GET method of the /following endpoint:

```
apiVersion: "rbac.istio.io/v1alpha1"
 kind: ServiceRole
 metadata:
   name: get-following
   namespace: default
 spec:
   rules:
   - services: ["social-graph.default.svc.cluster.local"]
     paths: ["/following"]
     methods: ["GET"]
```

In order to allow only the link service to call the method, we can bind the role to the link-manager service account as the subject user:

```
apiVersion: "rbac.istio.io/v1alpha1"
 kind: ServiceRoleBinding
 metadata:
   name: get-following
   namespace: default
 spec:
   subjects:
   - user: "cluster.local/ns/default/sa/link-manager"
     roleRef:
       kind: ServiceRole
       name: "get-following"
```

If, later, we need to allow other services to call the /following endpoint, we can add more subjects to this role binding. The social service itself doesn't need to know what service is allowed to call its methods. The calling services don't need to provide any credentials explicitly. The service mesh takes care of all that.

Another area where Istio can really help Delinkcious is with canary deployments.

Utilizing better canary deployments

In Chapter 11, *Deploying Microservices*, we used Kubernetes deployments and services to do canary deployments. In order to divert 10% of the traffic to a canary version, we scaled the current version to nine replicas and created a canary deployment, with one replica for the new version. We used the same labels (svc: link and app: manager) for both deployments.

The link-manager service in front of both deployments distributed the load evenly between all the pods, creating the 90/10 split we were aiming for:

```
$ kubectl scale --replicas=9 deployment/green-link-manager
deployment.extensions/green-link-manager scaled

$ kubectl get po -l svc=link,app=manager
NAME                                      READY  STATUS   RESTARTS  AGE
green-link-manager-5874c6cd4f-21dfn       1/1    Running  10        15h
green-link-manager-5874c6cd4f-9csxz       1/1    Running  0         52s
green-link-manager-5874c6cd4f-c5rqn       1/1    Running  0         52s
green-link-manager-5874c6cd4f-mvm5v       1/1    Running  10        15h
green-link-manager-5874c6cd4f-qn4zj       1/1    Running  0         52s
green-link-manager-5874c6cd4f-r2jxf       1/1    Running  0         52s
green-link-manager-5874c6cd4f-rtwsj       1/1    Running  0         52s
green-link-manager-5874c6cd4f-sw27r       1/1    Running  0         52s
green-link-manager-5874c6cd4f-vcj9s       1/1    Running  10        15h
yellow-link-manager-67847d6b85-n97b5      1/1    Running  4         6m20s
```

This works, but it couples canary deployments with scaling deployments. This can be expensive, especially if you need to run the canary deployment for a while until you are confident that it is okay. Ideally, you shouldn't need to create more pods just to divert a certain percentage of your traffic to a new version.

The traffic shaping capabilities with the subset concepts of Istio address this use case perfectly. The following virtual service splits the traffic into a ratio of 90/10 between a subset called v0.5 and another subset called canary:

```
apiVersion: networking.istio.io/v1alpha3
kind: VirtualService
metadata:
  name: social-graph-manager
spec:
  hosts:
    - social-graph-manager
  http:
  - route:
    - destination:
```

```
        host: social-graph-manager
        subset: v0.5
    weight: 90
  - destination:
        host: social-graph-manager
        subset: canary
    weight: 10
```

Doing canary deployments with Istio's virtual services and subsets is great for Delinkcious. Istio can help with logging and error reporting, too.

Automatic logging and error reporting

When running Delinkcious on GKE with the Istio add-on, you get automatic integration with Stackdriver, which is a one-stop shop for monitoring, including metrics, centralized logging, error reporting, and distributed tracing. Here is the Stackdriver log viewer for when you are searching for the `link-manager` logs:

Alternatively, you can filter by service name through the drop-down list. Here is what it looks like when specifying the api-gateway:

Sometimes, the error reporting view is what you need:

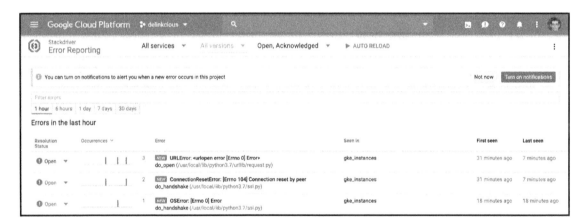

Then, you can drill down into any error and get a lot of additional information that will help you understand what went wrong and how to fix it:

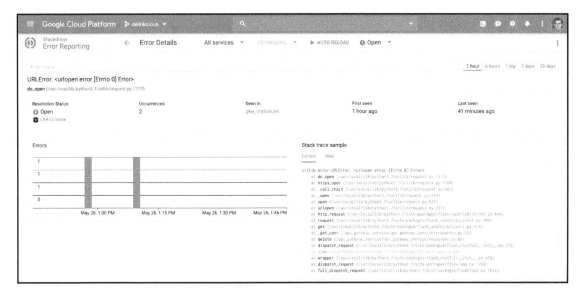

While Istio provides a lot of value and, in the case of Stackdriver, you benefit from automatic setup too, it is not always smooth riding – it has some limitations and rough edges.

Accommodating NATS

One of the limitations I discovered when deploying Istio into the Delinkcious cluster is that NATS doesn't work with Istio because it requires direct connections and it breaks when the Envoy proxy hijacks the communication. The solution is to prevent Istio from injecting the sidecar container and accepting that NATS will not be managed. Adding the NatsCluster CRD to the following annotation to the pod spec does the work for us: sidecar.istio.io/inject: "false":

```
apiVersion: nats.io/v1alpha2
  kind: NatsCluster
  metadata:
    name: nats-cluster
  spec:
    pod:
      # Disable istio on nats pods
      annotations:
```

```
        sidecar.istio.io/inject: "false"
    size: 1
    version: "1.4.0"
```

The preceding code is the complete `NatsCluster` resource definition with the annotation in place.

Examining the Istio footprint

Istio deploys a lot of stuff into the cluster, so let's review some of it. Mercifully, the Istio control plane is isolated in its own `istio-system` namespace, but CRDs are always cluster-wide and Istio doesn't skimp on those:

```
$ kubectl get crd -l k8s-app=istio -o custom-columns="NAME:.metadata.name"

NAME
adapters.config.istio.io
apikeys.config.istio.io
attributemanifests.config.istio.io
authorizations.config.istio.io
bypasses.config.istio.io
checknothings.config.istio.io
circonuses.config.istio.io
deniers.config.istio.io
destinationrules.networking.istio.io
edges.config.istio.io
envoyfilters.networking.istio.io
fluentds.config.istio.io
gateways.networking.istio.io
handlers.config.istio.io
httpapispecbindings.config.istio.io
httpapispecs.config.istio.io
instances.config.istio.io
kubernetesenvs.config.istio.io
kuberneteses.config.istio.io
listcheckers.config.istio.io
listentries.config.istio.io
logentries.config.istio.io
memquotas.config.istio.io
metrics.config.istio.io
noops.config.istio.io
opas.config.istio.io
prometheuses.config.istio.io
quotas.config.istio.io
quotaspecbindings.config.istio.io
quotaspecs.config.istio.io
```

```
rbacconfigs.rbac.istio.io
rbacs.config.istio.io
redisquotas.config.istio.io
reportnothings.config.istio.io
rules.config.istio.io
servicecontrolreports.config.istio.io
servicecontrols.config.istio.io
serviceentries.networking.istio.io
servicerolebindings.rbac.istio.io
serviceroles.rbac.istio.io
signalfxs.config.istio.io
solarwindses.config.istio.io
stackdrivers.config.istio.io
statsds.config.istio.io
stdios.config.istio.io
templates.config.istio.io
tracespans.config.istio.io
virtualservices.networking.istio.io
```

In addition to all of those CRDs, Istio installs all its components into the Istio namespace:

```
$ kubectl -n istio-system get all -o name
pod/istio-citadel-6995f7bd9-7c7x9
pod/istio-egressgateway-57b96d87bd-cnc2s
pod/istio-galley-6d7dd498f6-b29sk
pod/istio-ingressgateway-ddd557db7-glwm2
pod/istio-pilot-5765d76b8c-d9hq7
pod/istio-policy-5b47b88467-x7pqf
pod/istio-sidecar-injector-6b9fbbfcf6-fhc4k
pod/istio-telemetry-65dcd9ff85-bkjtd
pod/promsd-7b49dcb96c-wrfs8
service/istio-citadel
service/istio-egressgateway
service/istio-galley
service/istio-ingressgateway
service/istio-pilot
service/istio-policy
service/istio-sidecar-injector
service/istio-telemetry
service/promsd
deployment.apps/istio-citadel
deployment.apps/istio-egressgateway
deployment.apps/istio-galley
deployment.apps/istio-ingressgateway
deployment.apps/istio-pilot
deployment.apps/istio-policy
deployment.apps/istio-sidecar-injector
deployment.apps/istio-telemetry
```

```
deployment.apps/promsd
replicaset.apps/istio-citadel-6995f7bd9
replicaset.apps/istio-egressgateway-57b96d87bd
replicaset.apps/istio-galley-6d7dd498f6
replicaset.apps/istio-ingressgateway-ddd557db7
replicaset.apps/istio-pilot-5765d76b8c
replicaset.apps/istio-policy-5b47b88467
replicaset.apps/istio-sidecar-injector-6b9fbbfcf6
replicaset.apps/istio-telemetry-65dcd9ff85
replicaset.apps/promsd-7b49dcb96c
horizontalpodautoscaler.autoscaling/istio-egressgateway
horizontalpodautoscaler.autoscaling/istio-ingressgateway
horizontalpodautoscaler.autoscaling/istio-pilot
horizontalpodautoscaler.autoscaling/istio-policy
horizontalpodautoscaler.autoscaling/istio-telemetry
```

Finally, Istio, of course, installs its sidecar proxies into each pod (except Nats, where we disabled it). As you can see, each pod in the default namespace has two containers (2/2 under the READY column). One container does the work and the other is the Istio proxy sidecar container:

```
$ kubectl get po
NAME READY STATUS RESTARTS AGE
api-gateway-5497d95c74-zlgnm 2/2 Running 0 4d11h
link-db-7445d6cbf7-wdfsb 2/2 Running 0 4d22h
link-manager-54968ff8cf-vtpqr 2/2 Running 1 4d13h
nats-cluster-1 1/1 Running 0 4d20h
nats-operator-55dfdc6868-2b57q 2/2 Running 3 4d22h
news-manager-7f447f5c9f-n2v2v 2/2 Running 1 4d20h
news-manager-redis-0 2/2 Running 0 4d22h
social-graph-db-7d8ffb877b-nrzxh 2/2 Running 0 4d11h
social-graph-manager-59b464456f-48lrn 2/2 Running 1 4d11h
trouble-64554479d-rjszv 2/2 Running 0 4d17h
user-db-0 2/2 Running 0 4d22h
user-manager-699458447-9h64n 2/2 Running 2 4d22h
```

If you think that Istio is too big and complicated, you may still want to enjoy the benefits of a service mesh by pursuing one of the alternatives.

Alternatives to Istio

Istio has a lot of momentum, but it's not necessarily the best service mesh for you. Let's take a look at some other service meshes and consider their attributes.

Linkerd 2.0

Buoyant is the company that coined the term *Service Mesh* in 2016 and came out with the first service mesh – Linkerd. It was based on Twitter's Finagle and was implemented in Scala. Since then, Buoyant developed a new service mesh that focused on Kubernetes, called Conduit (which was implemented in Rust and Go), and later (in July 2018) renamed it to Linkerd 2.0. It is a CNCF project like Istio. Linkerd 2.0 also uses sidecar containers that can be automatically or manually injected.

Due to its lightweight design and tighter implementation of the data plane proxies in Rust, Linkerd 2.0 is supposed to outperform Istio and consume far fewer resources in the control plane. You can refer to the following resources for more information:

- **CPU and memory**: `https://istio.io/docs/concepts/performance-and-scalability/#cpu-and-memory`
- **Linkerd 2.0 and Istio Performance Benchmark**: `https://medium.com/@ihcsim/linkerd-2-0-and-istio-performance-benchmark-df290101c2bb`
- **Benchmarking Istio and Linkerd CPU**: `https://medium.com/@michael_87395/benchmarking-istio-linkerd-cpu-c36287e32781`

Buoyant is a smaller company and it seems to lag slightly behind Istio in functionality.

Envoy

The Istio data plane is Envoy, which does all the heavy lifting. You may find the Istio control plane too complicated and prefer to remove this layer of indirection and build your own control plane to interact directly with Envoy. This can be useful in some specialized circumstances; for example, if you want to use a load balancing algorithm offered by Envoy that Istio doesn't support.

HashiCorp Consul

Consul doesn't tick all the checkboxes for a service mesh, but it provides service discovery, service identity, and mTLS authorization. It is not Kubernetes-specific and isn't endorsed by the CNCF. If you already use Consul or other HashiCorp products, you may prefer to use it as a service mesh too.

AWS App Mesh

If you run your infrastructure on AWS, you should consider the AWS App Mesh. It is a newer project, AWS-specific, and also uses Envoy as its data plane. It is safe to assume that it will integrate the best with AWS IAM networking and monitoring technologies. It's not clear at this point as to whether AWS App Mesh is going to be a better service mesh for Kubernetes or if its main purpose is to provide service mesh benefits for ECS – AWS' proprietary container orchestration solution.

Others

There a few other service meshes out there. I will just mention them here so that you can pursue them further if you're interested. Some of them have some form of integration with Istio. It's not always clear what their value is since they are not open:

- Aspen Mesh
- Kong Mesh
- AVI Networks Universal Service Mesh

The no mesh option

You can always avoid a service mesh completely and use a library such as Go kit, Hystrix, or Finagle. You might lose the benefits of the external service mesh, but if you tightly control all your microservices and they all use the same programming language, then the library approach may work just fine for you. It is conceptually and operationally simpler and it shifts the responsibility for managing cross-cutting concerns toward developers.

Summary

In this chapter, we've looked at service meshes and Istio in particular. Istio is a complex project; it sits on top of Kubernetes and creates a type of shadow cluster with its proxies. Istio has outstanding features; it can shape traffic at a very fine-grained level, provide sophisticated authentication and authorization, enforce advanced policies, collect a lot of information, and help scale your cluster.

We covered the Istio architecture, its powerful capabilities, and explored how Delinkcious can benefit from these capabilities.

However, Istio is far from simple. It creates a plethora of custom resources, and it overlaps and extends existing Kubernetes resources in complex ways (VirtualService versus Service).

We also reviewed alternatives to Istio, including Linkerd 2.0, straight Envoy, AWS App Mesh, and Consul.

At this point, you should have a good understanding of the benefits of service meshes and what Istio can do for your projects. You may have to do some extra reading and experimentation to make an informed decision of whether you should incorporate Istio into your system right away, consider one of the alternatives, or just wait.

I believe that services meshes and Istio, in particular, will be very important and will become a standard best practice to incorporate into large Kubernetes clusters.

In the next chapter, which is the last chapter, we will continue our discussion about the future of microservices, Kubernetes, and other emerging trends, such as serverless.

Further reading

You can refer to the following resources for more information regarding what was covered in this chapter:

- **Istio**: `https://istio.io`
- **Hystrix**: `https://github.com/Netflix/Hystrix`
- **Finagle**: `https://twitter.github.io/finagle/`
- **Envo**: `https://www.envoyproxy.io/`
- **Spiffe**: `https://spiffe.io`
- **Configuration**: `https://istio.io/docs/reference/config/`

14
The Future of Microservices and Kubernetes

The software systems of tomorrow will be bigger, more complicated, will be able to handle more data, and will have an even bigger impact on our world. Just think about self-driving cars and ubiquitous robots. The human capacity to deal with complexity will not scale. That means that we will have to use a divide-and-conquer approach to build those complex software systems. Microservice-based architectures will continue to replace monoliths. Then, the challenge will shift into coordinating all those microservices into a coherent whole. This is where Kubernetes comes in as the standard orchestration solution.

In this chapter, we will discuss the near future of microservices and Kubernetes. We will focus on the near future, because the innovation pace is amazing and trying to look much further ahead is futile. The long-term vision is that AI will probably advance to the point where most software development can be automated. At this point, human limits of handling complexity may not apply, and the software developed by AI will not be understandable by humans.

So, let's leave the far future alone and, in the spirit of being hands-on, discuss the emerging technologies, standards, and trends that will be relevant in the next few years, of which you may want to become aware.

The topics we will cover include some microservices themes, such as the following:

- Microservices versus serverless functions
- Microservices, containers, and orchestration
- gRPC/gRPC-Web
- HTTP/3
- GraphQL

We will also discuss some Kubernetes themes:

- Kubernetes extensibility
- Service mesh integration
- Serverless computing on Kubernetes
- Kubernetes and VMs
- Cluster autoscaling
- Using operators

Let's start with microservices.

The future of microservices

Microservices are the dominant approach for building modern, large-scale systems today. But, are they going to remain the top choice? Let's find out.

Microservices versus serverless functions

One of the biggest questions regarding the future of microservices is whether serverless functions are going to make microservices obsolete. The answer is absolutely not. There are are many great benefits to serverless functions, as well as some serious limitations, such as cold start and time limits. Those limitations accumulate when you have functions invoking other functions. The execution time limits for function are very problematic if you want to apply retry logic with exponential backoff. A long-running service can keep local state and connections to data stores, and respond quicker to requests. But, for me, the biggest issue with serverless functions is that they represent a single function, which equates to a single endpoint of a service. I find a lot of value in the abstraction of a service that encapsulates a complete domain. If you try to port a service with 10 methods to serverless functions, then you'll run into management issues.

All those 10 functions will need access to the same data store, and multiple functions might need to be modified. All the functions will need similar access, configuration, and credentials to access various dependencies. Microservices will remain the backbone of large, cloud-native distributed systems. However, a lot of work will be offloaded to serverless functions, which makes sense. We will probably see some systems composed solely from serverless functions, but these will be forced and will have to make compromises.

Let's see the symbiotic relationship between microservices and containers.

Microservices, containers, and orchestration

When you break up a monolith into microservices, or start building a microservice-based system from scratch, you end up with a lot of services. You need to package, deploy, upgrade, and configure all those microservices. Containers address the packaging problem. Without containers, it is very difficult to scale microservice-based systems. As the number of microservices in the system grows orchestrating, the various containers and optimal scheduling requires a dedicated solution. This is where Kubernetes excels. The future of distributed systems is more microservices, packaged into more containers, which require Kubernetes to manage them. I say Kubernetes here, because in 2019, Kubernetes won the container orchestration wars.

Another aspect of many microservices is that they need to communicate with each other over a network. Where as in a monolith, most interactions are just function calls, in a microservice environment, a lot of interactions require hitting an endpoint or making a remote procedure call. Enter gRPC.

gRPC and gRPC-Web

gRPC is Google's remote procedure call protocol. Over the years, there were many RPC protocols. I still remember the days of CORBA and DCOM, and Java RMI. Fast-forward to the modern web, where REST beat SOAP to become the big gorilla in the arena of web APIs. But, these days, gRPC is beating REST. gRPC provides a contract-based model with strong typing, efficient payload based on protobuf, and is automatically generating client code. The combination is very powerful. The last refuge of REST was its ubiquity and the ease of calling REST APIs bearing JSON payloads from web applications running in the browser.

But, even this advantage is fading away. You could always put a REST-compatible gRPC gateway in front of your gRPC service, but I consider it a kludge. On the other hand, gRPC-web is a full-fledged JavaScript library that lets web applications simply invoke gRPC services. See `https://github.com/grpc/grpc-web/tree/master/packages/grpc-web`.

GraphQL

If gRPC is the REST killer inside the cluster, then GraphQL is the REST killer at the edge. GraphQL is simply a superior paradigm. It gives the frontend developers a lot of freedom to evolve their designs. It decouples the needs of the frontend from the rigid APIs of the backend and serves as the perfect BFF (backends-for-frontends) pattern. See `https://samnewman.io/patterns/architectural/bff/`.

Similar to gRPC contracts, the structured schema of a GraphQL service is very enticing for large-scale systems.

In addition, GraphQL solves the dreaded *N+1* problems of traditional REST APIs, where you first fetch a list of *N* resources from a REST endpoint and then you have to make *N* more calls (one per resource) to get related resources on each of the *N* items in the list.

I expect GraphQL to gain more and more mindshare as developers become more comfortable, awareness grows, tooling improves, and learning materials become more available.

HTTP/3 is coming

The web is built on HTTP. There is no question about it. It's pretty amazing how well this protocol fared. Here is a quick recap: in 1991, Tim-Berneres-Lee proposes HTTP 0.9 to support his idea for a World Wide Web. In 1996, The HTTP Working Group publishes HTTP 1.0 as the informational RFC 1945 to enable the internet boom of the late 1990s. In 1997, the first official RFC 2068 for HTTP 1.1 is published. In 1999, RFC 2616 adds a number of improvements to HTTP 1.1 and remains the dominant standard for two decades. In 2015, HTTP/2 is published, based on the SPDY protocol by Google, and all major browsers add support for it.

gRPC is built on top of HTTP/2, which fixes a lot of issues with previous revisions of the HTTP and provides the following features:

- Binary framing and compression
- Multiplexing using streams (multiple requests on the same TCP connection)
- Better flow control
- Server push

That sounds great. What will HTTP/3 give us? It offers the same feature set of HTTP/2. However, HTTP/2 is based on TCP, which doesn't offer streams. That means that streams are implemented at the HTTP/2 level. HTTP/3 is based on QUIC, a reliable transport over UDP. The details are out of scope, but the bottom line is that HTTP/3 will have much better performance and is always secure.

It may still take a while for broad HTTP/3 adoption, because many enterprises block or rate limit UDP on their networks. However, the benefits are compelling and gRPC over HTTP/3 will have even a bigger edge in performance compared to REST APIs.

Those are the primary future trends that will impact microservices. Let's see what is next for Kubernetes.

The future of Kubernetes

Kubernetes is here to stay. I will make a bold prediction and say that it will be around for decades. It is undeniably the current leader in the container orchestration space, but more importantly, it is designed in a super-extensible way. Any potential improvement can be built on top of the nice building blocks that Kubernetes provides (for example, service mesh) or replace those building blocks (such as network plugins, storage plugins, and custom schedulers). It is hard to imagine a brand new platform that will make Kubernetes obsolete, as opposed to improving and integrating it.

In addition, the industry momentum behind Kubernetes and the way it is developed in the open and managed by the CNCF is inspiring. Even though it originated from Google, there is no sentiment that it is Google's project. It is perceived as a true open source project that benefits everyone.

Now, consider that Kubernetes caters to the needs of the entire spectrum, from hobbyists playing with local Kubernetes on their laptops, through developers, testing locally or in the cloud, all the way to large enterprises that require certification and support for their own on-premises data centers.

Pretty much the only criticism there is against Kubernetes is that it is hard to learn. This is true at the moment, but it will get easier and easier. There is a lot of good training material. Developers and operators will gain experience. It's easy to find information and the community is large and vibrant.

A lot of people say that Kubernetes will become boring soon and will become an invisible infrastructure layer. I don't subscribe to this point of view. Some hard parts of the Kubernetes experience, such as setting up a cluster and installing a lot of additional software into the cluster, will become boring, but I think we'll see a lot of innovation across the board in the next 5 years.

Let's dive into specific technologies and trends.

Kubernetes extensibility

This is an easy call. Kubernetes was always designed as an extensible platform. But, some of the extension mechanisms required merging into the main Kubernetes repository. The Kubernetes developers recognized early the limitations and, across the board, introduced more loosely coupled mechanisms to extend Kubernetes and replace pieces that were considered core components in the past.

Abstracting the container runtime

Docker used to be the only container runtime that Kubernetes supported. Then it added special support to the now-defunct RKT runtime. However, later, it introduced the **Container Runtime Interface (CRI)** as a way to integrate any container runtime through a standard interface. Here are some of the runtimes that implement CRI and can be used in Kubernetes:

- Docker (of course)
- CRI-O (supports any OCI image)
- Containerd (became an CNCF graduate in February 2019)
- Frakti (Kata containers)
- PouchContainer (P2P image distribution, optional VM-based)

Abstracting networking

Kubernetes networking always required a **Container Networking Interface** (**CNI**) plugin. It is yet another CNCF project. It allows a lot of innovation in the networking and network security space.

You can find here a long list of platforms that support CNI (beyond Kubernetes) and an even longer list of plugins at `https://github.com/containernetworking/cni`.

I expect the CNI to remain the standard interface for networking solutions. A very interesting project is Cilium, which utilizes the **extended Berkeley Packet Filter** (**eBPF**) to provide very high-performance networking and security at the Linux-kernel level, which may offset some of the overhead of service mesh sidecar proxies.

Abstracting storage

Kubernetes has an abstract storage model, based on volumes and persistent volume claims. It supports a large number of storage solution in-trees. This means those storage solutions had to be built into the Kubernetes code base.

Early on (in Kubernetes 1.2), the Kubernetes team introduced a special type of plugin called FlexVolume that provided an interface for out-of-tree plugins. Storage providers could provide their own drivers that implement the FlexVolume interface and could serve as a storage layer without modifying Kubernetes itself. But, the FlexVolume approach was still pretty clunky. It required installing special drivers on each node and, in some cases, on the master too.

In Kubernetes 1.13, the **Container Storage Interface** (**CSI**) matured to **generally available** (**GA**) status and provides a modern gRPC-based interface for implementing out-of-tree storage plugins. Soon, Kubernetes will even support raw block storage via CSI (introduced as beta in Kubernetes 1.14).

The following diagram illustrates the place of CSI in the Kubernetes cluster and how it neatly isolates storage providers:

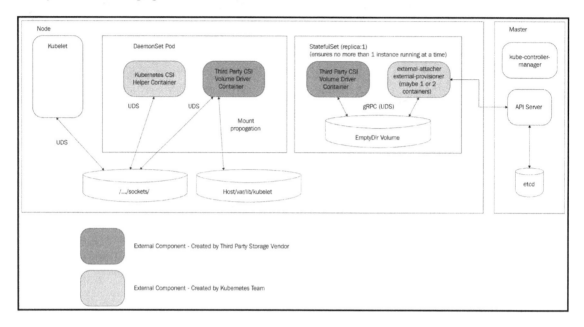

Container Storage Interface

The trend is to replace all the in-tree and FlexVolume plugins with CSI-based implementations, which will allow removing a significant chunk of functionality from the core Kubernetes code base.

The cloud provider interface

Kubernetes has seen a lot of success with cloud platforms, such as Google's GKE, Microsoft's AKS, Amazon's EKS, Alibaba's AliCloud, IBM's cloud Kubernetes service, DigitalOcean's Kubernetes service, VMware's Cloud PKS, and Oracle's container engine for Kubernetes.

In the early days, integrating Kubernetes into a cloud platform required a lot of effort and involved customizing multiple Kubernetes control plane components, such as the API server, the kubelet, and the controller manager.

To make things easier on cloud platform providers, Kubernetes introduced the **Cloud Controller Manager** (**CCM**). The CCM abstracts away, through a set of stable interfaces, all the parts that a cloud provider needs to implement. Now, the touch points between Kubernetes and the cloud provider are formalized and it's simpler to reason about and ensure that the integration is successful. Let's have a look at the following diagram:

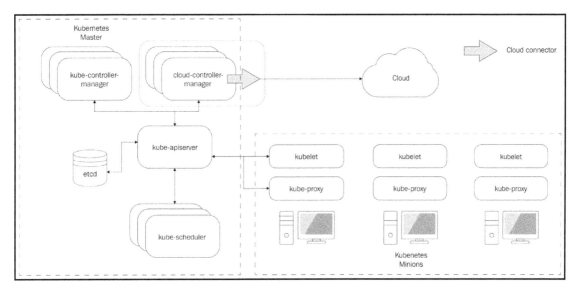

Cloud Controller Manager

The preceding diagram illustrates the interactions between a Kubernetes cluster and a host cloud platform.

Service mesh integration

I mentioned at the end of the Chapter 13, *Service Mesh - Working with Istio*, that service meshes are important. They complement Kubernetes and add a lot of value. While Kubernetes provides the management and scheduling of resources and the extensible API, a service mesh provides the next layer of managing the traffic flowing between the containers in the cluster.

This symbiosis is very powerful. On GKE, Istio is already just a button-click away. I expect most Kubernetes distribution to provide the option to install Istio (or maybe the AWS app mesh, in the case of EKS) as part of the initial setup.

At this point, I expect a lot of other solutions to consider Istio as a standard component and build on top of it. An interesting project to watch in this space is Kyma (`https://kyma-project.io/`), which aims to easily install a slew of best-of-breed cloud-native components. Kyna takes the extensible and open Kubernetes and adds an opinionated set of well-integrated components, such as the following:

- Helm
- Dex
- Istio
- Knative
- Prometheus
- Grafana
- Jeager
- Kubeless
- Loki
- Velero (formerly, Ark)
- Minio

Serverless computing on Kubernetes

As we discussed in `Chapter 9`, *Running Serverless Tasks on Kubernetes*, serverless computing is all the rage. There are many solutions out there. Let's distinguish between two separate solutions here:

- **Function as a Service (FaaS)**
- **Server as a Service (SaaS)**

FaaS	SaaS
FaaS means that you launch a function either as source code that gets packaged into an image, or as a pre-packaged image you build. This image then gets scheduled on your cluster and it runs to completion. You still need to mange and scale the nodes in your cluster and make sure you have enough capacity for your long-running services and your functions.	**SaaS** means that you don't need to provision and manage the nodes in your cluster. Your cluster auto-magically grows and shrinks according to the load. The Kubernetes cluster autoscaler provides this capability on Kubernetes.

Obviously, you can mix and match, and run the Kubernetes cluster autoscaler and also run some function as a service framework to get the benefits of both.

So far, so good. But, Kubernetes is often deployed on public cloud platforms that have their own non-Kubernetes solutions to the same problem. For example, in AWS, you have Lambda functions (FaaS) as well as Fargate (SaaS). Microsoft Azure has Azure Functions and container instances that use a virtual kubelet and you can elastically grow your AKS cluster. Google has Cloud Functions and Cloud Run.

It will interesting to see how the public cloud providers integrate their offerings with Kubernetes. Google Cloud Run is built on top on Knative and can already run either on your GKE cluster or on Google's infrastructure (so it's independent of Kubernetes).

I predict that Knative will become yet another standard component that other FaaS solutions use as a building block on Kubernetes because it is so portable and supported by major players, such as Google and Pivotal. It is designed from the get-go as a loosely coupled collection of pluggable components that let you swap in your preferred components.

Kubernetes and VMs

Kubernetes started as an orchestration platform for Docker containers. A lot of Docker-specific assumptions were built in. Kubernetes 1.3 added special support for CoreOS rkt and started the journey toward a decoupled runtime experience. Kubernetes 1.5 introduced the CRI, where the kubelet talks to the container runtime engine via gRPC. The CRI graduated to stable in Kubernetes 1.6.

As I mentioned earlier when discussing the abstraction of the container runtime, the CRI opened the door to multiple runtime implementations. One class of runtime extensions are lightweight or micro VMs. This may seem a little counter-productive because one of the biggest motivations for the container movement was that VMs are too heavyweight for dynamic cloud applications.

It turned out that containers are not fool-proof when it comes to isolation. Security concerns override any other concern for many use cases. The solution is to bring back VMs, but with a lighter touch. Now that the industry has some decent experience with containers, it is possible to design the next generation of VMs that will find the sweet spot between iron-clad isolation and high performance/low resource.

The following are some of the most prominent projects:

- gVisor
- Firecracker
- Kata containers

gVisor

gVisor is an open source project from Google. It is a user-space kernel sandbox that sits in front of the host kernel. It exposes an **Open Container Initiative** (**OCI**) interface called runsc. It also has a CRI plugin to interface directly with Kubernetes. The protection offered by gVisor is only partial. If there is a container breach, then the user kernel and a special secomp policy provide extra layers of security, but it is not a complete isolation. gVisor is used by Google AppEngine.

Firecracker

Firecracker is an open source project from AWS. It is a VM monitor using KVM to manage micro VMs. It is designed specifically to run secure multi-tenant containers and functions as as a service. It currently runs only on Intel CPUs, but support is planned for AMD and ARM.

AWS Lambda and AWS Fargate use Firecracker already. Currently, Firecracker can't be used easily on Kubernetes. The plan is to provide container integration via containerd. Refer to the link: `https://github.com/firecracker-microvm/firecracker-containerd/`.

Kata containers

This is another open source solution managed by the **OpenStack Foundation** (**OSF**), in the form of Kata containers. It combines technology from Intel's clear containers and Hyper.sh RunV. It supports multiple hypervisors, such QEMU, NEMU, and even Firecracker. The goal of the Kata containers is to build a secure container runtime based on hardware virtualization for workload isolation. Kata containers can already be used on Kubernetes via containerd.

It's hard to tell how it will all shake up. There was already some consolidation. There is strong demand for safe and secure container runtimes. All the projects can either be used on Kubernetes already, or there are plans to integrate them soon. This will probably be one of the most important, yet invisible, improvements to the cloud-native landscape. The main concern is that those lightweight VMs might introduce too much of a performance overhead for some use cases.

Cluster autoscaling

If you deal with fluctuating load (and it's safe to say that any non-trivial system does), then you have three options:

- Over provision your cluster.
- Try to find a magic ideal size and deal with outages, timeout, and slow performance.
- Grow and shrink your cluster based on demand.

Let's discuss the preceding options in more detail:

- Option 1 is expensive. You pay for resources, you don't fully utilize most of the time. It does buy you some peace and quiet, but eventually, you may run into a spike of demand that temporarily exceeds even your over provisioned capacity.
- Option 2 is not really an option. You may find yourself there if you opted for over provisioning and underestimated.
- Option 3 is where you want to be. Your cluster's capacity matches your workload. You can always satisfy your SLOs and SLAs and you don't pay for unused capacity. However, trying to elastically manage your cluster manually is a no-starter.

The solution is to do it automatically. This is where the cluster autoscaler comes in. I believe that, for large-scale clusters, the cluster autoscaler will become a standard component. There may be additional custom controllers that also adjust the cluster size based on custom metrics, or adjust other resources beyond nodes.

I fully expect all the large cloud providers to invest and address all the current gotchas and issues related to the cluster autoscaler and ensure it works flawlessly on their platforms.

Another prominent trend in the Kubernetes community that became a best practice is to provide complex components through Kubernetes operators.

Using operators

A Kubernetes operator is a controller that encapsulates operational knowledge of some application. It can manage installation, configuration, updates, fail-overs, and more. Operators often rely on CRDs to keep their own state and can automatically respond to events. Providing an operator is quickly becoming the way to release new, complicated software.

Helm charts are fine for installing the bits onto the cluster (and operators may use Helm charts for that purpose), but there is a lot of ongoing management associated with complex components, such as data stores, monitoring solutions, CI/CD pipelines, message brokers, and serverless frameworks.

The trend here is very clear: complex projects will provide operators as a standard feature.

There are two interesting projects that support this trend.

OperatorHub (`https://operatorhub.io/`) is a curated index of Kubernetes operators, where people can go and find well-packaged software to install on their cluster. OperatorHub was started by RedHat (now part of IBM), Amazon, Microsoft, and Google. It is very well-organized by category and provider and is easily searchable. Here is a screenshot of the main page:

Operator hub

Operators are very useful, but they require pretty good knowledge of how Kubernetes works, controllers, the concept of reconciliation logic, how to create CRDs, and how to interact with the Kubernetes API server. It is not rocket science, but it's not trivial either. If you want to develop your own operators, there is a project called the Operator Framework (`https://github.com/operator-framework`). The Operator Framework provides an SDK to make it easy to start with your operators. There are guides for writing operators in Go, using Ansible or Helm.

Operators significantly reduce complexity, but what if you need to manage many clusters? This is where cluster federation comes in.

Federation

Managing a single large Kubernetes cluster is not simple. Managing multiple geo-distributed clusters is much harder. It is especially difficult if you try to treat multiple clusters as one big logical cluster. Many challenges arise around high availability, fail-over, load balancing, security, and latency.

For many very large systems, multiple clusters are a necessity. Sometimes, it is necessary for smaller systems too. The following are some use cases:

- Hybrid on-premises/cloud
- Geo-distributed redundancy and availability
- Multi-provider redundancy and availability
- Very large systems (more nodes than a single Kubernetes cluster can handle)

Kubernetes attempted to address the problem with the Kubernetes Federation V1 proposal and implementation. It failed and never made it to GA. But, then came V2, at `https://github.com/kubernetes-sigs/federation-v2`.

All big cloud providers have products for a hybrid on-premises/cloud systems. These include the following:

- Google Anthos
- GKE on-premises - AWS Outposts: Microsoft Azure Stack

In addition, many third-party Kubernetes solutions offer cross-cloud and even bare-metal management of multiple clusters. One of the most promising projects in this area is Gardener (`https://gardener.cloud/`) that lets you manage potentially thousands of clusters. It operates by having a garden cluster that manages many seed clusters (as custom resources) that can have shoot clusters.

I see it as a natural progression. Once the industry masters the art of managing a single cluster, then mastering a collection of clusters will become the next challenge.

Summary

In this chapter, we looked at where microservices and Kubernetes are going next. All the indicators show that both microservices and Kubernetes will continue to be major factors when designing, building, evolving, and operating cloud-native, large-scale, distributed systems. This is good news. Small programs, scripts, and mobile apps will not disappear, but the backend systems will become large, deal with more data, and be responsible for managing larger and larger aspects of our lives. Technologies such as virtual reality, sensors, and AI will require ever-growing amounts of data to be processed and stored.

The short-term development in the microservices world will see gRPC emerge as a popular transport for inter-service communication, as well as a public interface. Web clients will be able to consume gRPC via the gRPC for web. GraphQL is another innovation that is a major improvement compared to the REST API. The industry still needs some time to understand how to design and build microservice-based architectures. Building a single microservice is simple. Building a whole system of coordinated microservices is a whole other story.

Containers and Kubernetes solve some of the hard problems that microservice-based architectures present. New technologies, such as service mesh, will gain mindshare very quickly. Serverless computing (both SaaS and FaaS) will help developers to deploy and update applications even faster. The merging of containers and virtualization will result in more secure systems. Operators will make bigger and more useful building blocks a reality. Cluster federation will be the new frontier of scalable systems.

At this point, you should have a good idea of what is coming down the line and what to expect. This knowledge will allow you to plan ahead and make your own assessments regarding which technologies to invest in right now, and which technologies need to mature some more.

In short, we are at the beginning of an exciting, new era, where we will learn how to create reliable systems at an unprecedented scale. Keep learning, stay on top of all the amazing technologies available to you, build your own systems, and contribute back to the community.

Further reading

The reading list is quite extensive because we discussed a lot of up-and-coming projects and technologies that are worth monitoring and following up on:

- **gRPC**: https://grpc.io/
- **The Frakti runtime**: https://github.com/kubernetes/frakti
- **Containerd**: https://containerd.io/
- **PouchContainer**: https://github.com/alibaba/pouch
- **Kata Containers**: https://katacontainers.io/
- **Kubernetes and Cloud Providers**: https://medium.com/@the.gigi/kubernetes-and-cloud-providers-b7a6227d3198
- **Extending Kubernetes**: https://www.youtube.com/watch?v=qVZnU8rXAEU
- **Azure Functions**: https://azure.microsoft.com/en-us/services/functions/
- **Azure Container Instances**: https://azure.microsoft.com/en-us/services/container-instances/
- **Google Cloud Run**: https://cloud.google.com/blog/products/serverless/announcing-cloud-run-the-newest-member-of-our-serverless-compute-stack
- **gVisor**: https://gvisor.dev/
- **Firecracker:** https://firecracker-microvm.github.io/
- **Kata Containers**: https://katacontainers.io/
- **Gardener**: https://gardener.cloud/
- **The Operator Framework**: https://github.com/operator-framework/operator-sdk
- **HTTP/3 explained**: https://http3-explained.haxx.se

Other Books You May Enjoy

If you enjoyed this book, you may be interested in these other books by Packt:

Kubernetes Cookbook - Second Edition
Hideto Saito, Hui-Chuan Chloe Lee, Et al

ISBN: 978-1-78883-760-6

- Build your own container cluster
- Deploy and manage highly scalable, containerized applications with Kubernetes
- Build high-availability Kubernetes clusters
- Build a continuous delivery pipeline for your application
- Track metrics and logs for every container running in your cluster
- Streamline the way you deploy and manage your applications with large-scale container orchestration

Mastering Kubernetes - Second Edition
Gigi Sayfan

ISBN: 978-1-78899-978-6

- Architect a robust Kubernetes cluster for long-time operation
- Discover the advantages of running Kubernetes on GCE, AWS, Azure, and bare metal
- Understand the identity model of Kubernetes, along with the options for cluster federation
- Monitor and troubleshoot Kubernetes clusters and run a highly available Kubernetes
- Create and configure custom Kubernetes resources and use third-party resources in your automation workflows
- Enjoy the art of running complex stateful applications in your container environment
- Deliver applications as standard packages

Leave a review - let other readers know what you think

Please share your thoughts on this book with others by leaving a review on the site that you bought it from. If you purchased the book from Amazon, please leave us an honest review on this book's Amazon page. This is vital so that other potential readers can see and use your unbiased opinion to make purchasing decisions, we can understand what our customers think about our products, and our authors can see your feedback on the title that they have worked with Packt to create. It will only take a few minutes of your time, but is valuable to other potential customers, our authors, and Packt. Thank you!

Index